# Precocious Charms

The publisher gratefully acknowledges the generous support of the Humanities Endowment Fund of the University of California Press Foundation.

# Precocious Charms

*Stars Performing Girlhood in Classical Hollywood Cinema*

Gaylyn Studlar

UNIVERSITY OF CALIFORNIA PRESS
*Berkeley · Los Angeles · London*

University of California Press, one of the most distinguished university presses in the United States, enriches lives around the world by advancing scholarship in the humanities, social sciences, and natural sciences. Its activities are supported by the UC Press Foundation and by philanthropic contributions from individuals and institutions. For more information visit www.ucpress.edu.

Materials in this book have appeared in different form in three previously published articles: "Oh, 'Doll Divine': Mary Pickford, Masquerade, and the Pedophilic Gaze" was originally published in *Camera Obscura* 16, no. 3.48 (2001): 197–227 © Gaylyn Studlar; "Velvet's Cherry: Elizabeth Taylor and Virginal English Girlhood" appeared in *Virgin Territory: Representing Sexual Inexperience in Film,* ed. Tamara Jeffers McDonald (Detroit: Wayne State University Press, 2010), 15–33. Copyright © 2010 Wayne State University Press. Used with permission by Wayne State University Press; "'Chi-Chi Cinderella': Audrey Hepburn as Couture Countermodel" was included in *Hollywood Goes Shopping,* ed. David Desser and Garth S. Jowett (Minneapolis: University of Minnesota Press, 2000): 159–78.

University of California Press
Berkeley and Los Angeles, California

University of California Press, Ltd.
London, England



Library of Congress Cataloging-in-Publication Data

Studlar, Gaylyn.
Precocious charms : stars performing girlhood in classical Hollywood cinema / Gaylyn Studlar.
p. cm.
Includes bibliographical references and index.
ISBN 978-0-520-25557-9 (cloth : alk. paper)
ISBN 978-0-520-27424-2 (pbk. : alk. paper)
1. Girls in motion pictures. 2. Teenage girls in motion pictures. 3. Motion pictures—United States—History—20th century. 4. Child actors—United States—History—20th century. I. Title.
PN1995.9.G57S65 2013
791.43'6523—dc23 2012029630

Manufactured in the United States of America

21 20 19 18 17 16 15 14 13
10 9 8 7 6 5 4 3 2 1

In keeping with a commitment to support environmentally responsible and sustainable printing practices, UC Press has printed this book on Rolland Enviro100, a 100% postconsumer fiber paper that is FSC certified, deinked, processed chlorine-free, and manufactured with renewable biogas energy. It is acid-free and EcoLogo certified.

*In memory of my parents, Irene and Joe Studlar,*
*with gratitude for their love and for the sacrifices*
*they made so that I could be an educated woman*

I suppose she must have looked rather delightful, for Mrs. Darling put her hand to her heart and cried, "Oh, why can't you remain like this for ever!"

—J. M. Barrie, *Peter Pan and Wendy*

# Contents

# Illustrations

# Acknowledgments

The publication of this book was dependent on many institutions and on many people. Dean Gary S. Wihl of the College of Arts and Sciences, Washington University in St. Louis, provided a much-appreciated book subvention. The University of Michigan provided generous funds and time off for my research. I owe many colleagues with whom I worked at the University of Michigan special thanks for creating a supportive environment. I especially want to thank Giorgio Bertellini, Jim Burnstein, Susan Douglas, Geoff Eley, Johannes Von Moltke, Eric Fredericksen, Bambi Haggins, Donald Lopez, Lucia Saks, and Terri Sarris. Katrina Mann ably served as my summer research assistant in the initial stage of this project. Phil Hallman made it possible for me to watch every Deanna Durbin film. Mary Lou Chlipala, Connie Ejarque, and Sue Kirby were cheerleaders for getting the book "on the girls" finished.

Special thanks go to the staff of the Margaret Herrick Library, at the Academy of Motion Picture Arts and Sciences, Douglas Fairbanks Study Center, and particularly to Barbara Hall and Janet Lorenz, who were wonderfully helpful and knowledgeable—as always. The Academy of Motion Picture Arts and Sciences allowed me to publish photographs of Mary Pickford from its core collection. Steve Wilson and the staff of the Harry Ransom Humanities Center provided assistance with the labyrinth of riches that is the David O. Selznick Collection. Permission to publish materials from that collection, including two photographs, has been granted by the Harry Ransom Humanities Center, University of Texas, Austin. I thank the Bridgeman Art Library for permission to publish reproductions of Sir John Everett Millais's *Cherry Ripe* and *The Woodman's Daughter*. Elisa Marquez kindly helped me secure publications rights from the Associated Press for a photograph of Deanna Durbin.

I wish to express gratitude to Matthew Bernstein, Janet Staiger, and Susan White for providing opportunities to publicly present my work in progress. Jennifer Bean and Diane Negra improved the chapter on Mary Pickford with their suggestions, and Tamara Jeffers McDonald did the same for the Elizabeth Taylor chapter. Virginia Wright Wexman was an astute and helpful manuscript reviewer. My colleagues at Washington University in St. Louis, including Bill Paul, Philip Sewell, and Todd Decker, took the time to chat about various questions raised by this project. They have improved this book by sharing their knowledge on topics as varied as film exhibition practice, radio programming in the 1930s, and tap dance. Elizabeth Childs has been an inspiration and a calming influence. Bradley Short helped me secure needed research materials. Mary Francis, my editor at the University of California Press, has been a model of patience while offering terrific advice. My gratitude goes to Constance Goodwin for more than forty years of friendship and professional encouragement and to my brother Donley Studlar for his enthusiasm for film.

Finally, I want to thank my husband, Thomas Haslett, for being funny, generous, supportive, and a wonderful cook.

FIGURE 1. Studio portrait of Mary Pickford for *Rebecca of Sunnybrook Farm* (dir. Marshall Neilan, 1917). Courtesy of the Academy of Motion Picture Arts and Sciences.

# Introduction

This book is about stardom and femininity and how six female stars figured in the inscription of girls and girlhood by Hollywood between the years 1914 and 1967. In this discussion I stress the importance of "juvenation" in the performances of girlhood by Mary Pickford, Shirley Temple, Deanna Durbin, Elizabeth Taylor, Jennifer Jones, and Audrey Hepburn.

What is juvenation? Referencing contemporary news media, John Hartley defines juvenation as "the creative practice of communicating with a readership *via the medium of* youthfulness."[1] He points to the ambivalent ways in which late twentieth- and early twenty-first-century popular media produce images of the young as a category of appeal defined by age but also inevitably by gender. Hartley explains how the overrepresentation of signs of youthfulness in journalism and electronic public media registers a preoccupation with boundaries of age and with the young, especially young girls. The latter, he says, are "up to their ankles, if not their necks, in public signification, becoming objects of public policy, public debate, the public gaze."[2] Hartley argues that the ubiquitous presence of this juvenating process can be located in various media-dominated spheres of culture that become juvenated discursively to facilitate enjoyment by viewers or readers, whether they are defined as adult or child. The reception of the juvenated leads to ambivalent or contradictory effects, says Hartley, because at the same time that adult-generated contemporary culture juvenates both subjects and consumers of media, there is an opposing drive to enforce age boundaries that define the differences between child and adult.[3] As a consequence, he suggests, these media images rarely celebrate the child but, instead, play up the taboo aspects of children's display—whether emphasizing victimization (such as sexual abuse) or pathologization (as with anorexia).[4] Hartley acknowledges in passing that juvenated images are not new in a democratized public sphere in which media define the "socially seeable," but he does not seem much interested in possible antecedents to this phenomenon in which age is strongly linked to feminization and eroticization.[5]

Using Hartley's identification of juvenation as a process important to understanding media representation of age as a springboard, I take the notion of juvenation in another direction, focusing on female stars during Hollywood's classical, studio-dominated era. I explore Hollywood's investment in creating fictions of girlhood that were defined by a different medium (film) in a different historical period (roughly the first half of the twentieth century), and via a different industry (American filmmaking). Given these differences, we cannot expect that performances of girlhood or the display of juvenile attributes by the female stars I analyze created the exact equivalent of what Hartley describes. In fact, some of these film representations could be seen as promulgating fantasies of girlhood with idealized or even utopian components. Nevertheless, the idea that we should investigate juvenation as a process linked to feminization and eroticization, and sometimes even to victimization and pathology, is a powerful one.

Juvenation suggests new avenues for approaching the construction of girls and girlhood in and through Hollywood stars and their film vehicles, as well as the cultural impact of stardom as it was constructed for public consumption across a number of media, including film, radio, print journalism, studio publicity, advertising, consumer product tie-ins, fashion, and public appearances. Thus, the juvenation of female stars by Hollywood was produced as a historically specific and semiotically contextualized process, one that demonstrates a remarkably long-lived attention to signifying girls and girlhood.

This means that along the way, this book deals with child stars, but it is not just about child stars. It analyzes adult actresses who played children or adolescents onscreen, but it is not just about these motion picture masquerades of youthfulness. Rather, it is about defining, constructing, and consuming youthful signs of femininity in Hollywood film and how that process was imbricated in the careers of six female stars. This process occurred during the time in which the studio system flourished as a dominating media influence on the U.S. cultural imaginary. As a consequence, this process of juvenating female stars was multifaceted, imagined as it was by a Hollywood system of filmmaking that was inseparable from the American culture that produced it.

In Hollywood's golden years the star system was a crucial aspect of the American film industry's appeal to viewers. As such, it became more than a mere marketing tool. After a fitful start in which U.S. producers withheld the names of "photoplay" actors, in the mid-1910s, by the time feature film was gaining a foothold, the star system was operating with highly organized strategies for creating and promoting distinctive screen "personalities." The fledgling industry hoped that film actors would be recognized by audiences from multiple film appearances and become box-office draws, thus expanding the appeal of motion pictures beyond branding films by studio name as a guarantee of quality. The beginning of the star system occurred when the industry moved beyond focusing on films as the almost exclusive site for explaining the "personality" of the actor.[6] By complicating the identity of film actors with reference to their offscreen, personal lives, viewers became "fans," and popular players became "stars." Hollywood did not invent this idea: it already reigned supreme in the theatrical world.

Viewer interest in knowing about feature-film actors as extrafilmic personalities emerged as a primary means through which Hollywood secured the fascination and loyalty of audiences. Audiences may not always have acknowledged that their favorite film actors and actresses were constructed (offscreen as well as on), but evidence of the disavowing complicity of viewers in the creation, marketing, and reception of Hollywood stars dates back to the 1910s.[7] Stars' images were used to sell films and secure Hollywood's domination of screens worldwide, but star identities often acquired considerable cultural complexity "at home," in the United States, as they were discursively constructed across many different media venues. Images and information about them circulated far beyond (and between) the release of individual films and the film-specific promotion and publicity that circulated to market specific movies.

The process of shaping and selling cinema stars was extremely important to the industry's economic organization. Stars were commodities, and their commercial significance was translated into the shaping of

Hollywood's aesthetic and narrative organization. Many films became "star vehicles," with narrative formulas and aesthetic techniques refined to meet the need of highlighting popular actors or actresses as a film's most important attraction. Stars were crucial to movies as a culture industry, with the star system's relevance extending beyond the selling of cinema as a consumer product or an artistic practice to assume a central role in Hollywood's hold over the cultural imaginary.

Stars were also recognized by their audiences as living persons with a unique relationship to Hollywood and its enticing make-believe. The stars of the Hollywood studio system lived for their fans, not only onscreen but also in publicity and film promotion, editorial columns, fan magazines, news, and appearances in other media like radio and live stage. Stars influenced the clothes women wore and the way men styled their hair, the music people sang and the way they made love.[8] They were envied and imitated, idealized and occasionally condemned. What they could not be was ignored. To be ignored meant that you were not a star.

Juvenated stars had a special connection to precinematic entertainment trends. Before film became a mass media, numerous entertainments involving "child-watching" were a favorite Victorian pastime in the United States and the United Kingdom, with the vogue for children performing onstage reaching a peak in the 1880s.[9] Among the many little girls who "trod the boards" in the late nineteenth century and early twentieth were Elsie Leslie, Maude Adams, Mary Miles Minter, Lillian Gish, and Mary Pickford. The last three made the transition to film stardom. Although it was largely perceived as representing the Victorian era's desire for embodied innocence, the transatlantic cultural phenomenon that idealized children, especially little white girls, was not without legal and sexual controversy when those children were professional performers.[10]

Building on established artistic, literary, and theatrical interest in the spectacle of children, by the 1910s the American film industry cultivated the presence of many child actors, male and female, even before Mary Pickford and her rivals were successfully impersonating juveniles in feature films. A significant number of children appeared in films during the first decade of features, but few of these child screen performers ever achieved star billing, much less became top box-office draws.[11] Sidney and Chester Franklin developed a roster of child actors at Fine Arts Studios who were generally supporting players. The Franklins, as well as many of these child actors, ended up at Fox studio and

FIGURE 2. Baby Marie Osborne, star of Balboa Productions, ca. 1915. Author's collection.

made several films with children as the leads, such as *Aladdin and the Wonderful Lamp* (1917), with Virginia Lee Corbin. *Motion Picture* featured Corbin's photograph in its "Gallery" and declared, "The day of the child picture star has come."[12] The popularity of children in movies was registered in the fact that studios extended the marketing tags or monikers accorded adult female stars such as "The Imp Girl" and "The Biograph Girl" to child actors, including Corbin, who was advertised as "The Youngest Emotional Star"; Magda Foy, who was advertised by the Solax studio as "The Solax Kid"; and Marie Osborne, also known as "Baby Marie" or "Little Mary Sunshine."[13]

In the 1920s, Hollywood capitalized on the cultural emergence of "the priceless child," the child who was valued for his or her emotional rather than economic value.[14] Big-eyed Jackie Coogan made box-office hay playing an orphan waif in Chaplin's *The Kid* (1921), *My*

*Boy* (1922), and *The Rag Man* (1925).[15] "Baby Peggy" Montgomery's films *The Darling of New York* (1923) and *Captain January* (1924) also relied on the heart-tugging motif of the lost or orphaned child who finds an unlikely companion and protector, usually male.[16] The trajectory of Montgomery's career anticipated Shirley Temple's, with the child starting in short comedies and doing uncanny imitations of adults.

Although Coogan and Baby Peggy became stars, it was not until the 1930s that child and adolescent actors were ubiquitous on the screen, with Jackie Cooper's appearance in *Skippy* (dir. Norman Taurog, 1931) sometimes regarded as the beginning of the trend.[17] In the early 1930s, as Shirley Temple shot to prominence, at least one newspaper commentator suggested that the motion pictures' dependence on child players was merely a revival of the 1910s; their popularity was also linked to the Production Code Administration's clamping down on violence and sexuality in Hollywood feature films.[18] Certainly, one thing remained the same: the American film industry continued to attach its child performers, onscreen and off, with traditional values of sentimentality and displays of familial affection. Of the 1930s, Tino Balio says, "Child and adolescent stars led the polls throughout the decade."[19] The youthful Janet Gaynor was box-office "queen" in 1934, with Will Rogers taking the top ranking among men, but Gaynor was not a teenager as Balio implies. Her screen persona was often juvenated, however, and she starred in remakes of two Mary Pickford titles, *Daddy Long Legs* (1931) and *Tess of the Storm Country* (1932). In the late 1930s adolescent performers began to gain traction at the box office, especially in musicals and comedies.

In the chapters that follow, I consider a specific kind of stardom—juvenated and female—within a specific period of time defined by the studio era of Hollywood cinema and its product, "classical Hollywood cinema." The latter, as Bordwell, Staiger, and Thompson define it, depends on "a distinct mode of film practice with its own cinematic style and industrial conditions of existence."[20] By emphasizing the signifiers of juvenated femininity, I seek to complicate the study of female stars by rejecting a monolithic categorization of female representation in cinema that ignores age or downplays age connotations. To study juvenated femininity and its existence in star personas calls attention to how differences in age are implicated in all representations of sexual difference within patriarchy and, more specifically, how the rhetoric of classical Hollywood cinema—as the most influential mass media of the first half of the twentieth century—constructed femininity in relation to age and gender expectations. By focusing not just on characters represented onscreen but also on a methodology that emphasizes the interplay between the star performer and her roles, between films and culture, we can read something more from cinema than images and do more than construct a taxonomy of stereotypes. My goal is to investigate, through an approach that is simultaneously analytical, historical, and theoretical, how embodiment by movie stars is incorporated into film to elicit fascination with girls and girlhood through femininity aligned with juvenated qualities, whether physical or psychological.

In focusing on the star images of Mary Pickford, Shirley Temple, Deanna Durbin, Elizabeth Taylor, Jennifer Jones, and Audrey Hepburn,[21] I argue that the textual and extratextual strategies that produced these stars not only gendered them as female but also constructed them (at one time or another in their careers) as possessing attributes, behaviors, and characteristics associated with the childish, the juvenile, and the youthful. The point is that whether they were actually young or not, these stars appealed to film viewers "via *the medium* of youthfulness."[22] In a fashion similar to that I used in my book *This Mad Masquerade: Masculinity and Stardom in the Jazz Age,* I use this series of chapter-by-chapter case studies to make linked points within a large historical framework.

That they were stars means by definition that these actresses were popular with audiences across a number of films. This means, in turn, that a significant number of viewers invested in them as performers who offered an engaging or enjoyable performance of femininity. It should be recognized that they are, of course, not the only stars affiliated with juvenation during the era of classical Hollywood cinema, but each of these actresses was important for several reasons. Not only did each one achieve the status of having her "name above the title," Hollywood's credit indicating an actor or actress who can sell a film and has marquee value recognized by the public, but Mary Pickford was American film's first female superstar. Shirley Temple was a box-office champion and beloved child star that remains recognized as a star icon. Elizabeth Taylor was much acclaimed as an actress and a beauty whose entire life, after the age of twelve, was played out in the spotlight. The general public has largely forgotten Deanna Durbin, but she was critically acclaimed as well as extremely popular. At the height of her career she became the highest paid actress in Hollywood. Her fan club, the "Deanna Durbin Devotees," still exists.[23] Jennifer Jones won an Oscar for her first major film role and was quickly catapulted into the top rank of screen actresses. Audrey Hepburn's image still circulates in popular culture as an exemplar of youthful elegance. All of them received Oscars, whether for lifetime achievement (Pickford, Temple), for acting in a single film (Pickford, Taylor, Jones, Hepburn), or for their accomplishments as a juvenile performer (Temple, Durbin). Because each star's career unfurled at different times and under particularized circumstances, with varying aesthetic, economic, and cultural influences brought to bear, I will discuss those differences, as well as emergent patterns of shared characteristics.

In selecting these stars I have attempted to offer significant chronological coverage. These stars emerged diachronically across the history of American cinema when it achieved its greatest cultural influence and popularity. Their careers extend the coverage of my analysis over the full range of classical Hollywood cinema. As both a textually based aesthetic practice and an industrial one dependent on complex processes and material structures, classical Hollywood cinema was sustained from early years in the 1910s into the 1960s, when the studio system received the final blow to its very existence. The U.S. Supreme Court forced the studios to divest themselves of their theaters; what was left after divestiture was sold off to corporate conglomerates.[24] Stylistic influences from overseas "new waves" impacted emerging U.S. filmmakers and their aesthetic approach to narrative cinema. Nevertheless, the conventions that defined Hollywood's style of moviemaking during the classical era remain a relevant area of inquiry.[25]

The actresses represented in this study also demonstrate how an emphasis on girls and girlhood impacted different genres, including romantic comedy, musicals, and melodramas. Even when they share generic territory, character types, or narrative formulas, they demonstrate distinctively different talents: Pickford—silent comedy; Temple—dancing and singing; Durbin—operatic singing; Taylor—beauty; Jones—"serious" emotional acting; and Hepburn—the display (or "modeling") of fashion in romantic comedy. These stars present both unexpected continuities and interesting differences in their pleasurable embodiment of juvenated femininity in classical Hollywood cinema. They all had distinctive star personas, formed out of their onscreen performances but also from the extratextual discourse that discussed their performances, private lives, public appearances, and "personal" pronouncements.

Star personas were not immune to change. The genres and plots that sustain a star persona may lose their impact after repetition and variation, replaced by other trends in production and storytelling. Musicals may be out; social problem films may be in. For actors representing female juvenation, the challenges may be greater since, as we know, styles of femininity change. Everyone ages. If the aging process was fraught with box-office peril for female actors whose films depended on their portrayals of young girls or adolescents, it contained even greater challenges for child actors. Girls grow up—and out. Child actors required a retooling of their star image when they grew up and no longer resembled the "self" that the public loved. Certainly, this was regarded as one of the difficulties that Shirley Temple faced. In 1934, just as she was starting out at Fox, the *Los Angeles Times* prominently featured an article on "Child Prodigies" that listed the many movie-based child actors who had vanished "seemingly into thin air," among them Virginia Corbin and Richard Headrick. Baby Marie Osborne, the article noted, had held on in the business but only as Ginger Rogers's stand-in.[26] In 1937, when Temple had been a star for three years (and was nine years old), a review in *Life* asked, "What's to become of Shirley Temple? She has lost some of her early prettiness and all of her babyish cuteness."[27] Physical changes make the teenager of sixteen look very different from a twelve-year-old. In general, the maturation of female stars caused greater disruptions in their careers than those of male stars. At the other end of the age spectrum male stars might still play romantic leads when female stars of the same age are consigned to the roles of mothers (or grandmothers).

To consider the relationship between stardom and signifiers of the juvenile in the sonic and visual figuration of the female body tells us a great deal about what may otherwise seem like Hollywood's overly familiar business of telling stories about, to, and through those who are gendered female. In each successive chapter I address the central conceit of a star who was affiliated with cinematic depictions of girlhood, whether during a relatively short period of time in an extraordinarily long career (as with Taylor) or across a lengthier part of her screen work (as with Pickford). I am especially interested in what happens in Hollywood film and to its viewers when there is a blurring of the boundaries between girl and woman, child and adult. At the center of each chapter is an interrogation of stardom's construction of girlish femininity in light of cultural, historical, and theoretical concerns. In a system in which typecasting and genre were so important in framing stars for public consumption, it is important to understand how performing females came to represent qualities interpreted as juvenated at particular historical moments and in certain kinds of films. I focus on the cultural influences referenced in these star-centered Hollywood performances of girlhood or a girl's transition to womanhood and how viewers were primed to respond to these qualities.

Many scholarly studies have addressed the historical and theoretical complexity of specific star identities, as well as the more general process of their construction. The latter involved not only their appearances as actors in films but also their inscription across the broader field of extratextual discourses engaged with film viewing as a social and consumer-oriented experience. Star-centered studies have shown a great deal of interest in issues of gender and sexual identity and have provided illuminating treatments of the complexities of race and ethnicity in the construction of women stars.[28] The relationship between screen actors and the treatment of stardom across different media, such as radio and television, has emerged as another important arena of consideration.[29]

Less attention, however, has been given to stardom and questions of age in relation to gender and sexuality, consumption, and social identity. Rather than investigate the impact of cinematic representations of maturity and immaturity, attention to adult femininity has held pride of place in feminist film history and theory for three decades, with the subject of youthful or juvenated femininity receiving very little notice. The primary representational concern of film studies, especially of feminist film studies, has been the middle-ground of an adult femininity left amorphously defined at best.[30] Whether filtered through the lens of stardom or not, the study of girls, adolescents, and the juvenation of femininity in cinema has been confined largely to the margins of our field, with few sustained attempts to fill this gap.[31] An exception to this neglect is found in the historical analysis of audiences, however, where scholarship by several authors has significantly enriched our understanding of various historical periods in which girls, usually defined collectively as young women rather than as schoolgirls, were responsible—as a powerful audience demographic—for moviegoing trends, with significant impact on film industries and the social realm in the United States and abroad.[32]

To date, no single-authored volume explores the convergence between representations of youthful femininity—whether juvenated as child or adolescent—and the phenomenon of film stardom. This book makes a gesture toward filling that gap. My title, *Precocious Charms,* may seem paradoxical, since not all the stars considered in this study were chil-

FIGURE 3. Shirley Temple, box-office champ, in costume for *The Little Colonel* (dir. David Butler, 1935). Author's collection.

dren, but a measure of paradox or play is my intention. *Precocious* usually refers to something ahead of its time, extraordinary, and thus unexpected. *Charms* is suggestive of qualities that create pleasure or satisfaction that is not serious, intellectual, or important but pleasing, delightful, and attractive. Charms are usually assigned to the feminine, and precociousness is frequently used to describe the young. If a six-year-old child, like Shirley Temple, tap dances with precocious skill, we understand that her performance exceeds our expectations for a child her age. What gives it the power to please or even delight? Certainly, as I argue in chapter 2, Temple's box-office status as number-one draw suggests that it does have that power. Yet *power* is a term rarely attributed to the juvenated or to feminine charms, and power's origins and its affect must be considered and understood.

If fifteen-year-old Deanna Durbin warbles a Puccini aria with amazing musicality, we know we are experiencing a precocious musical performance. But what does that precocious musical ability do to her embodied femininity? Is a powerful, disciplined voice a register of charms? What if thirty-something Mary Pickford pretends to be a little girl leading a gang of ragamuffins, or if thirty-something Audrey Hepburn kisses a man in a manner that suggests that she has never locked lips with a human being before? What do those representations signify in terms of circulating norms of feminine sexuality in relation to age—and power? Unlike Temple's and Durbin's performances, Hepburn's and Pickford's portrayals of energetically young or chastely innocent females are acting turns not likely to be labeled "precocious." But there is undoubtedly an edge of precociousness in these performances because the actress brings her "adultness" to the child or childlike character she portrays, thus making femininity in relation to age complex in its meanings. The representation of juvenated femininity acquires precocity through the actress's status as an adult woman.

The title of this book may seem old-fashioned, and in that respect, looking into the past is intentional. *Charms* may seem an anachronistic term, with little cultural currency, and notions of what constitutes the "precocious" are ever changing. Precociousness in one era may be accepted as the norm in another, but change may be slow to arrive in some cultural arenas and in relation to some deeply held beliefs about age- and gender-appropriate behaviors.

Although frequently lambasted for seeking sexual sensationalism and a tendency to take the moral low road, Hollywood classical cinema was actually rather conservative during much of its existence, a stance exacerbated by the Production Code Administration, the primary mechanism of industry "censorship" or self-regulation created in 1934. Hollywood's look back to established, often culturally elevated, traditions of representing juvenated femininity will be important to my consideration of these stars, especially in my analyses of the stardom of Mary Pickford, Shirley Temple, and Elizabeth Taylor. Classical Hollywood film was a twentieth-century mass media phenomenon, but Murray Pomerance has gone so far as to suggest that "Victorian conventions . . . guided filmmakers even through the refractive 1960s."[33] Some of my analysis in this book appears to confirm his rather bold statement.

From the various possibilities that emerge in the construction of female stardom against a changing historic-cultural background that contextualized and controlled Hollywood's interest in representing juvenated femininity, we can expect the long-standing association of girls and girlhood with sexual innocence and moral purity. It follows that this project is interested in how juvenated female star personas were used by Hollywood to address changing sexual mores, as well as issues of social transformation and class difference. At the center of my attempt to unravel the complexities of Hollywood's construction of star-embodied, juvenated femininity is my belief that such an exploration requires consolidating the strands of many discourses, from film texts to studio correspondence, publicity materials to seldom investigated literary and visual precursors.

Chapter 1 takes up the question of how Mary Pickford, one of the first superstars of the motion picture industry, built her twenty-year appeal to audiences on a star persona that incorporated the characteristics of both child and adult—a "child-woman." Born in 1892, Pickford worked in theater as a child actor under her birth name of "Gladys Smith." She started acting in motion pictures to earn extra money at American Biograph in 1909. There she appeared in a variety of roles. In the 1910s and early 1920s, instead of growing up onscreen, she turned more and more to child and adolescent roles, to the delight of audiences. Playing these juvenated characters, she solidified her position as one of the most powerful stars in the U.S. film industry. Drawing on Pickford's films, as well as on extratextual materials—including fan magazines, newspapers, and press books—I analyze the intricate and contradictory ways in which Pickford's masquerade of childishness made her so popular for such a long time. I examine the sentimental sources, such as girls' literature, that her masquerade of childishness drew on to create a screen persona that exploited the slippage between eroticized adult femininity and conventionalized inscriptions of girls as asexual. This creates what I call "the pedophilic gaze," a concept that I use to center my exploration of the multiple possibilities of identification and sexual desire created by Pickford's juvenated stardom for gendered spectators. Thus, Pickford's stardom suggests the complexity of film viewing in relation to an adult star's embodiment of juvenated femininity complicated by issues of embodiment and performance, historical intertexts and filmic representation, cultural change and nostalgia for girlhood.

Chapter 2 takes up the representation of femininity in the feature films of Shirley Temple, the world-famous child star who was one of the biggest box-office attractions of the 1930s. This chapter addresses the ways in which Temple's films provided a model of the "priceless child" associated with a major cultural revision of how children were valued by adults. At the same time, her films addressed more immediate anxieties related to national identity, most centrally, American men's responsibilities as fathers, an issue brought to the foreground during the 1930s by the economic disaster of the Great Depression. I argue that the need to claim masculinity for domesticity was one of Temple's primary functions on the screen. The emotional attachment connecting fathers and daughters is central to Temple's films, but I argue that this trope relies on antecedents and performative nuances that complicate film studies' current theorization of Temple almost exclusively as an erotic attraction for men. In constructing Temple's appeal, her films bear the marks of a wide range of influences, from Victorian family social practice ("cosseting") to the utopian conventions of the musical comedy. The result is that Temple's star persona positioned her as a liminal figure that unsettled binaries of gender, race, sexuality, and age. Although her femininity was used to solidify traditional structures of the male-dominated order, her stardom challenged stereotyped notions of simple "cuteness," as well as the view that her popularity rests solely on her association with a precociously eroticized femininity.

In chapter 3 I explore how the linked media of radio and film handled the contradictions created between the mature musical voice of Deanna Durbin and her juvenated star persona. Durbin's vocal masquerade of "womanliness" creates an aura of sensuality and sexual maturity that complicates her representation of sexually innocent adolescent femininity. Thus, the uncanny musical force of her vocal production raised questions about the "natural" connection between the body and the voice. In this respect Durbin's voice was freakish, an object of curiosity and awe, as well as pleasure. I argue that Durbin's films continually narrativize her vocality as a source of power over men who are seduced by and submit to her voice. Because of its operatic technique, Durbin's voice is not submerged in the female body; as a result, her stardom suggests a resistance to the limitations and vulnerability sometimes attributed to women's acoustic representation in cinema.[34]

Chapter 4 addresses the early screen appearances of Elizabeth Taylor. I am interested in the impact of her beauty in the nascent formation of her star presence in the 1940s. Like Durbin, Taylor represented a potentially dangerous erotic embodiment of the juvenated female. This chapter focuses on Taylor's appearances during the war years in two uncredited roles (in *Jane Eyre* and *The White Cliffs of Dover* [both 1944]) and her star-making performance in *National Velvet* (1944). The notion that Taylor's precocious beauty contributes to a queering of the text for female viewers is explored through an extended analysis of *Jane Eyre*. This chapter also charts how Hollywood drew on important Victorian high-art precursors in depicting popular representations of the beautiful English girl. This cultural heritage, I argue, contributed to the shaping of Taylor's early child roles in ways that either met or challenged culturally prevalent attitudes toward the eroticization of juvenated females. Understanding the implications of viewing pleasure attached to Taylor's beauty in films that focused on constructing Britishness complicates our view of Hollywood's representation of femininity during a time when shared Anglo-American values were emphasized by U.S. filmmakers because of World War II.

Chapter 5 focuses on the association of Jennifer Jones's star persona with hysteria and adolescence, a pairing that was important in the origins of psychoanalytic thought. I analyze the ways in which Jones's melodramatic performances of juvenated femininity, as well as her controversial professional and personal relationship with producer David O. Selznick, resonated with earlier discourses on adolescent hysteria. Her juvenated roles in melodramas were often in films aimed at women that registered the cultural interest in psychoanalysis demonstrated more broadly in U.S. culture during the 1940s. I devote particular attention to the hysterical inscription of juvenated femininity in *The Song of Bernadette, Since You Went Away,* and *Duel in the Sun.* The last film, a western, was the turning point in Jones's career that linked her screen persona to more transgressive female sexuality. Condemned as "filthy, debasing and insulting to the moral instincts of decent humanity," *Duel in the Sun* became a box-office smash, drawing the patronage of teenagers with the help of massive advertising and saturation booking.[35] As I contextualize her films within the changes occurring in the U.S. film industry's move toward more sexually liberal "adult" melodramas, I also consider the inscription of hysteria in her subsequent appearances in Michael Powell's and Emeric Pressburger's *Gone to Earth* (1951) and King Vidor's *Ruby Gentry* (1952). Like *Duel in the Sun,* these films centralize the presence of Jones in the role of a juvenated female who is a working-class or racial outsider devalued by society and sexually debased by men. Thus, this chapter is concerned with racial inscription in Hollywood melodramas that attempt to represent the female "rite of passage" at a time when U.S. culture was extremely anxious about female sexual delinquency.

Chapter 6 takes as its chief goal the understanding of Audrey Hepburn as a fashion commodity whose star persona participated in a number of cultural contradictions and tensions involving adolescent femininity. Simultaneously juvenated and "sophisticated," the star image of Audrey Hepburn in the 1950s existed in contradistinction to Hollywood's promotion of voluptuous, "sex bomb" femininity exemplified by Marilyn Monroe. Hepburn was juvenated through her androgynous and gamine qualities that her films and offscreen publicity emphasized. However, with her appearance in *Sabrina* (dir. Billy Wilder, 1954), the star also became associated with Parisian haute couture and the designs of Hubert de Givenchy. These fashions might have defined her feminine beauty as elitist and European, but these associations were mediated by her juvenated qualities and her films' use of fashion to facilitate the social elevation and sexual maturation of the heroine within a "Cinderella story" that often ends with marriage to an older man. Responding to disagreement concerning the response of youthful female viewers of the 1950s to the star as a role model, I argue that Hepburn's inscription of filmic fashionability attempts to solve the contradictions inherent in her films' transformation of the immature girl into an ideal of sophisticated woman that capitalizes on the nostalgic notions of Frenchness that helped fuel postwar interest in Parisian haute couture in the United States. Thus, my goal in this chapter is to show how Hepburn's representation in films and in extratextual star discourse made her a privileged cinematic signifier of a utopian consumer culture that could bring postwar femininity into appropriately domesticated—and unerringly fashionable—maturity. That maturity, however, was qualified by the star's juvenation on a number of levels and suggests ambivalence toward the move into full adulthood. While seeming to advocate for an elitist, fashion-centered identity, the star's juvenation, including the display of her flat body, may have appealed to some female viewers who regarded her as a liberating alternative model to the hypervoluptuous ideal of femininity that dominated midcentury America.

My conclusion addresses generalizations to be made from the alignment of stardom with juvenated femininity during the classical Hollywood era of filmmaking. I attempt to answer the question of why juvenated femininity appears to have such a persistent hold over movie viewers, often to the consternation of the stars who were typecast as girls or as girls in the transition to adulthood. What does this fascination tell us about the evolution of gender difference and the representation of female sexuality in mainstream commercial film? Using the six stars I consider as the foundation, I suggest related issues to be considered, as well as where study in this neglected area of investigation might usefully go.

FIGURE 4. Pickford studio portrait for *The Poor Little Rich Girl* (dir. Maurice Tourneur, 1917). Courtesy of the Academy of Motion Picture Arts and Sciences.

CHAPTER 1

# Oh, "Doll Divine"

## *Mary Pickford, Masquerade, and the Pedophilic Gaze*

Mary Pickford, doll divine,
Year by year, and every day
At the moving-picture play,
You have been my valentine.

—Vachel Lindsay, "To Mary Pickford, Moving-Picture Actress"

Mary Pickford was, arguably, the most famous woman of the first quarter of the twentieth century. Inarguably, she was one of the first major stars of the Hollywood film industry and one of the very few—female or male—able to sustain stardom for more than twenty years. Born Gladys Smith in Toronto, Canada, Mary Pickford became a stage actress at age six (published age "5"). She first appeared in motion pictures in one-reelers of American Biograph in the spring of 1909. In the 1910s the actress known as "Our Little Mary" quickly cemented her popularity through numerous films that coincided with the industry's shift to Hollywood and using the actor as a personality for drawing audiences to the box-office.[1] Pickford was promoted as "America's Sweetheart," "The World's Sweetheart," and, as poet Vachel Lindsay dubbed her, "The Queen of the Movies."[2] Her films for Famous Players in the late 1910s regularly netted more than a million dollars a year. In 1918 an article in *American Magazine* proclaimed what by then was obvious: "Our Little Mary" had become "the most popular motion picture actress in the world."[3]

What made her so popular? What exactly was the appeal of Mary Pickford and of her films? In attempting to answer these questions, it cannot escape notice that from the beginning of Pickford's film career, the actress's characters often are ambiguously inscribed with characteristics of both child and adult woman, as a child-woman.[4] As I will show, even when she ostensibly is cast as an adult, the grown-up Mary Pickford registers as an adolescent girl or a "child-woman," ambiguously poised between childhood and womanhood. As her career moved into the feature-film era, her screen persona grew even younger, until she was, for all intents and purposes, a child impersonator.

In 1914 an industry trade magazine, *The Bioscope,* published a review of the Pickford star vehicle *Tess of the Storm Country* (dir. Edwin S. Porter) that articulates one view of the actress's youthful appeal: "There are many young comediennes . . . but it is only Mary Pickford . . . who can create through the silent medium . . . just that particular kind of sentiment—ineffably sweet, joyously young, and sometimes, if one may put it so, almost unbearably heartbreaking in its tender pathos—which has become identified with her name, and with which we are all familiar."[5]

In *Tess* (as well as in its 1922 remake) Pickford was cast as an adolescent hoyden living in poverty. Many of the actress's other star vehicles, including *Rags* (dir. James Kirkwood, 1915) and *M'Liss* (dir. Marshall Neilan, 1918), followed the same formula, placing the girl in a small town or the country. A *Variety* reviewer of *Rags* thought that the basis of Pickford's popular appeal was already rather obvious: "she and her bag of tricks are so well established . . . [that] no matter what she does in a picture they [film followers] are sure to term it 'cute,' and in the current offering are many scenes that call for that expression."[6] Pickford regularly played "cute" girls who, in the emerging language of the time, fell into the category known as "adolescents."[7] In the late 1910s, however, her characters began to grow even younger. She became a child impersonator in *The Foundling* (dir. John O'Brien, 1916), *The Poor Little Rich Girl* (dir. Maurice Tourneur, 1917), *Rebecca of Sunnybrook Farm* (dir. Marshall Neilan, 1917), and *The Little Princess* (dir. Marshall Neilan, 1917). Audiences and critics responded with enthusiasm. She spawned imitators, like Mary Miles Minter, and wrote for *Vanity Fair* about the techniques and technical problems of undertaking child roles.[8]

The numerous textual iterations of the childlike "Mary Pickford" enabled her remarkable success. The model of young white femininity Pickford represented, sometimes fragile and imperiled, sometimes feisty and resilient, was not the only type available to audiences in the 1910s. In those same years Fox star Theda Bara was the most famous embodiment of the seductive power of the dark, orientalized vamp; and Pearl White and Grace Cunard exemplified the thrilling athleticism of the serial heroine who turned physical danger into high adventure.[9] Yet none of these stars achieved the sustained popularity of Pickford.

In searching for an explanation of Pickford's juvenation, one might be tempted to assume that it reflected the predictable typecasting of

FIGURE 5. Pickford as the mining camp hoyden in *Rags* (dir. James Kirkwood, 1915). Courtesy of the Academy of Motion Picture Arts and Sciences.

a popular actress by an exploitative, male-dominated industry. Such a view has to be tempered by the knowledge that, by the late 1910s, the actress was already exercising a great deal of influence over her film projects made through the Artcraft division of Famous Players–Lasky. She briefly moved to First National, where she enjoyed more control as her own independent producer. As one of the founders of United Artists in 1919, she was in the forefront of film artists who exercised absolute creative mastery over their vehicles, from concept through distribution.

In spite of Pickford's unprecedented control over her films, the formula for her star vehicles changed relatively little. In fact, not only did she continue to play ragged adolescents, but also during the years in which she exercised the most creative authority over her silent film career, many of her most important and popular films present her in the role of a child. These included, at First National, *Daddy-Long-Legs* (dir. Marshall Neilan, 1919) and, at United Artists, *Pollyanna* (dir. Paul Powell, 1920), *Through the Back Door* (dir. Alfred E. Green and Jack Pickford, 1921), *Little Lord Fauntleroy* (dir. Alfred E. Green and Jack

Pickford, 1921), *Little Annie Rooney* (dir. William Beaudine, 1925), and *Sparrows* (dir. William Beaudine, 1926). A commentator reacted to Pickford in *Through the Back Door:* "She stands absolutely alone in the portrayal of youthful roles, and conveys the impression of extreme youth, both through face and conduct as no other player ever has. . . . She appears with equal facility and conviction a child of eleven and a girl of seventeen."[10]

The notion of a grown woman playing a child and the specific techniques used to represent "Our Little Mary" on- and offscreen certainly raise a host of questions about the fascination that Mary Pickford inspired in a broad range of viewers. In spite of her enormous popularity Pickford's sustained association with child roles did not go without comment. "Why do people love Mary?" was a question often raised in the 1910s, but Mordaunt Hall's review of *Pollyanna* in the *New York Times* articulates the rather more nervous question that was asked especially often in the 1920s: "People have been asking recently *why doesn't Mary Pickford grow up?* The question is answered at the Rivoli this week. It is evident that Miss Pickford doesn't grow up because she can make people laugh and cry, can win her way into more hearts and even protesting heads, as a rampant, resilient little girl than as anything else. She can no more grow up than Peter Pan."[11]

The public strongly associated Pickford with child and "girl" characters, so much so that the actress was said to be expressing ambivalence toward her typecasting in juvenated roles as early as 1917; in 1921 she protested: "The world wants me to remain a little girl all my life. . . . I want to give the very best that is in me, but whenever I try to do something different, the public complains I have tucked up my curls and let off the short pinafores. To them, I am eternal youth, and they won't let me grow up."[12]

If juvenation of her onscreen image frustrated the actress's desire to widen her range, it did not become the basis of any sustained effort to remake her screen persona. Pickford did attempt a departure in Frances Marion's *The Love Light* (dir. Marion, 1921), a World War I melodrama. Cast as an Italian peasant, Pickford starts out as a village hoyden but quickly grows up when she falls in love with and marries a stranded sailor (Fred Thomson). He turns out to be a German spy. The film called for Angela, Pickford's much-suffering protagonist, to temporarily lose her mind. Pickford immediately reverted back to type in her next film, *Through the Back Door,* in which she plays a child abandoned by her socialite mother to be raised by Belgian peasants. She

FIGURE 6. Ernst Lubitsch, director of *Rosita,* with Mrs. Charlotte Pickford and Mary Pickford, ca. 1923. Courtesy of the Academy of Motion Picture Arts and Sciences.

did attempt dual roles, of mother and curly-headed son, in *Little Lord Fauntleroy,* also released in 1921.

Pickford's most famous departures from "type" came in two historical costume dramas. In 1923 the star sought to play Marguerite in an Ernst Lubitsch–directed version of *Faust,* but her mother objected to her daughter playing a woman who commits infanticide.[13] Instead, Pickford assumed the role of a coquettish young street dancer who catches the eye of a Spanish king in *Rosita* (dir. Ernst Lubitsch, 1923). The next year, Pickford starred in Marshall Neilan's *Dorothy Vernon of Haddon Hall* (1924), in which she played another coquettish adolescent, one who rebels against the dictates of her father to follow her heart.

The career stretch the actress attempted in these two star vehicles may appear to be a very conservative one. A thoughtful commentary in the *New York Evening Post* concluded that both *Dorothy Vernon* and *Rosita* offered only inconsequential differences from Pickford's usual screen work: "Our Mary herself is better and prettier than ever before. But for some unknown reason, she seems to insist on sticking to a type. . . . This, of course, tends to monotony. We believe that this is recognized by Miss

Pickford, and probably gives her many uneasy moments. . . . However, it isn't exactly fair to criticize Miss Pickford for her lack of versatility. She has so firmly established herself in the affection of a large army of movie fans that, perhaps, there would be disappointment if Mary turned out in some picture to be anyone else than Mary."[14]

Most critics were quite positive about Pickford's performances in productions that were more sexually sophisticated than her usual vehicles. Both films made money. Pickford, however, regarded *Rosita* and *Dorothy Vernon of Haddon Hall* as failures. Perhaps their lack of resounding box-office success worried the star that she would inevitably lose some measure of her popularity if she were not "Little Mary" in her pictures. Shortly after *Dorothy Vernon of Haddon Hall* was released, Pickford warned her fans that she might be forced to take radical action: "I created a certain type, which has been worked out now. It is finished. It is possible to do another type, of course, but the public wants me only in one character, that of Mary Pickford. Now I have finished that and I think it is time to quit."[15]

Contrary to her published remarks, Pickford didn't quit, and she did not quit her little girl roles. In a letter to a family member she blamed others for her return to type: "Everyone seemed to resent so much the two grown up parts of Rosita and Dorothy that I felt I had to return to a little girl role."[16] Did her loyal public constitute "everyone"? If so, how did the public articulate this resentment if not at the box office? We do not have access to evidence (such as troves of angry fan letters) that might support Pickford's claim, but in a letter to *Photoplay,* in 1925, a female fan emphasizes the powerful conflation of Pickford with her child characters that no doubt influenced the star's decision to stay true to her juvenated type:

> My Dear Little Mary:
>
> The idea that you are "just a little girl" is so firmly established in my mind that any attempt to discard it is resented. . . . Only a great actress or one who is really a child at heart, could make those little characters so natural that they become our friends, and we refuse to give them up when another "Mary Pickford" appears in the role of an older girl. We love Dorothy Vernon, too, but we never, never associate her with our own little Mary, Rebecca, and Pollyanna.[17]

To the letter writer "Little Mary" is yet another little girl among her favorite Pickford characters. A virtual collapse had occurred between "Our Little Mary" onscreen and "Mary Pickford" the actress.

FIGURE 7. Annie (Mary Pickford) leads her gang in *Little Annie Rooney* (dir. William Beaudine, 1925). Courtesy of the Academy of Motion Picture Arts and Sciences.

In the same issue in which this letter appeared, *Photoplay* published a poll listing the roles that its readers wanted Pickford to play. The magazine claimed, "Almost twenty thousand readers spoke with a clear majority that was overwhelmingly in favor of roles [for Pickford] depicting childhood."[18] We do not know the age of those who responded or if the majority were girls and women, but their top choices seem to indicate a familiarity with girls' literature. Readers wanted Pickford to play Anne of Green Gables, Heidi, Alice in Wonderland, Cinderella, the Little Colonel, and Sara Crewe. As if in capitulation to the tastes of her fans, Pickford was back on the screen in the next year as a feisty Irish American tenement girl leading a multiracial neighborhood gang in *Little Annie Rooney* (dir. William Beaudine, 1925). Mordaunt Hall's review was appreciative but aware of the intractability of the Pickford screen persona: "Viewing Miss Pickford in such a role is like turning the clock back as this charming actress has not changed perceptibly since the early days of pictures."[19]

## MARY'S MASQUERADE AND GENDERED SPECTATORSHIP

Mary Pickford engaged in a masquerade of childishness with significant implications for gender-determined spectatorship. Pickford's juvenation, I will argue, complicated the erotic and identificatory responses of gendered spectators in reaction to femininity embodied by an adult star. Pickford's child-woman characters function as an object of identification but also of desire—whether as an object of the spectator's desire or of other characters. The spectator must negotiate the subtleties of a complex masquerade in which an adult star who represents feminine aesthetic perfection also embodies a girl whose juvenated qualities suggest that she is too young to know what desire is. This notion of a masquerade of childishness bears some structural similarities to the masquerade of femininity often cited in feminist film theory. The latter is derived from Joan Riviere's psychoanalytically based theory of womanliness. In her 1929 essay "Womanliness as a Masquerade" Riviere offers a psychoanalytic case history and argues that the cultural codes of womanliness or femininity are assumed rather like a masquerade to allay anxiety and deflect patriarchal criticism of the woman patient's demonstration of masculine traits such as intellectual prowess.[20]

Pickford's adult masquerade of childishness makes acceptable, perhaps even inevitable, the sexualization of her child-woman. Rather than performing the cultural codes expected to construct womanliness, Pickford assumed the signs of childishness. Pickford was diminutive (slightly over five feet tall), but her height alone does not explain why she so successfully embodied the child-woman. Many female stars in this era were petite; the movie industry believed that the camera was unflattering to taller women who also might look overwhelming beside many leading men.[21]

Although she often portrayed girls who were strong-minded and vigorous rather than silly and delicate, Pickford's masquerade of childishness undercut her potential to be a sexual subject. That masquerade of childishness reflects a nostalgia-driven, Victorian-influenced cultural determination of femininity. Pickford's films were often drawn from late nineteenth- and early twentieth-century literature about children but not necessarily addressed only to them. Adults frequently read this literature. Many of the novels and plays adapted by Pickford to film were by women writers who offered the adventures and triumphs of independent little white girls whose behavior rebelled against expected norms of feminine refinement.[22] Although largely adhering to expectations for the development of rambunctious girls into refined women, sometimes this literature was critical of gender inequalities. The inscription of the girl's immaturity and her transition to adulthood gave her "permission to behave in ways that might not be appropriate for a woman."[23]

Certainly all this is true of Pickford's title character in *Rebecca of Sunnybrook Farm,* adapted from the book by Kate Douglas Wiggin. The mother of the title character cannot afford to raise her daughter, so she ships Rebecca off to live with two dour aunts. Rebecca demonstrates remarkable independence and intelligence as she adapts to living with them. She is a tomboy who climbs trees, uses an umbrella like a sword against a bothersome girl, and assertively manages other children in a backyard circus performance. Her antics invariably get her into trouble at school, at home, and at play.

In spite of qualities that might also suggest a nascent "New Woman," Rebecca/Pickford is brought to the brink of a virtuous womanhood by two familiar aspects of the Victorian model of femininity—altruism and illness.[24] It is of some interest, nevertheless, that her actual transition to a traditional model of white womanhood—one in which demure sweetness will replace brazen outspokenness—is never shown by the film. After recovering from her illness, Rebecca is shipped off again—to boarding school. She returns visually transformed, a beautiful young woman (of seventeen) ready to forgive her dying Aunt Miranda (Josephine Crowell) for her occasionally harsh treatment of her. But her character retains enough spontaneity (or rebelliousness) to run away when a neighbor, Adam Ladd (Eugene O'Brien), coded throughout the film as Rebecca's future husband, attempts to kiss her.

To theorize the complexities of gendered spectatorship in relation to Pickford's construction of childishness in a film like *Rebecca of Sunnybrook Farm* requires an acknowledgment of the star's actual historical audiences in the period of her greatest popularity. United Artist press books gave exhibitors of Pickford's films advice for movie exploitation, including contests and tie-ins, event ideas for community organizations ("Humanizing the Campaign"), and articles for local newspaper publication.[25] These all suggest that in the 1920s, children were regarded as a very important segment of Pickford's historical audience, but women were also identified as a key part of the star's fan base. A review of *Dorothy Vernon of Haddon Hall* noted, "It's a safe bet that women of every age . . . will crowd the Criterion Theatre for months to come and many a man will also find himself sharing the joy of the powder-puff brigade."[26] Pickford herself speculated

FIGURE 8. Aunt Miranda (Josephine Crowell) ends the backyard circus for Rebecca (Mary Pickford) in *Rebecca of Sunnybrook Farm* (dir. Marshall Neilan, 1917). Courtesy of the Academy of Motion Picture Arts and Sciences.

that the typical customer for her films was "a tired businessman who gets home, settles down when his wife says, 'Ben, it's Mary Pickford tonight—let's take the children.'"[27] Since "Our Mary" cultivated her films' "uplifting," "wholesome" appeal, her account of her audience may be regarded as a savvy marketing ploy seeking to incorporate the whole spectrum of the family into her box office; it also is convergent with the industry's belief that women determined family moviegoing habits in the 1920s.[28]

Perhaps some men had to be coaxed to go to a Pickford film, but male critics were intrigued with her. These included Mordaunt Hall, who admitted that he found her fascinating even when he did not like her film vehicles (one of his *New York Times* reviews bemoaned the fact that so many of her films were not "adult fare").[29] Many male critics and commentators blended an admiration bordering on worship with open curiosity about the source(s) of her popularity. In *The Art of the Moving Picture,* Vachel Lindsay repeated the question that was often asked in popular discourse of the time: "Why do the people love Mary?" His answer to this question captures something of the power of the Pickford image:

> Because of a certain aspect of her face in her highest mood. . . . The people are hungry for this fine and spiritual thing that Botticelli painted in the faces of his muses and heavenly creatures. Because the mob catch the very glimpse of it in Mary's face, they follow her night after night in the films. They are never quite satisfied with the plays because the managers are not artists enough to know they should sometimes put her into sacred pictures and not have her always the village hoyden. . . . But perhaps in this argument I have but betrayed myself as Mary's infatuated partisan.[30]

Lindsay's remarks may strike us at first as a strange accounting of the reasons for Pickford's popularity, for he articulates a fascination that reaches beyond the boundaries of the star's roles; indeed, he suggests that her roles and film vehicles frustrate rather than satisfy her audience.

Lindsay's "infatuation" with Pickford constitutes a useful route to the notion of a pedophilic gaze in relation to the construction of "Our Little Mary." The idea that Pickford had anything to do with sexual desire aimed at a child would have scandalized her admirers in the 1910s and 1920s. Yet how often is an aesthetic response to females, like that of Lindsay to his "doll divine," completely unconnected to a sexual one? Also speaking volumes about the unconscious sexual force of Pickford's blurring of the boundaries between her womanliness and a masquerade of childishness is a 1916 commentary by Frederick Wallace. Like Lindsay, he claims to seek the reasons for Pickford's popularity; after admitting that he has seen all her films and listing those traits she shares with other stars (personality, talent, beauty), he provides a telling answer: "What is this appeal? Frankly, I do not know, . . . [but] she is the most humanly irresistible thing I ever saw. . . . She is so adorably feminine, from her curls to her toes . . . in everything she does."[31]

FIGURE 9. Wistful portrait of Mary Pickford by Ira A. Hill, 1916. Courtesy of the Academy of Motion Picture Arts and Sciences.

I do not wish to argue that Pickford appealed to male admirers who were actual pedophiles. What I do wish to suggest is that Pickford appealed to and through a kind of cultural pedophilia that looked to the adorable and innocent "child-woman" to personify nostalgic ideals of femininity that were inseparable from erotic value but also moral value. In this respect Pickford's popularity also was related to a phenomenon located in Victorian and post-turn-of-the-century academic painting by Bram Dijkstra in *Idols of Perversity.* Dijkstra argues that the representation of young girls in academic painting of the time created a venue as much about and for the play of male sexual fantasy as it was an idealization of childhood innocence.[32]

Pickford's films and extratextual publicity functioned as a venue for the play of male fantasy that shares much with fin de siècle high-art representations of children. One could argue that the actress's screen impersonations of the little girl add another complication to the eroticization of female innocence. It may have provided a mechanism of disavowal ("I watch, I desire this child, but she is really not a child") to men who sought to deny such culturally prevalent sexual fantasies. As an added bonus for the play of sexual fantasy, the viewer might have rationalized any desire for the child or childlike character through the disavowing formula: "I desire this woman who looks/acts like a child because I know that she is not a child; still, she is as all women should be—innocent and childlike." By its overt performative status, Pickford's masquerade of juvenated femininity might have rendered her erotic potential safe for men.

The complex disavowal of Pickford's status as an adult woman was not limited to her screen vehicles. It was reinforced in extratextual discourse: advertisements, fan and general interest magazine articles, publicity photographs, and interviews that juvenated the actress as a star persona. Not all of these venues present Pickford in exactly the same manner, however, and as Lindsay intuited, the treatment of Pickford in publicity portraiture is different. It fixed in all its intensity the wistful, soft beauty of her juvenated star persona, a side of her that was frequently complicated or even compromised by her presentation as a wild hoyden or aggressively active child of the poor in many of her films.

In spite of these complications, within the cultural scenario of the 1910s and 1920s Pickford's portrayal of an old-fashioned girl, albeit one of high spirits, may have provided an erotic object more acceptable to many men than the overtly sexualized flapper, whose transgression of traditional feminine sexual norms was often perceived as more of a challenge than a promise. It is well documented that in the 1910s and 1920s the flapper and the New Woman symbolized American women's overturning of Victorian feminine ideals. Considered a radical subversion of American gender ideals, sexual agency among modern women was met with a great deal of cultural anxiety. As social historian Paula Fass has noted: "gazing at the young women of the period, the traditionalist saw the end of American civilization as he had known it."[33] Thus, the cinematic articulation of Pickford as an antimodernist, Victorian-indebted model of femininity served as one antidote to a perceived crisis in feminine sexual behavior.

## LIMINALITY AND THE ATTRACTIVE CHILD-WOMAN

Coming as it does during a time in which modernism and antimodernism waged a war of words over women and their desires, Pickford's impersonation of girls takes on sexual complexity, especially in relation to gendered spectatorship. That complexity is illuminated by remarks made by Martha Vicinus in another context. Vicinus argues that the symbolic function of the adolescent boy in fin de siècle culture was to "absorb and reflect a variety of sexual desires and emotional needs."[34] Pickford's astonishing popularity depends on a similar process. On the one hand, male fantasies were easily attached to her. She represented a dangerously attractive female whose masquerade of childishness appealed to adult men raised in the late Victorian period. In the 1910s and 1920s those men might find her enticing innocence a comforting alternative to the models of feminine sexual subjectivity offered by the flapper and the New Woman. On the other hand, Pickford's many child-woman protagonists also could serve an important identificatory function for women and girls who might view the screen actress as a comforting asexual figure of freedom whose youth released her from the demands—including the sexual demands—of adult femininity. Her characters' frequent placement in rural settings and alignment with older moral values added to the nostalgic identification that viewers, especially women viewers, might feel for a girl who is freed from having to face the confusions of modern urban living.

From the start of her film career Pickford's screen persona evidenced liminality with regard to the inscription of her age and sexuality. This is evident as early as D.W. Griffith's *The Lonely Villa* of 1909. In this house-invasion narrative Pickford plays the oldest child of a besieged suburban family. What is noticeable in this film is how Pickford is distinguished, visually, from the other female actors. She is extraordinarily beautiful. Her expressive face and large head, topped by long, soft curls, draw the eye and impress with their perfection. The sensitivity and mature beauty of her face suggest a contradictory relationship with her small body, rendered shapeless and childish by a loose, low-waisted, white dress. This typical mode of clothing for a middle-class girl of the time inscribes physical and fashion-coded childishness, but her wom-

FIGURE 10. Mary Pickford and Lionel Barrymore in *The New York Hat* (dir. D.W. Griffith, 1912). Author's collection.

anly facial beauty contributes an uncertainty as to her status: is she an untouchable child or a marriageable, sexual woman?

A similar uncertainty or ambiguity underscored many of her silent film performances—as child, adolescent, and adult—and unsettled the inscription of sexual boundaries in everything from Griffith's *The New York Hat* (1912) to *My Best Girl* (dir. Sam Taylor, 1927). In *The New York Hat* a motherless girl becomes the target of small-town gossip when she receives an anonymous gift of an elaborate, feathered hat. The hat, displayed in a store window, has been the object of desire of most of the town's female population. "Mary" is unaware that the minister (Lionel Barrymore) bought her the hat to keep trust with a poignant request left him by her mother, who was worked to death by her husband. The mother gave the clergyman a sum of money to buy her daughter "the bits of finery she has always been denied."

Is the daughter a woman or a child? Pickford spends most of the film dressed young and playing young. Although she wears the long dress of a woman, her attire is loose and obscures her figure. As if she has suddenly outgrown her clothes, her arms stick awkwardly out of her sleeves. Her attempt to look sophisticated by carrying gloves as she walks down the street makes her look even more childish. Learning through gossips that the minister bought the expensive hat, the church elders and Mary's father suspect the worst (seduction). In a fit of outrage her father destroys the hat. The girl reacts with muted horror. Reaching for the ruined remains, she attempts to put the broken feathers back into place on the crushed brim.

The minister comforts her and shows the father and the church officials the letter entrusted to him by Mary's mother. Suddenly, with the revelation of the minister's kindness, the girl is represented as being of marriageable age when, through pantomime, the minister suggests that they marry. The scene continues to register the tension between Pickford's girlishness and womanliness as her character whispers in her father's ear to ask permission. The film's ending confirms the possibility of a mature sexual union that the rest of the film seems to vigorously deny. The denial rests chiefly in the strength of Pickford's performance of the girl as just that, a girl who appears capable of an intense interest in a hat but not in a man.

The image of the eroticized child-woman is familiar throughout the work of D.W. Griffith, where it has often been associated with Victorian ideals of femininity. Pickford's hoyden shares much with that ideal and with Griffith's child-women, but her characters' physical assertiveness and determined mind-set tend to obscure these fundamental commonalities. Pickford herself sought to distinguish her heroines from Griffith's; she came to articulate her artistic differences with the director as revolving around the exaggerated effects that he demanded in portrayals of youthful femininity. In an interview late in life she claimed, "I would not run around like a goose with its head off, crying 'oooooh . . . the little birds! Ooooh . . . look! A little bunny!' That's what he taught his ingénues, and they all did the same thing."[35]

Mary Pickford's screen heroines, like Griffith's, exhibited qualities associated with juvenated cuteness that became an established part of the Pickford screen persona, but they were also different in important ways. *M'Liss* is exemplary in this regard. *Motion Picture News* called the film "the 'typical' Pickford picture" since it "shows her in rags and curls, in situations both humorous and dramatic."[36] The film is set in California mining country during the Gold Rush years. Pickford plays "M'Liss" (the nickname of "Melissa Smith"), a hoyden who does not just move among the rougher elements of the town of Red Gulch but is one of them, infamous locally for her wild ways (including her "cussing"). After the intertitle introducing "Mary Pickford as M'Liss," the film offers an iris-framed long shot showing a huge, flat, weathered rock in the middle of the piney woods. Suddenly, a ragged girl (Pickford) runs into the frame from offscreen right, leaping onto the boulder with a little bounce. She looks around. Her golden hair is backlit. A reverse shot (iris) shows a small tree shaking. Then, a full shot shows M'Liss pulling up her right arm in exclamation and then slapping it down roughly on her leather holster. She purses her lips as she pulls a slingshot out of the holster and fusses with her other hand to get a rock from a pouch. Another shot shows the bear she has just spied. M'Liss fearlessly (and foolishly) takes aim and dings it with a rock. The bear turns. Instead of reverting to a close-up, a long shot shows M'Liss's surprised reaction registered in other typical Pickford mannerisms: the quick, almost mechanical (doll-like?) movement of her arms up in a register of surprise with a little step taken backward. The scene ends with her taking off in a vigorous, crouched run back in the same direction from whence she came.

This scene demonstrates the physical mannerisms that were already well established in the Pickford screen persona. A newspaper review of *M'Liss* summarized how the film capitalized on the appeal of its star as "the ragged little Mary everyone first learned to know and love. All the inimitable little mannerisms which are so much her own are in evidence. . . . All dressed up and in a beautiful garden she is lovely, but in funny tattered little garments, with curls flying, she is—well, just 'our Mary.'"[37] As the review suggests, *M'Liss* offered signature elements of the Pickford screen persona that audiences and critics came to appreciate—and expect. Like many Pickford heroines, M'Liss is poor. She lives with her father, "Bummer" Smith (Theodore Roberts), a lovable drunkard who sleeps with Hildegarde, his prized hen, under his arm. Left to her own devices, M'Liss robs the local stagecoach for fun. She does this in a flawed disguise, covering her face with a bandana but leaving visible her distinctively ragged (and dirty) clothing. Throughout the film, in a comic touch, Pickford has M'Liss periodically hitch up her skirt like a working-class man hitching up his pants, especially in moments when she is nervously out of place (the local schoolhouse).

More than her ragged clothing, the star's distinctive mass of long curls establishes the visual appeal of M'Liss as an archetypal Pickford screen character and representative of ideal, Victorian-influenced femininity. *M'Liss* exploits the beauty of Pickford's blonde hair, featuring her famous sausage curls backlit in many scenes as she moves across the countryside by foot or on horseback. A completely gratuitous sequence highlights the importance of her long curls as a reminder that Victorian culture regarded women's hair, especially blonde hair, as the source of a woman's almost magical sexual power.[38]

M'Liss decides she will go to school in the wake of accidentally destroying her doll (stolen from the stagecoach) with her slingshot. With her doll she has buried her "little gal dreams," an intertitle tells us. The handsome new schoolteacher (Thomas Meighan) encourages her to become a part of his classroom. In the next scene we see M'Liss struggling like a small child against her father as he vigorously washes her hair.[39] This is followed by a full shot showing M'Liss sitting on a fence in a pastoral setting. She faces the camera, but her hair obscures her face as she bends forward to dry her waist-length mass of blonde curls in the sun. Suddenly, she swings her hair back and raises her head in one fluid motion that showcases the beauty of her hair, which is given an angelic glow by the backlighting. She purses her lips, sighs, and dreamily looks into the foreground—until she sees something (offscreen) that sparks a plan. In a moment she is once again scurrying across the countryside. This may seem a reversion to innocent childhood, but the erotic qualities of M'Liss foregrounded in the scene and her interest in the schoolmaster will ultimately end in a romantic coupling with him that confirms her entry into womanhood.

The camera's fascination with M'Liss's hair demonstrates how "Our Little Mary" was not just a cute and lovable wild child but also someone whom we see in the process of becoming a woman. The lighting in this scene and throughout the film suggests the kind of visual treatment of femininity that Richard Dyer describes in reference to Lillian Gish as a paragon of whiteness. He argues that the use of halo effects and glowing three-point lighting for Gish in *True Heart Susie* (dir. D.W. Griffith, 1919) emphasizes the fairness of the star's hair and skin so that her beauty becomes "a moral value" registering aesthetic and moral superiority.[40]

In Pickford's films, however, there is more tension created between this kind of visualization and her characters. In spite of M'Liss's youth, the display of the star's hair works as a sexual exhibition reminiscent of those attributed to mermaids and sea sirens, popular subjects of late Victorian paintings. As Gitter suggests, "the more abundant the hair, the more potent the sexual invitation implied by its display. . . . The luxuriance of the hair is an index of vigorous sexuality."[41] There is something quite erotic about this film's display of its star at this moment, and Pickford's star persona, like Gish's, was affiliated with goodness, pathos, and whiteness. Yet her vigorous physicality made her seem much less fragile than Gish; she was often not just active but rambunctious and aligned in her films with working-class hardiness.[42]

As *M'Liss* and *Rebecca of Sunnybrook Farm* show, Pickford's heroines were less vacuous and hysterical and more assertive and hardheaded than Griffith's virginally pure child-women, but they still depended on the titillating vulnerability of the female innocent whose beauty was rarely complicated by sexual knowledge. Pickford's many motherless or orphaned heroines, like those in *Tess of the Storm Country, M'Liss, Little Annie Rooney,* and *Sparrows,* are placed within narratives that almost guarantee that a measure of pathos will be attached to the beautiful hoyden. In *M'Liss* the heroine first mourns her broken doll but then faces a life-changing loss when her father is murdered and the teacher she has come to love is accused of the crime. Little Annie Rooney also unexpectedly loses her father, a policeman. She hides at home under the table, hoping to surprise him on his return from work for his birthday celebration, but instead, another policeman comes with sad news. Orphaned, Annie is taken in by kindly Jewish neighbors.

No doubt the orphan-heroines Pickford often played appealed to many viewers as a poignant reflection of social reality; one in ten children of the time did not live with her or his parents.[43] Yet the codified strategies typically used to secure the audience's sentimental response to the plight of Pickford's character also reflected the influence of turn-of-the-century girls' literature. Casting Pickford as a neglected, orphaned, or poor child was a conventionalized avenue for empathetic identification with fictional girl protagonists. However, the girl protagonist's difficult circumstances also allowed her to have adventures that emphasized the enjoyable and humorous dimensions of her independence. That independence would normally be repressed in an intact nuclear family, especially a middle-class one with a watchful mother. Thus, women and girl viewers could guiltlessly rationalize the self-sufficiency of Pickford's characters since it often was acquired at the cost of home and family. Viewers might revel in Pickford's display of childhood freedom as an alternative space, a site of resistant female pleasures that slip away under the pressure of woman's cultural destiny.

After the film allows viewers to enjoy the girl's freedom, the Pickford heroine often suffers an accident or serious illness. Remarking on the appearance of this convention in girls' literature, Sally Mitchell claims that this trope functions not to reform the girl (since she is already good)

FIGURE 11. Judy Abbott (Mary Pickford) leads a revolt against prunes at the orphanage in *Daddy-Long-Legs* (dir. Marshall Neilan, 1919). Author's collection.

but to soften her tomboy qualities and induce "demonstrations of love from other characters as a delicious reward of subjugation."[44] Within Pickford's oeuvre the invalidism of Stella Maris, the illness of Rebecca of Sunnybrook Farm, and the paralysis of Pollyanna adhere to this model. In *Pollyanna* Pickford's heroine saves a child from being run over by an automobile, but she does so at the cost of being crushed under the wheels. Pollyanna's legs are paralyzed. Her aunt's emotional reserve has prevented her from showing her love for the child forced upon her, but after the accident she tenderly cares for Pollyanna. With the help of the local doctor Pollyanna is able to take her first halting steps under the gaze of all who have come to love her, including Aunt Polly.

The girl's endurance of grief, illness, or physical incapacitation is a precursor to her acceptance of a more restrained womanhood. Growing up may signal loss of freedom, but many Pickford films hold out the promise of romantic love as compensation for their heroines' lost childhood. Typical in this regard is *Daddy-Long-Legs*, which Kevin Brownlow has called "the archetypal Mary Pickford film . . . [having]

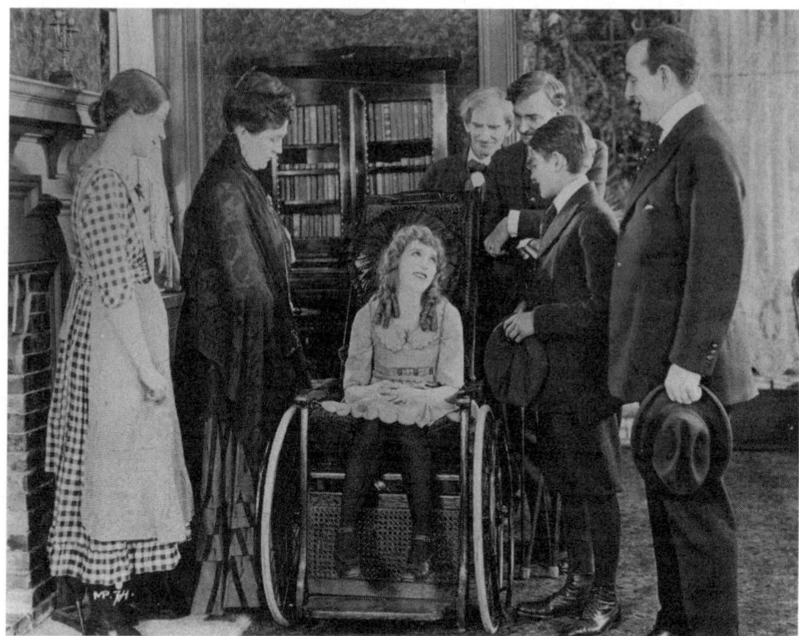

FIGURE 12. Altruism and illness bring the orphan (Mary Pickford) open expressions of love in *Pollyanna* (dir. Paul Powell, 1920). Courtesy of the Academy of Motion Picture Arts and Sciences.

all the elements an audience could hope for: a baby rescued from an ash can, an orphanage run like a penitentiary, hilarious and touching comedy, much pathos, and a lover waiting in the wings for Pickford's character to grow up."[45] The "lover waiting in the wings" certainly applies to Pickford films as early as *The New York Hat* and comes to be the expected formula for resolution in many of her feature films. In *Rebecca of Sunnybrook Farm,* Rebecca dons her Sunday best to sell soap door-to-door. Her goal is to secure a soap company prize (a lamp) to give to a poor family in town. During this door-to-door campaign the assertive Rebecca unexpectedly reverts to babyish confusion when Adam Ladd (whom she calls "Mr. Aladdin") shows her attention. In *Little Annie Rooney* the title character's escapades in leading her tenement gang of rock-throwing children end suddenly when she runs into Joe Kelly (William Haines), a grown man. He laughs at her, which makes her angry, but, of course, he will ultimately be her mate because, as the intertitles tell us, at this first meeting of child and man, she feels something for him that she cannot identify.

In spite of such moments the child's heterosexual love interest is quite marginalized in many of Pickford's films, for the heroine's bonding to other children takes precedence in her emotional life. Sometimes the heroine is simultaneously a motherless child and a child playing mother. This reproduction of mothering is poignantly offered in *Daddy-Long-Legs*. Judy Abbott (Pickford) steals a beautiful doll from a spoiled rich girl to lend to a sick orphan. Orphanage officials chase Judy in a scene that is played for comedy, but after they catch her, she is brutally punished, burned on a stove. Later that night, Judy cradles the sick orphan in her arms. She attempts to comfort the little girl with another doll, a crude, homemade one that Judy has obviously fashioned herself. The little girl only wants her "mama." An intertitle says: "Out of the great unknown the mother hears the call and comes with loving arms to take her baby home." Judy, who was left in an ash can as an infant, lightly holds her hand over her heart as she looks down on the bundle in her arms. Realizing the child is dead, she silently looks up to the heavens. Judy is still a girl, but her capacity for love affirms her potential to attain a superior womanhood in terms that resonate with the era's most traditional, family-centered values.[46] This scene suggests the "glows of feminine portraiture" suggested by Dyer as visual signifiers of the moral and aesthetic virtues of womanhood.[47] *Variety*'s reviewer correctly observed that "the punch of the picture is not in the love story of Judy grown up falling [in] love, . . . but in the pathos of the wistful little Judy, with her heart full of love, being constantly misunderstood."[48]

While figuring in *Daddy-Long-Legs* in this poignant scene, the talented orphan's ability to help other children forms the entire plot of *Sparrows*. "Mama Molly" (Pickford) is established as the oldest orphan at a Florida baby farm. A baby arrives, and Molly decides it "doesn't belong" because it is obviously well fed and so must be from a caring family. To keep the baby from being killed, Molly decides that all the children must escape. Though a mere adolescent in pigtails, she leads them in a harrowing journey across alligator-infested swamps to safety—and a new life. That life serves only to reinforce our confusion about her sexuality and age. In the mansion of the baby's widowed father Molly continues to look after the tiny child who motivated the escape. The wealthy father agrees to adopt the other children, but his relationship to Molly remains unclear: will she be another adopted child or his new wife?

Whether it was important to her audiences that Pickford's characters found romantic success in her films is uncertain. Often, as in *Sparrows*,

*Rebecca of Sunnybrook Farm,* and *Pollyanna,* her maturation into marriageable womanhood remains ambiguous. We cannot be certain that nascent or overt romance in these films necessarily held the most important appeal to her viewers, including to specific demographic segments (like women) of the audience. Or perhaps Pickford intuited that, after masquerading as a child, she should not completely spoil the illusion of girlhood that she had worked so hard to perfect. The final scene of *Daddy-Long-Legs* shows Rebecca discovering that Jarvis Pendleton (Mahlon Hamilton), the wealthy older man who has courted her, is also "Daddy-Long-Legs," the benefactor who has anonymously paid for her college education. Indirectness dominates the film's romantic conclusion: a huge wingback chair blocks the audience's view of Rebecca and Jarvis as they embrace and kiss. Only the changing rhythm of Rebecca's legs swinging over the side of the chair suggests what may be happening between them. Evidencing even greater avoidance of adult eroticism, the last shot of *Rebecca of Sunnybrook Farm* shows Rebecca running off into the distance to escape the kiss of Adam Ladd. Through different means Wiggin's original story registers its discomfort with making its seventeen-year-old heroine grow up into a sexualized adult. The novel reveals Adam's perspective on Rebecca: "He had looked into her eyes and they were still those of a child; there was no knowledge of the world . . . no passion, nor comprehension of it."[49] Similarly, at the end of *Little Annie Rooney* Annie says she "might wanna marry" Joe, but this will have to wait until the future, "when I grow up." Perhaps the love story in Pickford's films was important chiefly to signal that the heroine will be properly recognized as "priceless," as someone who deserves to be appreciated, understood, and cared for—whether by family or future husband.

Even without a romantic ending, however, the inscription of Pickford's adolescent heroines in these rags-to-riches scenarios had plenty of built-in appeal to women viewers, who could readily identify with Pickford's character as a girl who manages to eek out a great deal of fun from her rather miserable childhood. Pickford's films are remembered for their comedy but also for their pathos. In spite of the sentimental investment of her audiences in the actress and in her many "cute" screen characters, Pickford's films are also rather insistent in their emphasis on the effects of economics on girls. This resonated with cultural changes toward children and reformist efforts to improve their lives, most particularly, to release the young from the burdens of labor. An unexpectedly uncompromising approach to this issue is evident in two films in which Pickford refused to follow her own oft-repeated formula signaling the transition between girlhood freedom and womanly submission to love. As the plain Cockney laundress in *Suds* (dir. John Francis Dillon, 1920) and as the homely slave, Unity Blake, in *Stella Maris* (dir. Marshall Neilan, 1918), Pickford used character roles to depict girlhoods of drudgery and deprivation. In these films childhood losses are not, as in so many other Pickford films, redeemed by blossoming beauty and the promise of a loving—and economically comfortable—marriage.

## THE "DOLL DIVINE" AS A NEW WOMAN

As I have argued, in Pickford's films women were allowed to relive the pleasures and pains of girlhood and to identify with "Our Little Mary" incarnated as a feisty, irrepressible tomboy and altruistic little mother. However, these characters simultaneously carried an identity as the beautiful and successful adult actress and powerful New Woman known as Mary Pickford. Through star discourse the masquerade of childhood that Pickford played out in the plots of her films was extended and served as a means of disavowing or neutralizing the revisionary or emancipatory values contained in the distinctively New Woman elements of her career and personal life, including her business acumen, her immense wealth, her divorce and remarriage, and her childlessness.

As the star system developed, a gap between the fictitious screen persona and the offscreen "real" star persona was acknowledged and sometimes encouraged. The juvenating publicity surrounding Pickford coexisted with and often contradicted widespread public knowledge of the more adult particulars of the actress's private life as a grown woman.

In the early years of her stardom, signs of childishness were represented through publicity and promotion to be indicative of Pickford's "real self." The actress was depicted as an innocent adolescent girl who practiced piano and obeyed her mother, Mrs. Charlotte Pickford. In 1913, when Mary was twenty-one years old, *Cosmopolitan*'s "An Actress from the Movies" declared her to be an "unsophisticated believer in fairies" and the "pet of playgoers all over the country who don't even know her name."[50] Charlotte Pickford was regularly depicted as the driving force in her daughter's career and life, a strong, caring mother who served as Mary's business manager. One article described Charlotte as having "a rugged and unafraid personality."[51] In 1915, *Ladies' Home Journal's* "The Most Popular Girl in America" offered Mary supposedly in dialogue with her "girlfriends" (or more exactly, her fans); the actress notes that her "mother will not let [her] eat candy."[52] *Photoplay*'s 1917 article "Speaking of the Actress" declared of Pickford: "If everybody was as pureminded as she, there would be no sin in the world."[53]

Yet by 1916 it was also common knowledge that "Little Mary" was married (and had been since 1911) to Owen Moore, an actor she had met at Biograph.[54] Movie mogul Adolph Zukor says that during this time, when Pickford was contracted to Famous Players, Moore's "name did not creep into Mary's copy," and the actor was excluded from his wife's public appearances because the studio wanted to perpetuate the impression that Pickford was "a teen-ager."[55] There was also an ambiguous representation of Mary's domestic life in star discourse, as in "Before Nine and after Five with Mary Pickford" (1917). The fan magazine article leaves the impression that Mary is "a girl" who still lives with her beloved "Mumsey"; her mother is "her constant companion both at work and at play," but the existence of Owen Moore is acknowledged. He is absent, however, because "on many occasions the camera calls him to another part of the globe."[56] A photo accompanying the article shows Pickford writing her husband. Thus, Mary Pickford remains juvenated, bound in her home life to her mother rather than to a man.

Publicity sought to constitute the established "truth" of Mary Pickford's star persona in girlish innocence, but Pickford's relationship to both truth and innocence was called into question in 1918, when the actress faced the possibility of a career-ending sexual scandal. In that year superstar Douglas Fairbanks separated from his socialite wife, Beth Sully, mother to his nine-year-old son, Douglas Fairbanks Jr. Rumors flew that Pickford, who had joined Fairbanks and Charlie Chaplin on Liberty war bond tours in 1917, was the cause of his marital breakup. Mrs. Fairbanks initially told reporters that her husband was involved with an actress she would not name.[57] The breakup of Fairbanks's marriage was followed by Pickford's divorce from Moore, but Leonard J. Fowler, attorney general of Nevada, accused Pickford of collusion and of falsifying her Nevada residency to obtain her divorce. He brought suit to annul the Pickford-Moore divorce.[58] Once that embarrassment was settled, Pickford and Fairbanks hastily married in March 1920.

The scandal of adultery and divorce threatened to ruin Pickford's carefully constructed star persona and its claim to authenticity in a childlike femininity largely removed from sexual agency. Because her behaviors could be interpreted as showing a lack of respect for marriage and uncontrolled female desire, Pickford was in danger of being linked to the sexually transgressive modern women condemned by social conservatives. In *Century Magazine* the philosopher Will Durant wrote that history would look back on women in the 1920s and observe how marriage, "[an] institution which had lasted ten thousand years, was destroyed in a generation."[59] Thus, the ability of Pickford fans to accept the sudden revelation of the family-shattering desire of "Our little Mary" for a married man and vice versa might suggest an amazing wholesale disavowal of whatever might mark the "doll divine" as an adult or interfere with the comforting collapse/merger between the onscreen child and adolescent and the offscreen actress. This disavowal should not be taken for granted as a natural occurrence. The constructed discourse of stardom was crucial to Pickford's ability to weather the storm of scandal.

After the scandal broke in 1918, the Pickford publicity machine went into overdrive to re-juvenate the actress, realign her with an ideologically conservative view of femininity, and curb negative public reaction against the actress's offscreen behavior. Indeed, a change in the Pickford family discourse in virtual simultaneity with Fairbanks's separation from his wife suggests a conscious intervention. Displacing the specter of scandal, this discourse encouraged the filmgoing public to see Mary Pickford as a woman who deserved compassion, not condemnation. The rearticulation of her relationship to her family was key: through reference to her childhood of hard work and unhappiness, publicity justified Mary Pickford as a woman seeking romantic happiness with a married man.

At the center of this rearticulation of the Pickford family discourse was the revision of Mary Pickford's relationship with her mother. Charlotte's formerly dominant role with her daughter was altered to call attention to Mary as a dutiful daughter to an emotionally supportive but financially dependent mother. Mary is portrayed as the working-class daughter who, at an early age, takes on the role of breadwinner—thus sacrificing her childhood—to keep her family together.[60] This strategy is apparent as early as 1918, when an article in *American Magazine* claimed, "We all didn't know until recently that Mary Pickford was a breadwinner at the stupendous age of five."[61] The author recounts how Pickford's mother, struggling as a stage actress in second- and third-rate theatrical companies, was accompanied by Gladys, then aged five, to a rehearsal of the famous play *Bootles' Baby: A Story of the Scarlet Lancers*. With the role of the baby suddenly vacated, Gladys/Mary volunteers to audition. Ranck recounts the child standing in "patched and worn shoes, her legs encased in intricately darned stockings—eyes bright and serious. . . . 'I'll do it,' she piped up."[62] Gladys's clothes suggest poverty but also register the mother's care of her child through attention to the little girl's "intricately darned" stockings. The child's own eagerness to act absolves Charlotte of an inappropriate desire to force her child to work. Instead of being the stereotypical "stage mother" who perversely turns from domesticity to the entertainment business in order to live out her own ambitions through her child, Charlotte is a caring, albeit struggling, young mother. The daughter's talent becomes, as the informed reader knows, the key to relieving the family's poverty.

Public commentaries by Pickford on her girlhood began to follow trends in contemporary reformist discourse about the evils of putting children to work. Using her own "miserable" childhood as a stage actress as an example of what required reform, Mary Pickford's life story as standardized in articles throughout the 1920s followed lines similar to the sentimental discourse on girls that had long structured her films. The fan or reader is emotionally instructed to shed a tear over Pickford's past as a working child. Pickford appeals to readers' feelings in one newspaper interview from March 1921: "Even childhood is a terrible thing. I had one of the dearest mothers in the world, but I was an unhappy child."[63] In another from around the same time, she is quoted: "I've been acting since I was five years old. I'm glad I was able to help my mother. We had no man to look after us, but I missed all the sweet things of childhood that other people have to look back on. . . . It's rather a cruel life for a child."[64]

The actress condemns the practice of children acting in films to support adults who could work, but she makes her own work as a child actress a different order of experience. That difference is based on her loving relationship with her mother. Pickford's autobiography, serialized in 1923 in *Ladies' Home Journal,* tells a story that could be taken from one of her films. Mary relates how a rich doctor wanted to adopt her and that her mother allowed her "to choose for myself." She preferred "mother above riches," but that meant working: "I had to give up my own childhood, but it was necessary in my case—either work or be separated from my mother."[65]

Because she was depicted as a woman whose responsibilities to her mother and siblings meant she never knew happiness as a girl, Mary's scandalous remarriage to Fairbanks was portrayed as her reward for years of service as a dutiful working daughter. This sentiment was expressed in the *Los Angeles Times:* "No one, I'm sure, speaking humanly, who sees these two together could possibly wish to take their

FIGURE 13. Fan photo of Mary Pickford after she cut her hair, ca. 1928. Author's collection.

happiness from them—Mary, especially, perhaps, with her years of conscientious, hard labor, when as a mere child, she was mother to all her family, Jack, Lottie, even her own mother."[66]

In the 1920s, as more commentary asked when she was going to "grow up," Pickford's portrayals of childhood were increasingly attributed to her personal need to experience a childhood she had missed because of work. There is acknowledgment that her extreme youth is a construction, but its fictionality is disavowed, as is its function as a commercial tactic. Instead, juvenation is justified by the authenticity of Pickford's emotional need to create for herself a "true" childhood, even if belated and confined to the movie screen. Like her second marriage, her portrayal of girls on the screen became a sign of the actress's wish-fulfilling reach for the happiness that had eluded her in her difficult childhood. In a newspaper article of 1923, "A Character Study of the Real Mary Pickford: Woman and Genius," the author recounts the actress's accomplishments, her intellectual power, her "genius" as an artist. Her ultimate attainment, however, remains securely feminine: it is her "power to give happiness," which is linked to her own girlhood of economic deprivation and premature assumption of responsibility: "You may note a somewhat wistful look in her eyes as she tells you that among other things that she has missed in life was a REAL CHILDHOOD . . . [so] she decided to weave a fictitious one for herself on screen."[67] Such an article signals a desire to justify Pickford's masquerade of childishness by establishing its etiology in the actress's life history.

Yet, this would not be the last explanation for the persistence of Mary Pickford's girl roles. In 1928, after the death of her mother, Mary cut off her famous curls. Adela Rogers St. Johns claimed in *Photoplay* that not only had "the long beautifully arranged curls" been "Mrs. Pickford's idea" but that Charlotte had lovingly dominated Mary, keeping her in curls and little-girl roles because she refused to recognize that her daughter and times had changed.[68] St. Johns absolves Pickford of responsibility in sustaining her child-woman roles as she marks a turning point in the star's career. As in earlier fan discourse, it is Mary's love for her mother that governs her choices. She is, above all, a good, obedient, loving daughter. Only after her mother's death could Mary Pickford grow up as an artist and a woman.

## LOST GIRLHOODS

Commentary like Lindsay's on Pickford, the "doll divine," suggests the sustained power of the late nineteenth-century idealization of the child-woman as a sentimentalized object of desire. Pickford's popularity drew on powerful cultural attitudes that sentimentalized and eroticized the emergent sexuality of girls and adolescents at a time when women's more assertive and self-determined sexual desires were regarded as an intrusion into the traditional male domain of sexual subjectivity and a threat to the primacy of the family. Within the historical context of this widespread social discourse, Pickford's textual and extratextual construction exemplifies an antimodernist rearticulation of the Victorian child-woman as a sexually controllable and idealized version of beautiful white femininity with origins in fin de siècle attitudes toward the "sacred child."

While we might assume that the conscious intent of Pickford's films was *not* to create such a sexually enticing figure, the construction of the actress's appeal still serves as a model for broader late nineteenth- and early twentieth-century representational trends in the sexualized representation of "the girl" or very juvenated femininity. Here I should acknowledge that there is always a danger for film scholars working with historically remote materials of reading back into an earlier era the preoccupations of our own—including sexual preoccupations. That said, we should not forget that Western culture has frequently rendered a woman masquerading as a child or with culturally coded childlike qualities as sexually enticing in ways that a male masquerading as a child is not.

In reading textual and extratextual materials attached to the star over a number of years, it seems apparent that Pickford's juvenation as a curly-headed girl of the lower class created all the required elements to permit a disguised sexual enjoyment for male viewers of the 1910s and 1920s. Nevertheless, the pedophilic aspect of male viewing should not be regarded as the only pleasure available to men in watching Pickford's moving pictures or gazing at her image. Male viewers may have shared a host of feelings that Pickford's films also made available to women, including reform-minded concern for children, nostalgia for childhood, and identification with the child's freedom to make mischief.

We might first consider it unlikely that men, like women viewers, would experience a nostalgic pleasure in looking back on the lost freedom of an "asexual" girlhood through Pickford's films. However, Catherine Robson has argued that girl-lovers of the late nineteenth century were middle-class men looking for their own lost girlhoods, that is, for their feminized origins in early childhood, before the demands of Victorian masculinity alienated them from their truer lost selves. She argues that such a masculine investment in identifying with the girl "complicates narratives of pedophilic desire that have habitually been employed to explain the work of some of the nineteenth century's most infamous girl-lovers," such as John Ruskin and the Reverend Charles Dodgson (Lewis Carroll).[69] If this kind of investment also held true for Vachel Lindsay and other heterosexual men in the early twentieth century, Pickford's image (onscreen and off) might have offered some male viewers pleasure in identifying with the pure young female, in addition to the pleasure of finding a confirmation of aesthetic perfection and spirituality in a child-woman whose erotic promise elided the threatening sexual agency of modern women. Thus, Pickford's image—both textual and extratextual—proved liminal enough to negotiate a wide range of sexual desires and identifications.

The multiple possibilities of how Mary Pickford was received by her historical audiences—male and female—suggest that Pickford's persona as the erotically attractive but juvenated female functioned culturally and psychologically for her audiences in potentially far more complex and contradictory ways than is generally acknowledged. Pickford's on- and offscreen masquerade of childishness and the slippage between eroticized adult femininity and her inscriptions of aesthetically perfected children were attached to some meanings that appear to be quite historically and culturally specific to the waning days of the "cult of the girl" and the "age of the child." Other meanings may have lingered or been rearticulated in a different cinematic form in subsequent eras with different cultural forces and economic imperatives operating. After all, we should not forget the Great Depression and that other sacred child of the screen, Shirley Temple, who made several films based on the same source material as Pickford vehicles. Temple, who rose to stardom shortly after Pickford's retirement in 1933, raises equally interesting but necessarily different questions about the performance of childhood on the screen and the pleasures it offered. Temple's stardom and its representation of juvenated femininity in the 1930s will be addressed in the next chapter.

The star persona of "Little Mary" was produced in ubiquitous representations intended to represent innocence but implicated in a sexualized gaze fixed on the screen fiction of the girl-child played by a woman. Pickford's stardom and its relation to sexuality also resonate with the contemporary phenomenon of shifting boundaries between child and adult. Those shifts are manifested in both a pervasive fear of and campaign against sexually explicit material depicting children; simultaneously, they are manifested in ubiquitous display of images of juvenated sexuality that characterize much twenty-first-century media culture. Contemporary perception of the child and current cultural practice often produce a sexualization of representations of childhood, even in discourses that ostensibly seek to prohibit it.[70] This provides an echo of Pickford that may not be the exact semiotic equivalent of her effects but is related to them. Thus, we might be led to conclude that the interplay of gender, power, and sexuality in the construction and reception of Mary Pickford is more relevant to our own experience of mass media than Vachel Lindsay, adoring poet, might ever have imaged of his own "doll divine."

FIGURE 14. Shirley Temple, movie star, in costume for *Curly Top* (dir. Irving Cummings, 1935). Author's collection.

CHAPTER 2

# Cosseting the Nation; or, How to Conquer Fear Itself with Shirley Temple

"What a charming child!" This last was perhaps because Miss Mignon, finding her time had come . . . put two soft arms round his neck, and gave him such a genuine hug of friendship that the old man's heart was quite taken by storm.

—John Strange Winter, *Bootles' Baby*

In 1940 the photographer Arthur Rothstein was sent by the U.S. Farm Security Administration to California. His task was to record images of camps set up by the federal government for migrant farm laborers and their families. F.S.A. officials wanted positive images of this controversial program they hoped would ameliorate the deprivation of thousands of dispossessed rural poor. Rothstein took almost two hundred photographs of residents in a camp set up near Visalia in Tulare County. He showed these people in everyday activities and taking advantage of newly built community facilities. In an unusual approach for an F.S.A. photographer, Rothstein also took close-up portraits of some of the residents standing in front of a wall. Among the subjects photographed was a chubby-cheeked white girl of uncertain age.[1] The child's head is crowned by a tousled mass of blonde curls, some laced over her forehead and others framing her round face.

When this photograph was taken, in March of 1940, the migrant-camp child, with her blonde curls—in their color, length, and profusion—would immediately have recalled another little girl—Shirley Temple. Rothstein's portrait—taken in an unlikely corner of American society—offers an uncanny rearticulation of the movie star's signature blonde curls but also her whiteness, her round face, and her sturdy tomboy plumpness. The striking resemblance between the highly paid movie

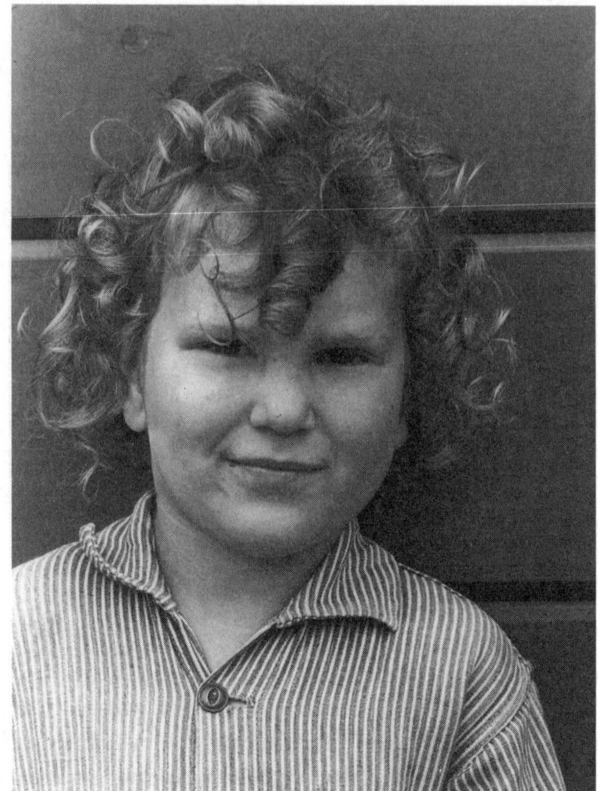

FIGURE 15. Migrant girl. Tulare migrant camp. Visalia, California, ca. 1940. Photograph by Arthur Rothstein. Courtesy of the Library of Congress, Prints and Photographs Division, FS-OWI Collection, LC-USF23-T01–024210-D DLC.

star and the migrant child does not diminish the importance of qualifying differences. Rothstein's photographic subject appears more androgynous than we may choose to remember Temple ever being. We may not even be able to discern, unequivocally, that the subject *is* a girl.[2] The collar of the child's shirt resembles those typical of girls' apparel, but the homemade striped shirt of rough cotton ticking contributes gender ambiguity through its lack of refinement, as does the fact that the shirt buttons like a boy's. Perhaps this child of the displaced poor is wearing a hand-me-down shirt from a brother. With lips held tightly together, the migrant girl fails to present the conventional, unambiguously friendly facial expression associated with pleasing femininity. Her smile lacks the open expressivity characteristic of Shirley Temple as the general public remembers the latter's quintessential "Oh, my Goodness!" expression of big eyed, pursed-mouth surprise or her famously dimpled smiles.

In spite of these differences—or perhaps because of them—could there be more poignant testament to the impact of Shirley Temple during the Great Depression? In all likelihood, the migrant girl's Templesque curls were more than a coincidence. The imitation of Temple's signature curls suggests that either the little girl sought to emulate the movie star or that her mother purposefully cultivated her daughter's likeness to "America's darling."[3] Who could blame the mother if she arranged her child's hair for the visit of the government photographer? She would join the army of Depression-era mothers who groomed their little girls to resemble "The Baby Who Conquered the World," whether they sought infant curling solutions, put their offspring in dresses modeled on Temple's costumes, encouraged them to sing and dance to the star's musical numbers, or took them to the era's many Shirley Temple look-alike contests.[4]

The Visalia camp mother may have hoped that her child would be discovered by Rothstein, just as Temple, with the support of her own mother's ambitions, had been discovered by talent scout and Poverty Row director-producer Charles Lamont.[5] Not long after Temple's stardom was confirmed by her feature-film success in *Little Miss Marker* (dir. Alexander Hall, 1934), the *Los Angeles Times* reported: "mamas everywhere are casting a speculative eye upon bright baby girls . . . and wondering just what is the precious recipe for producing a super baby star."[6] As studio publicity, fan magazine, and newspaper discourse often discussed, that recipe was held by Shirley's mother, Mrs. Gertrude Temple, who groomed her only daughter for success.[7]

With the help of her mother and the American film industry Shirley Temple had "conquered the world" just as Franklin Delano Roosevelt was encouraging the American people "to conquer fear itself."[8] As Rothstein's portrait shows so poignantly, America's children had plenty to fear as they became the innocent victims of widespread deprivation that occurred in the United States between 1929 and 1941: during these years, between one-third and one-half of American children suffered from some combination of malnutrition, inadequate clothing, substandard housing, and lack of medical care. While Rothstein's photograph of the migrant child in a government camp suggests a glimmer of hope in difficult circumstances, so, too, Temple's iconic screen persona came to represent childhood in its essential hope, the hope for the beleaguered nation's brighter future. At the core of that appeal was

FIGURE 16. Shirley Temple and her proud mother, Mrs. Gertrude Temple, ca. 1934. Author's collection.

Temple's screen persona, which offered 1930s cinema audiences a fantasy investment in and enjoyment of a symbolically loaded figure who supports traditional "family-centered values" but also excites through her unsettling of age, gender, and sexual boundaries.

In this respect Shirley Temple—America's "super baby star"—epitomized what Amelie Hastie has called, in another context, a "new generation, represented symbolically by the child."[9] According to Jennifer Bean, the child or juvenated woman star might embody this generation as "one able to discover fresh meaning in a world grown weary of the empty promises and failed machinations of industrial modernity."[10] Writer and humorist Irvin S. Cobb pointed to such a symbolic function when he wrote of Temple: "Darling, when Santa Claus bundled you up, a . . . joyous doll-baby package, and dropped you down creation's

FIGURE 17. Bill Robinson and Shirley Temple dance in *The Little Colonel*. Author's collection.

chimney, he gave to mankind the dearest and sweetest Christmas present that ever gladdened the hearts and stirred the souls of their weary old world."[11] Whether photographed as highly groomed film star or disheveled waif, beautiful little girl or daring tomboy, Temple became a symbol of cheerful resilience and America's most powerfully persuasive common values. In her films she embodied the promise of a more perfect future as an energetic, mischievous trouper offering song, dance, toughness, and sweet love within musicals fueled by a utopian sensibility.[12]

Commodified for a public that, even in hard times, proved eager to buy her image, Temple was placed in continuous cultural circulation after her first major role in a feature film, Fox's *Stand Up and Cheer!* (dir. Hamilton MacFadden, 1934). Her films are now regarded as strictly children's fare, but that was not the case in 1934, when *Time* magazine said of the new star, "Three months ago Fox discovered that she was excellent adult entertainment in the otherwise mediocre *Stand Up and Cheer!*" Star appeal to audiences was constructed and cultivated by Hollywood to reach the broadest possible range of viewers in the studio era.[13] A broad appeal was especially important during the

Great Depression, when box-office revenues took a beating. The combined force of children and their parents could make for potent box-office results, but children were expected only to dominate Saturday matinee screenings.[14] Not until the end of Temple's contract at Fox was a change in her appeal to adults recognized when *Variety* suggested that *Susannah of the Mounties* (dir. William A. Seiter, 1939) was "part of a pattern of vehicles increasingly aimed at juvenile audiences rather than at the adult public which first made her a star."[15]

Temple quickly went from featured player to "the name above the title" in vehicles shaped for her. Writing in the *Los Angeles Times* on the hastily made *Baby Take a Bow* (dir. Harry Lachman, 1934), the film that marked Temple's first star billing, Edwin Schallert tried to isolate the reasons for the child actor's broad audience appeal: "[*Baby Take a Bow* will] . . . bring huge joy to both adults and children; possibly even infants, and certainly grandmothers. . . . It's a clean little picture without being namby pamby. . . . Audiences will be going to see Shirley Temple, with her laughing eyes, and the droll smile that hovers about her mouth, her curls and her cute 'whoopee.' If anyone can resist the lure of this youngster he or she must have a heart of stone."[16]

Schallert's reference to a "clean little picture" hints at how Temple's films would form part of a significant—and defensive—industry trend. Seeking to avoid a boycott by the Catholic Legion of Decency and fearing increased "political" censorship at the local, state, or federal levels, the film industry allowed Will Hays of the Motion Picture Producers and Distributors of America to create the Production Code Administration as a new means of regulating morality in feature films starting in mid-1934. New production trends and new stars were required to meet the demands of this more systematic form of industry self-regulation. Temple was one of those new stars, a remarkably charismatic juvenile musical-comedy performer whose vivid physical presence few could resist.

Shirley Temple eclipsed the success of all previous child actors to become a cultural phenomenon, as well as a movie star. She was the number-one U.S. box-office draw for four years in the mid-1930s and was ranked within the top-ten list of box-office attractions for a record seven years by the *Motion Picture Herald* exhibitors' poll.[17] Temple appeared in almost two-dozen features while she was under contract to the Fox Film Corporation, which was reorganized in 1935 as Twentieth Century–Fox. Her profitability at the studio was tremendous. Her star vehicles generally cost less than $300,000 to produce but were reputed

FIGURE 18. The child star commodified: Shirley Temple doll and Shirley Temple, ca. 1936. Author's collection.

to gross from $1 million to $1.5 million on first-run showings alone.[18] Temple's image and endorsements were used to sell a wide range of consumer goods aimed at children and their parents, including dolls made in her image, toys, glassware, packaged food, books, girls' clothing, school supplies, and sheet music.

Few screen actors could boast of inspiring a similar degree of the public's expressed affection and sustained interest. Congress declared the curly-headed moppet to be "the most beloved individual in the world."[19] Temple was a distinctly American star whose joyous confidence, exuberant optimism, and apparent vitality were crucial to her popularity, as they were to Franklin Delano Roosevelt's. No wonder that President Roosevelt was quick to praise Temple's film appearances as one of the great morale boosters of the Depression era: "When the spirit of the people is lower than at any time during this Depression," he proclaimed, "it is a splendid thing that for just 15 cents, an American can go to a movie and look at the smiling face of a baby and forget his troubles."[20]

Through her films Temple addressed the anxieties, fantasies, fears, and consciously held hopes of audiences in the 1930s in her construction as a remarkably vigorous if contradiction-laden "national body." My interest in Temple as a national body is in keeping with contemporary scholarly accounts of stardom that dwell, as Barry King has observed, primarily with "the moment of consumption," that is, the realization of the value of the star based on the imperative of social or ideological "wants and needs" as opposed to the performance-centered "moment of production."[21] I am also very much interested in the moment of production, and I believe speculation regarding the reception of the star needs to be rebalanced with more emphasis on the specifics of her films and film performances.

Temple's films came to construct her as the symbolic body of the nation that redeemed masculinity for domesticity. She embodied hope for the future but also reasserted traditional values. She was a modern child whose films incorporated appeals, like cosseting, that rearticulated older rituals of familial bonding. Cosseting has almost been forgotten, but in the late nineteenth century it was applied to the situation in which the man (usually a father) was treated as if he were a lamb, a house pet who was indulged with pampering, petting, and attentive spoiling by the girl child, who typically climbs onto the lap, lavishes him with undivided attention, and accommodates his need to be touched, caressed, hugged, patted, talked to, and heard.[22] At the same time that cosseting or "petting" served to strengthen the love of the father for his child, the family ritual met emotional needs that middle-class adult men might otherwise be too reserved to admit. Sexual difference was inscribed in these demonstrations of bodily sentiment in that this high-Victorian domestic practice served also to train the girl to attend to the emotional and spiritual requirements of the father.[23]

Cosseting was highlighted in plays and literature centered on girl-man relationships such as John Strange Winter's *Bootles' Baby: A Story of the Scarlet Lancers* and Annie Fellows Johnston's book series, The Little Colonel. The former formed a virtual blueprint for many of Temple's film narratives, and the latter was adapted into one of her most beloved star vehicles. Whether cosseting is presented as a spontaneous event or an established family ritual, it is crucial in the emotional reawakening of the man. For example, in *The Little Colonel,* the first book in the beloved series, the title character is Lloyd Sherman, the mischievous, temperamental granddaughter of an unreconstructed Confederate colonel. Lloyd's mother, Elizabeth, is estranged from the old colonel because she ran off to marry a "Yankee." The grandfather is alone, his wife dead, his only son killed in the Civil War. With little money Lloyd's mother returns to Kentucky to live in a small cottage near her father's plantation house. By accident, during her daily adventures with her black playmates, Lloyd runs into her grandfather, who is overwhelmed emotionally by the encounter, even though it starts as a confrontation between two quick-tempered people. The book offers insight into the affect the little girl creates in the old man:

> When the last flutter of her dress had disappeared around the bend of the road, he walked slowly back toward the house. . . . He could feel her soft little fingers resting on his neck, where they had lain when he carried her to the gate. A very un-Napoleonlike mist blurred his sight for a moment. It had been so long since such a touch had thrilled him, so long since any caress had been given him. . . . Something very warm and sweet seemed to surge across his heart as he thought of the Little Colonel. He was glad, for a moment, that they called her that; glad that his only grandchild looked enough like himself for others to see the resemblance.[24]

This sentimental moment of the grandfather's longing and loneliness would be understood and appreciated by adults, likely more than children, and it should be remembered that adults, as well as children, regularly read literature of this type, which was wildly popular. Sentiment involves the body, and the colonel's body responds to the emotional affect Lloyd has created in him. Lloyd and her grandfather will continue to squabble, but their love for one another will never be in doubt.

As I suggested in chapter 1, dating from the 1870s a major cultural change occurred as the child's emotional and moral value to adults replaced economic usefulness in paramount importance.[25] This transformed notion of the value of children guided child-centered labor reforms and the institutionalization of improved safety and schooling standards.[26] By the 1930s, the valuation of the sentimental child was well-established, and the country was primed to respond to Shirley Temple and other screen representatives of childhood.

At the same time, the growing acceptance of adoption in the United States also reflected the perceived importance of children as the emotional glue of families. Instead of functioning as a static nineteenth-century narrative trope offering the pathetic image of the unwanted child, orphans and the possibility of their adoption acquired other symbolic and social meanings. Barbara Melosh has gone so far as to claim that adoption became a "quintessentially American institution" reflecting belief in "the possibility of a more expansive community."[27] Temple's characters are orphaned in many of her films, including *Little*

*Miss Marker* (1934), *Bright Eyes* (dir. David Butler, 1934), *Curly Top* (dir. Irving Cummings, 1935), *Heidi* (dir. Allan Dwan, 1937), *Stowaway* (dir. William A. Seiter, 1936), *Captain January* (dir. David Butler, 1936), *Rebecca of Sunnybrook Farm* (dir. Allan Dwan, 1938), *Little Miss Broadway* (dir. Irving Cummings, 1938), and *Susannah of the Mounties* (dir. William A. Seiter, 1939). Her films play on the idea that adoption was of great emotional benefit to the adoptive parent(s). This is expressed directly in *Curly Top* when Aunt Genevieve (Esther Dale) responds to the news that her nephew has adopted Elizabeth (Temple) from the local orphanage: "Nothing makes a home so happy as the sound of a child in laughter."

Without the benefit of contextualization or historicism it is easy to assert cultural superiority over sentimental entertainment that focuses on children—their beauty, innocence, and vulnerability. In keeping with such an attitude of superiority critics often dismiss Temple's films as pure escapism, overly sentimental and cloying. Jeanine Basinger says they have "little to recommend them" because they are the emotional equivalent of a "sentimental bath in a kiddie pool."[28] Yet Shirley Temple's films drew on established, as well as emerging, cultural meanings attached to the priceless child during a period of tremendous economic upheaval that threatened the social fabric of the United States.

The Great Depression was an economic crisis unprecedented in the history of the nation. For a large portion of the U.S. populace day-to-day misery was the norm and survival, even in its most basic form, uncertain. The difficulties of contemporary life that impacted children and families in the 1930s were not ignored by Temple's films and, indeed, formed the central conceit of one of her first feature films, *Stand Up and Cheer!* in which the U.S. government creates a "Secretary of Amusement" to hire unemployed performers. Shirley Dugan (Temple) charms the Secretary (Warner Baxter) into hiring her unemployed father Jimmy Dugan (James Dunn), a widowed song-and-dance man. Contemporary economic and familial difficulties appear in other Temple films, including *Our Little Girl* (dir. John Robertson, 1934), *Just around the Corner* (dir. Irving Cummings, 1938), and *Young People* (dir. Allan Dwan, 1940). Temple sang songs with Depression-era themes like "Look on the Sunnyside," in *Little Miss Marker;* "Be Optimistic," in *Little Miss Broadway;* and "The World Owes Me a Living," in *Now and Forever* (dir. Henry Hathaway, 1934); in the last film the song, taken from a Disney Silly Symphony animated skit about a lazy grasshopper and industrious ants, highlights a physically aggressive performance by Temple that is used to comment

FIGURE 19. Shirley Dugan (Shirley Temple) charms the U.S. Secretary of Amusement (Warner Baxter) in *Stand Up and Cheer!* (dir. Hamilton MacFadden, 1934). Author's collection.

on the charming high-class thief (Gary Cooper) who tries to assume responsibility for his motherless daughter (Temple).

Temple's films often speak to the historically specific needs and concerns of the 1930s through displacement that shifts and simultaneously registers the era's extraordinary economic and political challenges.[29] Almost half of Temple's films for Fox were set in the nineteenth century.[30] For example, *Dimples* (dir. William A. Seiter, 1936) is set in a "depression" occurring in the 1850s. Shirley, an orphan ("Dimples"), and her grandfather (Frank Morgan) earn a living through her street performances and his illicit activities. Other films with nineteenth-century settings include *The Little Colonel* (dir. David Butler, 1935), *The Littlest Rebel* (dir. David Butler, 1935), *Wee Willie Winkie* (dir. John Ford, 1937), *Heidi, The Little Princess* (dir. Walter Lang, 1939), *Susannah of the Mounties,* and *The Blue Bird* (dir. Walter Lang, 1940). Like *Dimples,* these films resonate with concerns of the Great Depression that impacted children: displacement from home, loss of family livelihood, and the death of parents.

With estimates that up to 25 percent of the nation's male breadwinners became jobless during the Great Depression, enormous strain was placed on traditional familial structures in the United States.[31] Men who were out of work sometimes left their families and took to the road or the rails rather than face the humiliation of being unable to meet the needs of their dependents.[32] If they remained at home, despondency, abusive behavior, and alcoholism might threaten domestic accord. The very survival of the American family was called into question.[33] A *Commonweal* editorial of 1931 declared that "the importance of children to the nation is . . . primary."[34] Perhaps this reminder was necessary since, during the Great Depression, the child's emotional value was brought into difficult circumstances as children were often called on to motivate the economic rescue of their families through their employment.[35]

Children's emotional importance and the need to improve fathering in the United States were intertwined issues in the 1930s. Increased focus on the "priceless child" was broadly registered, including the attempt of modern psychology and sociological studies to systematically improve parenting. Emerging by the 1930s, the concept of "The New Fatherhood" was linked to concerns about the development of children as "personalities" and "individuals." This line of thinking maintained that fathers needed to be modern companions to their children, "pals" who were role models and playmates instead of the overbearing authority figures of olden days.[36] An article from 1932 in *Parents' Magazine* declared the existence of a national crisis in the American family: "It is fatherless."[37] The article argued that fathers needed to be more present in the lives of their children and do more than supply income for their families. In keeping with this discourse, Temple's character in *Poor Little Rich Girl* (dir. Irving Cummings, 1936) tells her father: "This house wouldn't be so lonesome if you'd stay home once in a while." More concern with father-son relations was often expressed in parenting discourse than with fathers and daughters, but the latter also came under scrutiny, with some experts holding to the belief that fathers were supposed to function in the classical Freudian/Oedipal way, that is, allowing a daughter to "transfer her emotional focus from her mother to her father as an intermediate step preparatory to its final resting in her husband."[38] In spite of such pronouncements, a great deal of advice to parents in the 1930s seemed to smooth out the distinctions between raising girls and boys, especially in their early years, with recommendations to middle-class parents stressing the need for children to receive good nutrition, exercise, and a balance of play and moral training.[39]

The enthusiastic reception of the screen performances of Temple and other child actors in the 1930s reflected this culturally complex interest in American children and their fathers. If, as Shawn Johansen argues, "emotion has to be considered as one of the defining characteristics of middle-class father-child relationships,"[40] then sentimental screen depictions of the love between girl and man are worth exploring, especially as they appear during a period when American family relations were in particularly difficult circumstances. Looking at the 1930s, it is useful to remember Andrew Bergman 's remark that Depression-era audiences "did not escape into a void each week" because "people do not escape into something they cannot relate to."[41]

It follows that Temple and her films played a pleasurable role in reassuring adult viewers and perhaps children, too, that not only were the latter still "priceless" but masculinity could be made devotedly paternal and irrevocably domesticated at a time when the ties between men and their families were particularly fragile and the disintegration of families commonplace.[42] Her films built a utopian sensibility around the presence of her stardom and its power to create a family by securing men into happy domesticity. This made her stardom particularly meaningful and pleasurable within the particular historical context in which it appeared, for, as Ralph LaRossa argues, the 1930s may have put debilitating strains on the American family, but "the period also sparked intensified efforts to sanctify relations with children."[43]

## PEDOPHILIA OR COSSETING?

The pleasure value of Shirley Temple's popularity as a child star has become contested and controversial in film studies. After years of scholarly neglect her stardom has become the subject of attention that has an almost exclusive focus: the star's erotic appeal to men.[44] It is true that Temple made a considerable impression on the imaginative lives of many men, evidenced in admiring reviews and commentary in the 1930s, including those of Irvin S. Cobb, Frank Nugent, Mordaunt Hall, and Gilbert Seldes. *Time* reported in 1937 that Temple was one of the few female stars among men's favorites.[45]

Yet, of all the extensive commentary on Temple from the 1930s, almost none of it is remembered or cited in contemporary film scholarship except the remarks made by Graham Greene. In a review of *Captain January* Greene wrote that the star's appeal depended "on a coquetry quite as mature as Miss Colbert's and on an oddly precocious body as voluptuous in grey flannel trousers as Miss Dietrich's."[46] Writing in 1937, he continued to find her appearance in *Wee Willie Winkie* in disturbing erotic complicity with pedophilic masculine desires: "infancy is her disguise, her appeal is more secret and more adult. . . . Watch the way she measures a man with agile studio eyes, with dimpled depravity."[47] He attributed prurient motives to her handlers at 20th Century–Fox and asserted of her viewers: "Her admirers—middle-age men and clergymen respond to her dubious coquetry . . . because the safety curtain of story and dialogue drops between their intelligence and desire."[48]

Greene's response was clearly outside the normative reactions of commentators to Temple in the 1930s. In 1937 Greene was sued by Fox for libel, and a British court ruled against him, concluding that he had libeled the young star and committed a "gross outrage" against her.[49] Modern feminist-inspired criticism has been inclined to side with Greene, though, in spite of the fact that more than one of his contemporaries thought him to be obsessed with sex, and his observations regarding Temple's thighs and bottom are in line with similarly fetishistic remarks he made in other film reviews about the body parts of a number of adult female stars.[50] Also, there is evidence that Greene's own fictional writing was preoccupied with the idea of grotesquely precocious children. For example, in *The Power and the Glory* (1940), Greene described the young daughter of his main character, a lapsed priest: "He caught the look in the child's eyes which frightened him—it was again as if a grown woman was there before her time, making her plans, aware of far too much. . . . The child suddenly laughed again knowingly. The seven-year-old body was like a dwarf's: it disguised an ugly maturity."[51] Other strange children inhabit Greene's fiction, as well, including Hansel in *The Third Man,* whom he also associates with a precociously adult gaze.

Relying on Greene's commentary, feminist film criticism has viewed Temple as what one scholar calls, "the pedophile's muse."[52] As if she is channeling Greene, Jeanine Basinger labels Temple "an out-and-out baby sex pot" and writes of the star's performance in *Captain January:* "Her voluptuous thighs encased in sailor's slacks, she giggles and winks and chuckles and dimples away until, finally and utterly, she is irresistible."[53] Molly Haskell refers to Temple in passing as "an ideal post–Production Code sex kitten" and claims (without offering a shred of proof) that the star "was always a greater favorite with adult males than with children."[54] Nadine Wills discusses how "many of Temple's performances are particularly difficult to watch today because of the constant construction of paedophilic desire placed on her body."[55]

The almost obsessive desire to prove the singularly pedophilic quality of Temple's appeal is exemplified by James Kincaid, who asserts the pedophilic sexualization of almost all contemporary representations of children, regardless of gender, in Western culture. In *Erotic Innocence: The Culture of Child Molesting,* Kincaid uses language that appears purposefully provocative when he refers to Temple as having "a fat, round face with nothing in it and a body to match—like Ms. Potato Head. . . . Had this Miss Piggy been beautiful, she would never have done so well."[56]

Contemporary film scholarship presumes Temple's films and screen persona to be pedophilic in their textual construction and primary appeal, yet her films are barely analyzed, and at other times, when they are discussed, moments and scenes are often distorted to support generalizing claims.[57] An example of this occurs with Kincaid's claim that Temple's performance of the song "The Good Ship Lollipop" in *Bright Eyes* is staged "under the lustful looks of men."[58] Yet if one actually looks at this scene, what is striking is how the chorus boys seated within the crowded confines of an airplane appear to be directed to do everything *but* gaze lustfully—or even intently—at the little girl who is the singing musical star whose performance must be staged and supported but deferred to. Dominated by medium shots and objective views unmediated by male characters, the scene seems intent on preventing the spectacle of the child's prepubescent femininity (sexually taboo) from being read as the equivalent of the erotic spectacle of white adult femininity (acceptably desirable) often encoded in Hollywood's treatment of leading ladies, especially in musicals.

Numerous musical and nonmusical film sequences in Temple's films emphasize her interaction with men, such as "The Codfish Ball" dance number in *Captain January* and Priscilla's drilling with the troops in *Wee Willie Winkie,* but these scenes do not obviously eroticize Temple through a so-called cinematic "male gaze" but complicate her film presence in ways that mitigate a pedophilic interpretation. As I will argue, the whole point of Temple's films is their textual attempt to construct the love between a little girl and a man (a father, a grandfather, a father-in-the-making) as being of a different order than that of pedophilia. The idea of a unique, pure love of a father for a daughter and a daughter for her father based on "sweet sentiment" perpetuates a cultural myth, some would say. Yet the possibility of tender feelings across gen-

FIGURE 20. Lloyd Sherman (Shirley Temple) bonds with her grandfather (Lionel Barrymore) in *The Little Colonel.* Author's collection.

der and generation that challenge self-interest is the basis of a modern family-centered social model, one that changed social life in general in the Western world.[59]

I do not presume that children can be separated from adult desire or childhood sexuality, however inchoate the latter may be. In her analysis of children's literature that is really for adults, Jacqueline Rose says "innocence" should be regarded "not as a property of childhood but as a portion of adult desire."[60] This remark certainly is relevant to Temple's films, which were written by adults and aimed at adult viewers, as well as children. The difficulties in conceptualizing child sexuality apart from the demands of adult desire and gendered spectators are real, but unlike emotional investment in the pleasure of literary representations of children, responses to the representation of juvenated femininity in Temple's star vehicles depended on the subjectivity of a living performer, Shirley Temple. The child body of Temple was distinctively different from that of an adult, but it was still influenced by adult desire, expectations, and training. Temple's iconic qualities as a performer-subject had their origins in many sources, including her own abilities and sensibilities, her dance training and musical traditions, and the influence of her directors and her mother, Gertrude Temple.[61] Her screen performances operated within established generic and filmic conventions. Although it might have been impossible for any female—including a little girl—to escape a degree of sexual objectification in Hollywood film and its ancillary enterprises, Shirley Temple engages the camera as a child-subject who generates affects that cannot be completely accounted for if we regard her only as a female object whose presence counts for nothing in the process. Instead, Temple must be approached as an intermediary and complicating presence poised between the adult originated film fiction and the viewer.

## DOMINATING INNOCENCE

Film critic Frank Nugent wrote in his review of *Dimples:* "Why they bother with titles or with plots either is beyond us. . . . The sensible thing would be to announce Shirley Temple in 'Shirley Temple' and let it go at that."[62] Temple's stardom relied on the audience's awareness and appreciation of her as a juvenile who in some sense performed herself, a charming, clever child actor rather than a fully developed character.[63] Temple, like many other child stars, was not regarded as a real actor but as something else—a child trained to pretend and to present her pretense in terms of the naturalness and spontaneity that audiences traditionally demanded from child actors.[64] This is in contrast to Pickford's star acting, which centered on an adult who controlled and disguised her adult body to perform juvenation.

Temple's stardom demonstrates the inscription of sentimental, child-centered values on a physical body that spoke cultural notions of asexuality and innocence even while challenging or complicating assumptions about children through the star's dominating screen presence. Reviewing *Little Miss Marker,* Norbert Lusk of the *Los Angeles Times* wrote of her impact on movie audiences: "Every scene she plays, every word she utters, evokes response from spectators. . . . She dominates the picture."[65] In response to *Rebecca of Sunnybrook Farm, Variety*'s reviewer noted: "Any actress who can dominate a Zanuck musical with Jack Haley, Gloria Stuart, Phyllis Brooks, Helen Westley, Slim Summerville, Bill Robinson, Randolph Scott, Franklin Pangborn, etc. can dominate the world."[66] But why was Shirley Temple such a dominating screen presence?

In an astute essay," Two Great Women," drama critic Gilbert Seldes compared Temple to Mae West. The basis of his comparison was not that the two stars were similar in their erotic appeal but that they shared characteristics of a dominating personality. Temple's cuteness and dimples, said Seldes, "have very little [to] do with her real power," which, he said, was dependent on her "air of command." He admitted that this power tended to be "dissipated as soon as Miss Temple talks," but it could be restored by her look and by her gestures that communicate "the hard core of a personality which will not be bunked in any of the major moments."[67] Seldes also noted "something rude and rowdy in her characteristic expression" that could elicit a "growl of satisfaction" from men in the audience; this "growl" was not a sexual response, as some film scholars have claimed Seldes is reporting, but one of admiration for and perhaps identification with the child's unbunkable personality.[68] Seldes speculated: "Women may gasp at her charms because it is traditional to care for the sweetness of all children," but men offered her "their roar of approval [which] is not for what is sweet, but for what is mocking and hearty and contemptuous."[69] Seldes says it was this not-sweet quality that allowed Temple to assume the mantle of box-office favorite vacated by Mae West in the wake of the Production Code Administration crack down on screen sexuality. As a star intended to appeal to adults as well as children, Shirley Temple rose to fame by appealing to the family at precisely the moment when Hollywood was attempting to clean up its screen product in response to public protests against movie immorality. Film commentators of the 1930s regarded Temple's stardom as a welcome return of the innocence of childhood to the screen, but as Seldes points out, there was something more to her appeal than cuteness or one-dimensional innocence.

The complexity of her presentation as a star with a "personality which will not be bunked," to use Seldes's phrase, is central to Temple's fascinating screen presence. Demonstrating the complexity of that screen persona, especially as it relates to the filmic inscription of her relationship to grown men, is *Little Miss Marker,* one of Temple's early hits when she was on loan to Paramount. The film is set in a Damon Runyonesque world of nightclubs and small-time crooks. "Sorrowful Jones" (Adolphe Menjou) is a middle-aged bookmaker with a sad face and sagging suit. In the second scene of the film we see Sorrowful turning down man after man who attempts to place a bet with an I.O.U. instead of cash. Then, a man steps up to bet. He seems middle-class, well groomed, and has a refined cadence to his speech, but he is nervous as he asks for a twenty-dollar bet on "Dream Prince" with an I.O.U. Sorrowful refuses his bet even though the man complains he has already lost $500 to the bookie: "I wouldn't take a marker from my best friend. If I had a best friend." "You can trust me," the man begs Sorrowful. "No markers," responds Sorrowful. During this conversation the wire cage separating Sorrowful and the man will often be shown blocking one or both of them in a claustrophobic visual arrangement of shot/reverse shots. The visual argument of jailing seems to suggest both are emotionally constricted or otherwise limited. The betting man looks and bends down, a shot that shows him standing behind the wire and railing that separates the customers from the bookies. We see Sorrowful's back as he walks toward his office. Suddenly, we hear a light, high-pitched voice melodically say, "Hello." This prompts Sorrowful to slowly turn around. In an otherwise expressionless face, his eyes are wide with surprise. A reverse shot shows the man as he stands his small daughter (Temple) on top of the railing. Her father (Edward Earle) offers her as security for his bet: "Look, this is my little girl. I'll leave her here while I go for the money."

The gesture of leaving the child as a marker violates every principle attached to parents' proper treatment of the priceless child. The little girl who stands on the railing is attired in a plain coat thrown askew over an extremely battered, torn checkered dress. Her father's hands are around her middle, and the child's stance on the rail, with one leg straight and the other bent is strangely unchildlike. There is an adult-like quality of her hip-cocking stance (perhaps related to Temple's dance training?) that makes especially resonant Sorrowful's next line, "I ain't taking no dolls for security," for the child is a "doll," a female in the shady adult world of "guys and dolls," as well as in the more conventional sense of a miniature reproduction of an adult.

The pretty blonde girl looks at Sorrowful. A shot from behind her shows her pointing as she says in a childish voice: "Look daddy, he's running away. Is he afraid?" The line reading seems oddly singsong but decidedly childlike and spontaneous. Sorrowful starts to get mad: "Get down off of there. You get down off of there," he says as he slowly walks up to the little girl, who stands at eye-level with him. "You're afraid of my daddy," she smiles and giggles; then a reverse close-up on her (over the shoulder of Sorrowful) accompanies her line: "Or you're afraid of me." This line is given an oddly unchildlike reading, as Temple cocks her head and almost smirks. A reverse close-up of Sorrowful shows him looking her up and down. Then another reverse close-up focuses on her face as she continues with a rather wistful and almost sympathetic line reading: "You're afraid of something."

Her smile vanishes into a pensive expression that continues in the next shot, a remarkable two-shot close-up of the child and Sorrowful in profile as they silently look into each other's eyes as he holds her up to get her off the railing. The close-up continues as he lifts her up in his arms to set her down, and the gesture makes it appear as if he might be bringing her forward to him to kiss her. But this is a fleeting moment, and it is important that their faces (still in profile) are absolutely impassive, still, and rather sad looking. There is a restraint here that signals the seriousness of the meeting of man and girl in the narrative.

Does the moment construct Temple as the object of a pedophilic gaze? If so, is it Sorrowful's or the audience's? Certainly, the film brings the attractive child into close physical contact with an unrelated male, a stranger. The danger of pedophilia is perhaps implied (unknowingly by her) in the child's taunt: "You're afraid of something." Sorrowful's lifting Marky to take her down is an ambivalent gesture registering anger (he's been insulted; she's found out his weakness) and emotionally charged attraction. Her hands are on his shoulders as he puts her on the floor beside her father, an action matched on a full shot from behind her. In a full shot Sorrowful lets her go and walks back to his office. Suddenly, Sorrowful turns to the camera and barks at his assistant in the cage: "Take his marker. Little doll like that is worth twenty bucks, any way you look at it." The camera holds on the scene as Sorrowful goes into his office and the father puts his hand on the child's back.

This is a scene that registers the emotional promise of Shirley Temple at her most complex. Some might see only sexual danger or pedophilia barely veiled, but the film is after the redemption of masculinity, with the saving grace (of love for the child) as something that requires risk, that requires overcoming fear. It means opening the heart, which is in keeping with the scene in Johnston's *The Little Colonel* when the old colonel is moved by his granddaughter' s touch. Considering that it is the father and child who are in economic straits, for the little girl to intuit the possibility of Sorrowful's fear is a remarkably powerful moment: she cracks Sorrowful's tough-guy veneer even as she echoes Roosevelt's imperative to conquer "fear itself." The child's inflection is mocking, a dare, but Temple's voice is so childish that it is rendered almost comical, though not so comical as Sorrowful's retrospective explanation of why he violated his long-standing rule of no I.O.Us: "The doll bluffed me into it," he says in a monotone, attributing a precocious shrewdness to her that justifies his capitulation to her charm and his own feelings.

Marky's father puts her on a bench before he leaves and tells her to

FIGURE 21. Sorrowful Jones, the orphaned Marky, and Bangles in *Little Miss Marker* (dir. Alexander Hall, 1934). Adolphe Menjou, Shirley Temple, and Dorothy Dell in publicity photo. Author's collection.

"be a good little girl and daddy will be right back." "I'm not afraid," the child replies. Her father will never return. When Dream Prince does not win the race, he commits suicide. Resistant at first, Sorrowful succumbs to the charm of "the gorgeous rascal" and keeps her beyond the initial ploy of using her as the clean owner of record for racehorses owned by the cheating Big Steve Holloway (Charles Bickford). Cosseting figures in Sorrowful's growing attachment to the child. Sorrowful puts Marky to bed after she has broken down in tears because, as she bawls to his poker game mates, "He doesn't like me." He sits on a chair beside the bed and gets out the daily race results. "What's that guy's name?" he asks. "King Arthur," she asserts. He starts to read the daily race results in the language of the Arthurian tales that she loves. She takes her left arm from under the bed cover and puts her hand around his neck. Sorrowful keeps reading as she falls asleep. He smiles, folds the paper, and tucks her arm back under the cover. The scene starts as one in which the adult comforts the child, but it functions as cosseting because of the sweet comfort that Marky's relaxed embrace gives to Sorrowful, the crotchety, middle-aged man who has been forced by circumstance to take care of her. Sorrowful's life changes. He is domesticated because of Marky. Not only does he buy her (and himself) new clothes, but (under duress) he also teaches her to pray and declares his love for a gangster's moll, Bangles Carson (Dorothy Dell), who, also responding to Marky's influence, wants a different life—a family life. That possibility is temporarily endangered by an accident that threatens Marky's life. In the end, however, Marky is saved, and it is clear that the orphan will have a new mother and father, Bangles and Sorrowful.

Did Temple's employers know they were "playing with fire" in sexual terms? In *Little Miss Marker* there is a scene in which Marky is talking to an African American man, "Dizzy" (Willie Best), who sweeps the floors at the gambling establishment where her father has just left her as his I.O.U. Dizzy asks Marky whether her father often leaves her, and she tells him in a chirpy voice that once a man was arrested after he found her at the circus when her father lost her. Shocked beyond words by her story, Dizzy literally falls into the door.

We may be offended that a joke is made at the expense of the child's innocence or that it uses a black man as its comic foil, but this scene clearly depends on its audience's knowing about pedophilia, defined as the sexual abuse of prepubescent children. In the 1920s the notion of the "sexual psychopath" came into prominence in the United States. In 1932 the Lindbergh baby kidnapping heightened fears of criminal—although not necessarily sexual—threats to children. Two years later, Americans were confronted with the arrest of Albert Fish, accused of gruesomely murdering a ten-year-old New York City girl many years earlier, in 1925. After police traced a taunting letter he wrote to the child's parents in late 1933, they arrested him. It was revealed he had sexually abused numerous children and committed multiple child murders although police had had him in custody on other lesser charges several times and released him.[70]

Fueled by wire service coverage, such crimes left the impression that dangerous perverts were imperiling all America's children almost at will, an impression seared into the public imagination in 1937 by police crackdowns, especially in urban areas.[71] The social attitude regarding child predators that took hold in the United States in the late 1930s was based on localized but well-publicized crimes, like Fish's. In spite of evidence that contradicted the depth of this problem, an incipient moral panic over sexual offenses perpetrated by pedophiles began to grow.[72] Although this was not the first time such a moral panic had occurred in the United States, by autumn 1937 the latest sex offender crisis became the subject of articles in numerous national magazines such as *Newsweek, The Nation,* and *Time.*[73]

The scene between Marky and Dizzy acknowledges the "stranger danger" scenario that Americans in the 1930s would come to regard as the essence of pedophilic behavior. It is useful to keep in mind that this scene also shows that Temple's films are aware that not all man-child interaction is the same, even if what they seek to create falls under the category of what Michael Solomon calls "sweet kitsch," appealing to the audience's tender feelings within a benign and beautiful demonstration of pure innocence; such a demonstration of feeling is frequently dismissed as "false" and "sentimental" because "it gives us a picture of ourselves that is too pure, too ethically one-sided."[74] Yet, as I have shown in the case of *Little Miss Marker,* Temple's films can inscribe the potential danger in the relationship between a girl child and an adult male while choosing to assert the triumph of idealized paternal feeling over the pedophilic.

Modern scholarship sees her impact almost exclusively in terms of the erotic response of grown men to the child star, but the film industry, as well as movie reviewers, of the 1930s thought Temple's appeal was primarily to women and children. These two linked constituencies were identified as the main audience for Hollywood's juvenile performers and for Temple in the 1930s. With adult women long established by Hollywood industry lore as the arbiters of family film attendance, Temple's films were the kind of family fare that needed to appeal first to women and children.[75] The tastes and desires of women and children were thought to be the main determinant in the commercial success of juvenile-centered films. This was in keeping with the belief that these two groups were the most consistent consumers of stage and literary articulations of childhood in the late nineteenth century and the early twentieth.[76] A *New York Times* review called *Baby Take a Bow* "a delightful show for the large audience at which it is aimed. Women and children were in the majority at the Roxy yesterday; they liked Shirley and they liked the picture."[77] In response to *Curly Top, Variety* thought the film would be "cinch b.o. for almost any house. Should be a matinee cleanup (the mamas and kiddies) and almost just as good at night. Holds plenty for almost every type of audience."[78] Contrary to the view that children did not like Temple, Sarah Street affirms that children were fond of comedies and musicals and that Temple was a favorite.[79]

Temple's films invite child and perhaps also women viewers to identify with the star/girl Shirley Temple as a feisty and irrepressible tomboy, as well as a precociously talented and beautiful "feminine" little girl in stories in which the chief goal is the redemption of masculinity. Concerns of the Great Depression, including masculinity in flight from commitment to family and dealing with economic and emotional hardship, might have exerted a powerful attraction to women audiences who wanted to believe in the power that innocent femininity could exert over masculinity during a time of widespread familial stress.

Temple's status as a priceless child linked her to earlier screen representations of juvenated femininity that were popular with women and children, like Mary Pickford's. However, the cultural function she played and the overdetermined quality of her performances—inscribed in her physicality, onscreen personality, and musicality—meant that Temple's star vehicles presented a very different ordering of viewers' experience of girlhood, as well as a very different framework for fantasy and film pleasure than Pickford's. As we saw in chapter 1, the child or adolescent heroine's emotional value to adults was undoubtedly one appeal of Pickford's films. The movie audience's allegiance to the Pickford heroine typically was established very quickly (as with the introduction of Pickford in *M'Liss*), with dramatic suspense then priming viewers for the satisfying moment when the girl—neglected, orphaned, abused, or just underappreciated—is revealed as the "priceless jewel," and other characters acknowledge exactly how dear the young heroine is to them.

Many of Temple's star vehicles were associated with familiar sentimental tropes and with girl-centered narratives, but her films could hardly be considered duplicates of Pickford's, including the four that are ostensibly based on the same source material: *Curly Top, The Little Princess, Rebecca of Sunnybrook Farm,* and *Poor Little Rich Girl.* First of all, they could not be coming-of-age stories since it was impossible for the petite child to convincingly impersonate even an adolescent. Temple's *Curly Top* was based on the Jean Webster story that was made into Pickford's *Daddy-Long-Legs* and then a talkie with Janet Gaynor (dir. Alfred Santell, 1931).[80] As I detailed in chapter 1, Pickford's film shows the orphanage as a place of emotional and physical deprivation, sometimes ending in death for innocent children. Temple's version of the story cultivates a very different tone. Orphaned Elizabeth (Temple), the daughter of vaudevillians, may get into mild trouble because of her high-spirited antics (including the singing of "Animal Crackers in My Soup"), but the orphanage allows her to keep a pet pony and duck. Her older sister (Rochelle Hudson) is a teacher at the school, which is expansive and bright, with at least one highly sympathetic attendant (Jane Darwell).

In spite of the fact that both Pickford and Temple films upheld traditional values of family, juvenated female innocence, and the sentimental value of the child, Temple's films are very different from Pickford's. Plots do not constitute films, and narrative tropes and character types, even the most popular and resilient, are not frozen in time. Sentimental figures such as that of the orphan or the willful hoyden were recirculated but also reshaped to the requirements of Temple's age and specific talents, as well as for the tastes of her historical audience and generic norms attached to the musical. Temple's films were embedded in historical conventions and established entertainment practices, but her films were also impacted by the construction of a Hollywood fantasy of childhood that was not fixed but adaptive.

## THE DUAL RESCUE OF "DADDY-BOY" AND CHILD

Undoubtedly, Temple's films depended on the rich tradition of representing children and, more specifically, of representing the small girl or the so-called infant or baby as a highly conventionalized figure of longstanding and powerful appeal to audiences. In 1936 *Variety* suggested that *Poor Little Rich Girl* reflected the typical storyline of a Temple star vehicle: "the formula is daddy-boy meets child, loses child and wins back child."[81] Where did this sentimental trope come from, and how was it represented in Temple's films?

Temple's films depend on stories that are formulaic and character-types that may seem trite, but we need to recognize that they nevertheless possessed considerable cultural, ideological, and psychological traction. Recruiting men for happy domesticity and proving the power of girlhood to secure that commitment was a familiar task given to adorable little girls in popular culture—fulfilled again and again for more than a half century in many literary and performance venues: Shirley Temple would continue to trade on the currency of securely established conventions in literature, theater, and film for representing the girl child even while her stardom expanded or revised those conventions to meet new social and historical imperatives. In Temple's films it is not the transformation of the girl into a woman or the journey of a girl to the verge of womanhood that is emphasized but the impact of a little girl on an adult male who is transformed into a parent by his love for the priceless child, whether she is his own offspring, an orphan, or just a lonely little girl.

Long before the advent of film, the orphan's reliance on a male benefactor was a well-established part of literature centered on children, especially girls. George Eliot's *Silas Marner: The Weaver of Raveloe* (1861) was a key Victorian text built on this premise: after her mother drops dead in the snow, the golden-haired toddler, Eppie, wanders into the hut of the weaver, Silas Marner. Eppie replaces Silas's stolen coins to save him from a lonely life. *Silas Marner* exemplifies the popularity of the foundling trope in nineteenth-century sentimental fiction, which was prefigured, claims Carolyn Steedman, by Goethe's *Wilhelm Meister's Apprenticeship* (1795–96) as an urtext in the story of a man rescuing a female foundling, in this case, when the hero buys a little female acrobat, "Mignon," to save her from cruel treatment.[82]

Even without the orphan who requires rescue, the central conceit of many child-centered texts of the Victorian period was the child rescuing the man from himself, whether the latter is besotted with drink or merely selfish.[83] That has led one scholar to claim that Victorian temperance literature has a special affinity with Temple's films.[84] In such narratives, little girls' caresses and kisses "convert their drunken fathers into good, temperate men."[85] Temperance literature, with its melodramatic extreme of conversion and sacrifice, was but one strand in a much broader discursive tradition that shaped changing cultural expectations regarding man-and-child narratives and the power of innocence in relation to domesticity. In temperance fiction, as in much nineteenth-century melodrama, the typical little girl was a sad, frequently doomed creature. She had little in common with the joyous, triumphant "super baby star" embodied by Temple in films that resonated with the pleasures of man-child bonding.

While the rescue of the man is central in Victorian temperance literature, the rescue of the child is not. In contrast, Temple's films depend on what I call "the dual rescue" that creates emotional reciprocity between man and child. This dual or mutual rescue liberates the child from oppressive circumstances but also liberates the man from being emotionally obstructed. The dual rescue becomes foundational to the utopian formation of a new family and emerges as a critical convention of the form of child-man centered narrative that Temple's films exemplify.

A key precursor to Temple's films in this respect is *Bootles' Baby: A Story of the Scarlet Lancers,* one of the late nineteenth century's most famous and influential comic plays about little girls and man-child bonding. In its tenor, tone, and articulation of the trope of man and foundling girl against the backdrop of a male-dominated setting, *Bootles' Baby* provided the blueprint for many subsequent articulations of the dual rescue story that focuses on the love between a little girl and a grown

FIGURE 22. Captain Algeron Ferrers finds a baby in his bed. Frontispiece to John Strange Winter's *Bootles' Baby: A Story of the Scarlet Lancers* (1891).

man. Emphasizing comedy and sentimentality rather than intense melodrama and a suffering child, the highly successful play was written for the stage by Hugh Moss in 1887. Moss adapted his stage play from the 1885 novel by Henrietta Eliza Vaughan Stannard, who wrote under the male nom de plume "John Strange Winter."[86] Stannard's story is hardly original, indebted, as it appears, to the libretto penned by Jules-Henri Vernoy de Saint-Georges and Jean-François Bayard for Donizetti's *Daughter of the Regiment*, a comic opera of 1840. In the opera a sergeant of the twenty-first regiment finds a baby in a blanket and raises the foundling.

Working predominantly within a comic vein, *Bootles' Baby* demonstrates the force of the priceless little girl who is appreciated by a man ensconced in an all-male community separated from women, chil-

FIGURE 23. Priscilla (Shirley Temple) and her grandfather (C. Aubrey Smith) in a scene of cosseting. *Wee Willie Winkie* (dir. John Ford, 1937). Author's collection.

dren, or the expression of emotion. A similar emphasis on a community of men (often in a military setting) will be evident in many Temple vehicles including *Little Miss Marker, Bright Eyes, The Little Colonel, The Littlest Rebel, Wee Willie Winkie,* and *Susannah of the Mounties.* Stannard's story focused on Captain Algeron Ferrers, a.k.a. "Bootles," a thirty-five-year-old British cavalry officer described as rich, handsome, and pleasant. He walks into his quarters one night to find a blonde, curly-headed two-year-old girl sitting on his bed.[87] He is confounded by her presence and by the note written by an unidentified mother who thinks she has left the child in the room of its father.[88] Bootles grumbles to his compatriots: "It's a plant. I know nothing about the creature."[89] He soon finds himself thoroughly captivated by the winning ways of the young foundling he calls "Miss Mignon." He keeps her.

Like Sorrowful Jones in *Little Miss Marker,* Bootles turns from cynical skepticism to total devotion in a spectacle of child-centered sentimentalism that narrativizes the emotional impact of the tiny girl on the grown man. *Bootles' Baby,* like Temple's *Wee Willie Winkie,* emphasizes an extreme contrast in size between the man and the "baby," increasing a sense of the unexpected emotional power the child wields over the man. Bootles becomes the "favourite plaything" of the preternaturally energetic and intuitive baby.[90] In the end Bootles wins the woman of his heart (who turns out to be Mignon's mother) and refuses to give Mignon up, even when he learns that her biological father, now dead, was an officer who hated him.

In representing the dual rescue, *Bootles' Baby* is rife with cosseting as a key element that transports the father figure into an affective state of greater emotional openness and paternal feeling.[91] In one scene Bootles goes back to his room after being rejected by the woman he loves. He finds Mignon there:

> "Will Mignon *always* love Bootles?" he asked.
>
> "Always," was the confident reply. "Mignon will *always* love Bootles."
>
> . . . The little child crept closer and closer into his heart . . . and the clasp of her little arms about his neck seemed to take away the sharpest sting of defeat. The touch of her baby lips upon his aching forehead—and it *did* ache—brought him a larger measure of comfort than any other living thing had power to do at that moment.[92]

Through cosseting, the man is pulled emotionally into the intimate world of the child as an escape from the pressures of the separate, masculine sphere representing work but also sexual competition. The little girl's "petting" of the father figure may seem to imitate a woman's expression of love, but sympathy and tender touch are offered by a "baby" who can barely talk in full sentences. "The clasp of her little arms about his neck" and her declaration of lasting love secure Bootles to domesticity in a way that adult femininity cannot. The resemblance of this scene to Sorrowful's reading of the race results to Marky in *Little Miss Marker* and numerous other moments in Temple's films is striking. Although now subject to interpretation as eroticized signs of pedophilia, the force field of familial cosseting depends on behaviors between girl child and man that once were regarded as normative—and, indeed, desirable—within the family.

## "HELLO, LITTLE BOY!"

Although it is important to understand the cultural inheritance in which her films were grounded, Temple's star vehicles were more than just a repetition of the gendered conventions, narratives forms, and cultural values associated with the past and earlier cultural texts about idealized little girls and the men who come to love them. Her films were also impacted by Hollywood's construction of a fantasy of childhood, one that in the 1930s had as much to do with Depression-era uplift of national morale as with the moral uplift of men, with the values of the 1930s musical comedy and American consumerism as with the values inscribed in Victorian girl-centered literature and other sentimental discourses. Committed to optimism and a utopian sensibility, Temple's films offered escape into a potent cultural fantasy in which the adult world is no match for the power of the child, who transcends age, sex, and gender and sometimes race. She overcomes difficulty and defeat through a complex play of charm, determination, and luck. This fantasy was very much dependent on the personality conveyed by the child actor. At its most effective, Temple's screen persona flowed effortlessly between masculinity and femininity, comedy and pathos, blackness and whiteness, adult-enticing beauty and child-identified cuteness, middle-class manners and working-class resilience, innocent vulnerability and erotically charged power.

Temple is established as transiting the boundaries of gender as perhaps only a little girl may be allowed to do, that is, as a "tomboy." Temple's dominating child heroines are always engaged in an oscillation between stereotyped masculine and feminine behaviors. At some moments she seems to occupy both positions at once, suggesting an ambiguity in her relation to masculinity and femininity. However, this is not accomplished just by the screenplay or costuming. There is something in her attitude (as Seldes recognized) and in the child's physicality and "raucous," adventurous spirit that distinguishes her character. It is interesting that Temple was regarded as a tomboy offscreen, with stories circulating that she was nicknamed "Butch" by member(s) of a film crew, and, as some stories related, the nickname was sustained by her classmates at Westlake High School.[93] Making her an orphan or motherless in many of her films offers the opportunity of her being rescued by a man but also the freedom to identify with masculinity, to mimic it, even gently satirize it, and to cultivate those "rude and rowdy" qualities that Seldes admired in Temple and thought other men also appreciated.

In *Bright Eyes* "Shirley" (Temple) is a mascot for aviators: one, Loop Merritt (James Dunn) battles to adopt her after her mother dies. Shirley hangs out with aviators; the audience's first glimpse of Temple is as she walks down the side of a rural road. She is hitching for a ride to get to the airport to visit her friends. Clothed in aviator's pants, leather jacket, and headgear, and with only a hint of her blonde curls peaking from under the cap, she might, indeed, be taken for a boy. Temple's rolling

FIGURE 24. Paul (Buddy Ebsen) and Star (Shirley Temple) get ready to dance in *Captain January* (dir. David Butler, 1936). Author's collection.

gait and swinging arms in this scene in *Bright Eyes* are typical of a little boy rather than a girl, and her gestures for thumbing a ride are snappy and practiced rather than girlishly refined or tentative. The gaze of the camera does not eroticize her or even definitively mark her gender as female. Her identification with masculinity extends beyond her costuming. At the airport she is teased by one of the aviators, who says, "Hello, little boy!"

Temple is affiliated with the tomboy of "presexual" latency. Because she is so young, the gender ambiguity she displays suggests the fun to be had in the liminal phase in which the child tries on different gender roles. Temple's heroines are inscribed as gender-stretching figures of preadult female freedom who seek the company of grown men and marginalized others—soldiers and crooks, children and servants of color, immigrants and indigenous others. The fun of this liminal phase is illustrated by *Captain January,* in which Star (Temple) has been raised by a lighthouse keeper, Captain January (Guy Kibbee). The captain rescued her from a shipwreck that killed her mother, an opera singer. *Captain January,* like so many other Temple films, uses the trope of the foundling to exploit the humorous appeal of the child's imitation of masculinity. At the same time, it stokes the sentimentality of the female child's unusually persuasive power to inspire the devotion of an adult male to her and to domesticity.

*Captain January* is filled with musical numbers, opening with one in which Star gets out of bed to greet the morning (and the camera). Another, one of the best song-and-dance sequences in all of Temple's films, occurs early in the film and registers male appreciation of the little girl who is accepted as one of them. Sent on an errand in town ("government duty," she calls it), Star strolls into the local general store. She is dressed in a sailor suit. Her nautical lingo and punchy, masculine mannerisms resemble those of the seamen who hang around the establishment watching Paul Roberts (Buddy Ebsen) dance. When she orders supplies for the lighthouse, Star aggressively stabs her chubby finger across the counter at the clerk and reminds him not to forget "our special price." When she exits the store, a sailor with a hand accordion starts Star's "special music." Paul puts her on top of a barrel. In a medium shot Temple starts to sing "At the Codfish Ball" with the assembly of men around her. Paul then swings her to the ground, where she dances while continuing to sing the comic song, which incorporates comic references to popular musical lyrics like "Shuffle Off to Buffalo" and "Minnie the Moocher," as well as playing on the double meaning of codfish ball, which is a dance of the fishes in the song but is usually a fish cake for eating.

Paul then joins Star. The camera tracks with them as they dance and sing side by side off the porch. They then start to tap dance across the boardwalk. They join arms but in comic parody of couple dancing (he is down on bent knees to match her height or standing up with his hand on her head as she is forced to do small, quick steps to move toward and back from him). After she dances up a raised pier, they start to dance cheek to cheek in what can only be taken to be a satire of Rogers and Astaire, since their exaggerated ballroom dancing poses are accompanied by the strains of a lush orchestral arrangement punctuated by cymbal clashes. The sequence ends with their wildly exaggerated steps as they use a large open door as a proscenium arch marking the end of the impromptu performance with a wave of their hands.

After taking applause, Star joins the men. She is told that to be a sailor, she must learn to spit properly. An expert spitter proceeds to teach her in a hilarious scene that builds on Temple's ability to mimic adults. This scene depends on Temple's comically childish, inadequate attempt to emulate the sailor, but it is funny, too, for his comic grotesqueness compared to Temple's cute stylized attempt to replicate

FIGURE 25. Star (Shirley Temple) learns to spit in *Captain January.* Author's collection.

his behavior. Unfortunately, a stuck-up truant officer (Sara Haden) is watching. She is scandalized, ostensibly by Star's truancy and spitting, but the little girl who acts and dresses like an adult sailor no doubt also is unsettling. Using her influence, the truant officer will have Star taken away from the captain with the aim of placing her in an orphanage. Of course, since this is a Temple film, a happy ending will solve all problems and restore Star to the captain.

*Captain January* is but one of a number of Temple films that celebrate a male community that collectively embraces the child, contributing to her training—or perceived mistraining—as in *Little Miss Marker.* They celebrate the child's imitation of masculine toughness and humor, as well as her feminine emotion and affectionate softness. Even when Temple does have a living mother, as in *The Little Colonel* and John Ford's *Wee Willie Winkie,* her characters are miniature adventurers who chafe under the strictures of confined and conventionally refined adult female behavior.

*Wee Willie Winkie* is set in British colonial India in 1897. Because of financial problems, Priscilla Williams (Temple) and her widowed mother (June Lang) must travel to northern India to live with Priscilla's paternal grandfather (C. Aubrey Smith), a colonel at a British out-

FIGURE 26. Priscilla (Shirley Temple) drills with MacDuff's troops in *Wee Willie Winkie*. Author's collection.

post. Priscilla's mother is shown trying to curb her daughter's attempts to interact with native people and express herself without inhibition. Priscilla is demonstrably bored with sewing and playing with her dolls. She would rather drill with the troops led by Sergeant MacDuff (Victor McLaglen). Priscilla tells a young lieutenant that being a soldier would mean becoming one of those people her grandfather understands, and she wants her grandfather to like her.

Priscilla befriends Sergeant MacDuff, a mountain of a man, and he understands her desire to be a "full-fledged soldier of the Queen." Priscilla complains: "Whoever heard of a soldier called Priscilla?" "You couldn't take private Priscilla very seriously could you?" he replies. To remedy the limitations of femininity, MacDuff gives her a boy's name, albeit a fanciful one, "Wee Willie Winkie" from "an Old Scotch rhyme" about "a lad who always was getting himself into difficulties." Temple's character in *Wee Willie Winkie* is very much like the heroines of girls' literature, but the screenplay was freely adapted from a Rudyard Kipling story about a British colonel's six-year-old son. Born into his place in the British Raj as the pet of the regiment, Percival "enters his manhood" by bravely standing up to a force of "natives" bent on holding him and a grown woman for ransom.[94]

By way of contrast Priscilla earns the status of hero in Temple's *Wee Willie Winkie* through her feminine violation of the codes of the male community she joins. Her violation of those codes points to qualities of feminine empathy and values of tolerance very different from those celebrated in Kipling's story. Unlike Percival, Priscilla crosses class to demonstrate her devotion to MacDuff. In a moment of restrained cosseting, he shows her an old picture of himself, as "a little baby." She looks at the child in the kilt and exclaims: "Oh, I think you were just beautiful." MacDuff coughs and wipes a tear from his eye.

For Priscilla to be a soldier, she must have a uniform, and MacDuff and his men play a trick on a nasty little boy, conning him out of his new wool uniform, complete with kilt. They boil it down to fit Priscilla. Properly outfitted as a soldier (and resembling the child that was MacDuff), she works hard to become one of them. During drill, MacDuff does not spare her: "Snap into it, snap into it. Take that smile off your face. . . . Always the last man to obey the word of command, always the last man," he barks at Priscilla as she lags behind the other soldiers in moving into her place in formation.

The film seems intent on portraying events largely from the perspective of the girl child, who crosses gender boundaries to imitate the more active and interesting work of men. Nevertheless, Graham Greene used Ford's film to argue for the eroticization of Temple: "Now in *Wee Willie Winkie,* wearing short kilts, she is completely totsy. Watch her swaggering stride across the Indian barrack-square."[95] Greene seems to be projecting his own sexual preoccupations onto the film and Temple. Temple is a figure of identification rather than an erotic spectacle in the film. MacDuff also seems to identify with her, and he takes Priscilla's desire to submit to the discipline of the regiment and perform as a soldier very seriously. She is ridiculed by officers, however, including her grandfather, when she presents herself with the men and introduces herself as "Private Winkie." A close-up shows her puzzlement and hurt at not being taken seriously. She looks at her rifle and pulls at her uniform as if checking to see what might be wrong with her. What is wrong is that she is a little girl. The colonel punishes the unit with three hours of extra drill. He orders Priscilla in for a nap. She doesn't obey. Demonstrating the emotional and professional bond between girl and man, in two efficient and wordless shots (a full shot of Priscilla and then a long shot), Priscilla is shown following MacDuff and his men out on the punish-

FIGURE 27. Priscilla (Shirley Temple) is condemned to women's work in *Wee Willie Winkie*. With June Lang. Author's collection.

ment drill. She struggles to keep up with their quick march. When the men return, she is shown, again, in a wordless shot, in MacDuff's arms as he strides into the compound among his men. Worry is etched on the sergeant's face. We see only Priscilla's back, with her body unnaturally still, her arms and legs dangling.

Nothing is ever said about her collapse, but Priscilla is never allowed to drill with the men again. The next time we see her, she is knitting, sitting beside her mother, who sighs at the prospect of following one completed sewing task with another. Later, Priscilla watches MacDuff train his men to box. She asks him: "Can't we ever play together anymore?" The sentimental Scotsman explains in a broken voice. "No, lassie. You've got your orders and I've got my orders." "Old Boots" (her grandfather) has forbidden it. MacDuff starts to cry as he corrects the fighting stance Priscilla has assumed in hopes he will also teach her "the manly art of self-defense."

Priscilla's actions lead to startlingly different results from those in Kipling's original "Wee Willie Winkie" story. While the boy in the original story successfully threatens the natives with superior British military force until it actually arrives, Temple's heroine is a peacemaker.[96] Priscilla decides to visit the camp of an indigenous faction led by Khoda Khan

(Cesar Romero), whom she had befriended earlier. Patricia's grandfather walks alone into Khan's heavily fortified stronghold to rescue her, and she convinces the two leaders that armed conflict can be avoided if they talk. With bagpipes sounding, the film ends with the hope of a more peaceful future secured and a confirmation of the girl's power as a peacemaker. Priscilla is neither a chip off the old imperial block, like Percival, or condemned to be the passive woman captive whom he defends. Instead, Priscilla Williams, a.k.a. "Wee Willie Winkie," is the liminal, heroic girl blending qualities typically divided in conventional thinking about gender. Within the film's fantasy the child comes to represent the power to overcome difficulty and difference to find community, independence, love, and peace.

## SHIRLEY'S WAIF

The affective force of Shirley Temple as a star and the pleasures of her films must be mapped across her film performances as a star whose films drew on many sources, including the sentimental tropes of Victorian child-centered narratives and domestic practice. Although her films most often focused on securing masculinity into the family structure through the power of the little girl, they would not have been so popular in the United States and internationally if they had not been so polyvalent and, therefore, so powerfully open to a number of pleasurable responses from a wide range of viewers—men, women, and children. Part of that pleasure was produced by the performative uniqueness of Temple, whose childish body both defies and demonstrates the meanings culturally assigned to the girl-child. Also of importance is the star's amazing liminality, her ability to absorb and negotiate a host of cultural contradictions and paradoxes. Temple's presence thus contributed to the utopian potential of her films to temporarily resolve for her audiences the differences between old and young, masculine and feminine, black and white, the past and the present, progressive and conservative, the sexual and the asexual, poor and rich.

In light of her ability to negotiate contradictions it is interesting that writing about her life as an adult, Shirley Temple claimed as her own "all-time" personal favorite from among the thousands of photographs taken of her, one that depicts her as a "waif."[97] This photo from 1934, a posed publicity shot to support her appearance in *Little Miss Marker,* creates an unexpected convergence with the Arthur Rothstein photograph of the migrant girl. In the portrait Temple cocks her head and scowls directly at the camera in an uncharacteristic expression for her

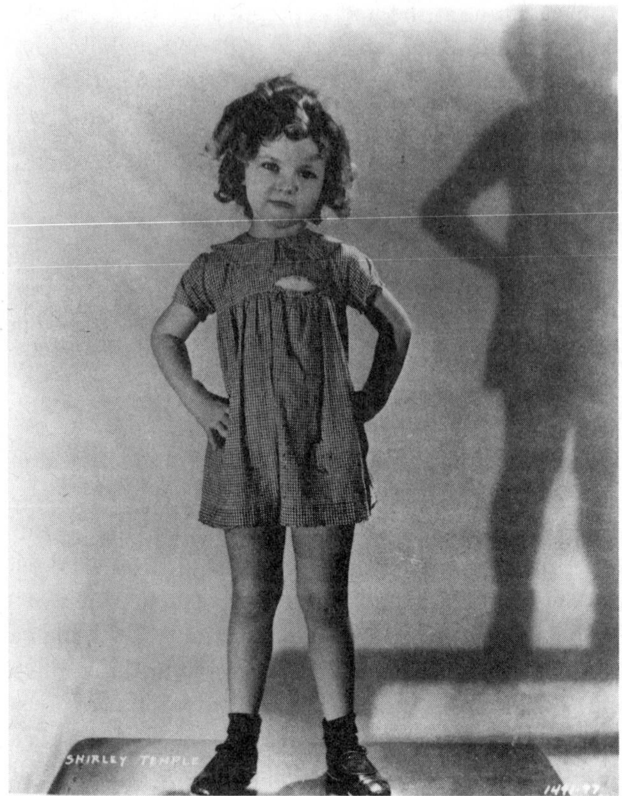


FIGURE 28. Shirley Temple as a Depression-era waif, photographed in costume for *Little Miss Marker,* ca. 1934. Author's collection.

publicity. It is a full shot of Shirley in a dirty, worn, checkered dress that she wears in the film and that a character later refers to as "rags." Her short dress has a broad Peter Pan collar, short sleeves, and an unraveling seam (or tear) across the bodice seam. Her hands rest on her hips. Her legs are bare. Utilitarian black shoes and drooping black socks add a lower-class touch to the outfit. Unlike portraits of Mary Pickford as a ragged waif, this portrait of Shirley Temple as a poor waif is anomalous, not only in relation to the overwhelming trend of how Temple was represented offscreen in publicity as a beautiful child star but also in relation to her appearance in films.

In this respect the publicity still is reminiscent of some of Lewis Carroll's photographs of his little girl friends that were very obviously posed with the child dressing up (or down to nothing) to portray a character or a type. In fact, the attitude that Temple displays, as well as the dressing up as a poor child of the Depression, recalls the conceit of fictionalized waifdom created by Lewis Carroll's photograph(s) of Alice Liddell as a beggar.[98] In toto, Temple's stance and straight gaze into the camera suggest a great deal more childish determination, defiance, and unhappiness than Rothstein's portrait of his Visalia child-subject. Determination was never lacking in Temple's screen persona, but here the portrait's backdrop changes the usually hopeful tone of most of her films: Temple is photographed against a blank studio backdrop; she casts a long shadow on the back wall. The signature blonde curls are in prominence, but the choice of full shot of Temple's entire body, as well as her pose, contributes to a more performative effect to the photo than Rothstein's headshot of the Visalia child, even though both appear to stare straight into the camera. The long shadow and empty background contribute also to the picture's theatricality, its status as posed fiction rather than being pulled from real life or even from a moment of action in a film.

This portrait of Temple seems to encapsulate, as perhaps in no other widely disseminated picture of her, the complexity of identification and desire in relation to the spectacle of childhood that she offered to viewers in the era in which she came to stardom. If we had only this single photo of her, we might presume that Temple and her films supported a reflection hypothesis that assumes a parallel relationship between Hollywood's cinematic presentation of childhood during the Great Depression and the hard realities of childhood experience suggested in Rothstein's photo. But we must be cautious in claiming that Temple's star persona reflected very much of the lived experience of contemporaneous children during the Great Depression, except as displaced and interpreted by the utopian fantasies projected in her films.

In spite of that, Temple's attitude toward this photo suggests her own identification with the lived experience of children who had to work to survive the Great Depression and the family troubles that characterized the historical period in which she came to fame. That attitude reminds us that Shirley Temple was a working child, and it was work and precocious talent that contributed to the unique cinematic power of her stardom that allowed audiences to confront their fears and ameliorate their anxieties through the screen presence of a little girl who served as a potent symbol of domestic happiness and national progress during hard times.

FIGURE 29. Deanna Durbin, film and radio star. Author's collection.

CHAPTER 3

# "The Little Girl with the Big Voice"

## *Deanna Durbin and Sonic Womanliness*

The important thing about Deanna is that she has "one of those throats." . . . Patti wasn't a prodigy. Neither was Bori. They happened to be born with something that occurs only once in a generation—a vocal equipment as fully developed as that of a grown-up singer. . . . Doctors who have peered down the little Durbin throat find that she too has that vocal rarity, a woman's voice in a child's body.

—Frederick Lewis, "The Private Life of Deanna Durbin"

Fourteen-year-old Deanna Durbin rocketed to stardom with the December 1936 release of *Three Smart Girls* (dir. Henry Koster). Universal cast Durbin as "Penny," one of three pampered sisters trying to save their estranged father from the clutches of a gold digger.[1] The studio revamped the script of what started out as a B picture to showcase Durbin's talents in a high-quality A-level production.[2] The plan worked. On its release the film became box-office dynamite. *Film Daily* represented the critical consensus: "Only on rare occasions has any newcomer scored so powerfully and decisively in an initial vehicle. . . . [Durbin's voice] finds itself running neck and neck with her personality, prettiness, poise, pep, and an amazing natural aptitude for acting."[3] MGM's Louis B. Mayer reportedly dubbed Durbin "The Little Girl with the Big Voice," but his studio dropped the little radio singer, originally named "Edna Mae," after her appearance in just one MGM musical short.[4] MGM's folly in releasing Durbin was soon apparent, as *Three Smart Girls* would become the model for a succession of critical and box-office hits that made Durbin Universal's biggest star and Hollywood's highest paid female performer.[5]

Durbin was a highly unusual movie star, not because she sang but because she was a teenager who sang in a preternaturally mature, lyric soprano voice evidencing classical training.[6] The voice creates a realm of signification that can create trouble, especially in relation to age and female sexuality. The contrast between Durbin's immature, adolescent body and the precocious maturity of her voice was the most intriguing complication of her stardom. Although her body and her voice changed over the years, Durbin's embodied voice continued to create contradictory sites of pleasure and cultural meaning in relation to her representation of juvenated femininity. As a result, in Durbin's film and radio appearances, comedy became an important part of the containment of unruly significations created by what Graham Greene described as "that unnaturally mature soprano voice."[7]

In all the venues in which she appeared—radio, film, and recordings—Durbin was affiliated with high-culture music through her vocal style and most of the musical selections she sang. Durbin was obviously not the first film star associated with an operatically trained voice, a classical singing style, or the attempt to popularize operatic singing in the movies. In the wake of synchronized-sound-on-film becoming the industry standard, American filmmakers attempted to exploit almost every musical idiom, including opera and operetta. Hollywood did not have a desire to film opera, but there was an interest in the operatic voice and in plagiarizing vocal music from grand opera.[8] After the arrival of the talkies spurred the production of musicals, Hollywood tried to lure famous opera stars to the screen. Laurence Tibbett, Grace Moore, Lily Pons, Gladys Swarthout, and Risë Stevens all achieved varying lengths and levels of crossover success in film.

In 1939 Fred C. Othamm called Durbin the movies' "greatest child singer [who] had earned the company [Universal] some 10 million dollars largely by steering away from kisses."[9] Although the exact extent of Universal's financial dependence on Durbin's extraordinary success is debated, the studio's bottom line was helped by the fact that her films were relatively inexpensive, in spite of her enormous salary.[10] Durbin's films and recordings enjoyed great appeal beyond the United States, reflected, for example, in her status as the number-one female box-office draw in Great Britain for four years running.[11] *Fortune* magazine took note of the "tremendous commercial significance" of Durbin's stardom in merchandising consumer products, with $2 million in sales attached to her image and endorsements in 1939 alone.[12] Her stardom had an impact on industry trends, challenging the common negative perception of the box-office value of adolescent screen actresses. Columnist

Sheila Graham wrote, "As a result of Deanna's unprecedented success, the 'awkward age' has been banished from the film vocabulary and studio doors are wide open to pretty girls with good singing voices."[13] Studios began to develop young sopranos who might replicate her box-office attainments: these included Susanna Foster and Gloria Jean at Universal, Jane Powell and Kathryn Grayson at MGM.

Durbin's impact was enormous, but her premature retirement from the screen in 1949, at the age of twenty-seven, and subsequent reclusive lifestyle have dimmed appreciation of the magnitude of her stardom.[14] Whereas her contemporary Judy Garland attained the status of cinematic and cultural icon, subject of a great deal of popular and scholarly commentary, Durbin, whose musical star shone just as bright (if not brighter), has been almost completely overlooked by film scholars.[15] That neglect may be related also to the general lack of interest in analyzing the stardom of classically trained sopranos in Hollywood, a claim made by Edward Baron Turk in reference to Jeanette MacDonald.[16] The few limited studies focusing on Durbin include an insightful appreciation written in 1976 by William K. Everson for *Films in Review*, a portion of a chapter by Jeanine Basinger in *The Star Machine*, and an article by Georganne Scheiner that addresses the reasons Durbin inspired adoration among teenage girls who were members of her fan club, "The Deanna Durbin Devotees."[17] All add to our knowledge, but none of these approaches addresses the central signifier of Durbin's stardom: her voice.

Durbin's characters were constructed within the familiar image of the "Miss Fix-It," who solved adult problems through childish machinations.[18] Whether rich or poor, darling daughter or plucky orphan, Durbin's "Miss Fix-It" was not the first strong-willed girl in films of the 1930s (Temple could be regarded as one), but she was the first who offered singing from nineteenth-century classical repertoire rather than from current musical trends. With the exception of the noirish *Christmas Holiday* (dir. Robert Siodmak, 1944), her films were lighthearted tales in which comedy dominated. Often, the only diegetic music in her films consisted of songs inserted in the story line for Durbin to sing solo in her classically trained style.

For a significant part of Durbin's screen career her voice and adolescent body combined to articulate a frisson that played on the gap between musical aestheticization and erotic sensuality, childishness and womanliness, cultural uplift and sexual taboo. Thus, the pleasure-giving effect of Durbin's voice contains both a danger and delight because visu-

FIGURE 30. Patsy's father conducts her singing in *One Hundred Men and a Girl* (dir. Henry Koster, 1937). Adolphe Menjou, Mischa Auer, and Deanna Durbin. Author's collection.

alizing the body of adolescent Durbin as a musical instrument unhinges the logic of the anticipated, normal relation of the cultured female soprano voice with an age-appropriate body. This makes for a listening and viewing experience in which the audience must cope with what Freud theorized as "unheimlich," the "uncanny" experience that registers the uncomfortable simultaneity of the familiar and the strange.[19] In this respect Durbin's voice evokes pleasure with an edge of disturbance: it may prove disconcerting or, as it was for many of her fans, tremendously exciting. For many it was very likely both.

In spite of her age and apparent physical immaturity, from the beginning of her film career Durbin's voice exerted the legendary seductive and intoxicating power of the adult female voice in song. Illustrating this intoxicating power, perhaps no male reviewer offered more rhetorical excess (and erotic suggestiveness) in response to Durbin than Patrick Galway. Writing in Britain's *New Statesman,* he remarked of the fourteen-year-old film star's appearance in her second feature, *One Hundred Men and a Girl* (dir. Henry Koster, 1937): "Useless to pretend that I am tough enough to resist the blandishments of Miss Deanna Durbin. The candid eyes, the parted lips, the electric energy, the astonishing voice; if they bowl over 50 million or so, surely a critic may be pardoned for wobbling a little on his professional cynical base."[20] Galway's comments suggest that Durbin's singing reveals an unexpectedly dangerous manifestation of adolescent female performance.

The uncanny pleasures of Durbin's singing extended beyond the presumed refining influence of operatically coded vocal production. They also exceeded the established boundaries of sentimentality in movies' textual construction of an innocent young girl in the 1930s, an era in which the "teenager" became a figure of cultural fascination in the United States. Teenagers drew a great deal of public attention in the States during the late 1930s, which one scholar attributes to "the growing visibility of high school students" and "curiosity about what 'youth' meant."[21] The heightened visibility of young people fourteen to seventeen years of age was related to the increasing size of this demographic in the United States; by 1940 the group was larger than it had ever been (more than nine million); soon these young people were given the label "teeners," "teensters," and "teenagers."[22] With their own music (swing), dialect ("jive talk"), and dance style (jitterbug), teenagers developed a distinctive culture that many adults thought was foolish—and irritating. Responding to this phenomenon, one prominent psychologist told readers of *Ladies' Home Journal* that American parents needed to show a sustained interest in their children and encourage them in more culturally elevated pursuits as an alternative to the addictive, mindless ones associated with teen culture.[23]

A national interest in teenagers was translated onto the screen in the 1930s and 1940s, with actors like Durbin, Judy Garland, Mickey Rooney, Shirley Temple, Jane Withers, and Bonita Granville playing adolescent characters who often were exasperating to authority figures but almost always proven to be fundamentally wholesome. This wholesomeness was exemplified by the Andy Hardy films and Durbin's musicals; in both, screen teenagers were more preoccupied with their families than with a separate teenage culture. Combining the cultural uplift of classical music with Durbin as an energetic, optimistic teen was sustained as a winning combination on movie screens during the late 1930s and early 1940s.

One scholar dismisses Durbin as a gingham-clothed ideal of adolescence that functioned primarily to soothe parental fears about teenagers' sexuality.[24] Such a view makes sense if one believes Durbin's classical music affiliation served only to support an image of wholesome, innocent (i.e., sexually repressed) adolescence operating primarily as a counter to female bobby-soxers in thrall to swing music. Certainly, a significant number of Americans regarded the latter as a perverse and degrading popular culture influence.[25] Such a view of swing music is expressed in Norbert Lusk's review of *One Hundred Men and a Girl:* "Virtually every music-lover who is carried away by her [Durbin's] lark-like voice, silently prays that it may never be desecrated by crooning and that she may never appear with a swing band or any of its derivatives. A great deal of her unique appeal is associated with good music, great music, and it [is] the fervent hope of many that her lovely gift may never be degraded."[26]

In an interview from 1953 Durbin says that she believes parents were her primary fans, but newsletters of the "Deanna Durbin Devotees" and Scheiner's research suggest otherwise.[27] It appears that young females made up a crucial element of her fan base, and those fans sometimes expressed their responses to her in terms that suggest a girl-on-girl crush. One remembrance by a female fan of Durbin is worth quoting at length:

> In the late 1930s, when I was about nine or ten, I began to be aware of a young girl's face appearing in magazines and newspapers. I was fascinated. . . . I realized that the face belonged to a very lovely singing voice beginning to be heard on the radio record programmes. The face and the voice belonged to Deanna Durbin . . . at the age of twelve. . . . At last I saw her [in *Three Smart Girls Grow Up*]. The effect she had upon me can only be described as electrifying. I had never felt such a surge of admiration and adoration before.[28]

This kind of youthful female response to Durbin's voice is raised also in the opening scene of her star vehicle *First Love* (dir. Henry Koster, 1939). Durbin's character, Connie Clinton, is an orphan whose best friend begs her to spend the summer with her and her family at their lake house; the friend, Wilma van Everett (Marcia Mae Jones), is giddy with praise for Connie: "Well, look at her, she's tops after all. . . . Honestly, she hits a high note and it sends chills up and down your spine!"

This suggests the kind of "coenesthetic" appeal of music that Roland Barthes describes. The voice in song "is connected less to an 'impression' than to an internal, muscular, humoral sensuality. . . . It passes over the entire surface of the body."[29] The breadth of Durbin's popularity suggests that, in addition to the sensual excitement she provided through her beautiful voice, her stardom may have spoken on another level to those who desired access to higher cultural values embodied by an emotionally accessible figure whose films and their comic narratives lifted the bar-

FIGURE 31. Deanna Durbin as a girl whose voice sends "chills up and down" the spine of her best friend. With Marcia Mae Jones (far left), Doris Lloyd, and Samuel Hinds in *First Love* (dir. Henry Koster, 1939). Author's collection.

rier of musical seriousness in a nonelitist mass media. With many people locked out of access to formal education because of the Great Depression, her appeal was part of the phalanx of technologies that reached out to provide the democratization of "good music" for U.S. audiences. The typical Durbin film would feature three to five carefully selected musical numbers; she almost always sang at least one operatic aria or a song from soprano recital repertoire (in English or its original language) or one based on a classical instrumental piece. She mixed the former with folk songs, hymns, patriotic songs, and newly written popular numbers, an approach that was familiar both to concertgoers and to radio listeners of the time in what Deems Taylor derided as "musical baby kissing."[30]

## PASSIONATE SOPRANOS, PRODIGIES, AND SONIC WOMANLINESS

The voice is a sonic signifier of many things, including the human body. As Barthes says: "The body—music—related to performance but also interiority—especially with singing—relation to breath, to shaping the mouth. . . . Music—is inevitably about the body."[31] Durbin's voice demands to be read as an extension of a body that functions as more than merely a musical instrument. Mladen Dolar argues, however, that the voice cannot be reduced to Barthes's description of the "grain of the voice" as an unproblematized extension of the body: "For to attach the voice to the body and to endow it with materiality involves all kinds of obstacles—one is ultimately faced with an unbridgeable gap, since the trouble is that the object never fits the body. . . . Music evokes the voice and conceals it, it fetishizes it, but also opens the gap that cannot be filled."[32]

The voice and body of Durbin represent a mass media commodification of this "unbridgeable gap" in which the aestheticized musical voice that represents the body becomes the "object [that] never fits the body." In this respect it becomes a fetish that substitutes for the lost or unobtainable object of desire. Characteristic of such a displacement of desire, the fetish is central in a fantasy process based on the disavowing formula, "I know [this is not the original object] but nevertheless [in this fetish] it is—and I have it."

Based on musical traditions that coalesced in the nineteenth century, to be a soprano is to be a woman, not a young boy or a castrato. The female soprano is associated with self-consciously beautiful sounds linked to the expression of emotionally heightened and erotically charged femininity—in other words, with aural representations that constitute "womanliness" within the musical realm. Also, to be a soprano in the modern era is to sing of passion, the passion of the body that is that of a woman, not a child. In Durbin's singing, sexual passion is articulated through the sonic register, as her voice becomes an acoustic signifier of "womanliness" produced through sonic aesthetic signs.

Taken from the psychoanalytic studies of Joan Riviere and Jacques Lacan, the term *womanliness* has been used in feminist film theory most often to refer to those behavioral and visual characteristics that are assumed by the female so that she might signify an acceptable, desirable femininity in patriarchal society.[33] To be a woman is not to be a man, to demonstrate the visual signifiers (such as excessively ornate clothes, hair, hats, or even flirtatious behavior) that connote a sexual difference that places femininity in opposition to masculinity—that is, not male or "castrated." Womanliness is often theorized as a masquerade. I am using the term *womanliness* in a slightly different sense from that often applied in film studies. Here I am using it to show how the

FIGURE 32. A startlingly successful debut at Universal. Deanna Durbin in publicity still for *Three Smart Girls* (dir. Henry Koster, 1936). With Nan Grey and Barbara Read. Author's collection.

voice signifies or flaunts femininity as desirable. I am not arguing, as Joan Riviere originally theorized from her case study, that womanliness functions in this specific context to deny the female's possession of masculine traits (including intellectuality) as part of an unconscious strategy of "masquerade" that turns aside reprisals that might be directed at the woman for possessing those characteristics that properly belong to men.[34] I am arguing, instead, that the sonic womanliness of Durbin is a strong appeal to audiences as a sexual fetish that, nevertheless, must be contained and controlled in order to keep it from undermining the star's juvenated qualities that signify not only physical and psychological immaturity but also sexual innocence and, therefore, moral goodness.

Womanliness plays on the conventional boundaries of sexual difference, but in film studies those boundaries are most often theorized without regard to the implications of age in constructing femininity as an acceptable object of male desire. Womanliness, however, implies a reference to age in its very name. To successfully represent womanliness is not to be a child but an adult female, one whose attractiveness and age confirm that she is an acceptable object of heterosexual desire within established cultural norms. Otherwise, the woman's desirability might be compromised by being either too young or too old (the child or the hag).

Because of its high tessitura, the operatically trained soprano voice is often considered the most distinctively female, indeed, the most womanly, of all voices. The voice of the modern soprano carries connotations related to gender difference and to sexuality because of the quality of sound produced but also because of the repertoire traditionally sung. Peter Brooks argues that "the operatic aria, like the melodramatic monologue, speaks the name of desire directly [and] may be the most unrepressed speech of desire that art allows."[35] Depending on the voice that functions in an oral mode affiliated with "the highest artifice," the classical or operatic soprano becomes the source of "the most professional highly trained imitation of passion imaginable."[36] Operatic arias are essentially melodramatic in their articulation of passion and the throes or thwarting of desire.[37]

This returns us to the question of the pleasures created for the listener by the adolescent soprano who sings classical music. Articulated through the sonic register, Durbin's voice is trained to produce sounds that are culturally coded to speak womanliness through melody and vocal embellishments, timbre, and tonal expression. The voice may contribute to masquerade, but it also is assumed to be natural in the sense of speaking the body of the singer as the instrument of vocal production. As a consequence, Deanna Durbin's voice speaks the body as womanly rather than childish. We should not forget that before she was signed by Universal, the Disney studio rejected thirteen-year-old Edna Mae Durbin as the voice of Snow White, claiming that she sounded too mature to represent their animated heroine.[38]

Durbin's singing forces the audience to bear witness to her as the child who astounds with her uncanny ability to produce the cultured sound of womanliness, its audible beauty—and its connotations of sexual desirability and mature passion. How could a schoolgirl produce sounds linked to technically, as well as expressively, difficult standards of nineteenth-century operatic or modern art song repertoire? Moreover, how could she effectively communicate the meaning of these adult texts in the sense of bringing complex emotions—which she, ostensibly, had never experienced—into performative expression?

There is a fetishistic significance in Durbin's voice and in her vocal performances. The voice in song evokes the body but also conceals and plays on a gap that, especially in this case, cannot be filled or accounted for because, as Mladen Dolar points out, it creates "an ineradicable ambiguity."[39] To account for Durbin's vocal gifts and implicitly address this voice/body schism, explanations for the star's voice made reference to the physical maturity of organs hidden within the female body. The operatic female voice in song has long been regarded as a mode of orality that speaks the feminine body as sexuality, with the throat and the larynx, the hidden physical organs of uncanny female vocal production, functioning as a metaphor or double for the female genitalia. This symbolization of the female vocal apparatus suggests some uncomfortable but not unprecedented sexual connotations that stereotypically have been applied to the female body and to the female voice as a reflection of feminine interiority.

Advancing a Lacanian reading of the voice, Britta Sjogren argues that an inevitable schism arises "between the voice and the corpus it inhabits" even as the voice embodies those losses that haunt the self.[40] The instrumental force of the female child who sings like a woman defies the expectation that such sublime sounds can only come from the mature female body that, as a result of age and experience, has known passion. Such a body—unlike Durbin's—is implicated in sexual as well as vocal maturity.

In keeping with long-standing fascination with the female body and its vocal apparatus, Universal publicity noted that doctors examined Durbin's throat and larynx and found them physically mature beyond her years. A caption accompanying a 1937 photo of Durbin notes, "Physicians find her throat to be fully developed despite her youth," and a fan magazine article claimed "her vocal chords had developed into a precocious maturity at 10."[41] According to such accounts, Durbin's talent is prodigious. It is a natural phenomenon originating in the body, but it is simultaneously unnatural, freakish. The freakish rarity of Durbin's singing relates to Rosemarie Garland Thomson's discussion of how "freaks" are framed in the cultural imaginary. They are those with extraordinary or "monstrous" bodies that are "sublime, merging the terrible with the wonderful, equalizing repulsion with attraction."[42] The mature voice of a female soprano, especially one classically trained, coming from a childish adolescent body suggests something uncommon and freakish because the throat and its hidden and unexpected powers are lodged mysteriously within the female body—just like women's sexuality.

FIGURE 33. A bossy, cute, cheerfully impulsive screen personality. Deanna Durbin and Eugene Pallette in *One Hundred Men and a Girl*. Author's collection.

Durbin is offered as a juvenated female with an extraordinary body, one that is sublimely monstrous or rare. In 1937 Frederick Lewis placed Durbin within a lineage of famous and famously young opera divas including Patti and Bori. These singers were not in the category of a "prodigy" who brings disciplined talents and a precocious artistic sensibility to classical music but, instead, were rare child divas whose extraordinary bodies were responsible for a vocal maturity that exists in contradiction to the apparent immaturity of the body it inhabits. Lewis reports: "Doctors who have peered down the little Durbin throat find that she too has that vocal rarity, a woman's voice in a child's body."[43]

Durbin's radio appearances and her film stardom were both constructed to defend against a mirroring (voice = vagina) conclusion but did so in slightly different ways. In her radio performances Durbin destabilized the intersubjective realm of the star in relation to listener expectations, primarily by the lack of an embodied voice and the body/sound mismatch that characterized the attempts at embodiment made through textual references, as well as extratextual publicity. In film the impact of Durbin's voice destabilizes the expectations of listeners/view-

FIGURE 34. A seventeen-year-old star's more complicated life offscreen: Deanna Durbin at the racetrack with future husband Vaughn Paul, May 1939. Courtesy of the Associated Press.

ers differently than it did for radio audiences because there is a direct visual representation of her body. The body is seen, known, visible—and juvenated. She also displayed juvenated qualities not permitted operatic stars: a cheerfully impulsive, decidedly adolescent screen persona.

As a consequence, central to my exploration of gender, sexuality, and age in Durbin's stardom are issues of visibility and invisibility as they relate to the acoustic signifiers of womanliness and the figuration of the juvenated body. Durbin's characters certainly are cute, with the star's bright, round face and her curls tucked under various hats (beanies, feathered felt, tams, and the like—hats that grew more outrageous as she grew older). Her schoolgirl outfits often feature coats carelessly thrown over plain blouses paired with skirts, socks, and sensible shoes.

In radio Durbin's age and physical immaturity might be elided or forgotten; in motion pictures they are reinforced visually at every moment. As a result, audience pleasures required negotiation of often contradictory and occasionally convergent signs of womanliness and juvenation put in play in the acoustic and visual realms in Durbin's films of the late 1930s. In the 1940s Durbin matured physically, but she often played characters younger than she was. Her frequently imitated signature boleros disguised a blossoming bosom as she grew up (and out).[44] In marked contrast, offscreen she was captured in candid photographs looking remarkably grown-up in fur wraps, smart hats and dresses, and high heels, as well as in the company she kept. From 1938 she was often shown on the arm of her boyfriend, Vaughn Paul, who became her first husband in 1941 (before Durbin turned twenty). Because a romantic relationship conflicted with her screen image, one fan magazine article reported that "her studio was admittedly scared to death when rumors of an impending marriage to Vaughn Paul were heard."[45] When Paul became ex-husband in December of 1943, another fan magazine declared that Durbin's marital unhappiness proved that "grown-up problems can belong to someone who still looks like a little girl."[46]

## MUSIC'S HIGH-CULTURE CROSSOVER

The American public (at least a sizable segment of it) first got to know Deanna Durbin—and her voice—through radio broadcasts. The *New York Times* noted in 1937 that Durbin had "started out at 13 as a radio singer."[47] Durbin appeared on local Los Angeles radio in 1935. MGM arranged for her—as one of its short-term contract players—to appear as a singing guest on three local KLBK broadcasts of the famous Los Angeles Breakfast Club Wednesday meetings. Durbin also appeared on the Los Angeles radio program "Young Stars over KFAC Tonight"—with Mickey Rooney as master of ceremonies—and on "Ben Alexander's Talent Parade" in May 1936.

Hollywood film stars, or even contract players like Durbin, were not always welcome on radio programs. Radio rejected the first overture of American film studios. Later, however, it embraced Hollywood as a means, says Michelle Hilmes, to bring "large audiences to the medium [that] was quickly recognized by sponsors and agencies—to the networks' frequent chagrin."[48] In 1921, advertising agencies including J. Walter Thompson moved into the forefront of radio. By the end of the decade these agencies were helping create variety shows such as *The Fleischmann's Yeast Hour* (1929) and *The Kraft Music Hall* (1933), which thrived in the 1930s along with numerous others that featured well-known stage and screen stars as hosts and in guest appearances.

This "Hollywood era of radio" reflected the influence of advertising agencies but also the desire of the American film industry to promote its talent and productions. Prime-time nationwide network radio offered highly advantageous publicity to film stars.[49] With the standardization of synchronized sound on film, Hollywood had an even greater incentive to use radio to promote Hollywood actors as vocally recognizable talent, especially musical talent.[50] Simultaneous with the advent of the talkies, the rise of radio variety shows reflected a major shift in programming away from the straight music programming that dominated the medium in the 1920s. In spite of this shift listeners retained a great interest in music on the radio. Variety show programming became one of the most popular venues for music, with musical numbers mixed with comedy narrative and banter between the host, regular cast members, and guests.

In her short time at MGM Deanna Durbin benefited from the studio's promotion of her talent on the radio. One of her earliest national network radio appearances occurred on the melodiously named *Shell Chateau Hour*, a variety show hosted by the non-too-melodious-voiced Wallace Beery. In the November 28, 1935, broadcast Durbin (then a few days away from her fourteenth birthday) performed "One Night of Love," by Victor Schertzinger and Gus Kahn. This was a song made familiar to audiences by the critically acclaimed and popular 1934 Columbia Pictures release of the same name starring Metropolitan Opera prima donna Grace Moore.[51]

By performing "One Night of Love," Durbin drew on listeners' familiarity with Moore's operatically centered film. "One Night of Love" is a song suggesting passionate adult femininity, expressed in Moore's film through the romantic plot, as well as in the music. In the film Moore appears as an aspiring opera singer who loses a radio show audition and impulsively moves to Italy. There, she settles in a tenement, works in a tavern, and falls madly in love with a handsome but dictatorial voice teacher who guides her to a stellar opera debut. While old enough to sing Moore's signature song from the film, Durbin was not old enough to play a similar screen role; in other words Moore's screen embodiment of a sexually inexperienced but willful adult woman who finds romance would be inappropriate for the thirteen-year-old who sings a song on the radio that expresses the passion that the adult character acts on in the film's story.

The half-grown girl (Durbin) and the adult opera star (Moore) sing in similar styles, and their performances might have been indistinguishable to the untrained ear. Without a visual aspect to Durbin's musical performance, questions arise about the radio broadcast. Can this *really* be a thirteen-year-old child singing? The female body evoked in the singing voice is rendered invisible by radio, so that the performance is purely acoustic rather than acoustic and visual as it would be in film or in live performance on the stage. There is no performing body to authenticate the performing voice to the radio audience through immediately visible transmission. This lack of a visible anchor to Durbin's precociously mature voice might have created what Michel Chion describes in another context: "The most familiar example [of] the 'mismatch' of an individual's voice and face [occurs] when we have had the experience of getting to know one of them well before discovering the other. We never failed to be surprised, even shocked, when we complete the picture. . . . Basically, this question of the unity of sound and image would have no importance if it didn't turn out . . . to be the very signifier of the question of human unity, cinematic unity, unity itself."[52]

If the listener knows that this is a child performing, attention would be drawn to Durbin as an unusual singer whose vocal talent defies the anticipated limitations of her age. In fact, some early Universal publicity said that Durbin's birth date was in 1922 rather than 1921, to make her appear even more musically precocious, a tactic that recalls Fox's shaving a year off of Shirley Temple's age. In addition, the musical link between Moore and Durbin suggests some of the sexual, age-related tensions that emerged in Durbin's stardom—across radio and film—but particularly pronounced in radio.

As Hilmes notes, "Radio's ability to escape visual overdetermination had the potential to set off a virtual riot of social signifiers."[53] Without the viewer's gaze to contain or define the female who is invisible to radio listeners, other strategies of containment were required to rein in meanings attached to the child with the voice of a woman. Otherwise, a host of dangerous significations might ensue. Those strategies are demonstrated in Durbin's nationwide network radio debut when Beery introduces "little Edna Mae," who is "under contract to Metro Goldwyn Mayer." Beery takes great pains to reassure radio listeners that the talented singer they are about to hear is really as young as he claims: "I know you won't believe it, but she's absolutely only thirteen years old." He talks to her as an adult talks to a child, asking her about her family, where she came from, and when she started singing. In her replies Durbin's speaking voice is light and childish as she responds in polite, short, measured, and obviously rehearsed answers. She offers a childishly blunt explanation of why her family moved from Canada: "My daddy got tired of being cold every day." Beery laughs and ends the banter. Durbin starts to sing in a marvelously mature soprano, with precise diction, exquisite breath control, and rounded, easily attained high notes. Even now, many comments posted on YouTube react with skepticism to a posting of this recorded radio episode, expressing doubt about the date of the recording of "One Night of Love" and the claim that Durbin was thirteen at the time of the recording/episode.[54]

## COMEDY, CONTROL, AND INVISIBLE DEANNA

A few weeks before Durbin's feature-film debut, her radio stardom took off in earnest with her September 20, 1936, appearance on the highly rated radio show *Texaco Town with Eddie Cantor.* Cantor, one of the highest paid radio personalities, in addition to being a Broadway and film star, hosted this variety program on NBC's Red Network. There was a buildup to Durbin's debut on *Texaco Town* with numerous publicity pictures of her on the train journey from Chicago to New York for her appearance on the program. This publicity visualized Durbin and helped to anchor her radio personality within traditional norms of girlhood. She was an adolescent in training as an adult. She was a girl who was excited to be singing beautiful music instead of devoting her time to the vapid preoccupations of teenage bobby-soxers: boys, clothes, swing music, and talking on the telephone.

These early publicity representations of Durbin did something else—at least for those who saw them. They mediated the invisibility of Durbin as one of radio's performing bodies and broadcast technology's existence as a dangerous realm in which the voice was independent of the body. Because of radio's invisibility, the authenticity of the assertion that Durbin was young—a vocal prodigy—had to be continually reinforced in order to contain the listeners' riotous production of meaning, including potential erotic responses to her vocalizations. As Paul Young suggests, radio "challenged the listener to recreate an imaginary mental picture from the aural stimulations transmitted," making the invisibility of its "acousmetric voice" especially dangerous with regard to women and African Americans; these groups might invisibly cross "the lines of sexual and/or interracial taboo" in a process in which "audio transmission made subversive voices even more threatening because they could manipulate vocal inflections and discursive framing to create even more convincing masquerades." Because the radio listener is not supplied with an image to anchor his or her response to the singer, the invisibility of Durbin as a vocalizing subject fits into radio's larger problem in that, as

FIGURE 35. Publicity shot of Durbin being helped by porters as she travels by train to perform on Eddie Cantor's radio program, ca. 1936. Author's collection.

Young says, the medium "is only symptomatic of a deeper struggle over who gets to decide what those sounds *signify,* the listener or the speaking subject."[55]

Taken in this context, the control of signification from Durbin's radio performances depended on multiple strategies to anchor their meaning and pleasure. For reasons of propriety, both familial and generational, asexuality or the presumed sexlessness of childhood was called upon in extratextual publicity and in radio's textual construction of her star persona to confirm the authenticity of a safely feminine identity; that is, "this *really* is a child singing." Textual strategies needed to be used to contain a listener's imagination and delimit subversive significations that might emanate from the seductive sonic maturity of Durbin's invisible "acousmetric voice." Her introductions, as well as the nature of the skits that involved her on *Texaco Town,* anchored her identity as a child or innocent teenage girl instead of allowing listeners' the freedom to interpret her singing as a reflection of a precociously mature vocal apparatus linked to a mature female sexuality. Nevertheless, we will see, as is frequently the case with such acts of textual censorship (whether conscious or unconscious), some eruption of the repressed occurred—even on a family-friendly variety show that aired on Sunday nights.

Eddie Cantor, as the "Mayor of Texaco Town," introduced Durbin in her first appearance on his program as "delightful, delicious, and delovely." She was featured singing "Il Bacio," which she had also sung in her first film appearance, MGM's "Tabloid Musical" short *Every Sunday* (dir. Felix Feist, 1936). Durbin's singing of a song whose title literally is translated as "the kiss" puts into circulation significations of womanliness. Then, too, what could be more flirtatious and feminine than the song's coloratura flourishes that demonstrate the overdetermined womanliness of the song and the voice that sings it?

The public's response to Durbin's initial vocal appearance on *Texaco Town* resulted in a barrage of fan letters—reportedly some four thousand.[56] Durbin's appearance on the program was no accident. Universal called on radio to help make a film star of Durbin. The studio pressed Cantor hard to feature Durbin as a guest star; he initially resisted, supposedly worried about how listeners would respond to her.[57] As if to inoculate his listening audience against negative reaction to what might be off-putting about a classically trained girl soprano, Cantor declares in his introduction of her in one program that it is not the type of music that determines popularity but how and by whom it is sung. In spite of Cantor's reservations Durbin's vocal style and her classical selections were not out of step with radio offerings in the 1930s.

In this period classical music no longer held pride of place as it had on radio in the 1920s, but network radio broadcasts and technologically improved recordings permitted this type of music a reach it had never enjoyed in the United States. By 1938, 80 percent of American homes possessed at least one radio, for a total of twenty-five million units.[58] Classical music appeared on the airwaves in numerous forms and venues, including CBS's Sunday afternoon concerts of the New York Philharmonic Symphony Orchestra. Starting in 1934, Texaco sponsored weekly broadcasts of the Metropolitan Opera. In 1936 David Sarnoff decided NBC radio needed its own symphony, and under the baton of Arturo Toscanini NBC's orchestra became one of the most famous cultural institutions in the United States.[59] American singers like tenor Jan Peerce and baritone Robert Merrill built their careers in radio broadcasts of operas anchored by the NBC Symphony Orchestra. Other classically trained vocalists took to the airwaves in the 1930s: Nelson Eddy had his own program, as did Grace Moore.[60] They, and other opera stars like Kirsten Flagstad, Gina Cigna, Marion Talley, and Nino

Martini, appeared on classical broadcasts like *The General Motors Concert Company* and were guests on variety shows like *The Chase and Sanborn Hour* and *The Jack Benny Show*.

Durbin was dubbed the "First Lady of Texaco Town" and appeared almost every week on *Texaco Town* for more than two years, from the fall of 1936 into late 1938; at the same time she churned out top-grossing films for Universal Pictures. On the program's weekly episodes, Durbin's repertoire included opera, concert, and orchestral pieces (the latter with added lyrics). The numbers she sang included "Giannina Mia," "The Blue Danube Waltz," "Carmen Vocal Waltz," "Un Bel Di" (in English), "Ave Maria (Bach-Gounod)," "The Merry Widow Waltz," "Vieni, Vieni," "Italian Street Song," and Verdi's "Brindisi" (adapted from *La traviata*). She also sang popular songs and show tunes such as "Summertime," "Smoke Gets in Your Eyes," "Alice Blue Gown," and "September," as well as traditional favorites such as "Your Mother Comes from Ireland, Mother Macree."

Durbin's youth was reinforced by publicity pairing her with Cantor as a father figure. Cantor declared her to be his "sixth daughter" (he had five of his own). They were shown in publicity photographs enjoying a soda at a dining counter in New York City and walking arm in arm on the street. They traveled to various sites all over the country, including to the Greater Texas and Pan American Exposition in Dallas, for nationwide radio hookup of remote broadcasts of the hugely popular program.[61] As the "mayor" of Texaco Town, Cantor praised "First Lady" Durbin as if he were a proud father (not a husband); in one episode of the program he reminded viewers of her visibility and her voice in sweet, sentimental terms. His praise implicitly refers to the missing element of radio, as well as to the symbiotic relationship of radio and film: "To hear her is to adore her. To both see and hear her is to take her to your heart for all time."[62]

In a classic demonstration of radio's pastiche of high culture and kitsch, Durbin shared space on the radio show with real and fictional Texaco town inhabitants, including "The Mad Russian" (Bert Gordon) and Oscar the trained flea (who had a tendency to disappear). She was often paired in song with another young vocal talent, Bobby Breen, Cantor's eight-year-old musical protégé, who sang in a smooth, tightly wound boyish soprano. In October of 1936 the *New York Times* depicted Durbin and Breen (who was at least a foot shorter than Durbin) singing at a shared radio microphone.[63] Radio's claims to their culturally uplifting, unusually precocious talent were authenticated in

FIGURE 36. Deanna Durbin as a star of radio. December 1936 cover of *Radio Guide*.

other photographs. They were shown together in *Motion Picture* magazine and described as "two potential opera stars."[64] In subsequent years the press reported from time to time that the Metropolitan Opera was interested in hiring Durbin away from Hollywood; her vocal coach, Andreas Perello de Segurola, was supposedly training her on the behest of the opera company. In 1937 the *New York Times* noted that Durbin "wants to be an opera singer, and voice experts say her voice will be fully developed in another year or two."[65] These items (likely planted by Universal) reconfirmed the star's high-art credentials—as well as her youth.

Because he was prepubescent, Breen's soprano voice could be mistaken for a woman's, but it could never be mistaken for a man's. Durbin's voice was much more mature, as were her radio persona and her speaking voice. When she and Breen converse on the radio, it is clear that he is a young child, but the precision of Durbin's diction, the richness of her voice, and the expressive maturity of her delivery might lead one to think she is an adult, except for the fact that announcing her immaturity and the precociousness of her vocal talent is, of course, part of the attraction—and imperative—of the show.

Radio scholar Matthew Murray notes that "sexual expression and sexuality were central to the processes of Golden Age radio comedy. . . . Sexual humor produced moments of excess and controversy, but it was also a regular and accepted ingredient of broadcast comedy."[66] *Texaco Town* reinforced Durbin's youthfulness to desexualize her, but, in keeping with Murray's remarks, they also drew attention to the sexual signification of the lyrics of her songs in order to call attention to and then defuse the erotic significations that might accrue around the "invisible" little girl who sings (and speaks) like a woman.

In the January 3, 1937, episode, after Durbin sings "Kiss Me Again," Cantor plays the title for comedy to ask her the name of her song as an excuse to kiss her again (on the cheek?). What might be read as a sexually provocative act (eliciting shock from the announcer, Jimmy Wallington) is defused by a distinctly Cantoresque move: he also plants a kiss on Wallington, an adult male. The emphasis on sexual innuendo is also evident in the December 29, 1937, episode; Bobby Breen announces in his Alvin the Chipmunk–like speaking voice that he wants Cantor to give him an allowance. Why? He wants it "for a license." "I want to marry Deanna Durbin," he declares, provoking the laughter of the audience. Then, again affirming his childishness, he asks Cantor to intercede on his behalf: "Will you ask her for me?" Eddie calls Durbin in, and she says to Cantor: "Tell him I'm too young. . . . Tell him I don't think he loves me enough anyway." It is important to note that her speaking voice, in contrast to Breen's, might be taken for that of an adult. Bobby declares: "I'll sing to her." Breen sings a love song to Durbin, concluding: "Well, Deanna, I told you my story. Now what do you say?" This leads her into the strains of "We Could Make Believe I Love You" from *Showboat*. Durbin sings in a lovely, mature soprano. "Well, Bobby, that's my answer," she says, and the girl and boy sopranos conclude with a duet, singing lyrics, " . . . couldn't you, couldn't I, couldn't we make believe our lips are blending in a phantom kiss," ending on a shared high note and thunderous audience applause.

A publicity photograph shows Cantor in his Texaco fire chief's hat standing between Breen and Durbin. He is raising his hand as if officiating at a marriage. A mock marriage between children is inappropriate and outrageous in that it suggests the social sanctioning of desire in those that culture says shouldn't have any sexual feelings. As Murray says, radio humor often worked "by reorienting aspects of everyday life in order to achieve a momentary mental confusion that upset audiences' commonsense assumptions and expectations regarding the conventions of language, standard behavior, and the organization of social relations."[67] Bobby is too young to know what desire is. He's a kid, and a small one at that. His register of desire for Durbin and a sanctification of that desire are inappropriate for a prepubescent boy who sings like a choir boy (or a castrato) with a soprano voice indicating male sexual immaturity. It is impossible to know if audiences took this as another element of radio's amusing defiance of common sense or as a dirty joke—or both.

In April 1937 *Radio Guide* noted Durbin's huge network popularity via her regular appearances on the airwaves; she was named "one of the best network stars of 1937," as well as "the most promising star." In these voter polls she ranked highly among classical singers and among popular singers.[68] But Durbin's appearances on *Texaco Town* would end in 1938 because of the heavy demands of her filmmaking schedule at Universal. She would then take up a pace of appearances on the radio more typical of other film stars, appearing on the *LUX Radio Theatre* program to promote specific film releases and making guest appearances into the 1940s on the *Gulf Screen Guild Theatre,* the *Edgar Bergen and Charlie McCarthy Show, Command Performance,* and *The Jack Benny Grape Nuts Flakes Show.*

## THE VOICE EMBODIED: DEANNA'S DISCIPLINARY EFFECTS

Wayne Koestenbaum defines operatic singing as dependent upon the classically trained voice that "is dexterous," which "strives to be strict in pitch and to obey the letter of the law; it projects, it forbids flaw." It is, he says, "the voice of Deanna Durbin, of Tito Gobbi, of Conchita Supervia" that "sings its training" and, to many, is an "I-affirming blast of a body that refuses dilution or compromise."[69] We may hesitate to call this combination of disciplinary effects and assertion of a musically centered identity either feminist or subversive of gendered norms, but surely it is useful to contemplate the unexpected or challenging effects that might accrue around Hollywood's visual and vocal assertion of this kind of distinct musical sound through the screen presence of Deanna Durbin.

Mass culture and new technologies like radio brought the problem of listening, production of meaning, and combining the popular and the serious to the foreground, but so did motion pictures.[70] Radio had made Durbin famous nationally, but as a "disembodied" medium, the sonic realm of radio highlights some of the complications and representational difficulties that accrued around sound, feminine embodiment, and age that would also play out—and require careful negotiation—in different but related ways, in Durbin's films. The motion pictures would make her an international star. They also had to give her a body.

Durbin's singing is an organizing principle of her films. The central importance of singing and Durbin's voice to her first feature film with Universal, *Three Smart Girls*, is inscribed from the opening moments of the film. The credits end with Hollywood's version of a birth announcement "and Universal's new discovery, Deanna Durbin as 'Penny,'" with a dissolve to a close-up of Durbin's bright countenance, with her mouth open as she sings a string of *la*s that introduce her coloratura embellished "On the Wings of a Song" delivered from the deck of a sailboat![71]

Although audiences would have been aware that the singer's voice and body may actually be separated through the process of dubbing (the sound is not really emanating from the adolescent girl as she is photographed), film still plays on the assumption that voice and body are not truly separable—but held in a paradoxical relationship. There is some irony in the fact that radio had primed film audiences to assume that Durbin's voice in film was hers and not dubbed by another person (as it was for a number of female stars, including Rita Hayworth, Ava Gardner, and Audrey Hepburn). This belief in the visualized body as the source of the musical sounds is especially important for Durbin, since her voice and operatic vocal style—even when applied to popular contemporary songs or folk numbers—communicates a more powerful, more mature, perhaps even more "culturally refined" body than that of the typical adolescent female and so would otherwise invite disbelief that this soprano voice is really produced by the young girl onscreen.

Established on the model of *Three Smart Girls*, Durbin's subsequent star vehicles often featured her in highly formulaic comedies centered squarely on the appeal of their star; her films were built around her singular vocal talent and her ability to project a charming, vivacious, and optimistic personality. Penny Craig is the first of many overconfident, overtalkative, and ultraenergetic meddlers who would become Durbin's

FIGURE 37. Thirteen-year-old Durbin with actor Lee Tracy at the "Parade of Talent" celebration at Universal Studios. Author's collection.

standard character type. Although Durbin's screen persona would be toned down slightly as she grew older (slowed down from her frenetic pace of movement and talking), its basics (assertiveness and action) would remain. Yet qualities signifying girlishness typically continued to disguise the equivalent of a human bulldozer who refused to take "no" for an answer or conform to nice-girl norms in most ways—except for her lack of sexual experience. Led by the power of her voice, Durbin is the dynamo, the young female not yet bound into all the rules of proper adult femininity, who blends charm with unruliness, exhibiting that energizing "verve" that critic Edwin Schallert thought she, alone, possessed in Hollywood.[72]

With an exception here and there, Durbin's films didn't contain choruses, luxurious costumes, or big production numbers; only one, *Can't Help Singing* (dir. Frank Ryan, 1944), was shot in color. Her star vehicles looked nothing like the lavish, Technicolor, multistar musicals that emerged from MGM's legendary Arthur Freed unit, but Durbin's pictures enjoyed high production values. Her films included expert cinematography, snappy scripts, and talented casts including the likes of Adolphe Menjou, Alice Brady, Robert Benchley, Kay Francis, Charles Laughton, Robert Cummings, Franchot Tone, Eugene Pallette, Ray Milland, Leatrice Joy, and Joseph Cotten. What they did not include was a roster of musical talent: the exceptions were when orchestra conductor Leopold Stokowski appeared as himself in *One Hundred Men and a Girl*, Jan Peerce's one scene appearance in *Something in the Wind* (dir. Irving Pichel, 1947), and the casting of Robert Paige as her only singing leading man in *Can't Help Singing*.[73]

Most of her films relied on Durbin as their sole musical talent, and why not? In the late 1930s Durbin possessed one of the nation's most famous operatically styled voices, in spite of the fact that she was not a star of staged opera or the concert hall. Durbin was, however, a radio and movie star. Her successful radio appearances demonstrated the symbiotic relationship between film and radio that came to full fruition in the late 1930s.[74] Durbin's performances must be understood in terms of the commodification of classical music in the United States in the 1930s that occurred through new and emergent technologies, such as the radio and ever improving phonographic recordings, as well as motion pictures.

The impact extended beyond profit: some cultural elites and "visionaries" supported classical music, as a means of improving people's lives during the Great Depression. Among the most important of these elite cheerleaders for musical uplift was Philadelphia Orchestra conductor Leopold Stokowski. Through his own pronouncements, radio broadcasts, and film appearances he supported the democratization of classical music. He was especially keen on radio's role in this cultural process: "No matter how far away our home is from cultural centers, we are in constant touch with them night and day by radio . . . it is a great privilege to be able to play music for the immense radio audience of millions of music lovers. . . . Radio is one of the greatest mechanical means toward evolution of Mind and Spirit."[75] In Stokowski's view broadcast performances of classical music contributed to the cultural uplift of American citizens—whatever their age, gender, race, or station in life. Such a view was not without controversy. Others regarded the same phenomenon as a regressive kitschification that turned "good music" into what Theodor Adorno dismissed as "musical goods."[76]

FIGURE 38. Patsy sings with Stokowski's orchestra in *One Hundred Men and a Girl*. Author's collection.

Durbin's second film, *One Hundred Men and a Girl,* not only benefited from the appearance of Stokowski as Durbin's elusive musical "object of desire" but also illustrates how Durbin's films differ from most musicals of the time that focused on romance.[77] Durbin's character is the daughter of a jobless trombone player (Adolphe Menjou). They are about to be thrown out on the street for nonpayment of rent, but after a number of setbacks and misunderstandings, a hard-nosed millionaire agrees to sponsor the radio performance of what Patricia, a.k.a. "Patsy," calls "my orchestra." The millionaire is not in it for altruism or cultural improvement but for the advertising value for his company—and the agreement hinges on Patsy getting a major conductor for her orchestra of unemployed musicians. The conductor she goes for is Stokowski. She sneaks into his rehearsal (producing the memorable shots of the feather on her tam bobbing between the rows of seats). She sings Mozart's "Alleluia" in an impromptu performance with his orchestra, and an impressed Stokowski talks to her about her voice. She wants to talk about *her* orchestra, but Stokowski's men laugh at Patsy when she describes how her orchestra rehearses in a garage. She yells at them for making fun of unemployed men and is basically thrown out. She goes home and cries, but she springs back with a plan.

That plan results in success, but it is not Patsy who actually persuades maestro Stokowski to conduct the Depression-impacted musicians but the music itself. In a last-ditch effort, after all her other machinations have failed, Patsy sends her orchestra to Stokowski's palatial home. At her command they start to play Liszt's "Second Hungarian Rhapsody" on his grand staircase. He goes out of his study and begs them to stop. He even turns to Patsy with anger, but the music ultimately overwhelms him. The film cuts between shots of him, Patsy, and the musicians (all men) watching him. Suddenly a medium two-shot of Patsy standing by Stokowski shows that his right hand is moving. He cannot help being drawn in to the rhythm of the music. Famed for conducting without a baton, Stokowski starts to conduct almost as if an unstoppable musical empathy or physical force is at work. The musicians, still in their hats and many in their coats, look at each other with happiness—and relief.

As farcical as it may seem, the sequence is exhilarating. Stokowski agrees to postpone his European tour to conduct the radio performance, which is the last scene of the film. At the end of the radio concert the maestro asks Patsy to say a few words, but she is tongue-tied. A taxicab driver who has befriended her yells down from the balcony: "How about singing, Patsy!" He beams with pride. She sings the famous Brindisi (drinking song) "Libiamo ne' lieti calici," from Verdi's *La traviata.* The power of cross-class values, cultural uplift, and the convergence of radio and film are affirmed through the voice—and will—of a girl.

*First Love* acknowledges the existence of the musical and cultural divide in the United States and uses Durbin to speak to it across the generations. Instead of going to her friend's house for the summer, Connie goes to the home of the rich uncle who has financed her education. Connie asks the butler if he likes singing. The butler scoffs in his clipped British accent that the answer is "Yes, I do and no, I don't" because "some people regard boop, boop, ditem, ditem zisss [as] an inspiring cantata." In response, Durbin launches into an amazingly relaxed, sexy, highly spirited version of "Amapola." It is the kind of Spanish song that might appear as the rousing finish to a recital. In this case it functions to literally stop the butler in his tracks. She sings directly into his face and then walks away in a subtle dance step; then she suddenly swishes around to face him, a movement she repeats in a teasing, enticing display of femininity. By the end she has charmed not only him but also the other servants, who become her working-class allies and the emotional

FIGURE 39. Forging working-class allies with song in *First Love*. Deanna Durbin and Charles Coleman. Publicity still. Author's collection.

support that will make this a modern Cinderella story—that is, a typical Durbin film narrative.

Just as Durbin's performances on the radio troubled the relationship of the female body to traditional operatic, soprano vocalization, her appearance in films in the late 1930s and early 1940s also created sexual trouble. In keeping with Durbin's singing on the radio, her songs in film, like "Amapola," often signify womanliness in their connotations of sensuality, sexuality, and the adult ability to produce a perfected, highly codified, and aesthetically disciplined expression of desire. This is demonstrated in a typically Durbinesque film sequence in *Three Smart Girls*. The scene is typical of how songs were inserted into her films and how those produced during her adolescent years constructed the vocal and visual appeal of the young Durbin. Penny Craig (Durbin) has run away from home to stop her father from marrying the gold-digger who wants him to send his three daughters away. Fighting all the way, Penny is hauled into a Brooklyn police station. She starts to sing "Il Bacio" as proof to the sergeant on duty that she is not the runaway "Craig girl" but an opera singer from Paris who is engaged to sing with the Metropolitan Opera. The girl, obviously a minor, stands in front of a police sergeant's high, imposing desk. She starts to sing without accompaniment. Harp chords in arpeggio steal in subtly on the soundtrack to provide a sonic bridge into a full orchestral accompaniment of the Luigi Ardita concert aria. Burly policemen start to gather around her. Beaming with joy, Durbin charms the authorities with her singing, as well as proves her high-art credentials. She ends with a coloratura flourish—and looks to one side of the room (of policemen) and then to the other. The policemen all applaud. A seasoned performer temporarily replaces the rebellious child, and her singing has created an atmosphere of sheer happiness and unity. She has proven her musical expertise, but it has not been enough to override the visual proof that she is a teenager. The police start to follow orders to return her home. She physically struggles, and the scene fades out as the sympathetic sergeant calms her down and starts to listen to why she came from Europe (to save her family).

In Durbin's films, almost everyone loves her singing, including men who are part of the workaday world: cops, cab drivers, domestic servants, even prison guards. This relates to how, in the 1930s, a radical change in classical music's traditional audience occurred in the United States. Susan Douglas details how radio made the enjoyment of "serious music" the province of new listeners who—whether because of education, income, location, or stereotypes of gendered behavior—would otherwise have had limited access to recitals and symphonies performed live by seasoned professionals. Although radio music programs were particularly popular with women, classical music no longer was associated exclusively with the feminine, on the one hand, and elevated economic status and urbanity, on the other. Listening to classical music was made "more available and more permissible" as a leisure-time pursuit, especially for working-class men.[78]

*Something in the Wind* plays on this trope in a clever way by offering the character of Tony, a prison guard who just happens to be played by the Metropolitan Opera's Jan Peerce. Warned that the female inmate is "frisky and tough," rather than "real pleasant and ladylike," Tony starts his singing practice in preparation for his performance at the policeman's ball. He is a working-class man who produces classical music. Instead of the jail matron with whom he usually practices, Durbin, the lone prisoner, joins him in singing the duet "Il miserere, 3rd act" from Verdi's s *Il trovatore* after she proves she knows it by recounting the scene's plot. Peerce starts the famous rhythmically implacable orchestral introduction and tells Durbin to follow his conducting. Slipping in from the soundtrack, an orchestra takes over the rhythm to provide the operatic orchestration. As they sing passionately, Durbin tries another slip: moving the jail keys from Tony's belt. At the end he kisses her hand, and she slips the keys away without his noticing. They agree that each other's singing is "magnificent" but then bickering starts over musical mistakes, and he says to her: "You belong in jail." When he goes to get the score to prove her wrong, she slips out of the holding cell to freedom.

Half the fun in this scene, like others in Durbin's films, arises from the unlikely circumstances in which the musical interlude occurs outside of a concert hall. It also depends on Durbin's acting ability that somehow makes her impromptu performance (usually solo) of difficult music seem the most enjoyable (if not natural) thing in a world in which serious music is democratized, not only by its audience but by Durbin's approach to singing. Because the musical numbers in Durbin's films arise primarily out of everyday situations, Durbin usually sings in street clothes, often to people of the working class. This is part of her films' democratization of serious music in terms that echo Leopold Stokowski's pronouncements about the value of music technologies in delivering classical music to Americans. When she does sing to the upper class (as in *First Love* and *One Hundred Men and a Girl*), the elitist implications of classical music as a part of high culture are deflated by comedy (ridiculing the upper class) rather than reinforced. Durbin represents the strenuousness of the musical body in this scene and many others in her films. She also represents the democratization of music through her working-class attitude toward its production.

## "HE WANTS HER FOR HIS FATHER"

Paying attention to Durbin's voice allows us to see her stardom as more complicated and interesting than those accounts, both contemporaneous with her stardom and subsequent to it, that tend to flatten her screen presence to a register merely of her characters' actions and attitudes.[79] In reference to bobby-soxer comedies and Hollywood's depiction of teenage girls' sexuality, Ilana Nash argues that "sexual innocence is merely the most literal method of rendering a heroine blank or hollow."[80] Although typically appearing to be sexually inexperienced, Durbin's screen characters are hardly "blank or hollow," and it is singing that asserts the power of her voice over the affairs of men while suggesting her emotional depth and complexity.

Durbin's high register/tessitura is an enveloping, inviting sound that

FIGURE 40. Deanna Durbin sings in *It's a Date* (dir. William A. Seiter, 1940). Author's collection.

also is sometimes piercing and penetrating (especially in singing opera). In this respect, and following Barthes on the voice's "coenesthetic" property, the sound of the star's soprano voice may challenge assumptions about our own nature in relation to its insinuating ability to cross age and gender boundaries, its power, and the production of pleasure. The female voice speaks more than castration or lack in the operatic mode of performance, even if one might argue (as some have) that texts/plots often mete out melodramatic punishment to the diva.[81] This is because the female soprano/character is on "par" with men in vocal terms. Her voice, fixed in the highest register/tessitura, produces an enveloping sound but also a potentially piercing, penetrating one.

Nevertheless, as Durbin entered her late teens, an overt problem in constructing the star's onscreen sexuality emerged. In 1939, the year of her official screen leap into romantic maturity (and her first kiss) in *First*

FIGURE 41. Holding the line against glamour: Deanna Durbin as the naive peasant girl, Ilonka, with Anne Gwynne in *Spring Parade* (dir. Henry Koster, 1940). Author's collection.

*Love,* critic Frank Nugent bemoaned Universal's new strategy for its seventeen-year-old star: "To suggest that this 'teenish miss is glamorous, with a leer ringing [in] the word, is not simply stupid but obscene."[82] Two years later, in 1941, the *Los Angeles Times* suggested that Nugent was not alone in wanting Durbin's juvenated self preserved. In "Deanna Durbin's Maturing Worries New York Critics," Richard Griffith claims that Universal was having difficulty figuring out how to handle romance in Durbin's films because of the desire of her audiences to make sure that the charming and winsome star "was still our little girl."[83]

Romance became a predictable feature of Durbin's films after 1939. Her schoolgirl attire gradually gave way to dresses that favored coverage of a modest and refined type for her hourglass figure. Yet, as critics pointed out, she "played young" in several films including the charming Viennese bonbon *Spring Parade* (dir. Koster, 1940) and the backstairs comedy *His Butler's Sister* (dir. Frank Borzage, 1943). Increasingly, in the 1940s, Durbin was sexed up with black satin and feathers. She wore fur-trimmed outfits, and her hair was dyed blonde in *Lady on a Train* (dir. Charles David, 1945). She wore more glamorous, grown-up clothes in *Because of Him* (dir. Richard Wallace, 1946), as a young woman who pretends she is the leading lady and mistress of a famous Broadway producer. However, the effect of this treatment is sometimes more comic than evocative of pinup-girl glamour, not only because of the star's solid, average figure but because of a continuing emphasis on the comic results of her actions and her established screen persona as the girl next door, whose only sexual mystery was her voice.

Rarely have musicals suggested so clearly that the man is the passive recipient of a feminine artistic endeavor. Durbin's characters continued to be impulsive, meddling tricksters, but she dominates men as well as women with her embodied voice, at once seductive and strenuous. True love is affirmed in these films only when the leading man/father figure/male audience is held in musical and sexual awe, virtually paralyzed by fascination with Durbin's radiant voice and her transformation into something she is only when she is singing—a glamorous diva. In *His Butler's Sister* Durbin sings Puccini's "Nessun dorma," from *Turandot,* to a large standing audience. Franchot Tone, identified as her romantic interest, stands in the back. He starts to move forward through the audience to Durbin as she reaches the climax of the aria. At the end, applause begins, and Durbin runs through the crowd to him (and toward the camera, which moves back in a tracking shot). At the end of the shot Tone steps into the frame to finish the film with an over-the-shoulder framing that shows Durbin's beaming face as she embraces him (there is no reverse shot). In *Because of Him* Durbin is alone in a room with theatrical producer John Sheridan (Charles Laughton). She has been pursuing him for a stage role, but he decides she is too inexperienced and steps out to get her a cab to send her away. She starts to hum and then sings "Danny Boy." Sheridan listens intently on the other side of a doorframe, with his back turned to Durbin. At the end of her song he strides in with a script: her singing has convinced him she has enough emotional depth and maturity to take on the nonsinging role of the heroine in his play. Her singing creates a scene of sonic seduction that allows the male to internalize and literally feel the female in song as her voice overcomes space and the separation of bodies, as well as emotional distanciation.[84]

Offering a variation on the straightforward courtship model that dominates most musicals of the time, Durbin's 1940s films continued to emphasize her emotional relationship with much older men, even after the star's age made her eligible for heterosexual romance.[85] Her music inspires deep feelings in men, but it has a particularly strong impact on older men, like John Sheridan, Charles Laughton's character in *Because of Him*. The pronounced Oedipal nature of many of Durbin's relationships to older men in her films increases our sense of the star's status as a girl who must be guided into adult sexuality.

Durbin's vocal impact on older men was established with her first film, *Three Smart Girls*. This impact is represented with particularly strange effect in the film, as if the appropriate boundaries for representing Durbin's vocal power in relation to a privileged adult male figure have not yet been worked out. In one scene "Penny" (Durbin) sings for her estranged father (Charles Winninger). She has interrupted him as he listened to his gold-digger girlfriend, "Precious" (Binnie Barnes), sing "Someone to Care for Me." Penny's father rushes out to investigate the loud noises emanating from his youngest daughter's bedroom. He discovers that Penny has been moving her bed, to avoid her snoring sister, she claims. This leads to a conversation. Her sisters join them and remark on Penny's vocal training. The father sits on the edge of his daughter's bed as she explains why his fiancée is such a bad singer. Penny mimics the poor vocal technique of Precious, and then she vocalizes how "Someone to Care for Me" should be properly sung. Her father gazes in rapt attention at her singing of this love song (which has slightly changed/censored lyrics). In much of the scene the father and child are shown in a two-shot with an over-the-shoulder angle emphasizing Durbin's face. Close-ups of Durbin then dominate, with reaction shots of Penny's father and two sisters. A repeated two-shot of Durbin and her father shows her leaning into him, as he holds her hands. As she finishes the song, he appears to move in to kiss her on the lips. She ends with a coloratura flourish and, in a flash, bids him goodnight and pops beneath the bed covers before he can kiss her. Penny/Durbin abruptly falls back on the bed to become a sexless child again.

Modern audiences react with disgust at the father's leaning forward to kiss his daughter. They read Penny's song and the paternal response as signaling the threat of incest and pedophilia. The staging of the scene suggests that the singing of the child diva might touch the sexual imagination of her father, as well as that of the viewer-listener. Durbin is singing the same romantic song as the woman who seeks to marry her father, but her version is more artistic, more beautiful, and more "feminine" than her rival's. Penny's singing blurs the differences between the appeal of Precious's femininity and hers. The former is associated with seductive (and deceptive) sophistication. The latter is supposed to be associated with asexuality, moral purity, and cultural refinement, but in *Three Smart Girls* Durbin's voice is a sensual lure that provides the greatest pleasure to her father as it does to Durbin's audiences. Aligning her with womanliness, her voice makes Penny erotically dangerous at the same time that she represents juvenated sexual innocence.

It is possible that audiences of the 1930s considered the estranged father's reaction as merely giving emphasis to the contrast between Durbin's astounding vocal precociousness and Precious's obvious vocal limitations. The scene is also in keeping with many of Durbin's *Texaco Town* radio appearances in that it ultimately disrupts and deflates the uncomfortable sexual implications it has created: laughter at Penny popping back into her bed registers a recognition and dismissal of the danger of the child's sonic womanliness, that is, how the voice's overwhelming beauty and seductive power could violate the separation between father and daughter, male and female, adult and child, to sweep away the barriers that define the social and sexual taboo, in this case, incest.

A similar paradoxical construction of sonic womanliness and juvenation occurs in *One Hundred Men and a Girl,* where Patsy Caldwell (Durbin) is "courting" Leopold Stokowski. While her voice is a lure to the older man, as it is in *Three Smart Girls,* comedy again defuses the potentially uncomfortable (and taboo) triumph of an Oedipal romance between a prepubescent young girl and a middle-age man. Here, the comedy is achieved primarily through the young girl's indefatigable energy and take-no-prisoners attitude toward achieving her purpose. Resolution arrives through sublimation: the mutual admiration of two extraordinary musicians, Stokowski and Durbin. Artistic sympathy replaces sexual intercourse.

Suggesting an interweaving of courtship and intergeneration models, *It Started with Eve* revolves around a hatcheck girl, Ann Terry (Durbin), who is grabbed by a rich young man, Johnny Reynolds (Robert Cummings), to substitute for his temporarily missing society fiancée. Johnny has returned to New York City from Mexico to attend to his dying father, millionaire Jonathan (Charles Laughton), who wants to see his son's fiancée, Gloria, once before he dies. Thinking it is a matter of minutes and wanting to make his father happy, Johnny grabs Ann off the street in front of her workplace and offers her fifty dollars to pretend she is Gloria. Meeting her, the father is charmed and rallies.

FIGURE 42. Deanna Durbin and maestro Leopold Stokowski in a publicity shot for *One Hundred Men and a Girl.* Author's collection.

The next morning, much improved in health, Jonathan wants to see "Gloria." Ann/"Gloria" is a singer, and after two frustrating years of trying to "meet the Heifitzes and Stokowskis" but failing to get anyone to listen to her singing, she has decided to use the money he gave her to return home to Ohio. Johnny frantically pulls her off the train platform and promises her another fifty dollars. Ann's roommate, Jackie, comments to their accompanying friend, "Don't worry Jenny, it's platonic, he wants her for his father." Jackie is not far wrong, for *It Started with Eve* is more of a love story between Ann and Johnny's father than between the girl and Johnny. As with Stokowski's and Durbin's characters in *One Hundred Men and a Girl,* it is music that cements the relationship.

*It Started with Eve* is a comedy that gives Jonathan Reynolds scenes

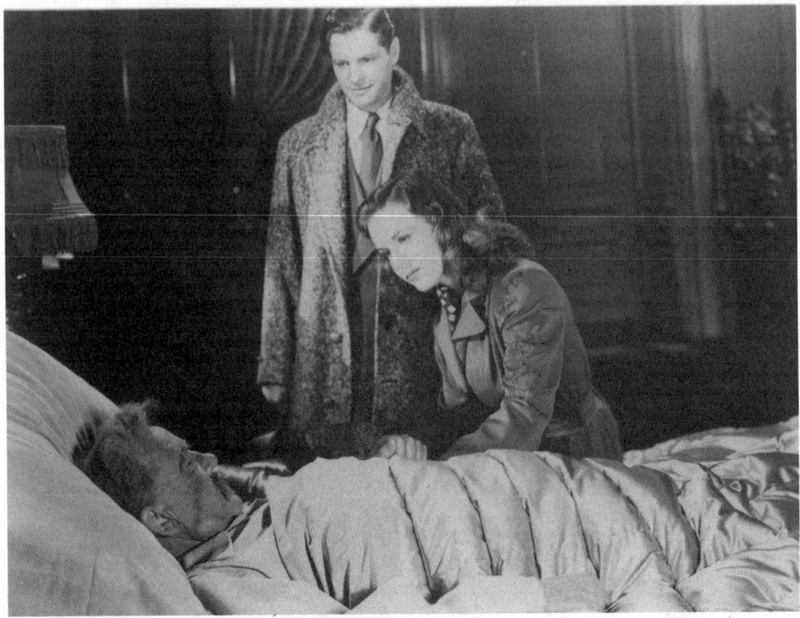

FIGURE 43. "Gloria"/Ann (Deanna Durbin) inspires Jonathan Reynolds (Charles Laughton) to live in *It Started with Eve* (dir. Henry Koster, 1941). Author's collection.

that one would normally expect to be played by a romantic leading man. It is he who wants Durbin in the family, yelling at his son to forgive her when she shows up after a supposed quarrel. It is he who goes to her apartment to retrieve her after the truth is revealed that she is not engaged to his son. The relationship between them is tender; they share a love of music, and they dance together (a comic conga). The development of Jonathan's tender relationship with Ann is much more interesting than her romance with the churlish and hysterical Johnny, which seems to exist only to secure Ann into the Reynolds household. The relationship of Ann to Johnny is pure screwball, marked by physical aggression (biting, pinching, chasing, forced kissing). This is typical of the subgenre, but the father, all tenderness and understanding—even love at first sight (confirmed by Ann's first voice)—renders the young people's aggressive courtship childish and slightly disturbing. However, in this film too, romance hinges on Johnny's delayed discovery of her voice. The possibility that this indecisive and immature son (who has had many fiancées) might fall in love with Ann is affirmed as she sings a robust "Cavalito." Jonathan's gaze guides the camera's as he assesses his son's feelings toward the woman that he prefers for him.

In later Durbin films, visual techniques associated with Hollywood's creation of the woman as an erotic visual spectacle bring Durbin's voice and visual appearance into adherence with more familiar Hollywood conventions to represent adult femininity. The most extreme instance of this in Durbin's films occurs in *Lady on a Train,* when Nicki Collins (Durbin) is literally flat on her back on a bed as she sings "Silent Night, Holy Night" to her father via the telephone. In this Oedipally charged moment her lips barely move as she sings, and her body moves not at all. The apparent work of the body in producing the voice is diminished. The camera takes up six different positions around her in succession, offering close-ups that are fetishistic, separating her body from her face as the primary erotic object of the camera.

Durbin was always most sensual and "glamorous" when she was singing, but this scene offers conventional Hollywood glamorization in a sequence that reinforces the strong Oedipal overtones apparent in Durbin's star vehicles from the beginning of her screen career. As in the scene from *Three Smart Girls* in which Durbin, in bed, sings to her father, the danger of sexuality is subject to comic deflation. The camera reveals that Danny (Allen Jenkins), a thug sent to rob Nicki of an important clue to solving a man's murder, has been listening. Reduced to tears, he has momentarily forgotten his nefarious task. Although she has not moved literally, the soprano in song has moved him figuratively.

## THE POWER OF EMBODIED SOUND

Durbin's vocality—the embodied sound produced by the star—offered audiences complex pleasures in two distinct but related forms of mass media: radio and film. The paradoxical cultural and gendered status of Durbin as a radio singer shows how her voice, possessed of cultural and musical force, was made uncanny by its embodiment in an adolescent female who was disembodied by radio, the preeminent invisible broadcasting medium of the 1930s. Radio attempted to reembody her through comic strategies that worked to contain the unruly (and erotic) significations of a voice that was of great interest to mass media audiences of the late 1930s and early 1940s.

The stardom of Durbin allows us to think about the female voice—complicated by womanliness, by musicality, and by the voice as an instrument—within a certain regime of aural and visual representation defined culturally, historically, stylistically, and technologically. In Durbin's films the visualization of the soprano makes music an embodied practice with an emphasis on a voice that has a diegetic and synchronized visual presence. An uncanny effect lingers, however, because Hollywood sought to mark Durbin as virginal while the voice of the star in song created potentially opposing effects. On one level Durbin's vocalization plays on the schism or disjuncture between what we see of her (either as adolescent or an innocent and sexually unsophisticated young woman) and the maturity of her voice, high-art implications, and operatically coded (i.e., passionate) femininity. This produces a vocal masquerade of womanliness, an aura of sensuality and sexual maturity that complicates her representation of juvenated femininity promoted in the nonmusical elements of her films.

In her early films, before nature took its course and Durbin turned into a buxom and beaming young woman, a womanly voice emanates from a body that is clearly not yet "woman." Her voice becomes the source of her glamour in ways that are not bound by Hollywood convention, even as her physicality is contained to suggest sexual innocence rather than a body that can respond to or seek libidinal satisfaction. Durbin's voice carried high-culture implications but also a sensualism that provided viewers and listeners of both sexes the pleasure of a shared bodily experience with the star.[86] In this respect the Durbin voice signals trouble, for, at the same time that it sings cultural uplift, it points to the sensate materiality and audible force of the juvenated body that Hollywood wished to hold in check within a historical moment in which the rise of teen culture exacerbated anxieties centered on adolescent female sexuality.

Durbin's vocal power exceeds her body through its disciplined artistry, vocal projection, and the penetration of its force, as well as its virtuosic range up and down the scale. Durbin's vocally produced sounds also offer the promise (and the threat) of creating an "internal sensualism" in the listener who responds to the singer's voice.[87] In line with Koestenbaum's assertion that the opera singer "discredits the fiction that bodies are separate," Durbin's vocal performances suggest a dangerous acoustic phenomenon offering pleasures that disturb the boundaries of age, gender, and sexuality.[88] Durbin's voice adds a significant and unacknowledged complication to our understanding of Hollywood's representation of juvenated femininity and how it might be affected by musical performance, for it is within the realm of the musical that Deanna Durbin assumes a "self" that is dependent on the power of the voice in song, a self that is embodied, emboldened, and perhaps even erotically empowered through its womanliness. Relying on musical technique, Durbin demonstrates how those who are among the least powerful in society become—at least momentarily—the source of disciplined, passionate, and sublimely beautiful sounds. This is no small accomplishment for any female in Hollywood film.

FIGURE 44. Elizabeth Taylor studio portrait, ca. 1944. Author's collection.

CHAPTER 4

# Velvet's Cherry

## *Elizabeth Taylor and Virginal English Girlhood*

"Isn't it a good job of work—just to be beautiful?"
—Velvet Brown (Elizabeth Taylor), *National Velvet* (1944)

The child actress was a staple of the Hollywood studio system by the 1940s. In the previous decade Shirley Temple had set a gold standard for child stars. Naturally, other studios tried to emulate Fox's success with Temple, but as I noted in chapter 3, the popularity of a juvenile female star was not replicated on a comparable scale until lyric soprano Durbin became a financial boon to Universal for a dozen years, starting in 1936.[1] In 1942, attempting to follow up on its success with Durbin, Universal offered a six-month contract to nine-year-old Elizabeth Taylor, whose parents had returned to the United States from Great Britain when war started. After appearing in one low-budget film, *There's One Born Every Minute* (1942), she was dropped by Universal. As movie lore has it, the studio's casting director who let her go justified his decision by remarking that Taylor did not appear enough like a little girl: she had the eyes and face of a woman.[2]

After Taylor was let go by Universal, her mother, Sara, a former stage actress, kept pushing for her daughter's Hollywood career. Taylor's next big break has been attributed to a chance conversation between her father, art dealer Francis Taylor, and MGM producer Samuel Marx as they both stood duty as wartime air raid wardens.[3] In 1943 MGM offered Taylor a small supporting role as an aristocratic English child in the film *Lassie Come Home* (dir. Fred M. Wilcox, 1943), starring the world's most famous collie. The film also featured British child actor Roddy McDowall, who, echoing the Universal executive, later remarked on his first glimpse of Taylor: "It was like seeing a tiny adult walking up with this exquisite face. She was the most beautiful child I ever saw."[4]

In this chapter I explore the cultural and sexual implications that accrued around the "beautiful" screen presence of Elizabeth Taylor as a child actress in the mid-1940s, as well as the relationship of three of her early screen appearances to their historical antecedents in other visual representations of little girls. The Victorian era was perhaps the most historically important manifestation of an Anglo-American cultural obsession with pure little girls. I examine how aesthetic codes, sentimental conventions, and thematic traditions associated with the representation of girls in Victorian genre painting influenced cinema's contradictory and complex representation of Taylor in the 1940s when she was under contract to MGM—including on loan-out. In this respect I am following Raymond Williams's observation: "In a society as a whole, and in all its particular activities, the cultural tradition can be seen as a continual selection and re-selection of ancestors."[5] I focus my analytical attention on the actress's uncredited but memorable screen appearances in *Jane Eyre* (dir. Robert Stevenson, 1944), in *The White Cliffs of Dover* (dir. Clarence Brown, 1944), and in her star-making title role in *National Velvet* (dir. Clarence Brown, 1944).

Elizabeth Taylor was not a cute moppet in the Temple mold but an unusually beautiful little girl. Her visual qualities might lead us to call her a womanly girl, whose womanliness, like that evoked by Deanna Durbin's voice, created both a problem and an opportunity for Hollywood. In this exploration I seek to answer how the mixture of childlike qualities and womanly facial beauty played into the construction of Elizabeth Taylor's early screen presence and ultimate stardom. I am interested in the signifiers of eroticism or even sexual agency that were inscribed in her screen performances in 1944. With regard to the construction of a womanly girl, I detail how these three films regulated the contradictions involved in presenting an eleven-year-old child who was marked as virginal or sexually taboo by story lines and by her juvenile physicality but whose film performances and visual presentation might suggest a femininity as desirable or precociously desiring. My argument is centered on how Taylor's early films reassert or reimagine the nostalgic visual conventions and thematic tropes used to represent the girl in sentimental paintings of the Victorian era, especially those of John Everett Millais. Finally, I explore the sexual anxieties and fascinations that might have been evoked by Taylor's early screen presence in the response of gendered spectators.

## APPEALING ANTECEDENTS AND FASCINATED FANS

As noted early in this book, the American film industry worked to associate moving picture child performers with middle-class values of sentimentality and familial affection from its beginnings. Women and children were frequently thought to be the primary audience for Hollywood's juvenile actors, but the emotional impact of child players on viewers could not always be predicted. In 1915 Betty Marsh, a four-year-old player for Reliance-Majestic Studios, received a letter from a New York man. In his self-declared "mash note" the "old bachelor" said he "never suspected [a] little girl could be so nice and appealing so I am going to wait until you grow up and then I will lay my heart and my fortune at your feet. . . . Please, oh please, do not promise to be a sister to me."[6] The letter was reproduced in several newspapers. Although it seems obviously pedophilic in content, no one appears to have used the letter's publication to comment on how this adult male fan's reaction to Marsh reflected a sexual response to the movies' profitable mass media spectacle of little girls.

Perhaps there was no comment because the "mash" letter was read as a confirmation of some of the more bizarre reactions that early movie culture could elicit from those suffering from "movieitis." The year before, a teenage male fan of Broncho Billy Anderson shot and killed a constable while acting out his "'wild west' proclivities."[7] The lack of comment to the Marsh fan's mash note might have been related to the fact that the spectacle of little girls was so familiar and male appreciation of it so deeply ingrained in society. As we saw in the introduction, minor females often graced the Anglo-American stage in the late nineteenth century. Even earlier, in the Victorian period, high-art visual representations of girls from both the upper and lower classes were made fashionable through countless artistic venues. As Lionel Lambourne has noted in his study of Victorian painting, "a flood of representations of childhood . . . reached tidal proportions by the early Victorian era."[8] Childhood themes appeared in the works of numerous artists who hailed from virtually all "schools" of artistic philosophy throughout the nineteenth century; these included Frederick Daniel Hardy, William Quiller Orchardson, Thomas Cooper Gotch, John Calcott Horsley, Charles Green, William Mulready, John Singer Sargent, and the era's most famous high-art interpreter of girlhood, John Everett Millais.

Unlike the theatrical use of children in the Victorian era, high art's reliance on little girls by and large lacked controversy. Millais remarked that appreciation of juvenile female beauty was so universal that "the only head you could paint to be considered beautiful by everybody would be the face of a little girl about eight years old."[9] Rather than being questioned or condemned, many of these artistic images of girls in rural settings or at domestic pastimes were the object of critical acclaim and wide public admiration. In reciprocal relationship with complicated cultural dynamics involving gender, power, and sexuality, these imaginings of eroticized but innocent girlhood were shaped by and yet also responsible for sustained, positive public response. This points to the potential of such imagery of girlhood, carefully controlled by male aesthetic sensibility, to satisfy multifaceted fantasies, including heteroerotic ones involving adult male viewers.

Although women might be fans of these pictures, as Leslie Williams reminds us, "the buyers of art, the market for these images of young girls, were men."[10] Artists like Millais relied on these buyers' appreciation of images of beautiful young girls to guarantee the marketability of their products, so the question of whether that appreciation rested on a sexual element was repressed. In fact, rather than raise questions about the sexual response of owners and viewers to these images of girls, artistic representations were called on to ameliorate fears about the sexual exploitation of performing, posing, or otherwise specularized children through their sentimentalization of childhood beauty. Viewers of sentimental "fancy pictures" that featured children were educated to respond with tender feeling or sympathy, especially to those prepubescent girls depicted as not only beautiful but put upon or suffering. Sir Joshua Reynolds is credited with originating the term *fancy picture* to refer to paintings by Thomas Gainsborough that presented themselves as a distinct genre revolving around children (often working class) in everyday scenes offered in a simple format with only one or two figures.[11] An exemplary case in this regard is Millais's *The Blind Girl* (1856), one of his most famous and popular works. The painting depicts a rosy-cheeked blind girl of uncertain age. She is apparently a beggar, who rests by a stream in a golden field in the English countryside. With her upright posture, shiny hair, and pale, smooth skin, she is dignified and beautiful. A concertina (an instrument often associated with the working class) is on her lap. A very small blonde girl, probably her younger sister, nestles into the older girl's left side, one hand entwined in her sister's. The younger girl turns to look behind, at a double rainbow stretching across the sky in the distant background over a village. A much smaller glory of nature, an exquisitely patterned butterfly, alights on the blind girl's rough shawl. These various elements increase the sense of the blind girl's isolation from her bucolic surroundings. The viewer's ability to see everything that makes the painting so exquisite, including the blind girl, is contrasted with her inability to see anything. Someone has placed a small sign around her neck that reads "Pity the blind." Millais does not need this sign to instruct his painting's viewers in the proper tender emotional response to what is shown. Instead, the sign adds to the pathos, indicating that in the world in which the blind girl lives as a vagrant, such a reminder may be necessary for those who come across her.

In their foregrounding of sympathy as the proper response to a thematic emphasis on childhood innocence and virginal girlhood, a sentimental Victorian painting of this type might also have worked to ameliorate fears about the possibility of children's sexuality, a topic to which Sigmund Freud would draw disquieting attention in the latter part of the nineteenth century with his theories of psychosexual development. That these paintings were expected to function, however unconsciously, in this contradictory manner of making the girl child a beautiful spectacle while rendering her innocent or asexual is given support by the negative response to another Millais painting, *The Woodman's Daughter* (1851), based on the Coventry Patmore poem that tells the story of a poor girl who grows up with a squire's son. She succumbs to his sexual overtures, bears his child, and then commits infanticide. Millais's painting foreshadows the eventual unchaste consequences in an earlier interaction between the young boy and girl as children in the forest. Thus, Millais's painting more overtly addressed the issue of childhood sexuality than was common.

Although representations of girlhood were ubiquitous by this time and Millais's painting was no less technically masterful than his other efforts, *The Woodman's Daughter* crossed the boundary between what was acceptable according to unspoken codes of representing girls as beautiful icons of erotic innocence and what was unacceptable, even repugnant to Victorian society in relation to them.[12] Patmore himself declared the otherwise "charming picture" based on his poem marred by the fact that "the girl looked like a vulgar little slut."[13] Patmore's assessment is not borne out by the painting, however; there does not seem to be any suggestiveness in the girl's bodily posture or costuming. It appears that the widespread negative response was triggered by something as subtle as the facial expression of the girl or perhaps her lack of beauty. Response to her may also have called up negative stereotypes of

FIGURE 45. *The Woodman's Daughter* (1851; oil on canvas), by Sir John Everett Millais (1829–96). ©Guildhall Art Gallery, City of London/Bridgeman Art Library.

working-class females. Attributing sexual precocity to a girl of the lower class would have been more easily justified than attributing sexuality to the squire's son, who, dressed in bright red and with his body rigid and unnaturally positioned, seems coded to represent the erotic in overt ways that the girl, with her hands shyly cupped in anticipation of his gift, is not. In any case, no one wanted to buy *The Woodman's Daughter* until it was finally purchased by Millais's half-brother, who many years later asked the artist to repaint the girl's face.[14]

*The Woodman's Daughter* teaches an important lesson about the subtle ways in which codes and conventions of depicting girlhood innocence as beautiful and sentimental had to be differentiated from those elements and techniques suggesting the sexuality of children that might more overtly implicate the viewer. As I will argue, almost a century later, the career of child actress Elizabeth Taylor would call attention to the boundary between the acceptable and the unacceptable in this regard. Her frequent casting as an English girl during the mid-1940s suggests both the long-lived appeal of and complexities in representing girlhood associated with both issues at play in *The Woodman's Daughter*—the English rural past and eroticized feminine innocence. As with Temple's films, Taylor's early screen appearances also attempt to guide viewers' responses in interpreting the sexual and symbolic connotations of the child, with performance, costuming, photography, and shot choice across these films from 1944, resulting in different but related meanings for the virginal girl child embodied by a star in the making.

## THE MOVIES AND CULTURAL ICONS OF GIRLHOOD

The Victorian "cult of the girl" was a cultural precedent that art historian Leslie Williams says has "complicated symbolic value as a meeting-point for subordinance and control, marketability and pricelessness, eroticism and innocence."[15] It was also a historically specific articulation of dominant social norms attached to childhood. Aestheticized and commodified, many of the iconic codes, sentimental values, and symbolic meanings attached to young females in the nineteenth century nevertheless continued to circulate in twentieth-century visual discourse. As I argued in chapter 1, Mary Pickford's popularity built on narrative and visual aspects of this "cult." Almost half of Shirley Temple's films at Fox were set in the Victorian period and exploited costuming, settings, and situations that would have been at home in the paintings of the Victorian period. Indeed, it could be argued that the "sacralization of the child" encouraged the use of immediately recognizable signs that would render little girls, even those impersonated by women (such as the adult Mary Pickford), clearly as one of the last cultural repositories of sexual innocence and ideal beauty.[16] Interest in the child primarily for its emotional rather than economic importance fused with antimodernist impulses that would logically look to the past for a repertoire of signs compatible with its values that might inform contemporary popular culture (including film culture). This explanation goes a long way in clarifying why, in representing girlhood, motion pictures came to rely on many visual conventions and sentimental narrative tropes that were ubiquitous in the Victorian period.

In working toward an understanding of the early star presence of

Elizabeth Taylor, we must recognize that into the 1930s and 1940s, Hollywood films continued to call on nostalgic visual traditions for representing girls who were sentimentalized in ways that suggest the persistence and power of Victorian antecedents. Explicitly demonstrating the impact of this representational heritage is the Shirley Temple vehicle *Curly Top* (dir. Irving Cummings, 1935). The film demonstrates how nineteenth-century representational norms as well as specific high-art references could attempt to control the overdetermined erotic meanings of girls in motion pictures. Although set in the 1930s, the film includes a scene that uses famous child paintings by Millais, as well as works by Reynolds, Gainsborough, and others that could be classified as "fancy pictures" emphasizing child-centered sentiment.

*Curly Top* centers on a very wealthy and handsome single man, Edward Morgan (John Boles) who becomes the youngest trustee of the Lakeside Orphanage. On a visit, he meets Elizabeth (Temple), an orphan who charms him with her lighthearted antics. Returning home to his mansion, Edward continues to think of the adorable child and sings a love song he has composed, "It's All So New to Me." As he looks around his music room at paintings, we see that the faces of the children are Shirley's/Elizabeth's, and the paintings come to life. She appears in Emile Renouf's *Un coup de main* (*The Helping Hand*, 1881). Appearing in Gainsborough's *Portrait of Jonathan Buttall* (*The Blue Boy*, 1770), she smiles and waves her hat. As the curly-headed girl sitting demurely on a church pew in Millais's *My First Sermon* (1863), she blows Edward a kiss.

The way in which the film cites nostalgic cultural icons suggests the orphaned girl has the beauty and charm possessed by idealized children in high art of the past. Although her parents were vaudevillians, her appearance as the subjects of these revered paintings confirms that she could be at home in the mansion of a millionaire. Because the idea of an adult male singing a love song to a child might seem sexually grotesque (like the letter to Betty Marsh), the high-art reference serves another important function. It suggests that the millionaire's appreciation of the attractive little orphan girl that he will eventually adopt is both emotionally and culturally elevated rather than pedophilic and perverse. *Curly Top* employs high art to guide the audience's interpretation of the adult male's appreciation of a beautiful, virginal girl as sexually benign. As we will see with Elizabeth Taylor's films of 1944, Hollywood's reference to cultural antecedents that guide viewers' responses to the little girl performer extends beyond merely citing paintings. When combined

FIGURE 46. Shirley Temple in *Curly Top*, posed in imitation of Sir John Everett Millais's *My First Sermon* (1863). Author's collection.

with an unusually beautiful child star—like Taylor—it may result in the inscription of the little girl as a sexually ambiguous presence with a power that complicates the romanticizing of girls as innocent, asexual objects of a sentimental gaze.

## WHO IS "CHERRY RIPE"?

To Hollywood screenwriters the English became especially appealing role models during the war years. British citizens' courageous response to the Blitz and their fortitude in standing firm against Nazi aggression aimed at their homeland appealed to American audiences, who identified with their allies. No doubt, they wished to imagine that, if called upon, they could represent Anglo-American ideals with equal vigor and resolve. British characters and subject matter were frequently accompanied in Hollywood films of the 1940s by a narrative return to the past, highlighting the conventional association of the British with quaintness or with an aristocratic or refined heritage. In addition, this pastness well suited Hollywood's desire to capitalize on romantic nostalgia as part of its ideological endeavor to remind wartime audiences "why we fight." In this respect children were an important part of Hollywood's construction of romantic nostalgia for the past used to support wartime morale. To be an English child onscreen during this period made for a special constellation of ideological meaningfulness.

Starting with *Lassie Come Home,* Elizabeth Taylor's career as a child actress at MGM was marked by her frequent casting as a pure and innocent English girl. In that film Taylor plays Priscilla, a refined little girl of unusually mature understanding. Her grandfather, the Duke of Rudling (Nigel Bruce), buys Lassie from a Yorkshire family left penniless by the depression. The dog keeps escaping his kennels. She encourages her grandfather to accept the fact that Lassie must be with Joe, the little boy (McDowall) the dog loves. Both *The White Cliffs of Dover,* based on a poem by Alice Duer Miller, and *Jane Eyre* were film melodramas aimed clearly at the U.S. female audiences so important to Hollywood's wartime box office. The former was a maternal melodrama chronicling the joys and sorrows of an American woman (played by Irene Dunne) whose English husband was killed in one war and her son in another. *Jane Eyre,* based on Brontë's novel, was gothic melodrama, delineating the by-now-familiar story of a governess who falls in love with her aristocratic but mysterious employer. In spite of their radically different generic origins, these two films, like many other Hollywood products released during World War II, were alike in drawing heavily on cultural ideals of personal courage, familial love, and sacrifice to duty. As women's films, they attached these ideals to adult female characters—and even to little girls. It is no wonder, then, that in all of Taylor's screen appearances of 1944—in *Lassie Come Home, Jane Eyre, The White Cliffs of Dover,* and *National Velvet*—the actress's young characters conform to sentimental notions of the "quintessential English little girl" of "timeless purity," a description applied by art historian Laurel Bradley to another iconic British figure, Cherry Ripe.[17]

This iconic figure is the juvenile female subject of Millais's *Cherry Ripe* (1879), a painting that became one of the most famous representations of childhood femininity in the late Victorian era. Paying homage to Sir Joshua Reynolds's 1788 painting of Penelope Boothby, Millais

FIGURE 47. *Cherry Ripe* (1879; oil on canvas), by Sir John Everett Millais (1829–96). Private collection/ Bridgeman Art Library.

depicted a big-eyed, dark-haired child in old-fashioned mobcap and countrified dress with a bunch of cherries on the bench beside her. The image circulated widely in popular culture through cheaply made reproductions. *Cherry Ripe* appeared in engraving as the commissioned centerfold of the *Graphic*'s Christmas annual of 1880 and, in mezzotint form, sold over a half million copies.[18] According to Bradley, "the pretty child in old-fashioned dress is meant to embody the positive attributes of English culture" at a time when Britain's influence was spreading throughout the world through imperialism.[19] This beautiful child appealed to nostalgia for a preindustrial, Edenic England and was constructed to address "the patriotic and emotional needs" of the cultural moment by aligning girlish purity and innocence with the rural past and "the timeless world of enduring values."[20] Pamela Reis has argued that the visual encoding of sexual connotations is attached to feminine sexual desirability in the construction of the painting's appeal.[21] This "pedophilic appeal," says Reis, is suggested in the artist's subtle display of the child—with her gaze rather boldly directed at the viewer and her hands cupped between her legs, as well as in the title of the painting, drawn from an early seventeenth-century poem by Thomas Campion. Campion's poem, "Cherry-Ripe," speaks of the sexual maturation of the virginal girl through reference to what became commonplace slang for the hymen:

> There is a garden in her face
>   Where roses and white lilies blow;
> A heavenly paradise is that place,
>   Wherein all pleasant fruits do grow;
> There cherries grow that none may buy,
>   Till Cherry-Ripe themselves do cry.

It is not unreasonable to suggest the ultimate compatibility of these two seemingly different approaches to the broad commercial appeal of Millais's *Cherry-Ripe.* Likewise, Taylor's representations of beautiful English girlhood frequently convey a conflation of ideological comfort and sexual suggestion; like Millais's painting, Taylor's films of 1944 expose some of the contradictions in Western culture's modern "eruptions" of the veritable worship of beautiful little girls and the particular power that such an eruption can acquire—for female as well as male viewers—during a time of ideological upheaval.

Just as Millais built upon but also revised earlier visual and literary representations of girlhood, the Hollywood studio system articulated standards of child beauty that incorporated visual and narrative conventions and did not undo, but built upon, the contradictions embedded in earlier representations. Taylor's early films often partake of that "reassuring aura of childhood, culture, and the English hearth" that Bradley finds in *Cherry Ripe* and that audiences no doubt found particularly reassuring in the context of the Anglo-American war effort. Although the product of a different historical moment, these films negotiated the presence of an extraordinarily beautiful little girl whose attractiveness echoes the overdetermined cultural and sexual complexities of Victorian girl painting in general and *Cherry Ripe* in particular.

Following the precedent of Millais's painting in their treatment of the precociously mature, womanly beauty of Taylor, these screen representations did not all present the child actress in exactly the same terms. From film to film, differences of presentation result in very different erotic affects attached to the beautiful, virginal, female child. Nevertheless, embodied onscreen by Taylor and envisioned by different creative collaborations, her characters consistently drew on conventions of representing juvenated femininity that predate cinema to suggest, like *Cherry Ripe,* the mysterious sexual power of the virginal young girl combined with nostalgia directed at the English past.

## HELEN BURNS AS THE "QUEER VIRGIN"

Nina Auerbach has identified the "charismatic union of childhood and death" as a ubiquitous feature in Victorian literature.[22] The classic Victorian fetish object, the child doomed to an early death, is found in many Victorian novels, including *Jane Eyre.* In Fox's 1944 film version of Brontë's novel, Elizabeth Taylor is cast as Helen Burns, who comes to embody this important Victorian narrative and sexual trope. As Jane Eyre's childhood friend at the Lowood orphanage, Taylor appeared in a handful of early scenes in the film: Jane's first day at the orphanage when she is publicly punished as a liar; a lighthearted scene set outdoors, away from the austere confines of the school; a scene in which the school superintendent, Mr. Brocklehurst (Henry Daniell), ignores Jane's pleas and cuts off Helen's curls; a nighttime scene in which Jane (Peggy Ann Garner) and Helen, laden down by heavy irons, are forced to walk in the cold rain; and a scene in which Jane overhears the doctor's prognosis that Helen will die and goes to her bedside. There is one more scene in which Helen figures posthumously and quite importantly in the film as she does not in the novel, one that undoubtedly resonated with wartime audiences made all too familiar with death and grief: Jane is found by the kindly Dr. Rivers (John Sutton) as she lies across Helen's unmarked grave. Distraught, she sobs: "I want to be with Helen." Dr. Rivers tells her not to succumb to despair. He encourages her to devote herself to her education in fulfillment of her duty to God. Sublimation of Jane's great despair over Helen's death becomes the fuel for Jane's remarkable self-improvement in her remaining years at Lowood.

The beauty of Elizabeth Taylor in her period costume and curls is reminiscent of the visual perfection of female children depicted by Millais and other sentimental Victorian artists. Brontë's novel, however, was considered, on its publication in 1847, far from sentimental, and its Helen Burns differs significantly from the film's. In the original novel Helen Burns is older (fourteen), pious, and not very pretty. She is described by Jane as having "marked lineaments . . . thin face . . . sunken grey eye."[23] Helen's lack of attention to the school's requirements results in humiliating punishments: the wearing of "the untidy badge" or of a placard that reads "Slattern."[24] In fact, on her deathbed her remarks to Jane show how much she has absorbed these damaging reprimands: "By dying young, I shall escape great sufferings. I had not qualities or talents to make my way very well in the world: I should have been continually at fault."[25] Brontë's Helen is physically unremarkable and downtrodden in almost every sense except the spiritual.

By contrast, Helen in the 1944 film is an erotically charged, if virginal, presence. This charge depends not only on Taylor's beauty and its visual presentation but also on a narrative that enhances her emotional importance to and intimacy with the young Jane Eyre. Thus, the filmic presence of Helen suggests her status as a "queer virgin," a term discussed by Theodora Jankowski in a different context, that of early modernism.[26] Applying "queer virginity" to a child rather than the category of "adult woman virgin," as Jankowski originally employs the term, allows a discussion of the film's presentation of Helen as an exemplar of the force of erotic innocence that moves beyond the "binary axis of homo versus heterosexuality" and acknowledges that this inchoate sexuality has physical consummation in a sexual act as its goal.[27]

Taylor's performative presence as an erotic object occurs because the film, even more so than the novel, makes the friendship between Helen and Jane much more intense through acting; the creation of new, emotionally charged scenes; and melodramatic visual and aural treatment. The resulting eroticization of Helen suggests an intriguing resistance to the heterosexual cultural positioning of the beautiful little girl as an object of male (pedophilic) lust.

As in the novel, Jane's unsympathetic aunt, Mrs. Reed (Agnes Moorehead), banishes her to the harsh Lowood School. Accused by Mr. Brocklehurst of lying, Jane is forced to stand on the "pedestal of infamy" in an assembly, with the students and teachers exhorted by the headmaster to shun this child of the devil. At this moment, Brontë's novel gives itself over to Jane's voice and to her articulation of her first glimpse of Helen, who moves past her, amid all the other students, and smiles: "Just as they all rose, stifling my breath and constricting my throat, a girl came up and passed me: in passing, she lifted her eyes. What a strange light inspired them! What an extraordinary sensation that ray sent through mine! It was as if a martyr, a hero, had passed a slave or victim, and impacted strength in the transit. I mastered the rising hysteria, lifted up my head, and took a firm stand on the stool."[28]

The film stages Helen's entrance for the film spectator, not Jane. While Brontë's novel emphasizes Helen's impact on Jane as imparting "strength," the intensity and tenor of the passage in the film suggests a sensual impact, largely through the choices in shot selection and the visualization of Helen. All the teachers and the other students file out. A lap dissolve collapses time. Jane is left alone on the stool. A long shot reveals the huge hall, its depth exaggerated through long lines of shadow that stretch to the background. Music begins quietly. The shot reveals the entrance of a small figure on the staircase in the background, the camera waiting as a girl gracefully walks down the stairs, casting large shadows on the wall. Thus, Helen (Elizabeth Taylor) comes from the back of the room in what can only be described as a star entrance. She walks into the midground and hands Jane a piece of bread: "I brought you this from supper." The very leisurely paced timing and depth-of-field shooting invite initially our curiosity and suggest the importance of Helen as a character who deserves the camera's (and the audience's) extended attention. When Helen comes into the midground of the scene, our wait to see her is rewarded when we see her beautiful face, her luxuriant hair, and her restrained but graceful movement. Elizabeth Taylor's Helen is a child but one with a sexual presence. Full shots, then a medium close-up that includes both girls, accompany Jane's dialogue. She recounts very emotionally and quite pitifully how she came to school wanting "people to love me." Close-ups are exchanged, while in a two-shot, Helen puts her hand over Jane's. "Eat your bread, Jane," she says, with a calm stillness that counterpoints Jane's hysteria.

In a scene in which dialogue is dominated by talk of love and the desire for acceptance, one child, a self-possessed, strikingly beautiful girl, creates a "sensation" in another little girl who is desperate, disheveled, and plain. The passionate friendship between Jane and Helen beginning in this scene is melodramatically effective because of a number of factors, not the least important being the convincing acting out of unhappiness displayed by Peggy Ann Garner, emphasized in several close-ups, and its contrast with the cool passivity of Taylor as Helen. Helen possesses that combination of "perfect beauty and tender expression" that Millais thought so crucial to "producing beauty" in child paintings.[29] Unlike Brontë's Helen, Taylor's Helen is grace and physical perfection personified.

In contrast to the novel, Jane and Helen are completely alone in the film's rendering of the scene rather than in the midst of others. There is an intimacy in their solitude, and Jane's disappointment in being taken for a liar and rejected is about relations, about love: "I thought school would be a place where people would love me." The stillness of her presence (vs. Jane's hysteria), the calmness of her reactions to Jane, and the measured tempo even of her placing her hand on Jane's all impose the attributes of an unexpected maturity and, therefore, womanliness on her status as a girl. Helen is an emblem of purity, of the female child whose purity is presumed to be spiritual (as innocent) and sexual (as untouched by men). Like a figure in a dream, this beautiful little girl comes out of nowhere to fulfill Jane's desire to have someone to love her.

Helen's erotic presence is readable as precociously mature and asserted through Taylor's performance of Helen, through the quality of her voice and in her delivery of her lines, as well as in the contextualization of her performance visually and aurally. Bernard Herrmann's hushed, romantic musical score conveys the tenderness of emotion that is valorized in this scene and confirms the importance of Helen's kindness to Jane. The music, the selection of shots, and their timing all combine to suggest a romantic sensuality to the scene that trumps spirituality and the presumption of children's asexuality. Although created by a largely male contingent of filmmakers, this romanticizing of the two girls' intense friendship to resemble something that looks like Hollywood's approach to romantic heterosexuality is made doubly interesting by the fact that it occurs in a film constructed to appeal to a largely female audience.

Another incident further reveals the film's evocation of the erotic in the girls' relationship: Mr. Brocklehurst's cutting of Helen's hair, which is "one mass of curls." Instead of taking care of Helen's persistent cough as the doctor instructs, Mr. Brocklehurst keeps the classroom cold and lashes out against Helen when he feels the doctor has questioned his authority. "What may I ask is the meaning of this?" he asks in reference to Helen's hair. He asks for the scissors and pushes Helen around so he can start cutting her hair. Helen is quiet, betraying emotion only through her eyes and only to the film audience, which she faces. Jane begs Mr. Brocklehurst to stop, to cut her hair instead. As discussed in chapter 1, in her analysis of Victorian aesthetics, Elisabeth Gitter has called attention to the importance of female hair as an erotic show or exhibition in Victorian art, with its luxuriance as a sign of sexuality.[30] In Victorian society the erotic charge that women's hair carried meant

FIGURE 48. The cutting of Helen's hair in *Jane Eyre* (dir. Robert Stevenson, 1943). Author's collection.

that only little girls were allowed to wear their hair long and flowing in public.

Under the repressed and repressive Mr. Brocklehurst, the girls of Lowood School are forced to wear their hair up or in pigtails or other restraining configurations. No wonder the horrible headmaster rails against Helen's natural curls as a sign of vanity—and nature—that must be conquered (i.e., cut). Helen's hair signifies the sexual nature of the feminine, and in an all-girls school this sexuality is dangerous. No wonder, too, that Jane begs that her own hair be cut rather than the curls of her beautiful little friend. The extreme reactions in this scene to Helen's curls, both in Brocklehurst's demands and Jane's impassioned defense, suggest an erotic charge to Helen and her curls that might subvert the order of things, including the conventional order that demands the repression not only of Mr. Brocklehurst's desire but also of Jane's inchoate love for her friend.

Mr. Brocklehurst reacts to what he calls "this insurrection" by sending both girls into the cold rain to march as punishment. When the doctor returns, he demands that they be brought in, but it is too late. Helen

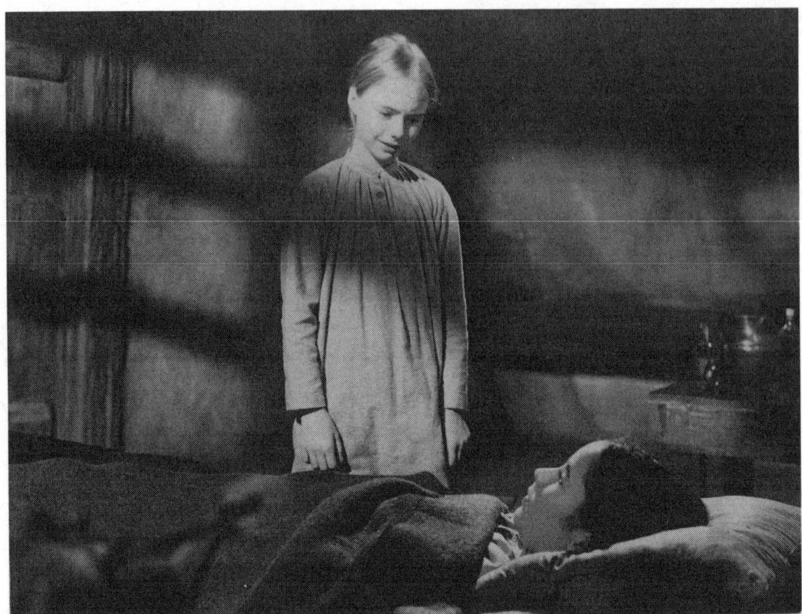

FIGURE 49. Helen Burns (Elizabeth Taylor) dying in *Jane Eyre*. With Peggy Ann Garner. Author's collection.

is felled by consumption. Jane overhears the doctor's prognosis of death and goes to Helen, who is as beautiful and calm as ever. "Don't cry, Jane. I don't want you to cry," she softly intones. She tells Jane to warm herself under the bed covers. Jane crawls into bed with Helen and falls asleep. A close-up of their intertwined hands is accompanied by the off-screen voice of Jane attempting to waken Helen; she squeezes her hand but then screams on realizing her friend is dead. This scene of intimacy and death is not in the novel, where Jane, still sleeping, is removed from Helen's bed and only later learns of Helen's death.

The identity and presence of Taylor's body are of the female as a little girl, for her body lacks the physical marks of womanhood—her flat child's chest and her diminutive physique indicate that hers is an unwomanly body, differing from that of a woman viewer, as well as from that of a male viewer. Yet Helen's certainty of purpose and mature grace conveyed in Taylor's performance as a pure little Victorian girl convey something otherworldly, erotically charged, and "not little girl."

Unlike Brontë's Helen, the impression that Taylor leaves is not of intense spirituality but of extreme femininity. Her hair, eyes, and skin, as well as her voice, function as heightened signs of conventional feminine beauty and refinement (quite clearly in contrast to Jane and the other girls). The result is that Helen's/Taylor's sexual difference is inscribed in ways partially associated with womanliness rather than completely with childishness. This preternatural womanliness is especially effective with regard to Helen's narrative function as that Victorian fetish, the doomed child. Because of the casting and visual treatment of Taylor, Helen is the child without a future (as a grown woman) who nevertheless conveys the woman she would have become. Thus, when she dies, post-Victorian viewers are encouraged to mourn her disappearance as both pitiable girl child and beautiful not-woman woman. To further support Helen's role in "queering virginity," both the narrative point in the story and the original historical viewing context for the film emphasize same-sex relations (female to female) rather than heterosexual ones.

## *CHERRY RIPE* REDUX

In *Jane Eyre* the sexual implications of Taylor's character are radical and unexpected and move into that dangerous territory where the sexual power as well as beauty of a virginal little girl might be wordlessly asserted. By contrast, in *The White Cliffs of Dover* and *National Velvet* Elizabeth Taylor's casting as a pure and innocent English girl is subject to very different strategies of visual display and performance nuance that work to discourage the audience's interpretation of her characters as possessing anything more than conventional girlhood innocence. However, these two films suggest the difficulties in presenting beautiful girlhood without also engaging in some of the sexual contradictions and discomfitures that long beset iconographic depictions of girlhood in and out of film.

In *The White Cliffs of Dover* Taylor plays ten-year-old Betsy Kenney, the daughter of English tenant farmers who live on the estate of Lady Jean Ashwood (Gladys Cooper). Lady Ashwood's widowed daughter-in-law, Lady Susan Ashwood (Irene Dunne) lives in the Ashwood manor house with her young son, John Ashwood II (Roddy McDowall). In one scene John and a male servant peruse the estate from horseback. They stop at the Kenney farm and are greeted by Betsy. The landscape and situation suggest a pastoral fairy tale but one with echoes of the erotic encounter of children of different classes depicted by Millais's *The Woodman's Daughter.* Unchaste associations are downplayed: Betsy appears in gingham pinafore and flowered bonnet. Betsy gazes with fascination at "Sir John," and exhibits flirtatious interest in him, holding on to the farm fence, stretching her arms as she bends into and away from the gate, moving her head in submissively feminine position and giggling.

Betsy's flirtations are gauche and unstudied so that her behavior appears excessively childish. Like Cherry Ripe in her mobcap, Betsy, in her gingham bonnet, is part of a pastoral idyllic landscape: a thatched-roof watermill is featured in the background. Unlike the little girls depicted in *Cherry Ripe* or *The Woodman's Daughter,* Betsy Kenney resists interpretation as precociously sexual even though the scene is obviously meant to suggest her romantic interest in another child. We are invited to consider her giddy, girlish, and silly.

In a later scene the boy, John, appears once again at the farm to say good-bye. He and his mother are moving to the United States. After conversing with her parents and shaking hands with a subdued Betsy, he walks off, but then he goes back to the fence, leans over it, and offers Betsy the ring, made of a horseshoe nail, he has been wearing. Over-the-shoulder shots and shot/reverse shot editing emphasize Betsy's more mature, subdued, and quite sincere reactions to John's attentions. Taylor is given two close-ups in shallow focus that emphasize her facial loveliness. She is bareheaded, dressed in a modest gingham pinafore apron, over a dress with a lace collar. Such materials would have signaled (at least to a female audience) self-respecting working-class feminine innocence. The sweetness of her verbal responses to John and her physical poise suggest something more than was expressed in the earlier scene between them. The gift of the ring recalls the girl's attempt to receive the offering of strawberries from the squire's son in Millais's *The Woodman's Daughter,* but here the nostalgic conventions of depicting childhood innocence are upheld rather than questioned. The moment prefigures a romance between them, a fairy-tale romance in which British class differences melt away under the force of Hollywood fantasy.

John and his mother decide to stay in England, and in the final scene of Taylor's appearance as Betsy, we see her, with John, on a windswept hill, gathering flowers as his mother prepares a picnic lunch. Although Taylor and McDowall appear no older, their stances are more mature. He holds her from behind lightly and points authoritatively into the distance as she smiles and holds a bouquet. A lap dissolve indicating the passage of time holds them in the same position but replaces McDowall and Taylor in close-up with more mature ingénue actors, Peter Lawford and June Lockhart. The latter, while clearly older than Taylor, appears less beautiful and significantly less sensual. At this moment viewers may realize that they have just witnessed how onscreen girlhood—embodied by Elizabeth Taylor—has threatened to speak the fragile boundary between adult sexual desire and the virgin child, the taboo object.

## "WHAT DOES IT FEEL LIKE TO BE IN LOVE WITH A HORSE?"

As I have argued of *The White Cliffs of Dover,* strategies of presentation and performance might work to discourage the audience's interpretation of Elizabeth Taylor's beautiful characters as possessing anything more than the innocence and purity conventionally associated with little girls. However, in Taylor's appearance in *Jane Eyre,* we observe strategies that move the film viewer into more dangerous regions where the sexual power of the virginal little girl is asserted. The result is that the sexual implications of her character's presentation become more radical and unexpected.

*National Velvet* negotiates these two positions in taking on the story of a twelve-year-old girl, Velvet Brown (Taylor), who wins an unwanted horse, "The Piebald," in a raffle and, disguised as a male jockey, rides him to victory in the Grand National. The film takes the ubiquitous girlhood fantasy in which prepubescent females obsess over all things "horsey" and places it within a pastoral dream version of a coastal English village in the 1920s. In this respect the film nostalgically contextualizes the girl's fantasy within a prewar world of familial and national contentment guaranteeing the purity and innocence of the fantasy to which this idyllic setting gives birth. It is a world for a beautiful childhood dream.

Unlike Alfred Hitchcock's *Marnie* (1962), which takes the "horse equals phallus" element of the girl's horse fantasy to psychosexual extremes, *National Velvet* constructs the girl's love of horses as both a natural phase ("all things in their time," as her mother says) and the positive psychological impetus for striving for greatness. It is because Velvet wants to show the world that her "Pie" is an extraordinary jumper that she concocts the plan to enter the Grand National and enlists the help of ex-jockey Mi Taylor (Mickey Rooney).

Her older sister, Edwina (Angela Lansbury), offers a sexual interpretation of Velvet's love for horses by asking, "What does it feel like to be in love with a horse?" The film raises the issue to dismiss it by making it the object of comedy: at another point, Mi touches Velvet's forehead to

FIGURE 50. A daughter's quest and a mother's memories: Elizabeth Taylor and Anne Revere in *National Velvet* (dir. Clarence Brown, 1944). Author's collection.

feel for a fever when she talks of horses and gazes in rapture at nothing. Nevertheless, *National Velvet* prompted the reviewer for *Time* magazine to suggest the transparency of the heroine's sexual obsession. He noted of the film: "it is also an interesting psychological study of hysterical obsession, conversion mania, [and] pre-adolescent sexuality."[31] Manny Farber detected a painful realism in the heroine's "childhood fanaticism" and suggested that she made him "wonder uncomfortably what her motives are when she says she wants to be 'the greatest rider in the world.'"[32] While Farber reads sexual motives into the heroine's desires, the film (like the book) justifies her desires by making Velvet part of a family of obsessive collectors and strivers: her brother collects insects; her younger sister, canaries; and sister Edwina, boyfriends. Her mother, identified as the first woman to swim the English Channel, encourages her entry into the Grand National as a "breathtaking folly" that everyone should have once in her life.

James Agee observed that Taylor was not only "rapturously beautiful" in the film but capable of expressing certain emotions, including "a mock-pastoral kind of simplicity" and "an odd sort of pre-specific erotic sentience."[33] Agee seems to be pointing to a precocious eroticism wed-

FIGURE 51. Mickey Rooney, Elizabeth Taylor, and The Pie in *National Velvet*. Author's collection.

ded to beauty, exactly those qualities that Victorian painting presented but also worked to contain. Containment is also crucial to this film. Velvet's intense feeling for horses remains a buoyant, uplifting emotion rather than a low sexual one. The film works to de-eroticize Taylor at key moments in the story, including the beginning, when she is introduced in a classroom of girls. Her childishness in this scene and later ones is emphasized in reiterated business involving a dental retainer for her bite and in the camera's and costuming's emphasis on her childish, flat body. However, later scenes of her riding The Pie in long shot capture something of rapture in her feelings for the horse and eroticize her by making her and the horse a powerful spectacle of graceful movement, as well as of emotional bonding. Of course, the film cannot suggest that an obsessive female rider actually experiences a sexual charge from the physical act of her horsemanship, as Farber's review alludes and Hitchcock's film ultimately articulates.

Similarly, there is no physical sexual relationship suggested between Velvet and Mi, but the film does suggest an emotional sympathy between them that has romantic potential, and the casting of the diminutive Rooney lends a kind of physical symmetry to the two (they are

FIGURE 52. The prepubescent girl and the diminutive jockey may be destined to be a couple. Elizabeth Taylor and Mickey Rooney in *National Velvet*. Author's collection.

almost the same height) that adds to the viewer's perception that they may be destined to be a couple. Their conversations are often held in private and played against the backdrop of intimate or confined spaces, as when Velvet goes to Mi's sleeping quarters in the barn to attempt to persuade him to stay with her family and work for her father or when the two of them attempt to nurse The Pie back from illness.

Farber complained, in fact, that MGM displayed a "lack of daring" because the relationship between the two, "one of the more interesting in current movies, is left untouched."[34] Obviously, Farber may be following the film's visual cues, but it is interesting that he is forgetting the taboo created by Taylor's age, as both prepubescent actress and character. Nevertheless, *National Velvet* acknowledges and satisfies the audience's perception of deep feeling between the young girl and the ex-jockey with the final shot of the film, in which Velvet, in extreme long shot on the back of The Pie, is shown stopping in the middle of the road to bid good-bye to Mi, who leaves to make his way in the world. In spite of the lack of conventional heterosexual romance in *National Velvet,* the film's advertising campaign offered posters with close-up portraits of Taylor and Rooney, leaning into each other, and called the film "M-G-M's Great Technicolor Heart Drama."[35] This is typical of Hollywood advertising of the time in emphasizing heterosexual coupling even in films that have it at the margins or almost not at all.[36]

In 1944 Elizabeth Taylor's screen presence challenged the desexualized cultural significance of the stereotype of the pure child and unhinged its moorings. Womanly qualities inscribed by narrative and visual strategies, as well as her own nuances of performance and physicality, complicated the child-actress Elizabeth Taylor's textual status as a pure child, an exemplar of virginity to be read as a conventional, sentimental sign of little sexual desirability and no sexual power. Especially through her screen appearance in *Jane Eyre,* we can observe how Taylor's beauty, in combination with specific textual strategies, has the potential to unfix her textual status as an asexual child.

As a consequence, the Elizabeth Taylor on screens in 1944 occupies a sexual space that disturbs established categories of sexuality in gendered, as well as generational, terms and raises the signifying problem of sexual difference in relation to childhood. Sexual power accrues to her by virtue of her eroticized innocence and the desire of others directed toward her, including the desire of the film viewer. As embodied by Taylor, onscreen girlhood threatened to speak in visual terms the fragile boundary between adult sexual desire and the virgin child, the taboo object. This calls into question the cultural fantasy of being able to separate desire for the pure child (taboo) from that for the impure woman (acceptable). Thus, Taylor's erotically charged feminine presence creates a tension between what is said and unsaid, openly conveyed and wordlessly implied about the possibilities of sexual desire at mid-twentieth century in a culture that would admit only to a sympathy for or appreciation of the beauty of little girls and so reverberated still with those disturbances in the sphere of sexuality that the Victorians knew so well.

FIGURE 53. Jennifer Jones assumes the role of a fourteen-year-old religious visionary in *The Song of Bernadette* (dir. Henry King, 1943). Author's collection.

CHAPTER 5

# Perilous Transition

## *Jennifer Jones as Melodrama's Hysterical Adolescent*

"That Trilby was just a singing-machine—an organ to play upon . . . a flexible flageolet of flesh and blood . . . and nothing more—just the unconscious voice that Svengali sang with—for it takes two to sing like la Svengali, monsieur—the one who has got the voice, and the one who knows what do with it . . . So that when you heard her sing . . . , you heard Svengali singing with her voice, just as you hear Joachim play a *chaconne* of Bach with his fiddle!"

—George Du Maurier, *Trilby*

In July of 1941, twenty-two-year-old Phylis Walker was studying acting in New York City with her husband, Robert, when super producer David O. Selznick agreed to give her a screen test. At the end of the try out Selznick signed the young actress from Tulsa, Oklahoma, to an exclusive, seven-year contract. In keeping with Hollywood practice, he soon gave her a new name, "Jennifer Jones." Jones was joining Selznick International's impressive roster of established stars, which included Joan Fontaine, Ingrid Bergman, Vivien Leigh, Gregory Peck, and Joseph Cotten.[1] Walker/Jones's thespian training consisted largely of work in her parents' regional "tent shows,"[2] but the fledgling actress knew what she wanted—the leading role in the film adaptation of *Claudia,* a hit Broadway comedy about a "gawky-little gamin[e]" of a bride.[3] Little over a month after signing her, Selznick fretted in a memo about the transience of her appealingly youthful femininity: "Already she has lost some of that eager, blushing quality that made her so enchanting when we first saw her and when she was just the girl from the tent shows. I am terrified that by the time we get 'Claudia' in work [*sic*] she will be wrong for it because the bloom will be off the peach."[4]

In his own characteristically hyperbolic and melodramatic way (he's "terrified"), Selznick feared the imminent loss of naive and nubile femininity in the married mother of two. The actress lost the lead in *Claudia*, and six months later, with no film for her, Selznick fumed about the amount he was paying an "inexperienced girl."[5] He arranged for her to audition for director Henry King for the leading role in 20th Century–Fox's prestige production of *The Song Of Bernadette* (1943), adapted from Franz Werfel's best-selling novelization of the life of Bernadette Soubirous. Jones was selected for the role of the fourteen-year-old French peasant girl who, in 1858, began seeing "a beautiful lady" standing in a niche above the Lourdes town dump. On its release the film about the visionary saint was declared a box-office and critical success, garnering twelve Academy Award nominations. *Time* called Jones's performance in *The Song of Bernadette* "one of the most impressive screen debuts in many years."[6] Jones won an Academy Award for best actress in a leading role. She was set on the path of stardom.

*The Song of Bernadette* was also the beginning of Jones's screen affiliation with juvenated femininity in female-centered melodrama. Like a number of other female stars of the period, including Joan Crawford, Bette Davis, Gene Tierney, Olivia de Havilland, Joan Fontaine, and Lana Turner, Jones was closely identified with Hollywood melodrama. While the label "melodrama" was applied to a broad range of Hollywood films, it was linked in this era to an important subgenre, the "woman's film." The latter cut across genres, but it was typically centered on a female protagonist, with whom women viewers might identify. During World War II, with female viewers crucial to U.S. box-office returns, the woman's film and its stars became even more important to the American film industry. In contrast to most other actresses affiliated with female-centered melodramas, however, Jones's portrayals frequently relied on age impersonations, exploiting the actress's uncanny ability to act and look young, a talent that had been central to the twenty-three-year-old's convincing performance as a fourteen-year-old in *The Song of Bernadette*.[7]

Although comedies, not melodramas, were the primary vehicle for exploring adolescent femininity during the war years, Jones's wartime films, *The Song of Bernadette, Since You Went Away* (dir. John Cromwell, 1944), and *Love Letters* (dir. William Dieterle, 1945), as well as many of her postwar releases, including her most controversial, *Duel in the Sun* (dir. King Vidor, 1946), presented her in roles in which female adolescence is portrayed as a condition associated with unpredictable sexuality as well as emotionally perilous transformations.[8] Her films emphasized a rhetoric of desire played out in melodramatic terms across the star's body and the psychological terrain of the family. Those that focused on females in transition from adolescence to young womanhood included *Since You Went Away, Duel in the Sun, Cluny Brown* (dir. Ernst Lubitsch, 1946), *Portrait of Jennie* (dir. William Dieterle, 1948), *Madame Bovary* (dir. Vincente Minnelli, 1949), *Gone to Earth* (dir. Michael Powell and Emeric Pressburger, 1950), *Carrie* (dir. William Wyler, 1952), and, in flashbacks, *Ruby Gentry* (dir. King Vidor, 1952), *Good Morning, Miss Dove* (dir. Henry Koster, 1955), and *Tender Is the Night* (dir. Henry King, 1962). Jones was also considered for or sought the youthful leading roles in stage or film productions of *The Constant Nymph, Laura, St. Joan, The Moon Is Blue, The Miracle of the Bells, Little Women, Roman Holiday, Trilby,* and *Tess of the D'Urbervilles.* On occasion Jones played a grown woman who experiences a delayed sexual "coming of age," as in *Love Is a Many-Splendored Thing* (dir. Henry King, 1955) and *The Barretts of Wimpole Street* (dir. Sidney Franklin, 1957).

Jennifer Jones was an adult woman who was often cast as adolescents or twenty-something females who were sexually inexperienced, but Jones's protagonists differed radically from Mary Pickford's—or, for that matter, from Deanna Durbin's juvenated heroines. They were not invested in the perpetuation of innocence or the idealization of the girl's attainment of womanhood. Instead, the move from sexual inexperience to experience as embodied by the star is psychologically, sexually, and socially traumatic, a fall rather than an attainment; frequently it is marked as fatal, with the premature death of the heroine in *The Song of Bernadette, Duel in the Sun, Portrait of Jennie, Madame Bovary,* and *Gone to Earth*, or of her lover, as in *Since You Went Away, Duel in the Sun, We Were Strangers* (dir. John Huston, 1949), *Carrie, Ruby Gentry,* and *Love Is a Many-Splendored Thing.*

What is more, Jones's screen persona came to represent adolescent "femaleness" that coalesced around long-standing psychoanalytic notions of hysteria and problems of identification and desire. This embodiment of juvenated femininity also reflected a complex interplay of filmic, historical, and personal influences that occurred at a time when adolescent femininity was under intense cultural scrutiny focused on sexuality. The result was that Jones's films inscribed adolescent female identity in terms traditionally associated with hysteria, including anomalies of sight, hearing, memory, and movement. These are suggested in *The Song of Bernadette* (visual hallucinations), *Madame Bovary* (blindness and illness), *Love Letters* (amnesia), *Gone to Earth* (visual and auditory hallucinations), and *The Barretts of Wimpole Street* (paralysis and illness). In numerous films in which Jones starred, symptoms of hysteria are also evidenced in oscillations of desire, psychological or mood instability, overly intense emotionality or hyperexcitability, contradictory identifications across gender, sensuality instead of sexuality, as well as the nascent assumption of so-called multiple personalities. Two of the most striking instances occur in her embodiment of the hysterical "performance of seduction" in *Duel in the Sun* and *Ruby Gentry,* an embodiment comparable to the early photographs of female hysteria made famous by Jean-Martin Charcot, whose patients' "hysterical performances" often included visual disturbances, most notably, sightings of things that were not there—including imaginary lovers.[9]

The problems of desire and identification attributed to hysteria function as the central thematic issue in most of Jones's films, even those that are equally if not more focused on a sympathetic male. The latter is illustrated by *Love Letters,* in which Jones plays Victoria, a "youngster" who completely loses her memory and, with it, her identity, when she discovers that her husband did not write the letters that made her fall in love with him. The man who did write the letters, Allen Quinton (Joseph Cotten), comes across his "pinup girl of the spirit," marries her, and seeks to solve the mystery of Victoria's repressed memories and the murder of her first husband. The hysterical symptom of visual hallucination commonly stereotyped as female is reversed in *Portrait of Jennie,* where Jones plays the title character, seemingly a ghost, who first appears as a child from the past to a down-and-out artist. Growing older and more beautiful with each fleeting appearance, Jennie inspires Eben Adams (Joseph Cotten) to paint his greatest work. As is to be expected of melodrama, the big and conflicted emotions of the characters are expressed in dialogue, but also in nonverbal elements. Exemplary of this mode of melodramatic expressivity, the final scene of *Portrait of Jennie* shows Jennie dying for a second time, literally swept out of Eben's grasp by a storm that is heightened sensationally with music, special tints, and, in selected theaters, a "cycloramic screen together with multi-sound."[10]

Others have suggested the relationship of hysteria to melodrama, to specific films in which Jones appeared, or even to the star's screen persona. However, the inscription of hysteria in Jones's films has not been linked to the juvenation of her characters. Hysteria, often defined in very broad, nonsexual terms, has been attributed generally to melodrama as a mode by scholars such as Peter Brooks, and to film melodrama by Geoffrey Nowell-Smith, Thomas Elsaesser, and others, who regard the

FIGURE 54. Jones as a ghostly girl who inspires a failing artist (Joseph Cotten). *Portrait of Jennie* (dir. William Dieterle, 1948). Author's collection.

visual and nonverbal aural language of melodrama as a process of signification comparable to that of hysteria.[11] In an influential theorization of the process Nowell-Smith identifies the source of the excessive, "hysterical" quality of film melodrama in terms evoking "conversion": "The undischarged emotion which cannot be accommodated within the action . . . is traditionally expressed in the music and, in the case of film, in certain elements of the mise-en-scène . . . [which] do not just heighten the emotionality of an element of the action: to some extent they substitute for it. The mechanism here is strikingly similar to that of the psychopathology of hysteria. . . . The energy attached to an idea that has been repressed returns converted to a bodily symptom. . . . A conversion can take place into the body of the text."[12]

Nowell-Smith's account is in keeping with Freud's understanding of hysteria as developed from his case studies. In one of the most important, Freud narrativized his analysis of fourteen-year-old Ida Bauer, whom he called "Dora" (after a servant girl) in his case study, "Fragment of an Analysis of Hysteria."[13] Ida Bauer suffered from various symptoms without organic causes, including a limp.[14] Interested in hysteria's sexual etiology, Freud became fascinated with Ida Bauer's rejection of the sexual advances of a middle-aged man ("Herr K."), whose wife was the mistress of her father. Revising his belief that hysteria was based on the repression of memories of sexual trauma (frequently the result of fathers molesting their daughters), Freud decided Dora's/Ira's hysterical symptoms were somatic expressions, the work of the unconscious that converted troubling ideation (her repressed desire for Herr K.) that the subject did not want to bring into consciousness.

Although much of film theory builds on Freud's concept of hysterical conversion to explain melodrama, the sexual etiology of hysteria is sometimes obscured in this scholarship. In his pioneering analysis of *Duel in the Sun* Robin Wood asserts that "the star image of Jennifer Jones is centred on hysteria"; Wood defines hysteria very broadly, "in its wider, popular sense." He sees hysteria almost exclusively as ideological, as women's instinctive breaking of patriarchal rules.[15] Wood's approach is in keeping with feminists such as Catherine Clément and Hélène Cixous, who celebrate hysteria as a woman's response to powerlessness rather than as evidence of the hyperbolic body that acts out an internal struggle over sexual desire and identity.[16]

While vital to targeting Jones's importance, Wood's analysis desexualizes hysteria in relation to the performance of femininity; this avoids theoretical challenges and historical complexities. Therefore, I am returning to a psychoanalytically informed definition of *hysteria* in which sexual conflict is at the core of the phenomenon. I will consider hysteria as a process that signifies, as one psychoanalyst suggests, both "an exaggerated feminine aspect—emotional, impulsive and infantile—a caricature of feminine nature" and crucial evidence of an internalized "battle between the sexes" that is somatically "enacted in the body."[17] I am operating from the assumption that, within midcentury film melodrama, hysteria was not necessarily an accurate representation of then current or past psychiatric thought but was exaggerated and mythologized as a rhetorical tool to address the troubled process of gendering women—especially adolescent or juvenated females—within a society that was anxious about youthful female sexuality.

Jones's films serve as a fictional model of hysterical, juvenated femininity that resonated with contemporary concerns. Psychoanalysis was popularized in the United States in the 1940s. As World War II put a strain on American social norms and shifted expectations for femininity, the use of psychoanalysis and psychology to monitor fighting men would be applied to females, including teenage girls, in and out of film. Concerns about female sexuality were reflected broadly in U.S. culture and in Hollywood melodrama as symptomatic of that culture.[18] After the war, interest in the new sexology was spurred by the first Kinsey Report of 1948 on male sexual response, which was followed in 1953 by a report on female sexuality. Viewed through this cultural lens, hysteria contains a useful repertoire of meanings that can be related to Jones's films as mid-twentieth-century women's films, influenced by convergent discourses of psychoanalysis, patriarchal ideology, sexology, and social anxiety directed at female adolescence.

David O. Selznick, whose involvement went beyond that of producer, was the immediate force that influenced Jones's films. His sexual desire for her was inscribed in professional as well as personal terms. As a result, Jones's films often suggest the hysteric's performance of an interrelation, of the "psychology of two," embodying an intersubjective process that is acted out in the performance of characters who are in the process of becoming women.[19] The result is that Jones's films often display powerfully disturbing visual and aural representations of juvenated—and overtly sexualized—femininity.

## WHAT ABOUT DAVID?

Jones's initial association with Selznick seemed unusually fortuitous as she attempted to build a career as an actress. Selznick was not just one of Hollywood's most successful independent producers, but he was regarded as having a special talent for making films with strong roles for women that appealed to female audiences. Fitting this model was his most famous production, *Gone with the Wind* (dir. Victor Fleming, 1939), but other Selznick productions were also important showcases for female stars: *Little Women* (dir. George Cukor, 1933), *A Star Is Born* (dir. William Wellman, 1937), *Garden of Allah* (dir. Richard Boleslawski, 1936), *Intermezzo* (dir. Gregory Ratoff, 1939), *Rebecca* (dir. Alfred Hitchcock, 1940), and *Spellbound* (dir. Alfred Hitchcock, 1945).

Jennifer Jones's creative input into her performances has been eclipsed by the role that David O. Selznick played in shaping her individual films and her career. Selznick's relationship to Jones has been described as "Svengali-like."[20] There is no doubt that the producer was a domineering and excitable man, even measured by Hollywood standards for moguls; his maniacal efforts to control every detail of his personal productions, especially *Gone with the Wind* and *Duel in the Sun*, became the stuff of Hollywood legend. Legendary, too, were his gambling, boozing, and Benzedrine addiction. His office, with its remote-control door lock, was infamous as a site of sexual predation.[21]

Selznick assumed a major role in developing Jones's screen persona before their romantic relationship developed in the mid-1940s, during the filming of *Since You Went Away.* Soon, media coverage constructed a narrative in which Selznick was "Svengali" with Jones as his "Trilby" who left her true love (first husband Walker) to embrace the chance for stardom held out to her by Selznick—Hollywood's version of George Du Maurier's monstrous but mesmerizing Jew. In Du Maurier's classic tale Trilby can only perform as a great singer ("la Svengali") when she is under hypnosis and channels Svengali's musicality. The Svengali/Trilby comparison extended to rumors that Selznick, like Du Maurier's character, not only exerted close control over Jones but also put his female protégé/wife under hypnosis to elicit her performances. Circulating in the 1950s, the rumors were repeated in Jones's obituary in 2009, in which Bob Thomas quotes Rock Hudson, her costar in *A Farewell to Arms:* "I heard fantastic stories about this girl, that she was neurotic, temperamental, under hypnosis by Selznick. Not a word of truth in any of it. From the first take, she's been cooperative with everyone—except reporters."[22]

Nevertheless, it appears that hypnotism figured in Jones's approach to acting, as it also did in a likely cultural referent to Du Maurier's famous character, Jean-Martin Charcot, who used hypnosis to analyze and treat hysteria in the 1870s and 1880s at the Salpêtrière, a Parisian hospital for madwomen. In one of her rare fan magazine interviews, from 1947, Jones applies another cultural referent. She is quoted as comparing her mental state while acting to that of Eastern mystics, not psychologically disturbed women: "I sort of hypnotize myself. I find myself really living the roles I play. . . . I think that my own mental state is something like a trance when I'm acting. If anything else, any outside thought or impulse, disturbs the spell by intruding into my consciousness, I have to break off and start all over again."[23] This account of her acting technique seems normal and natural compared with much of what has been written about Jones and Selznick in their professional and personal life together.[24]

After putting him off for several years, Jones became contracted to Selznick personally in 1949, when she became the second Mrs. David O. Selznick. In that same year Louella Parsons refers to the Trilby/Svengali–esque nature of their relationship when she notes Jones's willingness to be dominated by a man she thinks "is a god, controlling not

FIGURE 55. David O. Selznick and Jennifer Jones, ca. 1950. Author's collection.

only her career, but her life, her laughter, and even her tears."[25] Until his death in 1965, Selznick's attention was completely focused on the task of guiding the career of the woman he loved and regarded as one of the industry's finest actresses.[26] He personally produced her vehicles *Since You Went Away, Duel in the Sun, Portrait of Jennie,* and *A Farewell to Arms.* In addition, he reshot and recut two of her films, Vittorio De Sica's *Terminal Station* for its release in the United States as *Indiscretion of an American Wife* (1954) and Michael Powell and Emeric Pressburger's *Gone to Earth,* turning it into the U.S. release *The Wild Heart* (1952). Not all of the films she made were financially lucrative or critically well-received, but by the end of her career Jones had worked with many important directors and amassed five Academy Award nominations and one win.[27] She was a star with major hits (as well as misses) and amassed an enviable track record of challenging and serious roles. However, Selznick's reputation for overly complex negotiations and compulsive meddling in productions, as well as Jones's high salary and her unwillingness to participate in selling a film, may have negatively impacted her choice of roles.[28]

Jones enjoyed script approval starting in 1947, and Selznick was in her corner. It follows that she could have exercised a tremendous degree of control over her film appearances, as Mary Pickford did. Although she was ambitious and hardworking, it does not appear that Jones was willing to claim ownership or direct influence over her career. Pickford readily admitted that United Artists was *her* idea. The producer's archived papers articulate a great respect for Jones's judgment in professional matters, but Selznick worried that Jones was too modest, with the result that she conveyed the impression that she was not up to certain roles.[29] In contrast, Mary Pickford was renowned for her business acumen and her savvy cultivation of a star image that made her creative control over her productions acceptable to a public that perceived her as juvenated. As I suggested in chapter 1, her publicity used her mother Charlotte as a cover so as not to put too much contradictory pressure on Pickford's screen persona of a feisty, though wistfully innocent, child-woman.

Whether Jones used Selznick as her own cover or surrogate for getting what she wanted, we do not know, but to shackle Jones's performances to Selznick as if only he were speaking through her is to negate the ambition and embodied creative power of the actress, qualities attested to on a number of occasions by her film collaborators.[30] Soon after their marriage, Selznick recorded his desire that Jones never be forced or even persuaded to play a role she was not completely enthusiastic about;[31] production records suggest that some of the roles she played, such as Catherine Barkley in *A Farewell to Arms* (1957) and Elizabeth Barrett in *The Barretts of Wimpole Street* (1957), were ones that she had long expressed an interest in playing, and she pursued some roles with an assertiveness that many accounts of her would make seem almost inconceivable.[32]

As complicated as the particulars of their relationship, professional and personal, may have been, we have only one side—Selznick's. He was an unusually prolific writer of memos and cables to colleagues and to his staff. While Selznick produced voluminous memos recording his ever-changing thoughts, Jones rarely gave interviews or asserted her opinions in public, whether during the height of her career or in the forty-four years she survived Selznick. In 1946 Selznick admitted to his staff that Jones was "a star who loathes publicity" in response to ongoing complaints from them regarding Jones's uncooperative attitude toward radio appearances, publicity junkets, interviews, and sitting for stills.[33]

At the same time, commentary by colleagues like directors John Cromwell and John Huston, as well as costars Shirley Temple and Joseph Cotten, contribute to the central role popular notions of neuroses and hysteria play in the dual biography of Selznick and Jones. Cromwell recounted of *Since You Went Away:* "David seemed to get even more *hysterical* during this picture than I heard he had been during *Gone with the Wind*. . . . [He] was totally *obsessed* by Jennifer. . . . David's *neurotic* courtship of Jennifer kept her in a state of mild *hysteria*."[34] Whether outrageously insensitive or cleverly perverse, Selznick decided to cast Jones's estranged husband, Robert Walker, as "Bill," Jane Hilton's doomed love interest in *Since You Went Away,* a decision that suggests something of the complex psychosexual contextualization of Jones's performances. Speaking about the production, costar Shirley Temple recalls, "On one occasion we two sisters were being filmed in bed, carrying on a sentimental dialogue about [the character played by Robert] Walker. Beyond expressing the required sentimentality of her lines, she [Jennifer Jones] wriggled under the sheets, a slight twisting and rolling of her hips. Suggestive movements really had no relationship to her specific lines, so at first I read this as simple scene stealing, ingenious at that. When the scene finished, however, she leaped from bed, burst into unrehearsed, copious sobbing, and fled to her dressing room."[35]

Forced to play romantic scenes with her estranged husband at the same time she was romantically involved with her producer, Jones was left "in a highly nervous state," according to costar Joseph Cotten.[36] Inside accounts (Temple, Cotten, Irene Selznick) of the development of the Selznick-Jones romantic relationship all agree: Selznick was sexually obsessed with Jones, losing all sense of judgment, driving everyone, most of all, Jones, to the brink of "hysteria."[37]

The actress's emotional fragility and her relationship to Selznick became linked as the primary thematic core of Jones's offscreen image, to the exclusion of virtually everything else, including her acting skill.[38] But star discourse that affiliated her offscreen self with nervousness, neuroses, and implications of psychological instability started almost at the beginning of her stardom. One of the first mainstream press assertions of Jones's mental fragility occurred in 1944, when *Time* reported that winning the Academy Award "was a severe personal jolt" to Jones, and "sudden success made her nervous at work and timid with autograph fans."[39] An article *in Photoplay* in 1947 refers to her "tenseness and reserve" and details how the "sensitive" star visibly trembles as she walks down the red carpet at premieres, as if enduring a gauntlet.[40] Another fan magazine noted that the star pulled out strands of hair from her head while being interviewed.[41] Selznick, it was sometimes suggested, gave Jones plenty of reasons to be insecure and nervous. His overbearing perfectionism and mania for controlling every detail of his personal productions is said to have extended into his personal life with Jones.[42] Jones went into analysis and sought out Carl Jung to help her understand why she did not want to marry Selznick.[43] Irene Selznick and biographers of Selznick and Jones all claim that Jones attempted suicide at least twice.[44]

Remarking about the star system in general, Edgar Morin once said, "The star is not only an actress. The characters she plays are not only isolated characters. The characters of her films infect the star. Reciprocally, the star herself infects these characters."[45] In the case of Jennifer Jones this phenomenon seems to work on a literal level, since "infection" aptly describes how Jones's characterizations came to be perceived in relation to her offscreen persona as an artistically serious but psychologically fragile actress paired with a domineering yet psychologically unpredictable man. The neuroses, nervousness, passivity, and insecurities attributed to Jones infected her juvenated characters with something resembling hysteria. The *Time* review of *Since You Went Away* noted that Jones rewarded her mentor (Selznick) "with a nervous, carefully studied, somewhat over intense performance."[46] When she was making *Duel in the Sun,* director King Vidor worried about the "strange tricks she did with her mouth."[47] Negative critical reception of Jones's performances increased in the late 1950s and early 1960s with critics using terms like "neurotic" and "hysterical" to describe her performances and calling attention to her "alarmingly sick [facial] tic," "hysterical laughter," and "grimaces."[48] Her performance as a schizophrenic socialite in *Tender Is the Night* elicited a backhanded compliment from one reviewer: "She is well cast as a neurotic and does her best work in a decade."[49]

If Jones was marked as psychologically fragile onscreen and off, Selznick's behaviors in the 1940s and 1950s showed that he was a man who was in deepening psychological trouble. In the early 1940s, depression (and the urging of his first wife) drove him into a yearlong stint in psychotherapy with Dr. May Romm. With classic Selznick arrogance he soon decided he knew more than she did, and she broke off his analysis.[50] However, Selznick's interest in psychoanalysis was fueled rather than quelled by this contact, and he invited Romm to serve as a consultant on the production of *Spellbound,* starring Ingrid Bergman as a repressed psychoanalyst who falls in love with a deeply disturbed man who may be a killer. Romm also served as therapist to Jennifer Jones and consulted on the actress's role in *Love Letters* as Victoria/Singleton, the amnesiac who is mistakenly thought to have murdered her husband.[51] Selznick's interest in psychoanalysis, his own psychological complexity, and his emotional and professional investment in Jones's stardom means that he must be addressed as a complicating presence relevant to the representation of hysterical juvenated femininity as a persistent trope in Jones's star persona.

In dealing with this complicated issue, I will contextualize Selznick's role in the authorship of Jones's film performances in light of other examples of powerful males who authored narratives centered on females, the latter of whom were presented as neurotic, hysterical, and performative: Charcot and "Augustine," Sigmund Freud and "Dora," and the fictional Svengali and Trilby. Taking these male-authored narratives of female hysteria as a model will help us to understand how hysteria as an intersubjective "psychology of two" comes to be acted out in Jones's screen performances.[52] This model, comparable to the process of transference, allows for a consideration of the staging of male hysteria through the figure of the adolescent female that holds center stage in Jones's film melodramas. To consider Selznick and Jones together in this process is to suggest that a "psychology of two" unveils the complex intersection of film performance, textuality, and authorship that cannot be separated from Jones's melodramatic impersonations of becoming woman.

## THE ADOLESCENT VISIONARY: OBSCENE HYSTERIC OR CHASTE MYSTIC?

Reference to psychoanalysis and psychoanalytic concepts proliferated in American public discourse in the 1940s. This occurred partially in response to concerns about the psychological impact of World War II on American GIs.[53] The so-called psychoneurotic soldier was a national concern referenced in a number of films during and after the war, including *Since You Went Away,* Jones's second major film appearance. The film shows a psychiatrist treating a sailor physically and psychologically immobilized by guilt over his brother's death. However, the presence of a psychoanalyst was not a necessary precondition for a film's discursive alignment with psychoanalytic thought. Nor was a contemporary setting required, as demonstrated by the referencing of psychoanalysis to explain the religious visions of Bernadette Soubirous in *The Song of Bernadette,* set in 1858.

Franz Werfel's book, the basis of the screenplay, includes a chapter titled "Psychiatry Takes a Hand," which describes various "psychiatrists" and "neurologists" who examine Bernadette.[54] In the film these psychiatrists and neurologists are condensed into the town's lone physician, Dr. Dozous (Lee J. Cobb), who delivers his diagnosis of the visionary girl's apparent normality to Lourdes officials. In spite of this declaration, the difficulty of distinguishing hysteria from religious mysticism underscores the narrative, and, following Werfel's novel, the film's screenplay offers an explanation of Saint Bernadette's visions that references the crucial role that adolescent hysteria played in the origins of psychoanalytic thought.[55]

In the late nineteenth century Charcot, Freud, and Joseph Breuer often treated women and adolescent females who were thought to suffer from hysteria, a spectacularly physical or performative illness.[56] They did not dismiss hysteria as a female-specific malady, as many of their predecessors and contemporaries did, but Charcot gendered the phenomenon by making great distinctions between the causes of male and female hysteria; he always viewed the disease as primarily neurological.[57] He used hypnosis, regarded as rather disreputable, as a clinical procedure to reproduce states of hysteria for improved scientific analysis, and hysterical subjects (especially women) were objectified through a variety of modes of representation.[58] Charcot favored photography as the best way to arrest and catalog the symptoms of hysteria rushing across the body.[59] Nevertheless, this visual technology of mechanical reproduction could not guarantee objectivity, and Charcot was accused of coaching his patients to elicit their mysterious or obscene behavior.

Most famous among the hysterical patients that Charcot photographed was the pseudonymous "Augustine," a working-class female who came to Salpêtrière in 1875. Augustine entered the hospital as a prepubescent fifteen-year-old, before her first menstruation, but she was not a virgin: her stepfather had raped her.[60] In the many photographs Charcot had taken of her, Augustine often appears on her hospital bed, her rounded, youthful body barely covered by a loose nightgown; the camera captures various forms of her contorted or erotically coded physicality that Charcot identified with predictable stages of the disease.[61] Augustine was accused of acting, of creating dramatic performances of hysteria that drew on preexistent cultural signs from the stage, paintings, or religious iconography associated with distressed femininity.[62] She was certainly Charcot's most cooperatively performative and photogenic patient—until she ran away in the guise of a man in 1880.[63]

In one of the most famous of the photographs of her—captioned, "Attitudes passionnelles: Supplication amoureuse"—Augustine looks up with her hands placed together as if in prayer, but rather than religious visions, the girl's supplication is described by Charcot as her calling upon an invisible male lover.[64] Charcot notes that Augustine's entreaties were followed by her lying down and expressing erotic signs of "possession and satisfied desire. . . . Then come little cries, smiles, movements of the pelvis, words of desire of encouragement." [65] Religious visions, erotic deliria, the conflation of radically different emotions into one visible symptom ("ataxia"), and attacks of paralysis or physical contortion were all thought by Charcot to be typical of hysteria. For hysterical conversion to link religious imagery to sexual fantasy was not unprecedented or even unusual. In the history of the Catholic faith, accounts of divine favor in women mystics were commonly asserted through their curative powers and holy revelations, but also in trances and physical symptoms, from stigmata to ecstasies that were represented as bodily communication with Jesus, as either a man or a child.[66] Cristina Mazzoni notes, "The common discourse of religion and sex defines both of them as essentially mystical, as desiring an object (be it the propagation of the species or the attainment of the absolute ideal) that is essentially beyond the self."[67]

*The Song of Bernadette* also links adolescence to the somatic symptomatology of hysterical conversion and religious experience. The film uses visual argument to suggest that the spiritual visions of Bernadette may be a conversion of unconscious conflict based on adolescent sexual awakening. In the opening scene the camera views the night sky, reframing to reveal Bernadette sleeping in bed. Camera movement then shows the rest of the family sleeping within a one-room hovel, an abandoned jail, where they have been forced to live. This shot sets up the film's contrast between the heavens, associated with eternity and God, and Bernadette in her bed, an asthmatic child in a family barely surviving at the margins of society. This scene may suggest that Bernadette is a spiritual bridge between heaven and earth, but to focus on the girl in her bed is an overdetermined trope, with inescapable connotations of both illness and sexuality, that will be featured in a number of Jones's films (including *Since You Went Away, Gone to Earth,* and *Duel in the Sun*). It is a trope that surely has no equivalent in films of the time about adolescent males.

In both Werfel's novel and the film, Bernadette's mother (Anne Revere) links her daughter's religious visions to the physiological and psychological changes of puberty: "Girls your age often see things that aren't there, but it passes." In the mid-nineteenth century, puberty was regarded as "one of the most psychologically dangerous periods in the female life-cycle," with one British doctor calling female adolescence a "miniature insanity" that could completely change obedient girls into deceitful, promiscuous, and unhappy human beings.[68] By the 1940s, the view that adolescent females were creatures troubled by their emerging sexuality still had currency: a teenager quivering in the sexual overdrive of puberty might be unable to distinguish between fantasy and reality, with hysterical fabulation as the result.

The conflation of religion and sexuality is also illuminated by Julia Kristeva's notion of the "idealizing course of adolescent drives": the adolescent is the ultimate model of the person of faith because he or she is capable of being "enthralled by the absolute" and, like the religious believer, has a "passion for the object relation."[69] This does not explain adolescent hysterical fabulation, but it does explain the close relationship between the adolescent's fanatical investment in the ideal object and religious belief that underscores *The Song of Bernadette.* Bernadette's first vision occurs when she accompanies her sister, Marie (Ermadean Walters), and a female friend in gathering wood around the Lourdes dump, near the Massabielle cave. She falls behind because of her asthma and is sitting alone when the wind stirs. She shyly looks up; a heavenly light illuminates her face. She sees "the lady" in the grotto above the cave and takes out her rosary to imitate the woman's actions. Bernadette's companions call her. The girls see her from a distance across a pond. After Bernadette regains a sense of her surroundings, her friend Jeanne Abadie (Mary Anderson) asks why she was lingering: "Was somebody with you in that cave? . . . Oh, somebody was and you were praying for forgiveness."

Jeanne Abadie thinks that her friend has had a sexual encounter. Sex at a remote location followed by a teenager feeling regret would have been familiar in the 1940s as characteristic of sexual delinquency. In

FIGURE 56. Bernadette (Jennifer Jones) sees "the lady" for the first time in *The Song of Bernadette*. Author's collection.

Bernadette's case the situation is much more complicated. She may have experienced a heavenly visitation. Her family is disbelieving, and the authorities suspect some kind of mental problem or a hoax intended to help her destitute family. If the latter, Bernadette would not have been the first young woman whose celestial vision offered her something better than poverty, inequality, and an early death.[70]

Bernadette's parents find her embarrassing, not unlike the unhappy parents of bobby-soxers in film comedies of the 1940s. As discussed in chapter 3, bobby-soxers were middle-class white teenagers thought to be obsessed with swing music, "jive talk," and exploring their budding sexuality by stealthily circumventing parental authority. Bobby-soxer comedies became the primary venue in 1940s Hollywood film for expressing anxiety about adolescent female sexuality. Paradigmatic of the popular culture treatment of this phenomenon was the tremendously popular *Kiss and Tell*, which started as a play and then became a popular radio

FIGURE 57. Bernadette's father (Roman Bohnen) comforts his daughter (Jennifer Jones) as she yearns to see "the lady" in *The Song of Bernadette*. Author's collection.

program, a film (dir. Richard Wallace, 1945), and a television series. The plot focuses on bobby-soxer Corliss Archer (Shirley Temple in the film), whose parents are convinced (erroneously, of course) that their sexually precocious teenage daughter, who craves the company of soldiers, has become pregnant out of wedlock.

Although *The Song of Bernadette* does not seek, as Charcot did, to medicalize the experience of female religious visionaries and consign saints to the category of "hysterics," it seems to be contaminated by hysteria and its "natural" association with femininity and adolescence. In contrast with Augustine's spectacularly lewd "amorous supplications" that imitated the eroticized physicality of some female visionary mystics, Bernadette's visits to the lady are constructed as supplications notable for the girl's physical reserve and shyness.[71] Yet the film does not quite trust viewers to believe in the truth of Bernadette's visions without visual proof. The "lady" she sees in the grotto is shown several times to the audience to confirm that what Bernadette sees is based on real perception, not hysterical hallucination. Bernadette's parents forbid her to return to Massabielle after the threats of local authorities and her collapse at the dump site (which leads her mother to think her asthma has killed her).

FIGURE 58. Madame Soubirous (Anne Revere) and her daughter (Jennifer Jones) in *The Song of Bernadette*. Author's collection.

In response Bernadette cries herself to sleep every night and stops eating, behaviors that would not be out of place in bobby-soxer comedies.

Part of this film's hysterical edge is created by the insistent equation of religion and sexuality. Bernadette never claims to see anything but a lady, but others insist her visions are of the Virgin Mary. If this vision is a communication from heaven, the female intercessor has to be worthy, pure, chaste.[72] The natural order for girls of her class must be altered. To her mother Bernadette is a "big girl" who can still be cradled, but she tells her daughter she will soon be a woman who will marry and have a family. As belief in Bernadette's claims grows, her priest, Father Peyramale (Charles Bickford), tells her that she must choose God—as he has chosen her. She must become a nun. Through spiritual obedience that renounces her sexuality and consecrates her body to God, Bernadette demonstrates that she is extraordinary, that, indeed, she is a worthy intermediary between heaven and earth instead of a hysteric.[73]

Bernadette's choice between two irreconcilable paths is a typical melodramatic conceit. Many film melodramas of the 1940s like *Daisy Kenyon* (dir. Otto Preminger, 1947) focus on a female protagonist who must choose between lovers. Bernadette will not have the simple life of a married peasant woman anticipated as a possibility by her mother and the many acts of sympathetic interest and quiet devotion of her handsome young neighbor, Antoine (William Eythe). Continuing to visually reinforce the idea of the conversion of sexual energy into spiritual events, the film depicts the emergence of the spring that will make Lourdes the world-famous site of healing miracles by showing the water as a stream that trickles under the hand of Antoine as he sits contemplating Bernadette and the strange occurrences at Massabielle. That very afternoon she was led away to the laughter of the crowds after groveling in the dirt and eating weeds—in obedience to her visions.

Through such means *The Song of Bernadette* offers visual strategies that suggest that the religious visions of the teenager are a compromise, an unconscious, hysterical substitution for heterosexual desire. Bernadette chooses her visions instead of Antoine. Through her love for the lady, Bernadette participates in a religious rearticulation of the pre-Oedipal attachment to the maternal. There is no veneration of Christ by the girl who, in confirmation classes, did not know what the Holy Trinity is. The displacement of Bernadette's sexuality onto this mother/child, female-female relationship juvenates her even more. It is given its most melodramatic representation in the final scene of the film when Bernadette is on her deathbed, a victim of painful tuberculosis of the bone. Illness and eroticism merge through the rhetoric of melodrama and the trope of the bed-bound female. An unseen priest (exactly who is speaking is not clear) recites verses from the Old Testament's Song of Solomon, chapter 2 ("Arise my love, my fair one, and come away"). This is a strange substitute for the traditional rites of extreme unction. Through the recitation of verses from Song of Solomon, Bernadette's reunion with "the lady" in death is eroticized as a substitute for the heterosexual relations she sacrificed in life. Nevertheless, visual treatment tends to undercut this eroticization. Bernadette moves forward to her vision of the lady and then falls back on the pillow. Viewed in close-up, she now looks like an asexual child. Her head has fallen to the side. She wears a white, pleated cap and is surrounded by white. There is a slight smile on her face. Father Peyramale declares that her life will now begin. Bernadette has achieved her beatitude.

In spite—or, perhaps, because—of the rather unusual religious subject matter represented by the story of a visionary teenager, *The Song of Bernadette* struck a chord with wartime audiences.[74] The film reflected the country's understandable preoccupation with faith and the meaning of sacrifice in the midst of a war that impacted the collective national consciousness. It also traded on the interest in adolescent femininity in the United States that had been building since the late 1930s in Hollywood film, albeit primarily in lighter film fare. While *The Song of Bernadette* raises sexually based adolescent hysteria as an explanation for its protagonist's visions only to turn it aside again and again, this is just the first of Jones's three wartime melodramas that seek to explain behavior that looks hysterical in ways derived from psychoanalysis.

## HYSTERICAL ADOLESCENCE ON THE HOME FRONT

Like *The Song of Bernadette* Jones's next film, *Since You Went Away,* demonstrates that anxiety-driven bobby-soxer comedy was not Hollywood's only approach to adolescent female sexuality in the 1940s. Positive portrayals of the contemporary American way of life were demanded of Hollywood during the war years to lift national morale and reassure the Allies. However, a film intended to be uplifting and a positive reinforcement of conservative values might also reflect a considerable amount of anxiety regarding juvenated femininity.

Selznick quickly sought to distance Jones from her award-winning role as Bernadette. He told Darryl F. Zanuck that he was casting Jones as a seventeen-year-old high school girl in his personal production of *Since You Went Away,* to prove that the actress "is an extremely attractive young American girl not to be classified as simply a gawky, young, one-part character actress."[75] *Since You Went Away,* a home-front melodrama, was definitely a "woman's picture," with a strong core of female actors and a focus on their domestic and emotional concerns.[76] The film details the triumphs and tragedies of the Hiltons, mother Anne (Claudette Colbert) and her two teenage daughters, Jane (Jones) and Brig (Shirley Temple), as they cope with the war's impact, including the absence of the husband/father, who has been called to duty. The melodrama opens with a nighttime shot of their substantial upper-middle-class home accompanied by the intertitle: "This is a story of the Unconquerable Fortress: the American Home . . . 1943." Within such an idealistic framework, how was anxiety over the sexuality of female adolescents expressed in a melodrama claiming to reflect contemporary social reality?

FIGURE 59. Publicity shot of Jennifer Jones in costume for *Since You Went Away* (dir. John Cromwell, 1944). Courtesy of the David O. Selznick Collection, Harry Ransom Humanities Center, University of Texas, Austin.

Selznick wrote the screenplay in addition to producing Jones's second major film outing. He extensively built up the sympathetic role of Jane Hilton for his protégé. To help him shape the roles of the two teenage sisters in the film, Selznick brought in playwright F. Hugh Herbert, who created the country's most famous fictional bobby-soxer, Corliss Archer, and would pen numerous successful stage plays and film scripts focused on teenage girls as sex-teases.[77] Herbert was one of the culture industry's prime purveyors of the stereotype of the bobby-soxer as a perverse mix of sexual aggression and naivety, or as Corliss Archer was described at the time, "a strange and rather delightful mixture of child, woman, and she-devil."[78] Perhaps reflecting Herbert's influence on

FIGURE 60. Jane Hilton (Jennifer Jones) and other girls arrive at a soldiers' dance in *Since You Went Away.* Author's collection.

Selznick's screenplay, *Since You Went Away* perpetuates the stereotypes that one teenager bemoaned in a letter to *Seventeen* magazine: "some of these so-called magazines for the high school crowd . . . either have us in . . . pigtails . . . or seated at a bar in some swanky night club, fluttering false eyelashes at some Navy lieutenant."[79]

*Since You Went Away* sustains a similar bifurcated stereotype, one that resembles a hysterical division or disassociation between feminine identities by the fact that both types are placed within one character—Jane Hilton. Early in the film, Jane is put to bed by Fedelia, the family's domestic (Hattie McDaniel). With her hair in pigtails Jane clings to Fedelia's arm and softly bids her goodnight in a childish voice. In another scene, however, Jane is accused by her younger sister, Brig, of being "crazy about uniforms" when Jane, dreamily looking away from a card game, warms to the idea of taking in an officer as a boarder. She is recruited to attend a soldiers' dance and arrives, along with other young women, on the back of a truck. Greeted by the wolf whistles of servicemen, Jane ignores the throng of GIs. She flirts ineptly at the dance with her mother's former beau, Tony Willett (Joseph Cotten), an artist turned navy lieutenant.

Largely played for humor, Jane's feelings toward Tony are in keeping with the movies' stereotypical depiction of bobby-soxers' sexual impulsivity and the "false dawn" of teenage crushes.[80] The age difference between Jane and Tony is brought home in a good-bye scene before he leaves for duty. Sexuality and illness again merge around the trope of the girl-becoming-woman in bed. Jane is sick and confined to her bed. "Why do we children have mumps?" she moans on hearing her mother's diagnosis. When Tony knocks on her bedroom door and insists on saying good-bye, she wraps up her face (in a close-up) and tries to hide under the covers; she declares she looks "terrible." He says he loves her, and she perks up, interpreting this as adult desire, but he quickly adds, "from the moment you were born." "That's all," she sighs. She pouts when he predicts she will fall in love while he's gone. He kisses her forehead and declares that he wishes he were seventeen. Jane bursts into tears (in close-up).

In spite of the humor created at the teenager's expense, the scene is a reminder of the central role Oedipal fantasy would come to hold in Freud's mature theorization of hysteria. Jane places Tony in the imaginary position of the incestuous father, but Tony maintains the boundary that keeps Jane in her taboo place as the child who could have been his ("from the moment you were born"). It is yet one of a number of sexually charged but nevertheless "benign" bedroom interactions of a father and daughter in Hollywood film of the studio era, not only in bobby-soxer comedies but also, as we saw in chapter 3, offered with considerable erotic complication in Deanna Durbin's *Three Smart Girls*.[81]

What is Jane's sexuality? She has some qualities of the bobby-soxer, but these are held in check. Unlike Corliss Archer and other film bobby-soxers, like Susan Turner (Shirley Temple) in *The Bachelor and the Bobbysoxer* (dir. Irving Reis, 1947), Jane is not sexually aggressive. Rather than being insensitive and cruel, she is sensitive and empathetic. Her interest in officers is never shown entering the territory of the war years' other most anxiety-ridden stereotype of youthful femininity: the notorious "V-girl." These were identified as young women who raised the morale of the armed forces by making themselves sexually available to men in uniform.[82] Schoolgirls were not excluded: an article in *Reader's Digest* in 1943, "Trouble on the Street Corners," claimed, "Good-time girls of high school age are the army's biggest problem today as a potential source of venereal disease."[83] The idea of the adolescent female becoming a sexual delinquent pursuing erotic pleasure became a cultural nightmare, and, as Rachel Devlin notes, "the influence of the psychoanalytic paradigm for understanding female delinquency can hardly be overstated."[84]

A V-girl reference is made late in *Since You Went Away* in a climactic scene that suggests both the fear of the war's impact on adolescent female sexuality and the performance of emotion that would fuel critical perception of Jones's acting style as "intense" or "neurotic." Jane is shown resolutely coping with the death of her fiancé, Bill, who has been killed in the Allied campaign in Italy. She works as a nurse's aide at a government hospital, scrubbing bed frames, handing out ice cream, assisting physicians, and taking wheelchair-bound men into the sunshine. Emily Hawkins (Agnes Moorehead), a friend of Jane's mother, criticizes the idea of a "well-bred single girl" doing the kind of work that would put her in "intimate" contact with men of all sorts. Responding to her, Jane is shown in a reverse shot that resembles the full shot that served to introduce her at the beginning of the film. In that scene a star entrance featured Jane center frame and then moved into a close-up of her as she searched her mother's face for reactions to the departure of Jane's father for war duty. In that scene she was quietly intuitive. Here, Jane's emotionally charged anger offers an unusually frank acknowledgment of the V-girl phenomenon for a Hollywood film: "Don't worry, we're not V-girls, we're simply helping with the wreckage." She then laughs (in a high pitch that is almost a sob) and declares with a smirk and in a voice dripping with sarcasm that she and her younger sister are going to go play with their dolls. Brig leads her away.

The almost simultaneous laughter, sobbing, sarcasm, and emotional vulnerability in Jones's performance suggest the extreme emotional fluidity and temporal urgency of hysterical *ataxia*.[85] Robert Lang has called Jones's acting style "unique," describing it as "exquisitely controlled, hard-working, self-regarding and phony, and yet utterly sincere. The actress, perhaps like no other, achieves conviction through a kind of absolute intensity, in highly mannered displays of Hollywood acting conventions."[86] "Highly mannered displays" that are "phony, and yet utterly sincere" could be used to describe Hollywood melodramas in the 1940s in general, and Jones's intense, self-referential acting style was compatible with the genre at this historical moment.

The V-girl may be referenced as an outrageous effrontery to Jane's altruistic commitment to the war wounded, but the teenager's response becomes more melodramatic and hysterical, in part, because references to wartime's impact on young people's sexuality are so muted in the rest of the film. A rare reference is an earlier comic bit at the train station,

FIGURE 61. *Since You Went Away,* a film meant to mirror "perfectly the thoughts and feelings of the bulk of feminine America." Brig (Shirley Temple), Tony (Joseph Cotten), and Jane (Jennifer Jones). Author's collection.

where a soldier is shown bidding good-bye, with the exact same declaration of love, to a series of different young women. Dances, cocktail bars, and downtown streets at night are shown filled with young people, but erotic experimentation so feared at the time is almost completely disavowed. Jane's sister, Brig, is absolutely uninterested in "boys." Instead, she is preoccupied with helping the war effort, improving the social skills of her best girlfriend, and keeping the family's crotchety boarder, Colonel Smollett (Monty Woolley), happy. In constructing Brig's relationship to Col. Smollett, the film plays on the familiar sight of Temple cosseting an older man, albeit in a more restrained way.

Of course, the Selznick production was not meant to be an exposé of youthful sexual experimentation. It was designed to appeal to and flatter the large female audiences that dominated wartime movie theaters. Selznick described the film for his publicity department: "We think it mirrors perfectly the thoughts and feelings of the bulk of feminine America in these times. The story of you and yours in these times."[87] No other Hollywood woman's picture of the time is more carefully constructed as a tribute to the female-centered family than *Since You Went Away.* In keeping with the film's faith in American womanhood, Jane is shown transcending adolescent female stereotypes and the inscription of a teenager in the grip of a hysteric division of personality (child/woman). Jane's path to adulthood is maturation into civic-minded seriousness rather than release into pleasure-seeking irresponsibility. As a young sailor (Guy Madison) at the bowling alley says to Bill: "I know she's a nice girl. Anyone can see that."

Representing sweetness, sympathy, and understanding, Jane embodies an idealized view of young American women as healers and helpmates to men in an era in which home-front adolescents were, in the words of one, actually learning a much different set of values—"fear, hate and prejudice"—from newsreels, print media, school, and home.[88] In the film's last scene Jane is shown promising to write a serviceman who has been cured of psychoneurosis and is going back into battle. Resembling *The Song of Bernadette* in its emphasis on the healing power of an adolescent femininity that, at times, may appear hysterical, *Since You Went Away* ultimately redeems that femininity from hysteria and sexual delinquency to uphold wartime ideological imperatives and affirm the traditional role that women of all ages were told they would have to play in the postwar healing of the country—and the world.[89]

## HYSTERIA AND THE ADOLESCENT OTHER

Two models of femininity are frequently separated and regarded as antagonistic: the sexually inexperienced "innocent" and the dark sensual "Other." This was evident in star construction in the 1910s, when Mary Pickford represented the former, and Theda Bara, "The Queen of Vampires," represented the latter. Jones's screen persona was an important bridge between these two models. In her postwar films Jones's heroines frequently are identified as clearly adolescent or as women who are juvenated by their sexual inexperience. Yet her heroines also are often unequivocally seductive, attempting consciously or unconsciously, to eroticize their contact with others. One such scene is played for fun in Ernst Lubitsch's comedy *Cluny Brown,* when a plumber's niece, the eponymous heroine (Jones), answers a call to fix a stopped-up drain in an upper-class London apartment. Using unorthodox techniques, she fixes the problem. Slightly tipsy after she drinks a celebratory cocktail, she stretches out on the couch and imitates a Persian cat. The upper-class men are mesmerized by her, yet she seems completely unaware of her erotic impact on them.[90] Her uncle (Billy Bevan) interrupts the

FIGURE 62. An orphan (Jennifer Jones) who is passionate about plumbing cannot seem to learn her place in *Cluny Brown* (dir. Ernst Lubitsch, 1946). Author's collection.

scene. He decides to send Cluny away to be a domestic at a country manor because she obviously needs to learn "her place."

In this film and several of her postwar melodramas Jones embodies a sensual, eroticized femininity associated with "Otherness." Her protagonists frequently struggle with reactions to their lowly class origins, as in *Madame Bovary, Duel in the Sun, Ruby Gentry, Gone to Earth,* and *Carrie,* or with the social meaning attached to their racial difference, as in *Duel in the Sun* and *Love Is a Many-Splendored Thing,* but those reactions and meanings are always inseparable from their gender.[91] That struggle is central in their attempt to define and express their sexuality in the process of becoming a woman and, like Cluny Brown, find an identity in the world that moves beyond what others think their "place" should be.

Jones's postwar performances embodied the psychological complexities and sensuality of especially youthful femininity. In all but a handful of her star vehicles, her screen femininity was affiliated with moral innocence, sexual inexperience, and other qualities associated with juvenation, including psychological processes aligned with adolescence.[92] Unlike Jones's wartime films, her representation of femininity in postwar films is more centrally related to the signs of hysteria, with unusual levels of emotional urgency and physical vitality acted out by her characters. Jones's films are not merely about romantic love but the pain of attempting to discover what desire is. That desire is infected by hysterical anxiety, urgency, and the performance of sensuality as a substitute for sexuality. This, I would argue, is hysteria, with apparent sexual conflict intensified by its alignment in Jones's films with other types of conflict, often motivated by her characters' Otherness, inscribed as marginal class or racial/ethnic status.

In the process we see Jones's characters embody, melodramatically and hysterically, the transformation of the juvenated female into desiring—and suffering—adult femininity. In spite of gaining sexual experience, her characters are frequently left without a sexually coherent identity. The result is that it is impossible for Jones's heroines to achieve a meaningful womanhood: they either experience a kind of death in life in which they become genderless, are robbed of desire (as in *Ruby Gentry*), or die (as in *Duel in the Sun* and *Gone to Earth*). Often the heroine's unhappy end is signaled from the very beginning of the film: in *Gone to Earth* the opening scene shows Hazel Woodus (Jones) running furiously across the Welsh countryside as she tries to save her pet fox from the hunters and their hounds. This is turn-of-the-century Wales, and Hazel is a wild country girl, eighteen years old and part gypsy. Her character and the setting might initially seem reminiscent of Pickford's hoydens, but the scene is visualized in expressionist terms, the mood anxious, with the musical score contributing to the sense of life-threatening urgency. Hazel breathlessly enters her father's hovel and slams the door shut. She is framed within the sides of a coffin her father is building, one of his many odd jobs, including beekeeping and harping. The framing signals that Hazel's fate is already sealed. By the close of this sequence, the film has enmeshed the viewer in an atmosphere of anxious excitability, Oedipal fixation, and sexual ambivalence, all characteristic of hysteria. At the end of the film Hazel will once again try to save the fox from the hunters; she will fall (or leap) to her death into an abandoned mine shaft.

The presentation of hysteria in melodramas like *Duel in the Sun* and *Gone to Earth* revolves around an adolescent female; in other Jones films, like *Ruby Gentry* and *Madame Bovary,* the actress plays a young, sexually inexperienced woman who is not in her teens but whose sexual identity remains juvenated because it is rooted in adolescent psychic structures. Those structures are described by Julia Kristeva as a "syndrome of ideality" frequently subject to a crisis that takes the form of "the fantasy of an absolute Object as well as of the fantasy of its venge-

FIGURE 63. Hazel Woodus (Jennifer Jones) runs from the hunters in *Gone to Earth* (dir. Michael Powell and Emeric Pressburger, 1950). Author's collection.

ful destruction."[93] Unless sublimated and stabilized, this "propensity for belief" moves the adolescent along a path on which "the passion for the object relation is reversed, giving way to punishment and self-punishment," including somatic forms of destruction (as the conclusions of all these films suggest).[94]

Jones's heroines typically must deal with the dangers of sexual awakening, including but not limited to the dangerous oscillations of sadism and masochism lurking in adolescent ideation. Often these dangers are inscribed in ways that recall Joan Copjec's explanation of the meaning of innocence and seduction in melodrama: "The stereotypes of innocent, pre-Raphaelite virgins and fiendish rakes who take advantage of them are evidence that melodrama . . . is concerned with specularizing justice in a world which is unsure what justice should look like."[95] Justice proves elusive for Jones's characters in her postwar films.

Sometimes, the female forces the issue. In *Ruby Gentry,* Ruby Corey (Jones) is a lower-class white girl of the North Carolina backcountry. After an introduction that shows her in the present as an androgynous, gaunt, and aged figure, we see her in a flashback as she waits for her former high school love, just returned from a five-year absence. A son of Old South aristocracy, Boake Tackman (Charlton Heston) shows up for a hunting party at the run-down "lodge" of Ruby's father (Tom Tully). The sexual attraction is still there, expressed in physically aggressive, teasing behaviors. Their interaction is fraught with class tensions, as well as sexual antagonism. They renew the relationship, but Boake announces he is marrying a moneyed woman and there will be no place for Ruby in his life except as a backstreet lover. Ruby refuses. She marries a rich, older man. When she is widowed, Ruby uses her husband's financial power to ruin all the men in her town who, she says, "tramped up and down over my life."[96] Disaster ensues for Ruby after she offers Boake the gift of *not* ruining him if he will come back to her. He refuses. She floods his land with salt water. He then rapes her in her childhood bedroom. In a hallucinatory final scene, they go hunting in the swamp, and Boake is shot down by Ruby's brother.

The mimicking of the man's desire through seductive female behavior is particularly significant in hysteria. Seen in this light, Jones's performances in *Ruby Gentry* and *Duel in the Sun* may be used to complicate Mulvey's view of the de-eroticization of film melodrama's female protagonists. Mulvey claims that the norms of cinematic voyeurism are violated because "the melodramatic symptom tends to de-eroticise its female spectacle."[97] She does not explain exactly how this happens, but the question of what mid-twentieth-century film melodrama, especially that aimed primarily at women, does with the erotic spectacle of its female protagonists is worth reexamining. Could hysterical symptoms *eroticize* rather than de-eroticize the juvenated female as a cinematic spectacle in female-centered melodrama, as they seem to do in many of Jones's films? If so, what might this do to the pleasures of cinematic spectatorship? To answer these questions, I will look at Jones's most important and controversial postwar melodrama, *Duel in the Sun.*

## *DUEL IN THE SUN*: SEX, MELODRAMA, HYSTERIA

The public perception of Jones's screen persona would be forever changed with her appearance in *Duel in the Sun,* a sprawling, multi-star western epic and family melodrama. The Selznick production was Jones's fifth major film release (started before but released after the comedy *Cluny Brown*). One of the most controversial Hollywood features released in the immediate postwar era, it was notorious for its sexual content, as well as for its extraordinarily difficult production history.[98] It was denounced on the floor of the U.S. Congress by ultraconservative Senator John Rankin: "Hollywood commentators and critics refer to *Duel in the Sun* as stark realism—It is stark murder! It is stark horror! It is stark depravity! It is stark filth!"[99] Rankin was joined in expressions of outrage by censorship boards, religious leaders, and civic organizations; ridicule was heaped on the film before and after its release. In spite of largely negative response, however, *Duel in the Sun* was a box-office sensation; it went on to become one of the highest grossing westerns of all time.[100]

*Duel in the Sun* was produced and written by Selznick, who contemplated calling the film "Arizona Appassionales" or "Desert Appassionales," unusual titles both reminiscent of Charcot's labeling of the particularly seductive phase of female hysteria.[101] The film was a prototype for the female-centered western of the 1950s, and Niven Busch, the author of the original novel on which the film was based, became a key screenwriter in Hollywood's creation of highly Freudian/psychoanalytic westerns in the postwar years. Many of these, like *Pursued, The Furies, Johnny Guitar,* and *Rancho Notorious,* refocused the traditionally male genre onto women.[102]

Of all of Jones's films, *Duel in the Sun* is most often mentioned as constructing her screen persona to satisfy male erotic fantasies. David Thomson tells the story that Selznick was to the side of the camera engaged in heavy breathing during the shooting of love scenes, and Otto Friedrich discusses the first Mrs. Selznick dealing with the predictions that the film, starring her rival, was virtually "pornographic."[103] Molly Haskell describes Jones in this film as "suggesting not so much a woman as a walking libido" that confirms "women's worst fears of men's most lubricious fantasies."[104]

The film tells the story of an "Indian half breed," Pearl Chavez (Jones). Originally twelve at the beginning of Busch's novel, Pearl is depicted as a teenager in the film. In the first scene of the flashback (after the legend establishing her death), Pearl witnesses her father (Herbert Marshall), a Creole gambler, kill her Indian/mestizo mother (Tilly Losch) and her mother's lover (Sidney Blackmer) when he finds them in flagrante delicto. Pearl's father is sent to the gallows. In the next scene Pearl journeys to live with a tremendously wealthy but emotionally dysfunctional ranching family headed by a racist patriarch, Sen. Jackson McCanles (Lionel Barrymore). Pearl's father wanted her raised by McCanles's wife, Laura Belle (Lillian Gish), a woman he loved and lost. In spite of Laura Belle's best efforts, Pearl is alternately treated at the McCanles

FIGURE 64. Pearl Chavez (Jennifer Jones), a dark, working-class, hysterical heroine. Courtesy of the David O. Selznick Collection, Harry Ransom Center for the Humanities, University of Texas, Austin.

ranch as a racial and social inferior (not allowed to live in the house) or a member of the family (groomed and outfitted in virginal white for a public dance). The gentle McCanles son, Jesse (Joseph Cotten), loves Pearl, but she is forced into sex by the younger son, the spoiled and charismatic Lewt (Gregory Peck), whose "girl" Pearl becomes after Jesse rejects her, presuming she has made her "choice." Lewt turns outlaw and leaves. Pearl accepts the marriage proposal of a kind middle-aged rancher, Sam Pierce (Charles Bickford). The night before their marriage, Lewt guns down Sam in cold blood. Pearl decides to kill Lewt, but she succumbs to his seductive entreaties. Not until Lewt attempts to kill Jesse can Pearl resist him sexually. Her resolve set, she departs to hunt him down at his hideout at Squaw's Head Rock. Their "duel in the sun," mixing hate and love, ends with Pearl crawling up a mountain to die in Lewt's arms after they have fatally shot one another.

*Duel in the Sun* is Jones's best-known film and one of few of her star vehicles that have achieved any attention in film studies. Laura Mulvey reads *Duel in the Sun* from a feminist perspective, as a film in which "a woman central protagonist is shown to be unable to achieve a stable sexual identity, torn between the deep blue sea of femininity and the devil of regressive masculinity."[105] She argues that Pearl's identification is divided between eroticized femininity and active, phallic masculinity. Mulvey's analysis is extremely helpful in calling attention to the basic melodramatic division in the film's construction of its female protagonist; however, in spite of the obvious similarities between the oscillation she describes and discussions of hysteria, she does not mention the latter, perhaps in an attempt to avoid the political difficulty of using a term sometimes regarded as anachronistic or imposing patriarchal discursive and diagnostic control over women. Nor does she actually address how the film, beyond elements of the plot's representation of male/female as active/passive, actually presents an instability of female identity that she says oscillates or "splits" or what it might mean to be "torn between . . . femininity and . . . regressive masculinity." Mulvey also does not address Pearl's juvenation, Jones's star performance, or the melodramatic textual/visual arguments made in *Duel in the Sun.*

Hysterics, according to Freud and some contemporary psychoanalysts, experience the central hysterical dilemma of identification because they have not resolved their Oedipal conflict. They are locked into a problem of identification centering on the issue: "Am I a man or am I a woman?" This is a confusion of gender and sexuality based on identification with both sexes at one time and the wish to simultaneously occupy and act on both identifications. This hysterical identification resonates with the modern psychoanalytic definition of hysteria as an internal struggle between identifications (a "battle of the sexes") being enacted in the body of the hysteric who strives for a completeness or triumph over sexual difference symbolized in the androgyne. This kind of hysterical identification underscores the representation of juvenated femininity not only in *Duel in the Sun* but in many other of Jones's postwar films. Understanding Pearl's division of identification in relation to hysteria offers the advantage of understanding the melodramatic, performative, and psychological implications of Pearl's interactions with phallic masculinity (her father, Senator McCanles, Jesse, Lewt) as well as with submissive femininity (Laura Belle) and with phallic femininity (her unnamed mother).

In her oscillating identifications with masculinity and femininity

Pearl is an instrument of the hysterical psyche that plays out the battle of the sexes and the anxiety associated with it in the subject's body. The hysteric tries to find a compromise strategy to prevent being stranded between excitable sensuality and sexuality, and, as Kristeva argues of hysterics, between genders.[106] The hysteric experiences excitability related to anxiety that undermines the subject's phallic identification with the father. This identification normally underscores the relation to the symbolic, but the hysteric operates on the basis of a psychosexual compromise between cognitive action and "conversion or phantasmatic anxiety" that results in "radical excitability that cannot be symbolized, one that is experienced as a gap, as passivity, as female castration, as a narcissistic flaw, or as depressive disregard."[107]

The construction of female spectacle in many of Jones's postwar films is a neurotic defense that includes a self-conscious performance soliciting the male gaze. In this respect these films also register a refusal, a wish *not* to succumb to male desire like Dora with Herr K.[108] A primary example of this occurs in *Duel in the Sun,* when Pearl, rejected by Jesse, hears Lewt outside her window serenading her with his guitar. The camera takes a high-angle position over Pearl's bed, and shows her writhing back and forth, her hands to her head in a melodramatic display of suffering as she calls out Jesse's name, until she says, "If that's the way you want it, Jesse." Suddenly she bolts upright and shakes her shoulders back. She gets up and, with her hips swinging, and her head tossed back, walks across the room to the window.

In this scene Pearl rehearses the signs of sexual solicitation and marshals her tactics, like Charcot's hysterics, to meet the demands of the situation she has been dealt—her sexual "ruination," in Victorian terms. The scene suggests also that Pearl is trying to arouse herself. Trying too hard to ease the sorrow of her desire for Jesse, she hysterically replaces those feelings with an autoeroticism aligned with the castrated mother. Her own body becomes the oversensualized instrument for performing a desire that she does not desire. Like Augustine, Pearl has learned "the science of objectifying herself for another," as Didi-Huberman says in reference to hysterics, in which "her gesture becomes acting-out in the strong sense: an act beside one's self."[109] Pearl's sexual display is a self-punishment resembling Augustine's hysterical performances of seduction in the Salpêtrière, but Pearl's real desire is repressed; instead, there is only a contrivance of "jouissance in the replay of a torment," thus creating a symptom of "an even crueler violence to herself where her own identity, already so unhappy, was concerned."[110]

FIGURE 65. Pearl Chavez (Jennifer Jones) and her father's lost love (Lillian Gish) in *Duel in the Sun* (dir. King Vidor, 1946). Author's collection.

Pearl's performance of seduction suggests crude, obvious sensuality that reflects a misidentification based on mimesis: she presumes from her mother's behavior what men—like her mother's lover and Lewt—expect of nonvirgins, of "trash," as Pearl calls herself after Lewt sexually assaults her. Up until this point in the film, Pearl says over and over that she is "a good girl," in the typical hysterical overassertion. We take her meaning to be that she is a virgin, the definition of female goodness for someone of her age in white bourgeois culture. No doubt because of Pearl's color and her class, Lewt scoffs at her assertion. Pearl attempts to emulate the refined Laura Belle, who, her father says, "should" have been her mother because she embodies proper white, southern womanhood. But Pearl is not white, and her status as a "half-breed" orphan condemns her to sleep as hired or slave help, in a bunkhouse room without a lock.

In keeping with this rejection of her as a vulnerable young female deserving protection, she is often presented in tandem with the black servant girl, Vashti (Butterfly McQueen), whose desire to be married is ridiculed, even by the gentle Laura Belle. Like Vashti, Pearl cannot hope for marriage in this environment, at least not marriage to a respectable white man. Just as Lewt scoffs at Pearl's claim to be a virgin, Senator McCanles scoffs at the idea of Lewt's marrying her. Lewt's violent seduction of Pearl emphasizes her status as racial and class-bound Other. He walks into her room without knocking. He (and the camera) observe her from behind as she is bent over on the floor, scrubbing. This visual image might be interpreted as sexually and socially degrading, since it fetishistically emphasizes Pearl's buttocks. It is also anxiety provoking, however, as we know Lewt's intention, and the film has been constructed to align us with Pearl. Her physical position defines her sexual vulnerability, but it also conveys her status as working class, more specifically, as a member of the "colored" working class whose body is interpreted by the "master"/male to be freely available for the taking. A thunderstorm begins outside in melodramatic confirmation of the sexual danger Pearl faces: she attempts to elude Lewt's lustful grasp, but she cannot escape. In Lewt's tight embrace, she ultimately responds sexually to him.

Again and again in Jones's films, the actress's enormous energy is expended in performances in which the juvenated female's seductive behavior is a bodily performance registering the deeply divided psyche of the hysteric. It is useful to contextualize these performances within Julia Kristeva's explanation of the hysteric's seeking out "a maximal symbolic and psychic jouissance while simultaneously postulating the impossibility or the futility of this desire."[111] Yet, as Didi-Huberman argues and *Duel in the Sun* illustrates, the hysterical performance of seductiveness may serve to interrogate the gaze of the male spectator through exaggerated, lewd gestures and physical contortions, through the hysterical quality of the solicitation showing the female's pain, as well as her submission to the male's pleasure; in this respect, he says, the hysteric's performance may become a "challenge, farce, malice, mockery."[112] Whether Jones's performances also offer such a challenge to the viewer and mockery of desire may depend on the viewer's attunement to the ideological tenor of melodrama, as well as to his or her identification with Jones as a psychologically complex and sympathetic character. Nevertheless, these performances are often uncomfortable in their mix of anxiety and sensuality. They register the damage done to the female who makes herself over in an act of transference into the image of what she thinks is the desired object of the phallic man. In putting herself in his hands and making herself available to the man's will (and perversions), she wreaks havoc with her own identity and her own desire, which are impossibly divided at their core.

FIGURE 66. Luke McCanles (Gregory Peck) assaults Pearl Chavez (Jennifer Jones) in *Duel in the Sun*. Author's collection.

The second scene of the film illustrates the hysterical basis of Pearl's gender-divided identifications as a "battle of the sexes." This highly melodramatic, almost dreamlike sequence suggests a hysterical interpretation of the primal scene. Pearl dances in the street, which, as critics have pointed out, anticipates her mother's dancing and suggests identification with her mother. Yet Pearl's dance is childish and for children. She dances to a jaunty Mexican tune. She is approached by and rejects the sexual advances of her mother's lover. Pearl splays her body against a wall in a defensive move away from his looming presence. The camera follows the lecherous gambler into "The Presidio," an impossibly enormous and elaborate gambling hall where Pearl's mother dances on a massive four-sided bar, to music anchored by a primitive, pounding drumbeat. In a far, dark corner of the establishment sits Pearl's father, Scott Chavez. His poker companions ridicule him about his wife's exhibitionism. "Look at her!" they sneer. With his handkerchief at his mouth (to block the noxious smell of cigars), Chavez coolly looks at her from a distance as she finishes her dance and falls into the arms of her lover.

FIGURE 67. The anxiety and sensuality of hysteria: Pearl Chavez (Jennifer Jones) and Luke McCanles (Gregory Peck) in *Duel in the Sun*. Author's collection.

The sequence is visually unsettling as her head is upside down as the camera closes in on her as they embrace. There is a cut back to Chavez's impassive reaction to the spectacle of his wife's infidelity. He leaves the poker table after calmly buttoning his coat.

Outside, in the dark street, the mother and her lover are followed by Pearl; she sees them enter a house and reacts by lowering her head in shame. She turns and sees her father. The music is intense and strident, dominated by strings, as Pearl attempts to divert her father. She asks him to take her into the presidio. He tells her she shouldn't be in the presidio or the street, then apologizes to her. It is his fault, he says, "the sins of the father." She embraces him in medium close-up and starts to kiss his neck and then his face. "Not here," he says. "I'll be back in a little while." We see her move forward slightly, and then her father walks up to and enters the dark house. Only the huge window is illuminated. It becomes the stage that reveals the melodramatic enactment of a primal scene in which Chavez's wife and her lover will die. In medium close-up we see Pearl's body spasm in reaction to gunshots as her father, unseen, starts to kill the lovers, who then appear fleetingly as silhouetted figures in the window. Pearl's mother begs for her life: "Don't, don't I beg you." More shots ring out. Pearl cries out, "Paw, Paw, Paw," as she rapidly moves in and out of darkness, but always forward into an extreme close-up, so close that her face loses focus before it falls outside the frame.

Robin Wood does not discuss this scene, but it certainly validates his argument that *Duel in the Sun* "is not simply a film about a hysterical protagonist: by virtue of its melodramatic excess it must be considered one of Hollywood's hysterical texts."[113] Selznick wrote and insisted on adding this sequence to the film. It represents a melodramatic inscription of the child's interpretation of parental intercourse overseen and overheard. In this frightening primal scene, father is not just "hurting mother" but "killing" her. What position in this drama of "love" should the child wish to occupy? With whom should she identify? What is the meaning of sexuality?

The lesson for Pearl from "the primal scene" is that identification with femininity and female desire means alignment with symbolic castration, with death. Later in the film, Pearl's hysterical identifications suggest her attempts to repudiate a subordinated, suffering femininity and, instead, to identify with dominant masculinity; in the words of Maria Ramas in reference to Ida Bauer, she attempts "to repudiate the 'scene' itself and the sadistic meaning of the phallus . . . [in an] attempt to deny patriarchal sexuality."[114] This effort is doomed to fail because Pearl is adolescently fixated on her hysterical desire for the Ideal Object, just as she is continually drawn to one extreme or the other (s/m, masculinity/femininity).

This is a western, but it is also a woman's film. From the beginning the audience's primary figure of identification is Pearl, and it will remain Pearl throughout the film. Her father describes her as a "miracle . . . wonderful and strong," but we already see how many strikes she has against her, including her status as a "half-breed" and her uncertain upbringing. Her father recognizes his role in her problems ("the sins of the father"); we see what he does not: that she has an unusually erotic attachment to him: their physical interaction in the street, with her body up against his and his declaration for her to save her kisses "for later," seem more appropriate for lovers. Pearl's interactions with her father indicate an unresolved Oedipal complex and the role of seduction in forming the identifications of hysteria, including her strong identification with her father. Pearl's phallic identification will be revealed through more than her tomboyish ways (mastery of the rifle and horseback riding) but also in her psychological masculinization.

In the end Pearl's identification with her father and his acting out of phallic, murderous masculinity will be reasserted when she shoots

Lewt. She does not declare the appropriateness of her actions and her superiority over her lover as her father does in his statement to the jury. Instead, her identification slips into alignment with castrated primal scene femininity when she starts to crawl to Lewt.[115] Visualized largely as a movement across the rocks and downward, her spectacularly active crawl *up* the mountain evidences physical toughness and the power of her will. Pearl is at once phallic and castrated.

Pearl attempts to identify with Laura Belle as a substitute for her Indian mother, but no matter which mode of femininity she identifies with, she can only be affiliated with primal scene submission and masochism. After Lewt murders her fiancé, he visits Pearl in the middle of the night. She pulls a handgun out from under the bedcovers to shoot him, but he caresses her hair, takes the gun away from her, and they start to make love. Pearl is wearing a white nightgown with Laura Belle's name embroidered in large script on the bosom. As outrageously "pop-Freudian" as this moment may appear, it was the end of this sequence that was one of the most controversial moments in the film. Selznick advertised it as the "degradation scene" (shot by Josef von Sternberg from Vidor's instructions).[116] After they make love, Lewt tells Pearl he is going to go to Mexico, without her. Under the grip of passion she begs Lewt to take her with him. Pearl holds on to his leg and is dragged across the floor as she screams her adoration. He tells her to quit her "yammering." Charcot was not interested in what women hysterics had to say, and neither is Lewt.[117] The camera stays focused on Pearl's body as she is dragged across the room, until Lewt kicks her away. Pearl is left crying on the floor. She rolls over on to her back and stretches out in a position reminiscent of the painful ecstasies of Augustine.

This erotic spectacle's disturbing fusion of pleasure and pain has implications related to hysteria. As Didi-Huberman notes: "The anxiety of the hysterical body, the incessant motor anxiety, functions as *plastic obstinacy,* though always fragmentary, always guilty and painful. Thus this anxiety can nonetheless call to the gaze . . . by its very paradox of visibility. The paradox: the *attitude passionnelle* contrived a *jouissance* in the replay of a torment."[118] Hysteria indicates identifications that are impossible to reconcile except through compromise formulas that involve fantasy and conversion. Suggesting the neurotic defense and melodramatic structure of hysteria, oscillations of identification can only merge sexuality and anxiety. They cannot bring stability of identity or relief of suffering.

Oscillating between the hysterical extremes, Pearl acts out the adolescent crisis that demands action to complete the fantasy with the destruction of the absolute Object that has failed her. As she rides to Lewt's hiding place, Pearl assumes a physical rigidity and the impassive face that have become identified with the phallic determination of western heroes, including icons of the genre like Clint Eastwood. But her hysterical identification with sadistic masculinity does not offer the liberation and triumph conventionally associated with male power. She cannot disentangle the Object of her adolescent fantasy from her own hysterical identity. Destruction is inseparable from self-destruction.

*Duel in the Sun*'s fusion of anxiety and hyperexcitability, pain and pleasure in the hysterical, anxious, yet eroticized body may be used to argue that Jones's screen portrayals embody much more than a simple, pleasurable erotic fantasy for men. Jones's performances suggest the erotic complexity described by Kristeva: "The hysteric's presumed aspiration to endless pleasure is not sexual but sensual—an unlimited sensory and emotional excitability."[119] Hysteria-infused performances of seduction move the viewer into the territory of a film fantasy that centralizes the adolescent drive for ideality. There, as *Duel in the Sun* shows, Jones's performances of hysterical and melodramatically seductive femininity may be used to interrogate the spectatorial gaze even as they superficially appear to satisfy Hollywood's—and Selznick's—desire for sensational, highly marketable eroticism.

## TRANSITION AND TRANSFERENCE

The association of hysteria with the sexuality of female adolescence is crucial to understanding the gender ideology of Jones's films and how hysteria might function rhetorically in female-centered film melodramas of the period. The 1940s did not witness the kind of sexual revolution that occurred in the 1920s, when the system of dating and radical changes in young people's public behavior occurred, but the fear of precocious female sexuality and its impact on U.S. society was perhaps greater than at any other time since the Jazz Age. Wartime circumstances influenced the deployment of sexuality, especially as it related to young people. Female adolescence, often symbolically represented in the stereotypes of the V-girl and bobby-soxer, became a flash point in the 1940s, when cultural anxieties seemed to ignite in a kind of moral panic that would fully coalesce around the subject of teenage delinquency in the 1950s.

Jennifer Jones's films and her performances of juvenated femininity offer rich terrain for a consideration of female adolescence in Hollywood melodrama as a historically contingent form influenced by altered cultural perceptions of female sexuality, as well as by the popularization of psychoanalysis. As her films show, melodramas, including women's films, were often filtered through the lens of Freudianism and popularized notions of psychoanalytic discourse that took hold in American culture in the 1940s. In explaining the passions of women, psychoanalytically informed ideas were used by Hollywood to structure the erotic anxieties and pleasurable fantasies that circulated in a wide variety of films, not limited to psychologically centered murder mysteries like *Spellbound* or *Love Letters*, or films noirs.

Jones was constructed as a star whose performances clearly have "ontological priority." Her star persona was unusual for the time in its almost exclusive textual focus. As an offscreen persona she barely existed, other than in her association with Selznick and with the neurotic qualities attributed to her. Inscriptions of narrative, psychological, sonic, and visual excesses in films like *Duel in the Sun* and Jones's excessive, fragmented, and intense performances in them, suggest the compatible structures of melodrama and hysteria. The foundational essence of Jones's star persona was built on her ability to perform adolescent femininity in sexual transition. Unlike many other female star icons of film melodrama, Jones's presence complicated melodrama by juvenating the female protagonist, and her heroines frequently reveal the process of becoming woman in ways that brought erotic complexity to conventional tropes of the form, including the heroine's seduction or rape by the stereotypical rake.

That Selznick might channel his sexual anxieties and fantasies through Jones's onscreen performances certainly conforms to the Svengali narrative. Yet such transference is not without its dangers to the male. Svengali dies of a heart attack after trying to elevate Trilby's musical performances to yet another level of acclaim. Selznick, of course, also died of a heart attack a few years after the failure of *A Farewell to Arms* doomed his attempt to reassert Jones's star power and his preeminent place in the film industry. The man who uses the hysterical woman is not necessarily a hysteric himself, but there is much to suggest Selznick's hysteria. While men who demonstrate Don Juan–like, compulsive seductions act out hysterical tendencies, these men are also likely to project neurosis or perversion onto the woman. And, as we have seen, the hysterical woman is vulnerable to this kind of projection. Yet it is the female hysteric that Jones embodies in her films who claims the viewer's allegiance over and above the men who seek to dominate and judge her, whether benignly, violently, or through hysterical transference. This is the triumph of her juvenated heroines and of Jones herself, in all her Trilbyness.

FIGURE 68. Audrey Hepburn, Givenchy gown, and William Holden in publicity still for *Sabrina* (dir. Billy Wilder, 1954). Author's collection.

CHAPTER 6

# "Chi-Chi Cinderella"

## *Audrey Hepburn as Couture Countermodel*

"That's more than a dress—
that's an Audrey Hepburn movie."

—Jerry Maguire (Tom Cruise), in *Jerry Maguire* (1996)

Although the "mammary madness" of the 1950s represented by stars such as Marilyn Monroe, Jayne Mansfield, Jane Russell, Brigitte Bardot, and the adult Elizabeth Taylor has been much discussed, Hollywood's promotion of another, contrasting model of film femininity during the same period remains less examined. This "countermodel" to a voluptuous, hypersexualized femininity is found in the star image of Audrey Hepburn, who was described in 1955 as "flatchested, slim hipped and altogether un-Marilyn Monroeish."[1] Hepburn's stardom reveals the complex negotiation of age, gender, and star construction in mid-twentieth-century mass culture that the dominant model of screen femininity often suppressed. My goal in this chapter is to show how her representation in specific film texts of the 1950s and 1960s, and, more generally, in publicity articles, film advertising, and other extratextual materials, demonstrates the appeal of juvenated femininity as a hybrid blending innocence and sophistication. That appeal became part of a carefully modulated star persona crafted in the waning days of the Hollywood studio system and persisting into the mid to late 1960s, an era associated with a fashion revolution, as well as a sexual one.

As we have seen, during the war years V-girls and bobby-soxers defied traditional assumptions about how adolescent females should control their sexuality; in the postwar era the valuation of virginity in white, middle-class females remained a central tenet of American sexual ideology in spite of intensified pressures on that ideal. In 1953 *Sexual*

*Behavior in the Human Female,* by Alfred E. Kinsey, claimed there was a yawning gap between U.S. sexual ideals and common practice. The statistical analysis by Kinsey and the Institute for Sex Research at Indiana University reported that more than half of white American women were not virgins when they climbed into the marriage bed.[2] It followed that American teenagers in the 1950s were likely to have had a great deal more sexual experience than their parents wanted to know about; premarital sex was common, and it has been said that "the real difference between good teenagers and bad was a matter of appearance. Good teenagers kept their private lives private."[3] In such a social context, rife with contradiction, the appearance of sexual inexperience (or "virginity") in females still had cultural currency, even as screens were filled with women referred to as "sex bombs" and "sex goddesses."

Audrey Hepburn was not a teenager when she became a star in the wake of her appearance in *Roman Holiday* (dir. William Wyler, 1953), in which she plays a young princess, completely sheltered from the world, who runs away from her handlers while she is on a diplomatic tour in Rome. She meets a handsome young American journalist (Gregory Peck) who initially seeks only to score an exclusive story on runaway royalty. Of course, they fall in love. Hepburn most often was cast in light comedies, and she frequently played younger than her actual age as characters that experienced a sexual awakening. She was cast in one historical costume epic, *War and Peace* (dir. King Vidor, 1956), but Hepburn still played a sexually inexperienced adolescent, and one review suggested that the star, "with her precocious child's head set upon a swanlike neck, looks the part."[4] Only once in the 1950s did Hepburn attempt a radically different role that expanded both her acting and age range, that of Sister Luke, a Belgian nun, in *The Nun's Story* (dir. Fred Zinnemann, 1959). In spite of the occasional foray into different acting terrain, her star persona remained juvenated: thirteen years after her Hollywood feature film debut, she was still described as the "elfin, adolescently constructed star."[5]

Just as Deanna Durbin's voice complicated the gendered cultural meanings of the star's representation of innocent female adolescence, Hepburn's femininity was complicated by the insistent association of her juvenated star persona with fashion—more specifically, with Paris high fashion. In Hepburn's stardom, fashion became a privileged signifier of utopian consumer culture and sophisticated femininity. Director Stanley Donen went so far as to remark, "Audrey was always more about fashion than movies or acting."[6] Hepburn's alignment with fashion might have been unusual in its degree, but it was not incompatible with being a female film star.

Fashionability in American cinema was associated very early on with Paris design. The creations of French designers Paul Poiret and Erté were on display in U.S. feature films of the 1920s.[7] Other U.S. entertainments paralleled the movie industry's growing interest in foreign designers and what they could do for the female form. In the 1910s the Ziegfeld Follies relied on European haute couture fashions, albeit in the service of "glorifying the American girl." In 1915 Ziegfeld imported London designer "Lucile," Lady Duff Gordon to design clothes for his showgirls, who were known for their unusually tall stature and elegant mannequin-like walk that resembled haute couture modeling.[8] The emergent processes of constructing film stardom in the 1910s meant that female film players soon had to meet expectations of round-the-clock fashionability demanded of the Ziegfeld showgirl, who was required to keep up an image of graceful, dignified glamour offstage as well as on.[9] Admittedly, fashion did not have to become central to making a female movie star popular among women, but fan magazines, women's magazines, and newspapers served as print venues where film actresses regularly modeled everything from swimsuits to evening gowns.

This meant that even a star like Mary Pickford, who played a ragged adolescent hoyden onscreen, could become a fashion plate in the pages of a magazine without violating her screen image of extreme youthfulness. For example, in 1921, *Ladies' Home Journal* featured the recently divorced and remarried actress in a fashion feature that exemplified the continuing disavowal of her age and sexual maturity. Pickford models clothes clearly intended for an adolescent, and her poses suggest the shy demeanor of an ingénue; however, the feature copy suggests the distance between star and image in its statement that Miss Pickford "wishes to register a debutante." At the same time, the article collapses the difference between the twenty-nine-year-old star and her "registering" of youth by noting that these clothes for adolescents have been designed specifically for *her* by French high-fashion designer Lanvin. Appearing in a modest black afternoon frock and hat, Pickford could reinforce her star persona by using Paris high fashion to represent an old-fashioned nice girl alternative to the daring flapper.[10]

Fashion was never important to Pickford's star image, but it assumed a central role in the construction of her contemporary Gloria Swanson. Almost as diminutive as Pickford and younger, Swanson was known as a "clothes horse." She achieved fame for her roles in high-society sex comedies directed by Cecil B. DeMille: in *Don't Change Your Husband* (1919) and *Why Change Your Wife?* (1920) she was cast as a well-to-do woman dealing with modern sexual dilemmas such as adultery and divorce. These films offered her in wildly extravagant haute couture fashions that helped convince her fans that she was a sophisticated woman of the world. The "Continental sophistication" of Swanson's image was reinforced in the mid-1920s. First, divorce proceedings publicly recounted her numerous sexual infidelities. These revelations associated her with modern if not daringly Continental sexual mores. Following her divorce she set off to France in 1924, to produce an extravagant French-American coproduction, *Madame San-Gêne.* In Paris she reportedly spent a quarter of a million dollars on couturier furs and dresses (mainly at the House of Patou). She also acquired a new husband, French aristocrat Henri, Marquis del la Falaise de la Couraye, and persuaded Rene Hubert (who created the costumes for *Madame San-Gêne)* to come to the States to design for her.[11]

If certain silent movie stars like Swanson were privileged more than others as fashion commodities constructed to solicit the attention of their female audience's "shopper's eye," in the 1930s and 1940s glamorous female stars continued to function as fashion models for both adolescent and adult female spectators who watched their favorite stars' movies and associated the attainment of ideal femininity with the consumption of clothes.[12] Some stars could create a fashion trend with a single film, as demonstrated with Adrian's much copied "Letty Lyndon" dress designed for Joan Crawford or Jennifer Jones's off-the-shoulder peasant blouse and full skirt from *Duel in the Sun,* the latter adopted by teenagers.[13] However, the fashion tastes and goals of female viewers were not necessarily uniform or predictable. Kelly Schrum's research on teenage viewers in the 1940s suggests that we cannot assume that two seventeen-year-old females shared similar reactions to a film's fashions or its star-driven figuration of femininity. Schrum says that teenage girls often preferred the fashions and glamour displayed by stars in their twenties rather than identifying with those in their own age bracket, like Deanna Durbin or Judy Garland.[14]

In contrast to the current wall of praise for Hepburn's elegance and "sexual modesty," commentary on her stardom and reactions to her image in the 1950s as a fashion-centered film star were not univocal.[15] She became a fashion icon, but she did not represent the dominant ideal of female physicality in U.S. culture or films of the 1950s. Her stardom demonstrates how the fashioning of femininity in connection with screen stardom, juvenated or not, was a complex phenomenon, especially in the post–World War II era, when American film and its audiences—as well as fashion and femininity—were all undergoing significant change.

## "WOMEN-FLOWERS" OF THE NEW LOOK

To understand Audrey Hepburn as a fashion commodity, as well as a star commodity, we must start with a consideration of the state of haute couture at the end of World War II. In February of 1947 Christian Dior unveiled a collection that heralded the return of the French fashion industry in the world market. The impact of this collection was unprecedented. The "New Look"—as *Harper's Bazaar* editor-in-chief Carmel Snow dubbed it, constituted a revolution that would influence women's fashions for the next full decade.[16] If the success of the collection was soon strikingly clear, so was Dior's gender-defining purpose. That, he stated, was nothing less than to supplant the wartime era of "women soldiers built like boxers" with "women-flowers [with] soft shoulders, flowering busts, fine waists like liana and wide skirts like corolla."[17] Dior explained the quick acceptance of the New Look on both sides of the Atlantic as a reflection of his meeting a basic feminine desire: "Women longed to look like women again," he said, because there had been a "universal change of feeling."[18] Contrary to Dior's declaration of "universal" acceptance, there were some protests, especially in the United States, against the longer skirts hiding women's legs and the inappropriateness of the "wasp" waist for hale and hearty American women.

In spite of scattered resistance, however, Dior's New Look established the aesthetic norms of haute couture into the mid-1950s while it heralded an enthusiastic revival of Paris as the center of the fashion industry. In the 1960s its influence as a phenomenon went into precipitous decline as lady clients and their fortunes died out. At the same time, ready-to-wear clothing and a multiplicity of international design influences, often derived from youth-oriented "street" clothes (like mod and hippie styles), rose to prominence. This all occurred within a radically changing social atmosphere. Designer Cristóbal Balenciaga explained why he closed his fashion house in 1968: "The life which supported couture is finished."[19]

Never seeing that a shift was so near, in the late 1940s and 1950s, the glorious anachronism of haute couture, led by Dior's New Look, reestablished Paris's traditional domination of U.S. and European fashion trends. American manufacturers and retailers longed to exploit once again the status of superiority enjoyed by Parisian designers. What the war cruelly withheld from American women desiring Continental chic they were eager now to provide. French fashion houses were keenly aware of their postwar dependence on U.S. businesses that linked them to American consumers who could afford French luxury goods. By the mid-1950s it was estimated that 70 percent of haute couture clients were Americans. For those who could not go to France for fittings, enthusiastic retailers such as I. Magnin brought Parisian design to upper-class clientele at one-half the cost of Paris models, and an absence of meaningful antipiracy laws applicable to fashion made it possible in the United States to accommodate aspiring middle-class women with more affordable French-influenced wardrobe choices.[20]

Difference, of course, was sold as a key appeal in the New Look's design innovation. Plenitude replaced wartime austerity; exhibitionism replaced functionality. More to the point, long replaced short, billowing yardage replaced sparse wartime allotments, and diaphanous fabrics replaced sturdy materials of patriotic durability. The New Look short-circuited the evolutionary process of fashion as emergent designers such as Hubert de Givenchy emphasized "youthful" ideas and took mannish styles like the shirtwaist and gave them new, romantic life with delicate fabrics and impractical ornate detailing.[21] Throughout the 1950s, collections from Dior, Givenchy, Balenciaga, and other Paris fashion houses provided the continuous innovation expected of fashion but still sustained the spirit of Dior's postwar return to an elegant hyperfeminine fashion ideal inspired by the belle époque.

## HEPBURN AND THE SHOW WINDOW OF HOLLYWOOD

Hollywood became a key "show window" for selling the New Look and its image of femininity restored through revival of older ideals. As Maureen Turim has noted, Paris's high-fashion New Look was soon translated into homegrown Hollywood costume design.[22] The "sweetheart line" co-opted the New Look's full skirt, pinched waist, and dropped neckline (or, for nighttime, the strapless bodice). Its name reflected its bodice shape, as well as its association with youthful femininity that connoted Anglo-American romantic idealism rather than French sexual sophistication. The sweetheart line showed a great deal of a woman's neck and upper chest and drew attention to her breasts, but its name encouraged its acceptance as a style that offered an appropriate glimpse of the youthful physical charm of Americans rather than the erotically charged exhibitionism of overly sophisticated Continental women. In "How Low Will They Go?" *Modern Screen* suggested that Hollywood was more conservative than New York in advancing the "bosom art" of Paris-initiated fashion: "You don't catch those smart movie queens baring all!" declared the fan magazine.[23] In film the sweetheart line became the basic dress design used to symbolize the transformation of the immature bobby-soxer into a marriageable young woman in comedy-focused family films such as *A Date with Judy* (dir. Richard Thorpe, 1948) and *Father of the Bride* (dir. Vincente Minnelli, 1950). Highly appealing cinematic versions of the style, like Edith Head's glamorous flower-swathed party dress worn by Elizabeth Taylor's debutante in *A Place in the Sun* (dir. George Stevens, 1951), were popularized by affordable imitations in the U.S. ready-to-wear market.

Although Hollywood films referenced the New Look by the early 1950s, it was not until 1953 that French high fashion fully broke into postwar Hollywood costume design when Audrey Hepburn asked to add Givenchy designs to her wardrobe for Billy Wilder's romantic comedy *Sabrina* (1954).[24] Edith Head was credited with costume supervision and received an Oscar for the film's costume design, but the most memorable and imitated designs were Givenchy's: a slim, sophisticated town suit, a black satin cocktail dress, and a magnificent strapless white ball gown with black and gray embroidery and black ruffle. As a couturier Givenchy was relatively unknown in the United States when Hepburn asked him to provide designs for *Sabrina*, but that situation would soon change. The opening of *Sabrina* in Paris was timed to Givenchy's spring-summer 1955 collection; in the United States, Sabrina look-alike contests promoted both the film and the Givenchy look. The designer's success was assured: "*Sabrina* brought me more new clients then I could handle," he later remarked.[25]

*Sabrina* also marked the beginning of the public definition of Hepburn in which Givenchy fashions functioned as an important, recognizable component of her identity as a star personality. Hepburn and Givenchy would be linked inseparably, both onscreen and off. He would design her "costumes" for *Funny Face* (dir. Stanley Donen, 1957), *Love in the Afternoon* (dir. Billy Wilder, 1957), *Breakfast at Tiffany's* (dir. Blake Edwards, 1961), *Charade* (dir. Stanley Donen, 1963), *Paris When It Sizzles* (dir. Richard Quine, 1964), and *How to Steal a Million* (dir. William Wyler, 1966). It was reported that Hepburn turned down films that would not permit her to use him as her costume designer or consultant.[26] In addition, Givenchy would become the designer of choice for Hepburn's personal wardrobe for almost twenty years.[27] That fact was personal but not private: the star would become the subject of fashion news and featured on numerous occasions in Givenchy dresses, suits, ball gowns, and hats in elite fashion magazines such as *Vogue* (American) and *Harper's Bazaar.* Hepburn commented on her inseparability from high fashion and from Givenchy's role in shaping her image: "In a certain way one can say that Hubert de Givenchy has 'created' me over the years."[28]

Hepburn's association with Givenchy conformed to the established standards for an upper-class woman's relationship to her couturier. In American fashion magazines in the 1950s, anonymous models displayed new fashions, but special multipage layouts presenting haute couture were often reserved for women of the upper class. They were identified by their family connections as statesmen's wives, debutante daughters of the old rich, and members of European aristocracy. Hepburn joined the ranks of these social elite as a role model when, after her appearance in *Sabrina,* she was featured in *Vogue;* this arbiter of American fashion declared her to have "established a new standard of beauty and every other face now approximates the 'Hepburn look.'"[29] Whether overtly acknowledged or not, that "look" was a commodity and was subject to being reproduced. Throughout 1955 numerous models resembling Hepburn could be seen in fashion features and advertisements in *Vogue* displaying dark, cropped hair, swan-like necks, thick eyebrows, thin bodies, and wide-eyed youthfulness.[30]

Although not instigated by Givenchy or Hepburn, the latter epitomized the new high-fashion ideal body type as narrow and underdeveloped, a decided contrast to the shapely, buxom female stars of the 1950s. Givenchy proclaimed Hepburn to have "the proportions of the ideal woman" at 32–20–35; five feet, seven inches tall; and 110 pounds.[31] This standard seemed overly tall and decidedly underfed for America's cinematic and cultural norms. Continental-based postwar high fashion was said to be responsible. However, Americans had seen something like it before. In the 1910s Florence Ziegfeld commodified a showgirl ideal that also was tall, slim, and draped in haute couture fashions. However, the body of his ideal was womanly, described by Ziegfeld as "pulchritudinous," and she was advertised as the "Ideal American Girl."[32] Although the flapper was not an exclusively American phenomenon, her U.S. appearance was the type's most imitated and influential incarnation in the 1920s. Associated with a boyish flatness and muscular verve (displayed in jazz dancing), youth culture's ideal feminine body type in the Jazz Age was matched by flapper fashions that were narrow, straight, and short. They may have taken some cues from elitist haute couture, but they were widely accessible through the mass marketing of cheap ready-to-wear fashions in the United States.[33]

Contrary to earlier twentieth-century articulations of fashion meant for slim bodies, New Look haute couture did not depend on an American model. It made the physical ideal of the French mannequin—long, slender neck; slim-waisted body; and long legs—the increasingly desired physical type for fashionable clothes. In New Look fashions, inner dress construction (or padded bras and girdles) provided the necessary body shaping that would leave the long, graceful neck and thin arms intact. In the feminine physicality attached to the New Look, there was little association with Americanness, in spite of belle époque qualities that may have seemed compatible with the "sex bomb" voluptuousness of many Hollywood movie icons.

As the 1950s progressed, there was a discernible trend in New Look fashion toward suits and skirts that were less full (especially in the fall and winter collections). The pencil-slim suit, such as the one Hepburn wears in *Sabrina,* became one test of the appropriate body type for high fashion. Increasingly, too, there was less emphasis on the bosom and more on a straight signature silhouette: Dior introduced the sheath in 1953 and the A-line in 1955, Givenchy the chemise in 1956. These mid-1950s figure-revealing New Look developments demanded a slim body. By 1957 the *New York Times* remarked that Dior himself was growing fatter and fatter, but "his mannequins get thinner and thinner, straighter and straighter, flatter and flatter."[34] Satirizing this phenomenon, the fictional editor of *Quality* fashion magazine declares in Hepburn's *Funny Face,* "Who cares if the New Look has no bust!" In real life it was said that many American men did care—very much. Suffering from "Dior phobia," they vociferously protested the appearance of the flat look in their wives and girlfriends who followed fashion.[35]

The cinematic beginning of the Givenchy/Hepburn collaboration that decisively brought the New Look as designed by the French to American film was aided by the fact that *Sabrina* was one of the biggest box-office draws of 1954. A frothy, light comedy set in New York, it is a Cinderella story in which the title character, a chauffeur's daughter, Sabrina Fairchild (Hepburn), is sent to Paris for cooking lessons. Her father, who seems to be English, hopes that this transatlantic move will

FIGURE 69. Sabrina Fairchild (Audrey Hepburn) as a frustrated, ponytailed adolescent in *Sabrina*. Author's collection.

help Sabrina get over her teenage crush on David (William Holden), the playboy younger son of Oliver Larrabee (Walter Hampden), patriarch of the Long Island Larrabees, the wealthy family that employs Sabrina's father.

Months later, Sabrina prepares to return home. The audience has seen her homesick and an apparent failure in her cooking class, but she writes her father: "If you should have any difficulty recognizing your daughter, I shall be the most sophisticated woman at the Glen Cove Station." Such words would have normally struck fear in the hearts of American parents, for *sophisticated* carried connotations of sexual knowledge (and maturity) that many female teenagers (on- and offscreen) sought but parents firmly worked to curb. An article in *Seventeen* from 1946 noted the polymorphous meaning of the word but warned of its most dangerous connotations, which were sexual: "Sophistication has come to mean anything from black lace stockings to the right fork. . . . The visual signs of sophistication to boys translate as 'This is easy!'"[36]

When Sabrina returns from Paris, is she sophisticated in the possible ways suggested by *Seventeen*? Because the change in Sabrina's appearance is not visualized in the film's Paris scenes, the audience is surprised by her appearance at the train station. So is David, who initially does not recognize her. Sabrina is also much changed in attitude. She seems ready to capture the heart of dallying David, even after she appears to know he is to be married to a socialite to solidify the family business. This suggests the likelihood that Sabrina has gained sexual experience in Paris that the audience has not been allowed to see. However, ambiguity is cultivated in order to preserve the illusion of Sabrina's virginal innocence. Hepburn's enthusiastic, girlish manner undercuts the idea that her sophisticated Parisian fashion is matched by a new sexual sophistication also acquired on the continent.

*Women's Home Companion* was blunt in describing *Sabrina* as a movie in which the main character "learns how a girl dresses and talks to attract a man."[37] Obviously, fashion plays a central role in transforming Sabrina from a sexually frustrated adolescent with a ponytail "like a horse" into an immaculately groomed, chic woman who can jump across class lines into the arms of a fabulously wealthy suitor. Yet, as Rosalind Coward points out, there are more subtle sexual meanings attached to "Continental chic," the latter encompassing not only elements of clothing but "how they are arranged and worn, the style of the body and hair, [which] are geared to expressions of wealth and sophisticated sexuality."[38] Haute couture designers encouraged the idea that their products were meaningful in ways that rose above mass-produced fashion and mass taste.

Although Billy Wilder was not known as a director of "women's pictures," the film's emphasis on its female protagonist often takes a form that resembles a fashion show aimed at a distinctly female audience, even though men are marked as those who primarily look at Hepburn in the film. A *Hollywood Reporter* review recognized the fashion-centered feminine appeal of the film: "This is the best woman's picture since *Three Coins in the Fountain*. It is too bad that the storytelling wardrobe . . . has not been shot in color."[39] Throughout *Sabrina*, Hepburn's poses and the manner in which she is photographed suggest the conventions of high-fashion photography. When she appears at the Glen Cove train station in a pencil-slim Givenchy town suit, she adopts the chic pose and accoutrements (including a rhinestone-collared poodle) that female audiences would immediately recognize from the pages of *Vogue* or *Harper's Bazaar*, as well as from newspaper fashion and consumer product advertisements. This was because high fashion was big business in the 1950s, and its influence saturated the imagery employed for a wide range of consumer marketing. Women shaped like couture man-

FIGURE 70. Sabrina (Audrey Hepburn) returns home from Paris. With William Holden in *Sabrina*. Author's collection.

nequins, posed like them, and wearing clothes indebted to Paris fashion were used to sell a vast array of U.S. consumer products, from automobiles to lipstick. During these years, in the words of one scholar, "fashion was everywhere."[40]

The fashion show approach to presenting Hepburn is most memorably demonstrated in the party scene that marks her move from "over the garage" into polite society. On the veranda of the Larrabee mansion David looks for Sabrina as he dances with his fiancée, Elizabeth (Martha Hyer). He suddenly stops. A full shot that reverses the field of vision shows Sabrina sweeping up in a fast walk to the edge of the balustrade that defines the dance floor. Her movement suggests a model making an entrance on a fashion show runway. There are cuts to medium shots and close-up reaction shots of men looking in open-mouthed awe of her. Then we are offered a close-up of her face as she sways to the music. A cut back to David reveals him attempting to get rid of his fiancée. Sabrina is then shown in medium shot surrounded by men as David calls her name and reaches out dramatically to take her hand. An overhead long shot shows her dancing by herself, sweeping her dress's train around her as she moves to the orchestra's rendition of "Isn't It

Romantic." After they dance, she waits for David at the indoor tennis court, at his instruction; it is a plan that she, as an eavesdropping teenager, has heard him use with many women many times before.

Sabrina, like the film viewer desiring to take on the attributes of the beautiful, fashionable film star, has now become the woman that the handsome leading man desires. Her facial expressions remain open, soft, partaking of the big-eyed, startled innocence that often led the actress to be described as "fawn-like."[41] Her juvenated qualities counterpoint and mediate the sophisticated, womanly ones implied chiefly by expensive, exclusive high fashion. Now, too, there is a hint of sophistication in more than her gowns, since Sabrina recognizes and casually accepts the serial nature of David's sexual interests and her new status as the feminine object of his overpracticed romantic gestures. Those gestures become the object of comedy, culminating in the moment when their rendezvous on the tennis courts ends when he sits down on champagne glasses.

The star of this party scene is not just Hepburn, but Hepburn *in* Givenchy's evening dress. Jane Gaines has argued that costume was necessary in classical Hollywood film to create a pleasurable female spectacle but had to remain subservient to the dramatic content of the story and controlled so that it would not "divert the viewer's attention from the story itself."[42] Molly Haskell, writing of her teenage response to Hepburn, provides an interesting clue to this scene. She says: "Having no special clothes memory, I'm surprised at how vividly I recall design and detail of this dress."[43] That this scene would evoke vivid recall suggests that at this moment the film allows costume to overtake the normal conduits for advancing narrative. It is the dress, and the entrance of Hepburn in the dress, that provides the affective means for David (and the audience) to recognize the maturation of Sabrina into a desirable, fashionable, sophisticated woman.

The scene's violation of Hollywood norms in this regard may also account for the complaint voiced in one review of the film, which noted, "Her actual invasion of the dancing party on her return [from] Europe is basically a bad and incredible portion of the picture."[44] The Larrabee party scene may be "bad and incredible" from one perspective, but Haskell's vivid memories of Sabrina's ball gown support the conclusions drawn by Jackie Stacey from her interviews of British women who were avid consumers of American films of the 1940s and 1950s. Stacey indicates that these women actually enjoyed disruptions of classical narrative that permitted the foregrounding of fashion and star styles (clothing, as well as hairstyles and makeup).[45]

No wonder that Hepburn star vehicles, especially those reliant on contemporary fashion, would, at some level, all turn into fashion shows meant to appeal to women spectators interested in haute couture. Hepburn is fetishistically displayed for the male characters, as in the Larrabee party scene, but at the same time this scene and others, such as Sabrina's encounter with David at the Glen Cove train station, provide the film's female audience members ample time and a generous view so that they may study costume details and admire the heroine's enviable ability to use fashion to make her way down the traditional feminine path to social improvement and romantic happiness.

## FANTASIES OF A MORE FASHIONABLE FEMININITY

As Richard Dyer has noted, "Wearing Haute couture bespeaks luxury, wealth, refinement and, less obviously, power."[46] Givenchy's fashions sell Audrey Hepburn as an image of femininity that consistently enjoys these associations. *Sabrina* shows that fashion designs in and of themselves may have important appeal to women viewers, but, worn as costumes by specific stars in fantasy-evoking situations of the high life, they could form an even more potent attraction.

*Sabrina* offers the narrativization of a female consumer fantasy of fashion's transformative possibilities. Sabrina breathlessly responds to Mrs. Larrabee's revelation that she did not recognize her: "Have I changed, have I really changed?" In the film Hepburn is transformed from an invisible and miserable adolescent (who halfheartedly tries to commit suicide by carbon monoxide) into the ideal ingénue, combining high spirits with refinement and beauty. Like *Sabrina,* publicity on the actress offered a paradoxical duality of personality (adolescent but womanly, high-spirited but refined, innocent but sophisticated), as well as the duality of fashion, as an essential aspect of her star persona. An early *Life* photo feature on the star declared her to be "both waif and woman of the world . . . disarmingly friendly and strangely aloof . . . all queen . . . and all commoner."[47] Although this strategy of combining oppositions to create a personality was typical of discursive negotiations in the phase of star making, Hepburn's persona (onscreen and off) crucially retains qualities of the adolescent after she is transformed into a fashion plate. In her films the expressive medium of Continental fashionability is depicted as allowing beautiful, contented womanhood to emerge out of an adolescence that really does not end. Through the juvenation of femininity, haute couture is made approachable; it is naturalized as a fundamental articulation of the feminine self just waiting to be expressed.

While retaining her adolescent playfulness, Hepburn's character is sexualized within limits that are largely defined by her elegant haute couture dress and graceful, model-like physicality. Givenchy's designs establish Sabrina as womanly, but haute couture of the 1950s also would have connoted sexual discretion affiliated with social refinement—a private life kept private. These qualities were associated with the society debutantes and wealthy young married women (such as Jacqueline Kennedy) who graced the pages of high-fashion magazines in the 1950s. Continental chic not only signaled the presence of sophisticated tastes but a sophisticated sexuality based on "sensuality which is meant to come through wealth," achieved through individualized tailoring and the feel of expensive fabric that creates the "sensual pleasure in having the body touched [by clothes]."[48] This was a type of sophistication (achieved through the touch of silk lingerie, mink linings to coats, etc.) that few would ever know, lacking in knowledge of its potential pleasure—and the money to purchase the attire associated with it.

Parisian high fashion may express wealth and sexual sophistication—and, to some, snobbishness—but the plotlines of Hepburn's films and her characters' behaviors qualify or downplay these attributes. "This is where she belongs," says the Larrabees' cook of Sabrina's debut in high society. Sabrina must remain as good as she is beautiful, still dreamily adolescent in her desire for romance and monogamy. In this respect Hepburn retains characteristics of the *jeune fille,* the traditional middle-class French ideal of a girl who recalls simpler (prewar) times attached to conservative values and wistful, gentle femininity. As Sabrina dances with David, she smiles sweetly and waves to a group of servants who stand behind a hedge to watch her triumph. Later, the butler is so thrilled by her romantic success with David that he thrusts a drink tray at a guest to serve as he scurries away to tell the other domestic workers: "You should see Sabrina, the prettiest girl, the prettiest dress, the best dancer—the belle of the ball!" Although fashion's power provides the means by which Hepburn can enter the domain of the higher classes, the film is careful to establish that this glamorous transformation, with its promise of social mobility, does not cut off Sabrina's emotional connection to her original class represented by the servants who make up her "family." Sadly, their identification with her presumes she is automatically better off in the world of the rich.

Female audiences who were familiar with high-fashion magazines and news items on society's elite would immediately recognize that *Sabrina* visually presents its transformed heroine as the superior to her female rivals in terms of high-society standards of fashion and manners. David's fiancée is a shapely blonde clothed in a tulle black strapless sweetheart-design dress. Her appearance is coded as lacking the restraint appropriate for an unmarried society woman. Her blonde hair looks dyed; she is gloveless and perhaps wears more jewelry (pearl choker necklace and diamond bracelet) than would be proper for a young woman of "breeding" under the age of thirty.[49] She looks déclassé and decidedly nouveau riche compared to Sabrina, whose appearance at the dance demonstrates that taste cannot be bought: she has a more highly developed fashion sense than her financial betters.

David's prospective marriage is, above all, an economic enterprise, a merger based on wealth. His fiancée is the daughter of a man who owns the sugar plantations that the workaholic older brother Linus (Humphrey Bogart) must acquire for a multimillion-dollar business venture. Linus decides to keep Sabrina away from David, but the plan backfires when he falls in love with her. In spite of the fact that her two key displays of her fashion transformation into sophisticated womanhood are aimed at David, it is important that Sabrina not end up with David if she is to retain her youthful idealism. His impulsivity and practiced promiscuity are contrasted with older brother Linus's seriousness and disinterest in women. Linus's awkward courtship of Sabrina is meant to serve the interests of the family business, but comedy (generally about his age) takes the edge off his deception. When he brings out an ancient phonograph with a recording from his youth of "Yes, We Have No Bananas," Sabrina is charmed by the tune, and she then sings along. She wonders why she has not heard it before: the unspoken answer is that it was popular in 1921! The haute couture designs that attract David to Sabrina as a beautiful mannequin are contrasted with the more relaxed behaviors and casual fashions displayed when she is with Linus. In effect, Sabrina is more juvenated and less sophisticated in her relationship with Linus than with David.

In the end Sabrina will run off to Paris with Linus, not David. This Paris made for American escape suggests a fantasyland beyond Puritan moral strictures and the American obsession for making money, where the taboo-breaking romance between the aging businessman and the chauffeur's young daughter can flourish. As Vanessa Schwarz has suggested, in the 1950s American filmmakers used the cultural currency of

France to represent "high culture" associated with luxury, as well as art; they also represented Paris in clichéd but affectionate terms that marshaled "Frenchness" as a symbol of cosmopolitism. Just as Paris became the site where a girl of modest means like Sabrina could become a chic, desirable woman, it was also a place that could promise love and happiness to the most uptight American businessman/tourist (like Linus Larrabee).[50] It was where cosmopolitan freedom and pleasure could triumph over provincial judgment and repression.

The Cinderella theme of growing up through the gendered power of high fashion is an element of the Hepburn persona sustained through many of her films. In a way Hepburn's films offer a consumerist and fashion-oriented variation on the many Cinderella-themed films of Deanna Durbin, *First Love* being the most obvious example. In that film Durbin's character, Constance Harding, is an orphan who falls in love with a handsome scion of a wealthy family. She runs away from a society dance, leaving her slipper behind. In *His Butler's Sister* Durbin, an aspiring singer, decides that the best way to get an audition with a famous composer (Franchot Tone) is to become a maid in his household, since her brother is his butler. She hopes he will notice her voice as she sings while cleaning. As I noted in chapter 3, the romantic fate of Durbin's heroines is typically assured only when the proper romantic partner responds to her voice. Durbin has a bevy of eager suitors who are butlers, valets, and cooks, but *His Butler's Sister*, like *Sabrina,* holds out for class elevation that also assures its singing heroine a measure of musical compatibility. As in other Durbin vehicles, physical transformation, including through costuming, is irrelevant to romantic resolution. Only proper recognition of the protagonist's desirability—revealed in the womanliness of her singing—is required.

In contrast, Hepburn's commodification as an elegant, Continental-flavored ingénue depended on Givenchy couture clothes; it also drew on the aristocratic qualities embodied by the actress. Her upper-class, well-schooled accent, refined manners, and balletic carriage were important to defining the class to which her juvenated heroines *should* belong. It did not matter if the plots of *Sabrina, Funny Face, Breakfast at Tiffany's, Charade, Love in the Afternoon,* and *Paris When It Sizzles* did not allow her character to be wealthy. Hepburn still wore Givenchy by the end of the film, and her star persona provided proof that her character was someone who was properly attired in expensive fashion. It did not hurt that the actress bore a remarkable resemblance to the Vicomtesse Jacqueline de Ribes, one of the most famous (and aristo-

FIGURE 71. Audrey Hepburn as a "bedraggled book worm" who is not interested in fashion. With Kay Thompson in *Funny Face* (dir. Stanley Donen, 1957). Author's collection.

cratic) French fashion icons of the era, who, like Hepburn, spoke with a vaguely British accent.

Many of Hepburn's films reflected the nostalgic feelings that France held for American filmmakers in the 1950s. As a place that appealed to the artistic spirit, as well as the sensual, Paris became a favorite setting for American musicals.[51] Hepburn's characters also often end up in Paris, most memorably in *Funny Face*. In that film Hepburn plays Jo, described by *Look* magazine as a "bedraggled book worm."[52] Affiliated with anticonsumerist intellectualism, Jo denounces the fashion photography crew that invades her domain, the Greenwich Village bookstore where she works. The crew wants to use it as the backdrop for fashion photos, but she says the bookstore's owner "doesn't approve of fashion magazines. It's chi-chi and an unrealistic approach to self-impression, as well as economics." Her youthfulness and overly serious delivery render her weighty comment silly even as her loose tweed jumper, sensible

FIGURE 72. Audrey Hepburn celebrates fashion in *Funny Face*. Author's collection.

shoes, and shapeless hairstyle suggest that she shares the owner's opinion or, more likely, that the dismissal represents her own opinion. She adds that she thinks fashion photography consists of "men taking idiotic pictures of idiotic women."

The gender division of fashion photography will be at the center of a film that celebrates the process rather than condemns it; Jo's resistance is broken down rather quickly as veteran fashion photographer Dick Avery (Fred Astaire) is attracted to her and tenderly kisses her during the bookstore shoot. When she is alone, a high-fashion hat left behind becomes the vehicle for a musical reverie that signals she is not beyond being won over by fashion, as well as by heterosexual romance.

Like *Sabrina, Funny Face* insists on a transformation that affirms not only the heroine's acceptance of fashion but also her love for the new fashionable self that emerges. Jo succumbs to *Quality* magazine's desire to turn her into "the world's most glamorous mannequin." At

FIGURE 73. Frank Flannagan (Gary Cooper) with his juvenated lover, Ariane Chavasse (Audrey Hepburn), in *Love in the Afternoon* (dir. Billy Wilder, 1957). Author's collection.

first, she only wants to use the magazine's promised trip to Paris as a means of meeting her intellectual idol, a "philosopher" who is the darling of Left Bank beat culture. Jo's initial runway appearance in a Givenchy evening gown is, like the Larrabee party in *Sabrina,* a film-stopping moment. Maids and janitors applaud her along with all the fashion experts, putting the beautification-is-a-woman's-obligation-to-herself seal of approval on Jo's transformation into a "bird of paradise." By the end of the film Jo proclaims her love for fashion (represented by Givenchy), modeling, Paris, and the architect of her photogenic makeover, Avery.

As in *Sabrina,* the heroine's happiness in *Funny Face* depends on a romantic coupling with a much older man. This would be a formula followed in many other Hepburn films, including *Love in the Afternoon, Charade, War and Peace,* and *My Fair Lady* (dir. George Cukor, 1964). The extreme age difference between Hepburn's characters and her leading men creates a romantic coupling with overtones of incest exacerbated by the actress's juvenated qualities.

In *Love in the Afternoon* Hepburn plays a young music student, Ariane Chavasse, who lives with her father, a detective. Ariane makes up a history of amorous affairs to impress an aging American playboy, Frank Flannagan (Gary Cooper), who has seduced her on their first encounter after she adroitly rescues him from the gun-wielding husband of one of his lovers. She is depicted in one boating scene as literally being in pigtails, looking like a child in sweater and pants as she tells the jealous Flannagan, "You are the first American in my life." Flannagan educates Ariane, whom he knows only as the "thin girl," into the pleasures of secret afternoon assignations in his hotel room. In this film and others Hepburn's display of haute couture fashion suggests that she is sufficiently sophisticated to sexually appreciate and ultimately marry an older man. Her fashionability and beauty allow the aging man of a certain class and wealth to possess and proudly display her as a trophy wife. At the same time, her prepubescent body and shy expressions imply that she will likely not make significant demands (sexual or otherwise) on her aging lover.

## HAUTE COUTURE AS A YOUNG IDEA(L)

Perhaps more than any other Continental-flavored young female star in the 1950s, including American-born Grace Kelly, Audrey Hepburn's juvenated screen persona took the edge off haute couture's long-standing association with serious, dignified beauty and paved the way for a youthful feminine market for high fashion. In 1952 *Vogue* acknowledged this market of potential consumers through the debut of its "Young Idea" feature, aimed at readers seventeen to twenty-five years old.[53] In the postwar scene the broader emerging youth market was regarded as a distinct target for manufacturers of all size and stripe. In the Paris-based fashion scene it was represented more indirectly, as a nostalgic ideal represented in the romantic prettiness and delicacy of detail associated with the New Look, especially as practiced by Givenchy. Hepburn became an important marketing strategy for Givenchy, especially in his appeal to a more youthful clientele traditionally epitomized by the society debutante. But Paris design of the 1950s, while paying lip service to youthful styling, produced designs that rarely possessed qualities that obviously represented the ease and freedom of youth.[54] Fashion would have to wait for the influence of the mod and hippie movements and the alternative fashion beat of Carnaby Street before fashion became inextricably linked to qualities recognized broadly as adventurous or rebellious, daringly designed to free the youthful body from class-bound ideals, as well as binding clothing. As one commentary in 1966 suggested, not only was Hepburn "impeccably tailored" in her Givenchy outfits, but she also represented a "blueblooded mode" of dressing.[55]

Perhaps that is why, as we will see, there are some apparent contradictions in how Hepburn's films were marketed to and received by young female viewers. Hepburn's films did provide some sense of youthful freedom by setting off the traditional couture elegance and refinement of the star's costumes with her youthful physicality and lilting, rather adolescent voice, as well as her characters' often playful behavior. For example, in *Sabrina* Hepburn appears in the archetypal "little black dress," signaling Continental chic for Sabrina's dinner date with Linus Larrabee in Manhattan. Her Givenchy-designed sleeveless, black satin cocktail dress has a swing skirt, and it is beautifully accessorized by a small sequined hat and black gloves. Yet it is in this elegant outfit that she proceeds to spin around madly in Linus's executive chair until she is so dizzy that she collapses across his office conference table. Such moments illustrate how the comedic element of Hepburn's juvenated persona brought high fashion down to earth and made it emotionally accessible to young, middle-class women.[56] In spite of Hepburn's youthful aura, however, haute couture of the 1950s emphasizes the alignment of high fashion with elitist class norms that would not disintegrate in fashion photography and magazines until the 1960s and 1970s.

Although her haute couture attire sustains the ideals of New Look femininity, it is significant that Hepburn's appearance is tinged by boyishness and the suggestion of youthful physical immaturity. One British critic icily observed in response to *Sabrina,* "Surely the vogue for asexuality can go no further than this weird hybrid with butchered hair."[57] Molly Haskell has also remarked—albeit more positively—on Hepburn's androgynous qualities. She believes that Hepburn's onscreen representation of the "adolescent freedom" of a prepubescent-like flat female body evoked strong feelings of identification with young female audiences who longed to be free (again) of "those secondary sex characteristics designed explicitly to imprison them in the role of woman and mother."[58] For Haskell, Hepburn's appeal to adolescent girls resided partially in her ability to imply "the resolution of painful conflicts."[59] In contrast, Nora Sayre argues for a powerful element of conformity in the Hepburn image as it was received in midcentury America: "Many adolescent girls of the fifties were almost tyrannized by the image of Audrey Hepburn: Hers was the manner by which ours was measured, and we were expected to identify with her, or to use her as a model."[60]

Hepburn was a star who offered a model of the transition to adult femininity in which the transformation from child to woman depended on self-improvement defined largely as the cultivation of a fashionability linked to consumerism. However, instead of placing high-style fashion on a figure that adhered to the then current ideals of voluptuous femininity in American movies, Hepburn's transition into high-style fashionability was inseparable from a body that remained adolescent in physical characteristics and movement. Whether one comes down on the "side" of Haskell or Sayre, their comments on Hepburn's relationship to her youthful female audience supports Jackie Stacey's claim that film stars "representing cultural ideals of feminine beauty and charm played a key role in the processes of identity formation."[61] Certainly representing strong elements of a capitulation to feminine conformity, Hepburn's persona and its close association with haute couture nevertheless softens the oppressive blow of maturation into femininity by asserting fashion's romanticized status as an art form created almost exclusively in the twentieth century for the individual—and collective—enjoyment of females, youthful and otherwise. Thus, her female viewers might read Hepburn's films as a parallel reality where fashion was presented not as costume design of purely fictional origin and limited cinematic dimensions, but as having a real-world status in relation to feminine identity.

Female spectators were encouraged by Hepburn's films, extratextual promotion, and publicity to identify with the star as an ideal that represented a utopian fantasy of consumption. Stacey suggests that such a spectator fantasy did not necessarily depend on the actual purchase of clothing. Attaining an ideal self-image could be played out through gazing and fantasizing: "The desire to clothe your favorite star, to predict her taste and style," becomes part of the spectator's sharing of an "imagined intimacy with the Hollywood ideal."[62] Stacey's research also suggests that women spectators frequently copied movie fashions through adapting what they already owned, playing make-believe, or purchasing "styles which give them a feeling of connection with their ideal."[63] Girls and young women viewers could buy, copy, or creatively adapt designs associated with their favorite film stars.

The possibility of pursuing these avenues seems to be borne out by at least one significant element in the publicity attached to *Breakfast at Tiffany's*. *Photoplay* ran an article entitled "How Does a Girl Become a Woman?" in which Hepburn's Givenchy dresses for the film were compared to similar clothing and jewelry that promise "chic without the Givenchy price."[64] *Funny Face* advertising copy promised "All the Paris fashions of tomorrow in the picture that sets a new style in film musicals!" But, in contrast, the press book for *Funny Face* discusses a national magazine promotion and tie-in exhibitors' campaign based not on Givenchy's "Paris fashion" but on the designs of Edith Head that appear in the "Think Pink" sequence early in the film: "In its March issue, *Seventeen Magazine* is devoting 12 pages to the fashion theme, 'Think Pink,' with tie-in copy explaining its origin in 'Funny Face' and giving full picture credits. Leading department stores across the country are participating in this fashion promotion, which features fashions by 27 national manufacturers. Participating stores will back the promotion with fashion shows, window and departmental displays, tie-in ads, radio and television spots, and promotion and publicity based on the 'Think Pink' fashions."[65]

The "Think Pink" musical sequence in the film demands to be read as a satire on a then current fashion trend, but in the film's exhibition practice this very same trend is interpreted as having "feminine appeal [that] is so great that it's the basis of a national magazine promotion"; Edith Head appeared on Art Linkletter's CBS television program *House Party* to stage "a pink fashion show," and exhibitors were told to exploit *Funny Face*'s "bearing on the new fashions" by arranging local tie-ins with "department stores and shops that cater to women's fashions and beauty aids."[66] The only Givenchy design that appeared in the advertising campaign for the film was a wedding dress. In fact, the costumes from Hepburn's films that feminist film critics remember as important to them as adolescents infatuated with Hepburn's star appeal are not the haute couture of Givenchy that completes her characters' fashionable transformations but frequently those "antifashion" outfits (sometimes designed by Head) that clothe Hepburn in her adolescent, prefashion-model mode.

Within this context Elizabeth Wilson finds the dominance of haute couture in Hepburn's films "surprising" and recollects the impact that Hepburn's noncouture costumes had on teenagers. She remembers Hepburn as being "celebrated as a girl in black drainpipe trousers and a Left Bank sweater."[67] Hepburn wears Edith Head–designed trousers and sweater in her spontaneous "jazz" dance in a Left Bank underground nightclub. Black pants paired with a sweater or oversized shirt typified the clothes Hepburn donned for early photo features in magazines such as *Life* and in later candid shots.[68] The cover of *Life* for the December 7, 1953, issue features Hepburn sitting on the floor at home, with a telephone receiver in her hand. She looks straight into the camera. Her legs and feet are bare, and her very short pants are barely visible under an oversized white men's shirt. The shirt, as well as the telephone, would have recalled bobby-soxer attire and habits, but the shorts are rather daring. Such publicity could be seen as supporting Wilson's reading against the grain of *Funny Face* to see Hepburn as the "beginning of youth protest against cultural conservatism," even though the article on the actress in the magazine goes no further than suggesting that she is a very pleasant and hardworking young woman.[69]

In *Funny Face* high fashion is glorified visually and musically for bringing Jo a new identity as a mature and marriageable woman, but Wilson's memories and her undervaluing of haute couture's presence in this and other Hepburn films may be a testament to the power of female desire in relation to female film stars. Her memories of Hepburn's fashion appeal may also have their origin in the mixed signals that were sometimes sent by the star's film publicity. Most advertisements for *Funny Face* featured a dominating image of Hepburn in black sweater, pants, and loafers; she reaches for the sky as her face registers a blessed-out expression of soulfulness. Some advertisements acknowledged the musical score by George and Ira Gershwin (definitely names that parents—but not necessarily teenagers—would recognize), but others asserted, "When Audrey rocks—you'll roll!" Some advertisements went so far as to change the Hepburn "flat look" to meet the dominant cultural—and cinematic—feminine standard of buxom beauty.

The appeal to youth in the advertising campaign for *Funny Face* suggests the studio's recognition that haute couture may not have been of much interest to a large number of young people. *Teenager* was a term that came into popular use in the late 1930s and early 1940s, but it was not until the 1950s that the American film industry made "teenpics" aimed directly at this demographic. They did not feature teenagers in the wholesome fare offered in the prewar years and exemplified by Deanna Durbin's films and the Andy Hardy series starring Mickey Rooney. Instead, they were often cheaply made films formulated to exploit interest in the more controversial elements of teenage life: rock 'n' roll, hot rods, sexual delinquency, and social rebellion.[70]

Uncertainty about the value of haute couture as an appeal to changing audiences is evidenced in the advertising campaign for a later Hepburn vehicle, *How to Steal a Million.* On the one hand, the association of

FIGURE 74. Audrey Hepburn in mod fashion instead of Givenchy haute couture for advertising for *How to Steal a Million.* Author's collection.

Hepburn with Givenchy was so strong by 1966 that the trailer for *How to Steal a Million* declared one attraction of the film to be the "magnificent wardrobe by Givenchy." Like *Sabrina,* this film offers showstopping moments for Hepburn to display his designs, which alternate between looking dowdy and appearing to be virtual tongue-in-cheek parodies of high-fashion excess. In the exploitation plan, Givenchy designs were used in a tie-in with *McCall's* patterns for women who sewed at home and were featured in the July 1966 issue of *McCall's* magazine.

On the other hand, the film's advertising campaign suggests that high chic was not necessarily regarded as the most useful tool for selling Hepburn's image to a younger audience. All the advertisements featured her in clothes that do not appear in the film. These advertising-only costumes had a decidedly mod look, complete with fishnet stockings. Hepburn's hairdo was completely altered to conform more to popular mod standards, and she assumed an awkward (legs crossed while standing, one arm up) pose typical of 1960s sexualized high-fashion photography.[71] Like the flappers of the 1920s, mods were rebellious youth (of both genders, originally found in London) who appreciated how a carefully crafted fashion statement might publicly assert rejection of convention of all types.

This bifurcation of Hepburn's fashion commodification found in *Funny Face* and *How to Steal a Million* suggests the attempt to sell the star (and her films) to a broad female audience that was recognized as having potentially different fashion fantasies, some rooted in the current "youth cult" and others attuned to the older appeal of haute couture. Yet, contrary to Wilson, Hepburn's films and her stardom could be seen as a distinctly conservative response to current youth problems, especially the deployment of female sexuality. This was because Hepburn's star persona, like Deanna Durbin's, remained enmeshed in sexual inexperience and juvenated innocence, traditional aspects of idealized femininity, especially for Americans. Although Audrey Hepburn's juvenated persona was complicated by the star's alignment with high fashion and Continental sophistication, that alignment sometimes was asked to give way—however temporarily—to the current fashion(s) of youth rebellion.

## BUYING YOUR DESIGNER PERSONALITY

If fashionable clothes were defined in the mid-twentieth century as crucial to a woman's ability to attain her ideal self, in the case of Hepburn this consumer-centered phenomenon extended to the star herself. She voiced her undying gratitude for Givenchy's ability to give her true identity: "His are the only clothes in which I am myself," she was reported as saying in 1956. "He is far more than a couturier, he is a creator of personality."[72] These remarks seem to out-Trilby any statement ever made by Jennifer Jones in reference to a Svengali-like Selznick, and

Hepburn extended her tribute to the multifaceted influence of her favorite designer over her when she refers to the therapeutic effects of haute couture: "I depend on Givenchy in the same way American women depend on their psychiatrists."[73]

Hepburn's relationship to Givenchy was not constructed publicly as a crass commercial endorsement designed to profit the star but as a class and sex-stereotyped venture based on mutual appreciation and platonic friendship: he was the genius; she was his muse. In 1955 he hired a lookalike mannequin ("Jackie") to inspire him in her absence—and, also, perhaps, to remind his customers of his most famous celebrity client.[74] He named fabrics for Hepburn, dedicated collections to her, and created a perfume for the actress that, after a time, he graciously permitted other women to buy: advertisements for L'Interdit in *Vogue* in 1964 featured a wistful close-up of Hepburn's face surrounded by softly flowing tulle. Advertising copy reminded potential consumers of the product's exclusive origins: "Once she was the only woman in the world allowed to wear this perfume."

This advertisement resonates with established class alignments in high-fashion consumption. Unlike professional models (and movie stars onscreen), the aristocratic women featured in fashion magazines wore clothes that, it was implied, they were not just modeling but owned. Hepburn's appearance in couture followed this convention and also defined her relationship to Givenchy in terms apart from those normally associated with Hollywood designers and female stars. In November 1964, for example, Hepburn graced the cover of *Vogue* and was featured in a sumptuous ten-page layout in which she modeled "her favourites from the new Givenchy collection." The accompanying text declared that the featured evening gowns from the collection were ones that Hepburn might wear to the various major city openings (New York, Chicago, Los Angeles) of her newest film, *My Fair Lady.*[75] The fashions were followed by an article by Cleveland Amory titled, "The Phenomenon of *My Fair Lady*" and an advertising section in which models displayed fashions from Bonwit Teller and other major stores. This section was headlined "My Fair Lady: The Off-Screen Fashion Life" and was introduced by a cameo photograph of Hepburn in the Cecil Beaton–designed Ascot dress from the film. This introduction of the "*My Fair Lady* influence" of "purely contemporary prettiness . . . headlong charm . . . [and] heartbreaking allure" was followed by models photographed so as to appear to be in the foreground of various scenes of the film. The copy emphasized the film tie-in with taglines such as "Overture to a new Fair Lady in fashion" and "On the street where you live: the new romantics in costume form."[76]

In this multipage layout Hepburn's latest film vehicle was obviously being promoted through the exploitation of her association with high fashion and its department store offspring. It assumed her appeal to a potential audience of women with both an interest in fashion and the monetary ability to buy it in its more expensive manifestations. The status of Hepburn as fashionable and, moreover, as fashion setting (through the dominance of haute couture) was made the centerpiece to fantasy scenarios incorporating fashion as part of a female viewer's/consumer's romantic adventure that could incorporate elements of *My Fair Lady,* in spite of the film's period setting.

## AVOIDING AGE (AND FAT)

Audrey Hepburn grew older, but her characters and her cumulative screen persona barely aged at all. For many years her characters continued to be delineated as young, marriageable "girls" (usually without a profession). As late as *How to Steal a Million,* Hepburn (at thirty-six years old) plays a character that also lives with her "papa." She reacts to a kiss from Peter O'Toole with the wide-eyed confusion of an adolescent stirred by the first inklings of desire. Reviews of *How to Steal a Million* made an issue of the star's age, implying that she was stuck in an image of strained girlishness. One noted, "On occasion William Wyler shoots her through gauze, turning her even more into a brunette Doris Day."[77] Another, in a gentler spirit, observed, "Though not as young as she used to be, Miss Hepburn has lost none of her fey charm as a comedienne."[78] Another review called attention to the repetitive nature of her juvenated characterizations: "Audrey Hepburn is at it again, dressed to the nines by Givenchy, bejeweled by Cartier, terribly chic. . . . [She] responds with her usual selection of charms, looking girlishly amazed, standing slightly knock-kneed, walking with a tiny tiptoe teeter."[79] Apart from the reference to fashion, this review recalls the reactions of many critics to Pickford in the 1920s. It also anticipates Sayre's more pointed observation: "Hepburn blended cuteness and elegance with a sham innocence that almost insulted human nature. . . . No one over fifteen could have remained so sheltered as her screen personae—not even in the Fifties."[80]

Yet *How to Steal a Million* was a film of the 1960s, not the 1950s. Hepburn's juvenated innocence may have been wearing thin in the movies, but the Givenchy-Hepburn connection still had value in publicity.

"Co-Stars Again: Audrey Hepburn and Givenchy" details the long collaboration and even "love" between the star and her favorite designer and its role in securing Hepburn's exalted status on the list of best-dressed women in the world.[81] In typical star discourse that modulates the extraordinary with the ordinary, a great deal of time in this article is spent discussing how the actress's values remain based on care and thrift. Because she suffered from starvation as a child in the Netherlands during World War II, the actress, it is said, shows "the same careful respect for clothes as she does for food," and Hepburn is quoted: "I don't replace clothes until they can't be worn." She recycles the mink linings of her raincoats into other coats![82]

This strategy of referencing Hepburn's childhood deprivation to justify the wearing of fashions that literally cost thousands of dollars is reminiscent of the attempt to justify Mary Pickford's divorce and remarriage to Douglas Fairbanks as a reward for her sad childhood as a girl who either had to support her family or be given away. If the elite consumerism of haute couture seems hard to reconcile with the old-fashioned virtue of thrift, at least *How to Steal a Million* (which had a reported $30,000 budget for the actress's Givenchy wardrobe) approached Hepburn's association with the designer in a less maudlin way, with a cinematic in-joke.[83] Preparing to steal a statue from a museum, Hepburn's role in the caper requires her to don the unflattering attire of a charwoman. "That's fine. That does it," her companion in larceny, Simon Dermott (Peter O'Toole), says. "Does what?" Hepburn asks. He: "Well, for one thing, it gives Givenchy a night off."

Stanley Donen would soon give Givenchy more than a night off. Supposedly dismissing the designer's creations as "too chic," the director insisted that Hepburn could not use Givenchy for her costumes in his seriocomic analysis of a failing marriage, *Two for the Road*.[84] Although much of the film is set on the French Riviera, Hepburn donned ready-to-wear clothes for the first time onscreen. Her "swinging" new wardrobe was created by newly emergent or youth-oriented designers like American Ken Scott, Spaniard Paco Rabanne, London mod designer Mary Quant, and Michèle Rosier (a.k.a. "the vinyl girl").[85] The star's break from Givenchy made news as part of the film's strategic departure from Hepburn's established screen persona. The role of jet-setting Joanna Wallace was much more daring than the public had come to expect of Hepburn. Paralleling Hepburn's fall off the couture pedestal, her character would fall off the moral pedestal long associated with Hepburn's nice-girl heroines. In *Two for the Road* her character commits adultery, swears, and appears nearly nude. Hepburn would continue her association with Givenchy and appear consistently on "best dressed" lists, but her career trailed off simultaneous to the waning influence of Paris haute couture. She would return to the screen on occasion, as in Peter Bogdanovich's *They All Laughed* (1981), and appear middle-aged and chic, but her fashion influence was a thing of the past.

That is not to say that her androgynous, gamine image of undernourished femininity became passé. On the contrary, ultrathinness replaced the soft womanly curves of 1950s femininity as the feminine ideal. In the 1960s the teenage fashion model "Twiggy," otherwise known as Lesley Hornby, replaced Hepburn as the world's most famous thin girl. She became a chief representative of flat-bodied femininity, albeit one affiliated with Cockney cheek rather than Continental chic. With her short blonde hair and big eyes, Twiggy, like Hepburn, was androgynous and gamine.[86] With ninety-one pounds on her five-foot, seven-inch frame, Twiggy took thinness and the prepubescent female body to an even greater extreme as part of the youth quake that altered the relationship between fashion and feminine ideals. In mod or hippie-inspired fashions Twiggy embodied a rebellious break with fashion conceived as an elitist ideal aligned with Parisian elegance—the domain of the New Look, now old, and of Audrey Hepburn, whose ladylike refinement infused by playful innocence did not resonate with the increasingly bold demands of 1960s youth culture.

## THE KEY TO HAPPY ENDINGS

An analysis of Audrey Hepburn's image and its illustration of a convergence of stardom and fashion tells us a great deal about the cultural field of post–World War II America, its representation of youthful femininity for a mass audience, and the specific textual and extratextual means used to address the perceived desires of women in this era. The dimensions of meaning offered by Audrey Hepburn's "adolescent" body and elfin charm cloaked in upper-class haute couture depended on the specific historical circumstances that made Paris fashion an inspirational ideal for American women, who associated it with abundance, elegance, elite consumerism, and Continental sophistication. Hepburn's screen persona combined these associations with characteristics typically aligned with juvenile femininity to suggest the ways in which star images could contain—and benefit—from apparent contradictions. The shaping of Hepburn's screen persona suggests how the ubiquitous

1950s fashion culture for women, based on haute couture ideals, presented itself as enabling rather than constraining a coherent feminine identity, coherent although based on the primacy of a transformative capacity that must overcome cultural problematics inscribed in film—and fashion—in terms of class, gender, sexuality, and age.

Nevertheless, differences among recollected responses to Hepburn's bifurcated image suggest the variety of possible resistant readings of the star as haute couture icon, as well as a rejection, perhaps, of the film industry's presentation of her as the epitome of antielitist youthfulness at the same time she is presented as the exemplar of well-financed fashionability. In this there is the hint that adolescent female viewers, in particular, may have resisted identification with Hepburn's onscreen transformations into proper femininity through Paris high-fashion commoditization. Other viewers, however, may have accepted the films' textual and extratextual strategies of commodifying the star as a viable consumer-centered model for achieving ideal feminine identity, as well as the key to enjoying cinematic happy endings.

Elizabeth Wilson has suggested that fashion attempts to resolve at the imaginary level those social contradictions that cannot be resolved otherwise.[87] Hepburn's star persona manages to merge a number of apparent oppositions: she is playful but elegant, thoroughly American but faintly and aristocratically European, elite but democratic, androgynous but hyperfeminine, womanly but juvenated. More specifically, Hepburn's inscription of filmic fashionability succeeds in solving the contradictions inherent in the transformation of the playful adolescent female of androgynous body and immature sexuality into the securely heterosexual woman comfortable with conventional femininity. In this way Audrey Hepburn's stardom appears to have negotiated successfully the problem of woman's sexual difference and the dilemmas of becoming woman through a fantasy of feminine hybridity, class hybridity, and fashion hybridity. Through such means, her star persona accommodated the desire for a restoration of the prewar gender norms but also anticipated the winds of feminine change that would soon blow the petals of the New Look's "flower women" away.

# Conclusion

In 1922 Mary Pickford declared, "I play only one role, Mary Pickford. I believe that is the secret of my art—of all art."[1] This statement may seem slightly strange, coming from a motion picture actor of long experience and unquestionable success. It seems contrary to everything we want to think about what film, at least as "art," should be. Although it undermines the idea that audiences want something new and different in their filmgoing experiences, it also raises the question of what constitutes art in relation to acting—and stardom: what is the pleasure of seeing an actor perform her star persona, her "self"—especially if that constructed "self" is juvenated well beyond the time the actor is young? What does it mean to do so?

Spoken in a moment when she seems reconciled to her child-woman star persona, Pickford's comment suggests a keen understanding of the nature of stardom, including the skills it demanded and the limitations that ensued. Her statement also zeros in on the essential conundrum of film stardom: the persistent inseparability of most star personas from typecasting. Speaking to that issue, another film pioneer, Thomas H. Ince, defined stardom as when "some actor or actress . . . can portray a certain type better than any other actor or actress."[2]

The history of Hollywood film is filled with actors whose box-office appeal has been linked to the playing of "only one role." We might observe that it is the "secret of the art" of stars like Douglas Fairbanks and Pearl White in the silent era, John Wayne and Marilyn Monroe in the post–World War II period, Tom Cruise and Julia Roberts in more recent years. There may be stars who regularly perform widely different impersonations, in which they shift age as well as shape, like Lon Chaney, Paul Muni, or Meryl Streep. Such stars appear to revel in displaying a new accent or an altered visage, but the norm of stardom is focused on offering audiences something distinctive and pleasurable but also familiar, a star presence they recognize with ease and want to experience over and over again. Obviously, this phenomenon is not limited to juvenated females, but the issue of performing age complicates it. Why did viewers of classical Hollywood cinema enjoy juvenated female stars?

This book has suggested that there is not a single, simple answer to this question. Just as notions differ concerning what girlhood was, is, or should be, even in a narrow period of time (such as in the decade of the 1920s or the 1950s), the girls played by the six stars analyzed in this book varied considerably. Nevertheless, all of these stars showed the powerful appeal of juvenation linked to feminization and to eroticization, whether this appeal is thought of as speaking to anxieties, generating utopian fantasies about the nature of ideal girlhood, or constructing pleasures dependent on some element of contradiction (such as Durbin's voice in relation to her adolescent body or Taylor's startling beauty). Juvenated femininity may have changed considerably from the early years of stardom to the late 1960s, but, as this study has shown, the hold of these stars over the imaginations of their audiences was based on the specific embodiment of juvenated characteristics. Nevertheless, their films evidence the circulation of shared concerns, tropes, or themes associated with girls and girlhood. This persistence of tropes may point to the longevity of assumptions about the meaning of girlhood and cultural attitudes toward girls. In spite of changing standards of feminine conduct and alteration of the boundaries between the child and the adult (as clearly occurred during the 1920s, with the rise of the adolescent flapper), there seems to be a persistence of certain themes: the notion of girlhood as a distinct space, the girl's anticipation of virtues of womanliness (shown in her mothering of other children or in cosseting men), the need for the girl to grapple with loss or victimization, innocence as a counterforce to precocious sexuality, and the demand that the girl be recognized for her emotional and cultural value. As I have shown, however, in my comparison of Pickford's films to Temple's, the return to similar narrative elements may be given very different emphasis in the star vehicles of different juvenated actresses. They do not determine the meaning of the film or the star.

Each of the stars examined in this study participated in the performance of girlhood, but each actress gave the gendered process of juvenating femininity in Hollywood film a considerable range of inflection and meaning. The idea that the star persona becomes a screen type that could be created by Hollywood and the star system out of the imaginary realm and the industrial processes of stardom is important. As Mary Pickford's comments suggest, her child-woman was an imaginary construct, but so, too, were the juvenated star personas of every other actress I consider. Just as Pickford's beloved hoyden incorporated Victorian ideals of womanhood, tropes of children's literature, and cultural investment in the priceless child, other stars represented other well-established ways to mark the actress's age identity and its cultural resonance as a "type." In contrast to Thomas Ince, Pickford's notion of the star as a type includes a recognition that the star is supremely self-referential. A type or stereotype in film is often regarded negatively as an abstraction or generalization that extracts the specificity from human subjectivity. As this study has suggested, stars provide individualized embodiment—and fascinating specificity—to a type: the juvenated feminine.

If juvenated femininity was not all of a piece in Hollywood film, neither was it automatically or easily achieved—or sustained. As Pickford explained to readers of *Vanity Fair* in 1917, her film performances involved a great deal of carefully controlled acting so that she could succeed onscreen in "impersonating a child role." It was no easy task, she explained, even without the complication of the voice in silent motion pictures.[3] If a star specialized in juvenated roles, control of the performance onscreen was matched by the necessity of controlling public understanding of his or her private life. Careful construction of the particulars of that life were required, whether to keep Mary Pickford as the star commodity "Mary Pickford" or Shirley Temple as "Shirley Temple." The star persona could not become attached to facts about offscreen life that might make the portrayal of certain roles, such as innocent young girls, irreconcilable with the actor's public life. Mary Pickford could not be a home wrecker, and Shirley Temple could not be a child spoiled by fame.

Movies revised and recirculated stories and images of the juvenated feminine that were changed to meet the expectations of viewers engaged in the pleasures of different genres (such as the musical), different production trends (such as postwar "adult" melodramas), and different cultural and historical circumstances (such as the Jazz Age, the Great Depression, and World War II). In the end, borrowed spectacles and tropes of the juvenated resulted in shared, but also differentiated, articulations by movie stars who embodied and performed femininity in different ways for changing audiences with different expectations about the meaning of girls and girlhood.

Thus, Temple's stardom responded to Hollywood's perceived need to clean up its product. Her stardom, like Pickford's and Taylor's, drew on nineteenth-century texts and cultural practices but in stories of the juvenated female that, unlike Pickford's film narratives, sought to idealize the man/child relationship as a fortuitous dual rescue at a time when binding masculinity into domesticity was especially important. Durbin's stardom demonstrated the force of adolescent charm combined with cultured musicality. What might have seemed nothing more than a parent's dream of the sweetness of the half-grown girl actually produced an unexpected and exciting tension between sonic womanliness and girlish innocence. Elizabeth Taylor's child roles built on the rich iconographic heritage of sentimental Victorian paintings of little girls and their glorification of the child as an object of beauty. As embodied by Taylor, there was something more to these girls than sentimentality. Jennifer Jones's films problematized heterosexuality through the trope of hysteria attached to adolescence. Hepburn's stardom negotiated adolescence, consumerism, and class in the attainment of post–World War II womanhood through high fashion and romance.

We also need to recognize that classical Hollywood cinema represents an era of American filmmaking governed by the assumption that the audience included children and adolescents, indeed, people of all ages. The juvenation of stars was an industrial strategy that varied in popularity over the years, but the need for Hollywood feature films to appeal to a broad range of viewers did not (and has not) change(d). To speak to that broad demographic without offending, American cinema's overt expression of sexuality was held in check by the Production Code Administration from 1934 until it was replaced by a ratings system in the mid-1960s. All stars have the potential to be powerful role models, but the influence of female stars whose roles and star personas resonated with young people drew particular concern. Thus, the controversy surrounding a film like *Duel in the Sun* expressed a longstanding tension involving juvenation of a film's characters and of its audience. Postwar concerns that film could negatively impact the behavior—including the sexual behavior—of teenagers echoed responses in the 1920s to the movie industry's depiction of young women as flappers.

When Mary Pickford cut her curls on June 21, 1928, she was doing much more than getting a new hairdo. As I noted in chapter 1, star discourse shaped the event as marking a delayed rite of passage from girlhood after the death of her mother. Some regretted the loss of this crucial part of the star image of "America's Sweetheart" as a nostalgic reminder of the past; others rolled their eyes and wondered why it had taken so long.[4] Pickford's new haircut, which imitated modern flappers, was a statement that she was moving on from the childish femininity that she had both dismissed as behind her and vigorously defended so many times, as in the year before, when she declared, "Curls are the one distinctive tribute left to little girls"; she went on to reassure her fans that she was "dedicated to little-girl roles for the rest of my screen life."[5] By cutting her curls, Pickford symbolically killed her juvenated star-self; however, the juvenated "Mary Pickford" refused to die, even if, by 1928, it was obvious that public interest had turned decisively away from little girls in the Victorian mold to other female screen types, most notably the flapper.

Pickford had retained her curls and her little-girl roles past the time when, in the words of Adela Rogers St. Johns, "an entirely new generation had evolved an entirely new type of girl."[6] *Photoplay* noted that "fans are young and the new stars are young."[7] The audience's pleasures and fantasies were being influenced by a new form of juvenated female, the modern girl embodied by the screen flapper. Historian Frederick Lewis Allen remarked that the iconic flapper, the center of social controversy in the 1920s, was nothing more than "a flat-breasted, spindle-legged, carefree, knowing adolescent in a long-waisted child's frock."[8] The flapper's childish looks were combined, it was often said, with not-so-juvenated gin drinking, Charleston dancing, and cigarette-smoking exhibitionism. Although, as Allen suggests, the fashion ideal may have called for an adolescent or prepubescent look, flappers seemed to be redefining the sexual freedom of American women (of all ages) in the 1920s. In the movies, however, jazz babies typically made a last-reel commitment to traditional notions of marriage. The screen flapper suggests that there is a broad variety of juvenation that remains to be explored in Hollywood cinema.

Reflecting film's desire to both exploit and hold the flappers' rebellion in check, in 1929 a poll taken by the trade magazine *Exhibitors' Trade Herald and Moving Picture World* named the quintessential modern girl Clara Bow as the year's "most popular film actress," with archetypal flapper Colleen Moore in second place. Mary Pickford ranked sixth.[9] Displaced in popularity by the ubiquitous Jazz Age "dancing daughters" and "modern maidens" of the screen like Bow, Moore, and Joan Crawford, Pickford essayed her first all-talkie film role in 1929. She played a southern belle whose irresponsible flirtations lead to tragedy in *Coquette* (dir. Sam Taylor, 1929). The film, based on a stage play starring Helen Hayes, was advertised as presenting "a modern, grown-up Mary Pickford—with chic bobbed hair . . . lovelier than ever before, as an alluring little flirt, breaking hearts, playing with love!"[10] The advertisements made Pickford's role sound more daring than it was. In contrast to the original stage play, Pickford's flirt does not relinquish her virginity to a lower-class suitor. She stays all night at his cabin, but Norma Besant (Pickford) later sits on the lap of her "mammy," Julia (Louise Beavers), and assures her that she is untouched. This was a talkie, and perhaps because audiences were as curious about Pickford's voice as they were about the "modern, grown-up" turn in her screen persona, the film made more money than any previous Pickford vehicle. Even so, one New York reviewer expressed dissatisfaction with the results of the change: "The sophisticated Mary Pickford is not as compelling as 'America's Sweetheart.'"[11]

Pickford next starred as Katherine opposite Douglas Fairbanks's Petruchio in a talkie version of Shakespeare's *The Taming of the Shrew* (dir. Sam Taylor, 1929). Pickford gave a credible performance, and the film realized a modest return at the box office. She then took on the role of a French chorus girl with a yen for a recently divorced theater impresario in *Kiki* (dir. Clarence Brown, 1930). Although Pickford seemed to break even more radically with her established juvenated type, Mordaunt Hall wrote that the star made the naughty chorus girl into another Pickford "hoyden," the kind of "young imp of her early films," and that Pickford had "influenced Kiki a good deal more than Kiki has influenced her."[12] Thus, Hall recognizes what, in the wake of her mother's death, Pickford's publicity machine had worked to deny: the star's complicity in the sustained childishness of her portrayals that now infused roles that were far removed from the art of "Mary Pickford." *Kiki* flopped. In 1932 Claire Booth Brokaw (later Luce) wrote of this phase of Pickford's career in an essay that drips with disdain for the "sugared sentimentality" of the star persona that Pickford was attempting to change. She concludes with some satisfaction: "You cannot stay a child too long without paying the penalty of a devitalized maturity."[13]

Deanna Durbin also tried to escape juvenation, but like Pickford, she failed to do so. A British fan magazine, *Picturegoer*, breathed a sigh of relief that the seventeen-year-old star's introduction to screen romance in *First Love* managed to rise "above the polluting influence of Hollywood's diseased mind."[14] Universal's subsequent efforts to "glamorize" Durbin, as I noted in chapter 3, were greeted with alarm by many. Yet Durbin did not appreciate the juvenating restrictions on her image. She exhibited increased frustration with the studio system and with her star persona, which led to her suspension at Universal in October 1941, when she was just shy of her twentieth birthday. Durbin's rebellion is understandable if one takes for granted that stars who worked under long-term contracts in the studio system were given limited opportunities to experiment as actors and expand their range beyond their established and profitable type. When she finally resumed work, at the end of January 1942, Durbin had secured story and director approval, but she was never allowed to go on loan out, as she had wished, in the hopes of attaining more varied roles.[15] Durbin's most notable attempt to escape juvenation took form in the role of a cheap torch singer (a prostitute in Somerset Maugham's original story) in *Christmas Holiday.* She stated publicly that she allowed herself to be cast against type because of her desire to depart from "the youthful 'Durbin formula,'" which she described as eight years of "sweet and vapid ingénue roles."[16] Expecting, no doubt, to be shocked, audiences flocked to see the film, just as audiences had flocked to see Pickford as a new, sophisticated flirt in *Coquette.* But neither actress secured a new phase in her career. It appears that viewers' expectations that the star was aligned with idealized girlishness were too securely set.

Of course, the studio system often has been blamed for keeping Hollywood actors closely affiliated with their most successful roles in order to satisfy audience expectations and guarantee box office. Durbin's frustration with her career, leading to her early retirement, echoes public statements made by Mary Pickford when she was not defending her child/adolescent roles. Durbin, however, had significantly less control over her career than Pickford. It was undeniable, too, that audiences embraced the formula that Durbin dismissed, but as I have argued, her star presence may have been pleasurable not just because it rendered her "vapid" and "sweet" but because it offered complexity in the combination of Durbin's womanly voice and her visualization (and narrativization) as a charming but also surprisingly aggressive adolescent. That complexity may have provoked pleasures that appealed to the conscious desire for cultural uplift but also offered the star's audiences a model of chaste juvenated femininity made more exciting by its delivery of a frisson of erotic—as well as musical—pleasure.

While Pickford and Durbin struggled with the problem of whether and how to play roles beyond their juvenated type, a clear exception to being caught in a juvenated star persona was Elizabeth Taylor. Taylor's sensitive portrayals of virginal English girlhood were left far behind when, as a teenager, she developed a voluptuous physicality in keeping with the dominant feminine ideals of the postwar era. MGM quickly moved her into playing grown women, often outfitted in décolleté gowns based on the New Look. In her teens she was playing opposite older leading men, like Robert Taylor in *The Conspirator* (1949) and, later, in *Ivanhoe* (dir. Richard Thorpe, 1952). Taylor was funneled into a few comedies like *Father of the Bride* (dir. Vincente Minnelli, 1951), but she appeared primarily in melodramas, including *The Girl Who Had Everything* (dir. Richard Thorpe, 1953), based on the hoary Norma Shearer vehicle *A Free Soul* (dir. Clarence Brown, 1931), about a spoiled young woman who falls for a gangster. Although Taylor's voice remained breathy, high-pitched, and girlish for many years, she was sold to audiences as a desirable and desiring woman. All her films emphasized the spectacle of her facial beauty and womanly shape, even when she played women (as she did so often) who, by the machinations of melodramatic fate, longed for sexual satisfaction, as in *Cat on a Hot Tin Roof* (dir. Richard Brooks, 1958).

In spite of the popularity of teen stars like Deanna Durbin in the late 1930s, Shirley Temple had a difficult transition to adulthood onscreen. After leaving Fox, she made *Kathleen* (dir. Harold S. Bucquet, 1941) at MGM and then a B-film, *Miss Annie Rooney* (dir. Edwin L. Martin, 1942). Both movies died at the box office. She retired briefly before entering a new phase of her career when she signed as a Selznick artist in 1944. In her autobiography Temple recalls that Selznick tried to get her to bind her breasts because he thought her "too mature and curvaceous for the ingénue he visualized" in *Since You Went Away.*[17] She refused, and after her successful appearance as "Brig" in the Selznick production, Temple was typecast as a teenage bobby-soxer until her final retirement in 1950, at twenty-two years old.

For obvious reasons Selznick worked harder to keep Jennifer Jones from being typecast than he did Temple.[18] As I noted in chapter 4, Selznick expressed concern about this issue immediately following Jones's great success with *The Song of Bernadette,* but as we have seen, the star's roles were frequently juvenated, whether through psychological qualities or physical attributes. That juvenation was not aligned with the kind of mainstream bobby-soxer comedies that Temple succeeded in, but her star persona incorporated a strong affinity with juvenation attached to sexual victimization and pathology; the actress's ability to play young was called on as a kind of signature flourish to many of her roles: if not centralized in the plot, as in *Duel in the Sun,* then her skill in impersonating a girl was often emphasized with flashbacks to childhood and adolescence inserted into her films. Juvenation became a way to emphasize her skill as an actor.

As I suggested in chapter 6, Audrey Hepburn's juvenated qualities were sustained in considerably different ways from Jones's. Hepburn's juvenation was in some ways a throwback, emphasizing sexual innocence in an era that was worried about young people's sexual knowledge. It is of some interest, however, that Simone de Beauvoir lumped her together with a number of actresses, including Brigitte Bardot, as an "erotic hoyden."[19] This categorization, however, ignores the fact that Hepburn appealed to women and adolescents in a way that Bardot did not. Bardot was deeply disliked in France and regarded as an international embarrassment, an unwelcome confirmation of postwar sexual delinquency. Even if the characters of both stars often end up married to much older men at the end of their films, Hepburn's sexual awakening as a sheltered daughter contrasts sharply with Bardot's voluptuous and sexually precocious protagonists. Hepburn's characters are not only fashionable but so refined that even when director Stanley Donen used the spy comedy *Charade* (1963) to play with Hepburn's *jeune fille* star persona—making her prematurely widowed character the sexual aggressor in her relationship with a suave older man, Peter Joshua (Cary Grant)—the effect is comic rather than disturbing. The rite of passage to womanhood continued to be featured in many of Hepburn's films, including Donen's *Two for the Road* (1967), which depended on a multiple-flashback structure.

Pickford's statement quoted at the beginning of this conclusion may make us slightly uncomfortable in its assertion that playing one's constructed star persona is compatible with "art," yet as this study has shown, the process of constructing a star persona is not a simple thing, whether considered in relation to age, aesthetics, economics, audience expectations, or just about anything else. All these stars have a relationship to the imaginary realm, as well as to social reality and to social discourse. Working to define the interconnectedness of those arenas is an important, if not easily attained, goal in star studies, and it is certainly a worthy subject of future scholarship.

The world of classical Hollywood cinema is removed from ours, and speculating about the meanings and pleasures that stars created for their historical audiences is not only a necessary part of the reassessment of juvenated actors but also one of its most challenging aspects. Speculating about audience reception of specific performers and films demands piecing together evidence that is fragmentary and uncertain at best. In trying to locate the complexity of and nuances in the reception of stars' textual and extratextual construction, scholars like Annette Kuhn and Jackie Stacey have turned to interviewing aging filmgoers about their memories of Hollywood films and the appeal of actors who were their favorites in them. Such ethnohistorical attempts to recover and record cultural memories of star-centered pleasure are important, but conclusions drawn from this research approach are limited by the problem that these informants' expressions are consciously held and admitted reactions separated from the viewers' original responses by decades.[20]

In looking at the appeal of juvenated actresses and their films, this study has addressed girlhood as both the textual and extratextual construction of what is frequently a sentimental discourse that seeks to instruct the viewer in how to feel. Mary Pickford's use of a family discourse to justify her adultery, divorce, and remarriage is one instance of the industry's reliance on sentimentality as a means to control response to contradictions in a juvenated star persona deeply implicated in Hollywood's representation of girls and girlhood.

Because of its association with nostalgia and sentimentality, juvenated representation may appear to be an especially dangerous object of study, especially for feminists. Nostalgia is often considered a trap that leads to a denial of ideologically structured gender and sexual identity. It is undeniable that these star images show sexually and socially regulated femininity. Yet in many instances they call attention to that regulation even if they do not challenge it directly. Addressing film as a sentimental discourse centered on juvenation in relation to femininity is worthy of a great deal more study. In addition to illuminating texts, it seems to hold promise in opening discussion of how scholars and viewers should engage with film as an affect-engaged experience that moves us beyond the boundaries of many critical, historical, and theoretical methodologies.[21]

Instrumental to my study has been the attention paid to the textual specifics of female juvenation, how girls and girlhood were imagined—and "imaged"—through Hollywood classical cinema. Texts do not absolutely control how they are read, but they do "demand" to be read in specific ways, and analyzing the visualization of the juvenile is an important part of my argument. If we do not look at a film as a visual and aural experience, then we miss not only the performance element of stars but film's ability to make meaning through more than plots and dialogue.

This study has tried also to complicate notions of the cinema as a cultural field that produces stars and texts; stardom is inseparable from the force field of historical intertexts that inform film texts. I have also looked at the extratextual processes integral to the film industry's creation of films as economic products to be marketed and consumed. But films are more than consumables; they are experienced through the processes of reception. During the era of classical Hollywood cinema, reception did not begin or end with the film's exhibition. Like today, it would start with trailers or other advertisements and exhibitor promotions that would build anticipation for the film; after the film was seen, it reverberated in the actions and thoughts of viewers that might include a number of star-related activities that encompassed everything from buying a fan magazine to joining a fan club or recreating or buying clothing that resembled the star's. Such activities might be seen as primarily operating on the level of consumerism, but they had other emotional and psychological meanings, especially, as I discussed in chapter 6, in helping viewers, particularly female viewers, to negotiate their identities. Thus, stars and their historically and socially bound audiences are important to consider in understanding how film operates as a projected fantasy that might influence, consciously or unconsciously, a viewer's sense of identity, not only as a gendered subject but also as one bound into the social conventions linked to age-related aspects of identity.

My examination of these six stars shows that a complex interplay of cinematic and cultural dynamics is involved in constructing juvenated femininity as an appeal to viewers over a significant historical period in the cinema. The juvenated feminine is not just one unvarying type. It must be culturally contextualized, as well as placed within the aesthetic conventions, economic demands, and industrial processes of Hollywood film as a changing field, even within a stable period marked aesthetically as "classical Hollywood cinema" and industrially as "the studio system." Whether considered across time or at one particular moment in history, the varying responses to the precocious charms of a star like Shirley Temple or Audrey Hepburn show the need to contextualize responses to a given star image. The viewing pleasures attached to Hollywood's juvenated femininities are complex and variable, made more so by the prospect that some (whether men, women, or children) in the audience might draw on a distinct body of cultural knowledge (such as children's literature or orphan narratives or star discourse in fan magazines) that might make them preferred viewers and that might allow them to extend their pleasurable engagement with the star beyond the role the actor embodies onscreen.

The pleasures of that embodiment and their complex cultural meanings have been traced across the juvenated textual and extratextual inscription of six stars, but the implications are much greater in terms of considering gender and sexuality in the cinema. We need to move beyond considering feminine identity inscribed in the cinema as a matter only of representing "women." Juvenated femininity does not merely create a dismissible Other, the female who demonstrates age-based characteristics that keep society from confronting the complexities of adult women. The performance of girlhood has its own complexity, and we need to look in a more sustained and close way at the representation of age in screen femininity, just as film studies has benefited from being increasingly attuned to the complications created by race, ethnicity, and nationality.

It is not the intention of this study to suggest that gender juvenation is exclusively female in the cinema. The juvenation of masculinity is a subject for study that suggests altogether different but equally important cultural implications. As I have argued elsewhere, the juvenation of Douglas Fairbanks allowed him to figure as a powerful cinematic emblem of modern masculinity.[22] Aligned with the future rather than the past, Fairbanks's hyperenergetic, juvenated masculinity functioned very differently as a cultural icon during the same period in which Mary Pickford was representing juvenated femininity aligned with the past and with traditional values. There is significant difference between these two star icons also in the fact that as a male, Fairbanks was allowed to play an adult and still be juvenated, while Pickford's heroines are adolescents and children rather than adult women. This persistence of the juvenated in grown men seems to be normalized as an acceptable element of adult masculinity that is still seen today, especially in film comedies.

The stars and films examined in this study show us that we cannot keep to a narrow path in analyzing female stars in relation to mainstream culture. To be blind to the star embodiment of juvenation in different genres and periods is to ignore the adaptability of Hollywood to satisfy the desires of the collective imaginary. This study has suggested the need to explore those depictions of femininity that have been central to the pleasures of the cinema but escape the categories of analysis that have dominated our study of stars and of gender and sexuality in film. My study recognizes the need to be careful about categorizing responses to these cultural products through generalizations that fail to recognize the complexity of and differences in responses from men, women, and children to film when it is aimed at a broad demographic. We must acknowledge also that classical Hollywood aimed that product at white people. With the rare exception stars of color did not emerge on the screen as leads in major feature film productions until the 1950s, and all star personas, juvenated or not, were built on dominant assumptions about the value of whiteness as securely as they were founded on constructions of gender, sexuality, and age. More complex articulations of the performance of age and gender need to be explored, whether in relation to nationality, race, class, or other issues.

By studying juvenation attached to stardom, we are led to a greater understanding of how classical Hollywood films produced both meaning and pleasure through star images that were part of motion pictures as a stable but ever-changing aesthetic, cultural, historical, and industrial phenomenon. My hope is that this book provides a template for studying juvenation that occurs within but is not confined to film stardom in classical Hollywood cinema. Juvenation remains an important part of American culture and of visual media, in all its popular forms.

Clearly, with the presence of teens in every conceivable form of visual media, fascination with girls and girlhood continues to be registered today. Changes in culture and media have resulted in inevitable alteration of the qualities attached to girlhood. So, too, the relationship of juvenated femininity to stardom has changed, going so far in some media venues as to replace human performers with more controllable computer-generated or animated stars. Media convergence means that many teen stars are now visible and cross over from television or the music industry into film, but fragmented and diffused as it is, the creation of stardom now seems a process that is fitful at best, more inclined to create celebrities who are famous for being famous than stars whose performances onscreen are central to their popularity as "movie stars." Nevertheless, what the current fascination with female juvenation owes to classical Hollywood, when film was at its most culturally influential, textually prolific, and commercially popular, is what future studies must attempt to discover.

# Notes

INTRODUCTION

1. John Hartley, "'When Your Child Grows Up Too Fast': Juvenation and the Boundaries of the Social in the News Media," *Continuum: Journal of Media and Cultural Studies* 12, no. 1 (1998): 9–30, 15.

2. Ibid.

3. See ibid., 14–15, 20–22.

4. John Hartley, "Juvenation: News, Girls and Power." In *News, Gender and Power,* edited by Cynthia Carter, Gill Branston, and Stuart Allen (London: Routledge, 2000), 50–61.

5. Ibid., 48, 53–54.

6. On the transition from picture personalities to stars see the pioneering historical study by Richard deCordova, *Picture Personalities: The Emergence of the Star System in America* (Urbana: University of Illinois Press, 1990), 86, 98–116.

7. On this point see Gaylyn Studlar, "Theda Bara: Orientalism, Sexual Anarchy, and the Jewish Star," in *Flickers of Desire: Movie Stars of the 1910s,* ed. Jennifer Bean (New Brunswick, NJ: Rutgers University Press, 2011), 113–36.

8. Perhaps the most influential study from a cultural and theoretical perspective that emphasizes the semiotic dimensions of stardom is Richard Dyer's *Stars* (London: British Film Institute, 1979).

9. Anne Varty, *Children and Theatre in Victorian Britain: "All Work, No Play"* (Houndmills: Palgrave MacMillan, 2008), 9–16. Child-watching as entertainment has been addressed within a nineteenth-century British stage context by Varty, as well as by Carolyn Steedman, *Strange Dislocations: Childhood and the Idea of Human Interiority, 1780–1930* (Cambridge, MA: Harvard University Press, 1994); and Jacqueline Rose in *The Case of Peter Pan; or, The Impossibility of Children's Fiction* (Philadelphia: University of Pennsylvania Press,

1984), 90–102. Less attention seems to have been paid to this phenomenon in the States, although Viviana A. Zelizer discusses it briefly in her *Pricing the Priceless Child: The Changing Social Value of Children* (1985; Princeton, NJ: Princeton University Press, 1994), 6.

10. See Steedman, *Strange Dislocations,* esp. chap. 8, "Children of the Stage"; and Catherine Robson, *Men in Wonderland: The Lost Girlhood of the Victorian Gentleman* (Princeton, NJ: Princeton University Press, 2001), esp. 184–87.

11. For a popular-press discussion in the 1930s of how Hollywood defined a star, see George Shaffer, "How Real Film Star Packs 'em in without Aid," *Chicago Daily Tribune,* May 21, 1935, 16; and Rosalind Shaffer, "Movies Turn to Youngsters for Their Favorite Players," *Chicago Daily Tribune,* May 12, 1935, E12. On children working in films in the 1910s see Mary Abbott Lodge, "Children Who Support Grown-Up Stars," *Motion Picture,* Oct. 1917, 27–32; and Anonymous, "Christmas Letters from the Children of the Screen," *Motion Picture,* Jan. 1916, 121–23.

12. "Gallery," *Motion Picture,* Dec. 1917, n.p. In *Aladdin and the Wonderful Lamp* Corbin appears almost nude in an oriental bath. On Corbin see Katherine H. Adams, Michael L. Keene, and Katherine C. Koella, *Seeing the American Woman, 1880–1920: The Social Impact of the Visual Media Explosion* (Jefferson, NC: McFarland, 2011), 43–47.

13. Marie Osborne was also known as Helen Marie. Her status as a "leading lady" for the Balboa production company included direction by Henry King. See Anonymous, "What's Going On," *Green Book,* May 1916, 833. One of her monikers came from her appearance in *Little Mary Sunshine* (King, 1916). Foy's films for Solax studio included Alice Guy-Blaché's *Falling Leaves* (1912).

14. Zelizer, *Pricing the Priceless Child,* 11–13.

15. The plot of Coogan's *My Boy* resembles that of Baby Peggy's *Captain January,* which was remade by 20th Century–Fox, with Shirley Temple, in a version that actually eschews a great deal of the tearful sentimentality of the Baby Peggy film, in which the captain is very old and feeble and seems near death in the film's penultimate scene. Early in her career Temple was often compared to Jackie Coogan in the scale of her appeal. As Rob King has noted, the immensity of Coogan's popularity as a child star in the 1920s is now forgotten by the general public, which knows him primarily through his role as the grotesque "Uncle Fester" on the television series *The Addams Family.* By way of contrast, Temple's sound-era films for Fox have been rereleased in volumes of DVDs (after being on VHS for many years), and her dancing-star image has been imitated by little girls, especially on the kiddie beauty pageant circuit. See Rob King, "The Kid from *The Kid:* Jackie Coogan and the Consolidation of Child Consumerism," *Velvet Light Trap* 48 (fall 2001): 4–19.

16. On Baby Peggy's stardom and that of Jackie Coogan see the former's account of child actors in Diana Serra Cary, *Hollywood's Children: An Insider Account of the Child Star Era* (Dallas: Southern Methodist University Press, 1978), 45–70.

17. Tino Balio, *Grand Design: Hollywood as a Modern Business Enterprise, 1930–1939* (Berkeley: University of California Press, 1993), 260.

18. On the switch to child actors after the creation of the Production Code Administration see Jane Hampton, "Robbing the Cradle for Stars," *Photoplay,* Nov. 1934, 34–35, 98. On the 1930s repeating the 1910s in using children in film see Rosalind Shaffer, "Movies Turn to Youngsters for Their Favorite Players," *Chicago Daily Tribune,* May 12, 1935, E12.

19. See Balio, *Grand Design,* 146–47.

20. David Bordwell, Janet Staiger, and Kristin Thompson, *The Classical Hollywood Cinema: Film Style and Mode of Production to 1960* (New York: Columbia University Press, 1985), xiii.

21. Jones's feature film debut as "Phylis Isley" occurred in B films at Republic in 1939, but the studio quickly released her. As "Jennifer Jones" she began her successful film career in 1943 with the release of *The Song of Bernadette.* This means there is an argument to be made that Jones should come before Taylor in this chronology, but because the films I emphasize in the Jones chapter move beyond the wartime era and were released after those of Taylor I discuss, I have used this ordering.

22. John Hartley, "'When Your Child Grows Up Too Fast': Juvenation and the Boundaries of the Social in the News Media," *Continuum: Journal of Media and Cultural Studies* 12, no. 1 (1998): 9–30, 15. For a helpful overview of the representation of teenage girls in film and popular culture, mainly devoted to the 1930s through the 1950s, see Ilana Nash, *American Sweethearts: Teenage Girls in Twentieth-Century Popular Culture* (Bloomington: Indiana University Press, 2006).

23. Deanna Durbin Devotees was a fan club encouraged by Universal and given special access, on occasion, to Durbin during the height of her stardom. The fan club's current website is deannadurbindevotees.com.

24. The Paramount decrees handed down by the Supreme Court in 1948 declared vertical integration of production/distribution/exhibition to be monopolistic and required studios to divest themselves of their theaters. Vertical integration had been the backbone of studios' financial stability, allowing them to control the process of filmmaking from concept through guaranteed outlets for exhibition. For a summary of the case and other reasons for the demise of the old studio system see John Belton, *American Cinema/American Culture,* 3rd ed. (Boston: McGraw Hill, 2009), 82, 324–25. For an in-depth analysis see Michael Conant, *Antitrust in the Motion Picture Industry* (Berkeley: University of California Press, 1960).

25. Bordwell, Staiger, and Thompson, *Classical Hollywood Cinema,* 368.

26. "Films' Child Prodigies Must Make Hay While Sun Shines," *Los Angeles Times,* July 22, 1934, A1.

27. Review of *Heidi, Life,* Oct. 25, 1937, 104–5.

28. On female viewers' relationship to women stars see Jackie Stacey, *Star Gazing: Hollywood Cinema and Female Spectatorship* (London: Routledge, 1994); and, on the construction of masculinity in Hollywood stars of the 1950s, Steve Cohan, *Masked Men: Masculinity and the Movies in the Fifties* (Bloomington: Indiana University Press, 1997). On the construction of ethnicity in relation to stardom see Adrienne McLean, *Being Rita Hayworth: Labor, Identity, and Hollywood Stardom* (New Brunswick, NJ: Rutgers University Press, 2004);

and Diane Negra, *Off-White Hollywood: American Culture and Ethnic Female Stardom* (London: Routledge, 2001). On the social implications of a sexually transgressive star image see Ramona Curry, *Too Much of a Good Thing: Mae West as Cultural Icon* (Minneapolis: University of Minnesota Press, 1996).

29. See especially Diane Negra, "Re-made for Television: Hedy Lamarr's Postwar Star Textuality," in *Small Screens, Big Ideas: Television in the 1950s,* ed. Janet Thumim (London: I.B. Tauris, 2001), 105–17.

30. If we wished to trace the origins of this tendency, Laura Mulvey's influential article, "Visual Pleasure and Narrative Cinema," *Screen* 16, no. 3 (1975): 6–18, would be a good place to start.

31. See, e.g., Frances Gateward and Murray Pomerance, eds., *Sugar, Spice, and Everything Nice: Cinemas of Girlhood* (Detroit: Wayne State University Press, 2002).

32. See Shelley Stamp, *Movie-Struck Girls: Women and Motion Picture Culture after the Nickelodeon* (Princeton, NJ: Princeton University Press, 2000); Nan Enstad, *Ladies of Labor, Girls of Adventure: Working Women, Popular Culture, and Labor Politics at the Turn of the Twentieth Century* (New York: Columbia University Press, 1999); Antonia Lant, *Blackout: Reinventing Women for Wartime British Cinema* (Princeton, NJ: Princeton University Press, 1992). For girls' responses to mass media, including the music industry and television in the post–World War II era, see Susan J. Douglas, *Where the Girls Are: Growing Up Female with the Mass Media* (New York: Random House, 1995).

33. Murray Pomerance, "Introduction: Gender in Film and the End of the Twentieth Century," in *Ladies and Gentlemen, Boys and Girls,* ed. Murray Pomerance (New York: State University of New York Press, 2001), 5.

34. Kaja Silverman, *The Acoustic Mirror: The Female Voice in Psychoanalysis and Cinema* (Bloomington: Indiana University Press, 1988), 61.

35. "*Duel in the Sun,*" in *American Film Institute Catalog, 1941–1950, Film Entries, A-L,* ed. Patricia King Hanson (Berkeley: University of California Press, 1999), 661. For public reaction to Selznick's distribution and exhibition strategy for the film see Bosley Crowther, "The Screen," *New York Times,* May 8, 1947; and "The New Pictures," *Time,* March 17, 1947, 101.

## CHAPTER 1

*Epigraph.* Vachel Lindsay, "To Mary Pickford, Moving-Picture Actress (On hearing she was leaving the moving-pictures for the stage)," in *The Congo and Other Poems* (New York: Macmillan, 1914), www.gutenberg.org/files/1021/1021-h/1021-h.htm#2H_4_0042.

1. On the development of the "picture-personality" see Richard deCordova, *Picture Personalities: The Emergence of the Star System in America* (Urbana: University of Illinois Press, 1990), esp. 73–74; and Janet Staiger, "Seeing Stars," *Velvet Light Trap* 20 (summer 1983), repr. in *Stardom: Industry of Desire,* ed. Christine Gledhill (New York: Routledge, 1991), 1–16. On the early publicity surrounding Pickford see deCordova, 70–72; and Staiger, 5.

2. Vachel Lindsay, "Queen of My People," *New Republic,* July 17, 1917, 280–81.

3. Edwin Carty Ranck, "Mary Pickford—Whose Real Name Is Gladys Smith," *American Magazine,* May 1918, 35.

4. The term is used to describe Pickford in an article from 1917, detailing her generosity to charities, especially those seeking to improve the lives of children. See Edna Wright, "Mary Pickford Plus 'Silent Money Talk,'" *Motion Picture Classic,* March 1917, 21.

5. "The Charm of Mary Pickford," *The Bioscope,* April 1914, 753.

6. Review of *Rags, Variety,* August 6, 1915, 17.

7. G. Stanley Hall, *On Adolescence* (New York: D. Appleton, 1924), 241–42, 250–52, 262–64. See also John Demos and Virginia Demos, "Adolescence in Historical Perspective," *Journal of Marriage and the Family* 31 (Nov. 1969): 632–39.

8. On other child impersonators see "Screen Stars in Second Childhood," *Vanity Fair,* Dec. 1917, 74; and, in the same issue, Mary Pickford, "The Portrayal of Child Roles," 75.

9. On Bara's stardom see Gaylyn Studlar, "Theda Bara: Orientalism, Sexual Anarchy, and the Jewish Star," in *Flickers of Desire: Movie Stars of the 1910s,* ed. Jennifer M. Bean (New Brunswick, NJ: Rutgers University Press, 2011), 113–36; on stars who played serial heroines see Mark Garrett Cooper, "Pearl White and Grace Cunard: The Serial Queen's Volatile Present," in ibid., 174–95.

10. Unidentified newspaper clipping, May 17, 1921, n.p., in Scrapbook 35, Ms. Collection U-6, Mary Pickford Collection, Academy of Motion Picture Arts and Sciences (hereafter AMPAS). Her contemporary Edward Wagenknecht suggested that it was a mistake to identify Pickford "exclusively with a portrayal of children and young girls." He remarked, "It was not until after the beginning of the feature era that Miss Pickford became definitely associated with ingénue roles, and it was not until *The Poor Little Rich Girl* that she appeared all through a feature film as a child." Wagenknecht is correct that Pickford did not always play children, especially in the early years, when she appeared in numerous one-reelers. See Edward Wagenknecht, *The Movies in the Age of Innocence* (Norman: University of Oklahoma Press, 1962), 156.

11. Mordaunt Hall, "Pollyanna," *New York Times,* Jan. 19, 1920, 16 (emphasis added). Pickford acknowledges the frequency with which this question was asked in Mary Pickford, "My Own Story," *Ladies' Home Journal,* pt. 3, 128.

12. In 1917 a photo caption claimed that Pickford was already expressing ambivalence toward her youthful roles: "With one breath she announces her ambition to play only grown-up, emotional parts, and in the next little gasp she claims herself wedded forevermore to 'awkward age' impersonations." "Mary Pickford" [photo with caption], *Motion Picture,* Dec. 1917, 22. Mary Pickford, quoted in Evelyn Wells, "Big Film Roles, Four Babies, Pickford Wish," *San Francisco Call,* March 22, 1921, Scrapbook 29, Pickford Collection, AMPAS.

13. See Kevin Brownlow, *Mary Pickford Rediscovered* (New York: Abrams, 1999), 197–200. Pickford attributes abandoning the role in *Faust* to her own

realization that the part was too radical a departure for her. See Pickford, "My Own Story," pt. 3, 128.

14. "Photoplays: Miss Pickford's Universality, and Pola Negri's Comeback," *New York Evening Post,* May 10, 1924, Scrapbook 39, Mary Pickford Collection, AMPAS.

15. "Mary Will Quit Movies Because Type's Worn Out," unidentified newspaper clipping, April 24, 1924, n.p., in Scrapbook 39, Mary Pickford Collection, AMPAS.

16. Quoted in Brownlow, *Mary Pickford Rediscovered,* 250.

17. Avis McMakin, "The Winning Letter," *Photoplay,* Oct. 1925, 109.

18. Mary Pickford Awards," *Photoplay,* Oct. 1925, 45. Pickford played Cinderella (in 1914) and Sara Crewe in *The Little Princess* (in 1917). Mary Miles Minter essayed the role of Anne of Green Gables in 1919.

19. Mordaunt Hall, "Mary Pickford as of Old," *New York Times,* Oct. 19, 1925, 26; repr. in *The "New York Times" Film Reviews,* vol. 1, 280.

20. Joan Riviere, "Womanliness as a Masquerade," in *Psychoanalysis and Female Sexuality,* ed. Hendrik M. Ruitenbeek (New Haven, CT: College and University Press, 1966), 211–14.

21. In 1922 an advice book to women noted that the small girl (under five-foot-three) was the preferred "screen type" because "many leading men are not tall . . . [and] perhaps it is easier for the little girl to win sympathy." Quoted in Heather Addison, *Hollywood and the Rise of Physical Culture* (New York: Routledge, 2003), 59–60.

22. In a scenario file from the Pickford Collection at AMPAS there is a company memo listing writers who "write things that are considered Mary Pickford material." These writers include Kathleen Norris, Fannie Hurst, Edith Wharton, Edna Ferber, Corra Harris, Zona Gale, Willa Cather, Margaret Porter, Eleanor Gates, and Ruth Sawyer (Box 177, "188—Scenario" file, Mary Pickford Collection, AMPAS).

23. Sally Mitchell, *The New Girl* (New York: Columbia University Press, 1996), 25.

24. On girls' literature's use of illness as a vehicle to facilitate the transition from childhood to ideal womanhood see Anne Scott MacLeod, "The *Caddie Woodlawn* Syndrome: American Girlhood in the Nineteenth Century," in *A Century of Childhood, 1820–1920,* ed. Mary Lynn Stevens Heininger et al. (Rochester, NY: Margaret Woodbury Strong Museum, 1984), 97–119, esp. 110–12. See also Mitchell, *The New Girl,* 161.

25. A publicity article from 1924 noted that "millions of young girls—to say nothing of the boys and their elders—love the Mary Pickford of pictures, indicated by the letters received requesting photographs" (Joe Mitchell Chapple, "Flashlights of Famous People," *Brooklyn New York Times,* April 22, 1924, n.p., clipping in Scrapbook 39, Mary Pickford Collection, AMPAS).

26. "Subtle Mary Pickford, in New Film at Criterion Theatre Will Delight You, If—," clipping, n.p., in Scrapbook 39, Mary Pickford Collection, AMPAS.

27. Mary Pickford, quoted in press book for *My Best Girl* (1928).

28. This approach to marketing Pickford films in the 1920s seems indebted to the marketing concept of the "family party" promoted heavily by Pickford's

former studio, Famous Players–Lasky/Paramount Pictures, in the late 1910s and early 1920s in women's magazines such as *Ladies' Home Journal*. On women determining moviegoing see Dorothy Brown, "Making Movies for Women," *Moving Picture World,* March 26, 1927, 34; and Leo Handel, *Hollywood Looks at Its Audience* (Urbana: University of Illinois Press, 1950), 90.

29. Hall, "*Pollyanna,*" 16.

30. Vachel Lindsay, *The Art of the Moving Picture* (1915; New York: Liveright, 1970), 56. Adela Rogers St. Johns borrows heavily without attribution from Lindsay in "Why Does the World Love Mary?" *Photoplay,* Dec. 1921, 50–51, 110–11.

31. Frederick Wallace, "An Appreciation of Mary Pickford," *Motion Picture,* July 1916, 82.

32. Bram Dijkstra, *Idols of Perversity: Fantasies of Feminine Evil in Fin-de-siècle Culture* (New York: Oxford University Press, 1986), 182–98; see also Brownlow, *Mary Pickford Rediscovered,* 67.

33. Paula Fass, *The Damned and the Beautiful: American Youth in the 1920s* (New York: Oxford University Press, 1977), 25. On U.S. women asking for "the same promiscuity that society tacitly grants to the male" in the 1910s, see "Sex O'clock in America," *Current Opinion,* August 1913, 113–14.

34. Martha Vicinus, "The Adolescent Boy: Fin-de-siècle Femme Fatale?" in *Victorian Sexual Dissidence,* ed. Richard Dellamora (Chicago: University of Chicago Press, 1999), 83.

35. Brownlow, *Mary Pickford Rediscovered,* 67.

36. "*M'Liss,*" *Motion Picture News,* May 11, 1918, n.p., clipping in Scrapbook 31, Ms. Collection U-6, Mary Pickford Collection, AMPAS.

37. Virginia Dare, "News of Filmland: Moving Pictures," *Chicago Journal,* May 16, 1918, n.p., clipping in Scrapbook 31, Mary Pickford Collection, AMPAS.

38. Adela Rogers St. Johns, "Why Mary Pickford Bobbed Her Hair," *Photoplay,* Sept. 1928, 33. Elisabeth G. Gitter, "The Power of Women's Hair in the Victorian Imagination," *PMLA* 99, no. 5 (1984): 936–54.

39. A hair-washing scene also occurs in the 1922 version of *Tess of the Storm Country* to seventeen-year-old Tess, who is repeatedly told how pretty she would be if she was clean.

40. Richard Dyer, "The Colour of Virtue: Lillian Gish, Whiteness and Femininity," in *Women and Film: A Sight and Sound Reader,* edited by Pam Cook and Philip Dodd (Philadelphia: Temple University Press, 1993), 2–3.

41. Gitter, "The Power of Women's Hair in the Victorian Imagination," 938. On sirens and mermaids in Victorian painting see Dijkstra, *Idols of Perversity,* 258–71.

42. Dyer, "The Colour of Virtue," 2–3.

43. David MacLeod details the efforts of social reformers in the 1910s to improve the lot of children; see David MacLeod, *The Age of the Child* (Boston: Twayne, 1998), 119–30.

44. Mitchell, *The New Girl,* 161.

45. Brownlow, *Mary Pickford Rediscovered,* 157.

46. Adult misunderstanding of the heroine in late nineteenth-century

orphan-centered literature allowed the protagonist to demonstrate superior talents that benefit other children. See Claudia Nelson, "Drying the Orphan's Tear: Changing Representations of the Dependent Child in America, 1870–1930," *Children's Literature* 29 (2001): 52–70; and Joe Sutliff Sanders, "Spinning Sympathy: Orphan Girl Novels and the Sentimental Tradition," *Children's Literature Association Quarterly* 33, no. 1 (2008): 41–61.

47. Dyer, "The Colour of Virtue," 3.

48. "*Daddy-Long-Legs*," *Variety*, May 16, 1919, 54.

49. Kate Douglas Wiggin, *Rebecca of Sunnybrook Farm* (Boston: Houghton, Mifflin, 1904), 320.

50. "An Actress from the Movies," *Cosmopolitan*, July 1913, 265.

51. Julian Johnson, "Mary Pickford: Herself and Her Career," pt. 1, *Photoplay*, Jan. 1916, 43. Adolph Zukor recounts in his autobiography how Mrs. Pickford sat in on story conferences. She protected Mary and her screen image and "gained a reputation as a great salary negotiator" (Adolph Zukor, *The Public Is Never Wrong* [New York: G.P. Putnam's Sons, 1953], 111–12).

52. "The Best-Known Girl in America," *Ladies' Home Journal*, Jan. 1915, 9.

53. Ellen Woods, "Speaking of the Actress," *Photoplay*, Oct. 1917, 82.

54. Roberta Courtlandt, "Why Mary Pickford Married Twice," *Motion Picture*, Sept. 1916, 108–9, 168.

55. Zukor notes that in "Mary's public appearances her mother was always in evidence, but her husband, Owen Moore, hardly ever" (Zukor, *The Public Is Never Wrong*, 175).

56. Peter Gridley Schmid, "Before Nine and after Five with Mary Pickford," *Motion Picture*, Nov. 1917, 104.

57. Gary Carey, *Doug and Mary* (New York: E.P. Dutton, 1977), 62.

58. *New York Times*, April 4, 1920, 1. See also Carey, *Doug and Mary*, 77–78.

59. Will Durant, "The Modern Woman: Philosophers Grow Dizzy as She Passes," *Century Magazine*, Feb. 1927, 421. For other views of women's changing sexual desires see Joseph Collins, "Woman's Morality in Transition," *Current History* 27 (1927): 33–40; Edward Sapir, "The Discipline of Sex," *American Mercury* 16 (1929): 413–20; and H. McMenamin, "Evils of Woman's Revolt against the Old Standard," *Current History* 27 (1927): 30–32.

60. Many articles emphasized how hard Mary continued to work as an adult in the motion picture business. One newspaper article tells readers: "Think of Mary's sacrifices and then decide if you really want to become a star" ("Following Mary around the Clock," *Chicago American*, Feb. 19, 1921, n.p., in Scrapbook 29, U-6 Collection, Mary Pickford Collection, AMPAS).

61. Ranck, "Mary Pickford—Whose Real Name Is Gladys Smith," 34.

62. Ibid., 75. *Bootles' Baby* first appeared as a novel in 1885, was serialized in the *Graphic*, and then debuted as a stage play in London in 1889. The author of the original story of *Bootles' Baby*, novelist Henrietta Eliza Vaughan Stannard (1856–1911), came from a military family, and her writings, such as *Cavalry Life* (1881) and *Regimental Legends* (1883), reflected that background. However, her publishers thought, to assure public acceptance, the masculine

tenor of her work called for a male pseudonym, and she took on the nom de plume of "John Strange Winter."

63. Evelyn Wells, "Big Film Role, 4 Babies, Pickford Wish," *San Francisco Call,* March 22, 1921, clipping in Scrapbook 29, Ms. Collection U-6, Mary Pickford Collection, AMPAS.

64. *San Francisco California Daily News,* March 28, 1921, n.p., clipping in Scrapbook 29, Ms. Collection U-6, Mary Pickford Collection, AMPAS.

65. Pickford, "My Own Story," pt. 3, 9.

66. Grace Kingsley, "Europe Again Calls Star Duo," *Los Angeles Times,* March 3, 1921, clipping in Scrapbook 29, Ms. Collection U-6, Mary Pickford Collection, AMPAS.

67. Roger Lewis, "A Character Study of the Real Mary Pickford: Woman and Genius," *New York City Success,* June 1923, 90, clipping in Scrapbook 29, Ms. Collection U-6, Mary Pickford Collection, AMPAS.

68. St. Johns, "Why Mary Pickford Bobbed Her Hair," 33.

69. Catherine Robson, *Men in Wonderland: The Lost Girlhood of the Victorian Gentleman* (Princeton, NJ: Princeton University Press, 2001), 3–5, 13.

70. See John Hartley, "'When Your Child Grows Up Too Fast': Juvenation and the Boundaries of the Social in the News Media," *Continuum: Journal of Media and Cultural Studies* 12, no. 1 (1998): 10–11.

## CHAPTER 2

*Epigraph.* John Strange Winter, *Bootles' Baby: A Story of the Scarlet Lancers* (1885; London: Frederick Warne, 1891; repr. La Vergne, TN: Nabu Public Domain Reprints, 2010), 60.

1. The photo, held in the Library of Congress, is reproduced in *Documenting America, 1935–1943,* ed. Carl Fleischhauer and Beverly W. Brannan (Berkeley: University of California Press, 1988), 192. For an account of Rothstein's experiences at the Visalia camp see ibid., 188–205.

2. The child is identified in the Library of Congress catalog only as "Migrant Girl, Tulare migrant camp, Visalia, California." By the 1940s the fashion of long curls for very young boys had long passed and would have been doubly unlikely for a boy of this social class.

3. The advertising for Temple's film *Bright Eyes* used this phrase in prominent display on many film posters.

4. See advertisement by the Nestle-Le Mur Co. for baby hair treatment in *Parents' Magazine,* Sept. 1937, 60. See also "Buy Shirley Temple Branded Products and Be Sure of the Best!" advertisement (ibid., 72). In the film *Made for Each Other* (dir. Robert Bean, 1971) the little girl who grows up to be Renee Taylor's neurotic character is outfitted and groomed by her mother to look like Shirley Temple.

5. On Shirley's discovery see Philip K. Scheuer, "Being Mama's Little Elfy One of Those Things Child Prodigy Must Put Up With," *Los Angeles Times,* May 6, 1934, A1. See also Helen Harrison, "Tiny Girl, What Now?" *Motion Picture,* Oct. 1934, 39, 80–81; and Jeanine Basinger, *Shirley Temple* (New York:

Pyramid, 1975), 19. Patsy Guy Hammontree argues that it was not just any dance school in which Mrs. Temple enrolled Shirley at age two and one-half but the "Meglin Dance Studio," known in Los Angeles as a conduit for children's entry into the movie industry (Patsy Guy Hammontree, *Shirley Temple Black: A Bio-bibliography* [Westport, CT: Greenwood Press, 1998], 14–15).

6. Alma Whittaker, "Your Child, Too, May Be a Shirley Temple," *Los Angeles Times,* July 1, 1934, A1; see also Crete Cage, "Mothers Haunt Filmdom," *Los Angeles Times,* Jan. 22, 1938, A5; and John Scott, "Gangway for Avalanche of Child Talent!" *Los Angeles Times,* Sept. 9, 1934, A1.

7. Mrs. Gertrude Temple, as told to Mary Sharon, *How I Raised Shirley Temple* (Akron, OH: Saalfield, 1935.

8. Ibid. The subtitle of Mrs. Temple's pamphlet calls Shirley Temple "The Baby Who Conquered the World."

9. Amelie Hastie, "History in Miniature: Colleen Moore's Dollhouse and Historical Recollection," *Camera Obscura* 16, no. 3.48 (2001): 128.

10. Jennifer Bean, "Technologies of Early Stardom and the Extraordinary Body," in *A Feminist Reader in Early Cinema,* ed. Jennifer M. Bean and Diane Negra (Durham, NC: Duke University Press, 2002), 404–43, 442.

11. In the 1935 Academy Award ceremonies Cobb, a novelist, screenwriter, and actor, presented Temple with a miniature statuette for her outstanding contribution to movie entertainment in 1934. See "Miss Colbert Wins 1934 Screen Prize," *New York Times,* Feb. 28, 1935, 21. Cobb is quoted in Diana Serra Cary, *Hollywood's Children: An Inside Account of the Child Star Era* (1978; Dallas: Southern Methodist University Press, 1997), 210.

12. Richard Dyer, "Entertainment and Utopia," repr. in *Movies and Methods,* ed. Bill Nichols (Berkeley: University of California Press, 1985), 2:221–32.

13. "The New Pictures," *Time,* July 9, 1934, 48.

14. Agnes Benedict, "What's Ahead in the Movies?" *Parents' Magazine,* Sept. 1936, 30. Children were not believed to have control over families' entertainment dollars or considered capable of lifting a major "A level" feature film production to success. On matinee audiences in a British context that has relevance to U.S. practices see Sarah J. Smith, *Children, Cinema and Censorship: From Dracula to the Dead End Kids* (London: I.B. Tauris, 2005), 141–73. On U.S. film exhibition practices and children see Nicholas Sammond, *Babes in Tomorrowland: Walt Disney and the Making of the American Child, 1930–1960* (Durham, NC: Duke University Press, 2002).

15. "Temple Feature Fails to Excite Broadway," *Los Angeles Times,* June 28, 1939, n.p., *Susannah of the Mounties* clipping file, Academy of Motion Picture Arts and Sciences (AMPAS). This change was implicated in the decline of Temple's box office that led to an agreement between her parents and Fox to cancel her contract with the studio. See Douglas W. Churchill, "Miss Temple Rings the Hollywood Bells," *New York Times,* May 19, 1940, 133.

16. Edwin Schallert, "Child Shines at Loew's," *Los Angeles Times,* June 29, 1934, 11.

17. After Temple's ranking slipped to number five in 1939, Mickey Rooney replaced her as the industry's top box-office draw. On stars in the 1930s see

Tino Balio, *Grand Design: Hollywood as a Modern Business Enterprise, 1930–1939* (Berkeley: University of California Press, 1993), 146–47.

18. Robert Windeler, quoted in Balio, *Grand Design,* 147; "Cinema: Peewee's Progress," *Time,* April 27, 1936, 5, 29–32.

19. Quoted in Basinger, *Shirley Temple,* 86.

20. Quoted in Shirley Temple Black, *Child Star: An Autobiography* (New York: McGraw-Hill, 1988), 108. F.D.R., quoted in Ilana Nash, *American Sweethearts* (Bloomington: Indiana University Press, 2006), 119.

21. Barry King, "The Star and the Commodity: Notes towards a Performance Theory of Stardom," *Cultural Studies* 1, no. 2 (1987): 148.

22. Cassandra Cleghorn asserts the importance of "sentimental tropes realized through bodily touch" in relation to gendered narrative and the production of affect. Her primary reference is the famous case of Laura Dewey Bridgman, a blind and deaf girl who came under the care of Dr. Samuel Gridley Howe. See Cassandra Cleghorn, "Chivalric Sentimentalism: The Case of Dr. Howe and Laura Bridgman," in *Sentimental Men: Masculinity and the Politics of Affect in American Culture,* ed. Mary Chapman and Glenn Hendler (Berkeley: University of California Press, 1999), 163–80.

23. Jane H. Hunter, *How Young Ladies Became Girls: The Victorian Origins of American Girlhood* (New Haven, CT: Yale University Press, 2002), 123.

24. Annie Fellows Johnston, *The Little Colonel* (Boston: L.C. Page, 1922), 15–16 (also available at www.digital.library.upenn.edu/women/johnston/colonel/colonel.html).

25. Viviana A. Zelizer, *Pricing the Priceless Child: The Changing Social Value of Children* (1985; Princeton, NJ: Princeton University Press, 1994), 57. Reference to Zelizer's description of the "sentimental child" in relation to ideologies of work and the condemnation of children's professional acting is found in Karen Orr Vered, "White and Black in Black and White: Management of Race and Sexuality in the Coupling of Child-Star Shirley Temple and Bill Robinson," *Velvet Light Trap* 39 (spring 1997): 54–55.

26. David I. Macleod, *The Age of the Child: Children in America, 1890–1920* (New York: Twayne, 1998), 115–17.

27. Barbara Melosh, *Strangers and Kin: The American Way of Adoption* (Cambridge, MA: Harvard University Press, 2002), 11, 10. See also Julie Berebitsky, *Like Our Very Own: Adoption and the Changing Culture of Motherhood, 1851–1950* (Lawrence: University Press of Kansas, 2000). In the 1930s the comic strip *Little Orphan Annie* not only dealt with adoption but also responded to the impact of the Great Depression on children.

28. Basinger, *Shirley Temple,* 11.

29. See, e.g., ibid., 13; see also "Cinema: Peewee's Progress," *Time,* April 27, 1936, 32.

30. Temple's films, along with a slew of biopics and Will Rogers's films with John Ford, can be seen as why 20th Century–Fox earned the nickname "Nineteenth Century Fox" during the 1930s.

31. Russell Freedman, *Children of the Great Depression* (New York: Clarion, 2005), 4, 13–17.

32. T.H. Watkins, *The Hungry Years* (New York: Henry Holt, 1999), 68–69.

33. John Bodnar, *Blue-Collar Hollywood: Liberalism, Democracy, and Working People in American Film* (Baltimore: Johns Hopkins University Press, 2003), 41. See also Joseph M. Hawes, *Children between the Wars: American Childhood, 1920–1940* (New York: Twayne, 1997). For children's accounts of difficulties in family life see *Dear Mrs. Roosevelt: Letters from Children of the Great Depression,* ed. Robert Cohen (Chapel Hill: University of North Carolina Press, 2002).

34. Quoted in Zelizer, *Pricing the Priceless Child,* 49.

35. Glen H. Elder Jr., *Children of the Great Depression: Social Change in Life Experience* (Chicago: University of Chicago Press, 1974), 71, 80, 291. On children working part-time as a response to parental unemployment in the Great Depression see also Steven Mintz, *Huck's Raft: A History of American Childhood* (Cambridge, MA: Belknap Press of Harvard University Press, 2004), e237.

36. James Warbasse, "Fathers as Pals," *Parents' Magazine,* August 1936, 76.

37. Mary E. Overholt, "For Fathers Only," *Parents' Magazine,* July 1932, 39.

38. Lewis Leary, "A Girl Needs Her Father," *Parents' Magazine,* April 1936, 30, 61.

39. On how Temple's "million-dollar personality" and "beauty" were the result of her mother's extraordinary care in child rearing so that Shirley exemplified "a happy, healthy little girl," see Gladys Denny Shultz, "Mrs. Shultz Visits Shirley Temple," *Better Homes and Gardens,* Sept. 1938, 46, 70–73.

40. Shawn Johansen, *Family Men: Middle-Class Fatherhood in Early Industrializing America* (New York: Routledge, 2001), 138.

41. Andrew Bergman, *We're in the Money: Depression America and Its Films* (New York: New York University Press, 1971), 9–11.

42. Mintz, *Huck's Raft,* 236–37. My consideration of the cultural context moves beyond that of Charles Eckert, whose pioneering work in this area approached Temple's stardom through the lens of Marxism. He argued that the star's performance of "indiscriminate love" represented a politics of charity that fulfilled a conservative ideological agenda in the Great Depression. See Charles Eckert, "Shirley Temple and the House of Rockefeller," in *Jump Cut* 2 (July-August 1974): 1, 17–20, repr. and abr. in *Stardom: Industry of Desire,* ed. Christine Gledhill (London: Routledge, 1991), 60–73.

43. Ralph LaRossa, *The Modernization of Fatherhood: A Social and Political History* (Chicago: University of Chicago Press, 1997), 2.

44. Most recent scholarship on Temple does very little in textually analyzing how this occurs in her films. Kristen Lee Hatch attempts to build an argument that Temple appealed to the maternal instincts of men in the tradition of a long line of little girl performers, primarily in the Victorian era. See Hatch, "Playing Innocent: Shirley Temple and the Performance of Girlhood, 1850–1939" (PhD diss., University of California, Los Angeles, 2006), 153.

45. See "Cinema: Double Feature Down," *Time,* July 5, 1937, 24. Men's favorite stars were Clark Gable, Shirley Temple, William Powell, Wallace Beery, George Arliss, and Myrna Loy. Temple ranked as women's favorite star, followed by Robert Taylor and Clark Gable.

46. Quoted in Graham Greene, *The Graham Greene Film Reader,* ed. David Parkinson (New York: Applause, 1994), xxvii.

47. Graham Greene, "*Wee Willie Winkie, The Life of Emile Zola, Night and Day,*" repr. in Greene, *The Graham Greene Film Reader,* 233–34. On the lawsuit against Greene filed by 20th Century–Fox on behalf of Temple in British courts see ibid., xxv–vi. See also "Shirley Temple Wins," *New York Times,* March 23, 1938, 18; and "Dimpled Depravity," *Time,* April 4, 1938, 62.

48. Greene, *The Graham Greene Film Reader,* 233–34.

49. Ibid., 233–35.

50. Ibid., xxvii.

51. Graham Greene, *The Power and the Glory* (1940; London: Vintage, 2001), 67–68.

52. Ara Osterweil has adapted my notion of the pedophilic gaze in relation to Mary Pickford and applied it to Temple. She argues that Temple's films inscribed a "pedophilic structure of desire and identification" through which they "attempted to disguise their fundamentally white supremacist point of view" and "attempted to normalize and domesticate the project of black male castration" (Ara Osterweil, "Reconstructing Shirley: Pedophilia and Interracial Romance in Hollywood's Age of Innocence," *Camera Obscura* 24, no. 3.72 [2009]: 1–4). See also Haskell, *From Reverence to Rape: The Treatment of Women in the Movies,* 2nd ed. (Chicago: University of Chicago Press, 1987), 123; and Nadine Wills, "'110 Per Cent Woman': The Crotch Shot in the Hollywood Musical," *Screen* 42, no. 2 (2001): 129–30.

53. Basinger, *Shirley Temple,* 14, 52–53. Basinger declares, without accompanying citation, that many film viewers in the 1930s were uncomfortable with the interaction between Shirley and her father figures (54). See also David Parkinson's comments in Greene, *The Graham Greene Film Reader,* xxvii.

54. Haskell, *From Reverence to Rape,* 123.

55. Wills, "'110 Per Cent Woman,'" 129–30.

56. James Kincaid, *Erotic Innocence: The Culture of Child Molesting* (Durham, NC: Duke University Press, 1998), 120.

57. See, e.g., Basinger, *Shirley Temple,* 13.

58. Kincaid, *Erotic Innocence,* 118–21.

59. On "sweet sentiment" see Robert Solomon, "On Kitsch and Sentimentality," *Journal of Aesthetics and Art Criticism* 49, no. 1 (1991): 3. On the development of the family as a concept see Philippe Ariès, *Centuries of Childhood: A Social History of Family Life,* trans. Robert Baldick (New York: Vintage, 1962), 363–73, 398–404.

60. Jacqueline Rose, *The Case of Peter Pan; or, The Impossibility of Children's Fiction* (1984; Philadelphia: University of Pennsylvania Press, 1993), xii.

61. Stage mothers were subject to intense criticism, but Mrs. Temple fared better than most in public discourse. See, e.g., Sonia Lee, "Planning Shirley's Next Ten Years," *Motion Picture,* March 1936, 33, 66–67; and J.P. McEvoy, "Little Miss Miracle," *Saturday Evening Post,* July 9, 1938, 11–12. In 1936 *Time* magazine paid dubious tribute to Mrs. Temple's role in Shirley's success in one of its strangest covers ever. The cover depicts Shirley, in quasi-military uniform, on a stage, musicians in the background, during the production of *Poor*

*Little Rich Girl.* She bends over the edge of the stage, apparently to plant a kiss on a woman whose face cannot be seen. This woman is her mother, who is a gaunt and rather sinister figure in black dress and hat. The caption says, "Mrs. Temple & Daughter." See *Time,* April 27, 1936.

62. Frank Nugent, "The Screen," review of *Dimples, New York Times,* Oct. 10, 1936, 21.

63. On children's acting as pleasurable because it is viewed as limited and of a different order than adult performance, see Anne Varty, *Children and Theatre in Victorian Britain: "All Work, No Play"* (Houndmills, UK: Palgrave Macmillan, 2008), 10–17.

64. On Temple and pretending see Shirley Temple, as told to Marian Rhea, "Why I Like to Be in the Movies," *Motion Picture,* Jan. 1936, 27, 68. On child acting as "masks" and "faces" assumed without an awareness of the meaning and form of the performance, as well as the expectations of spontaneity and naturalness as applied to child performers, see Varty, *Children and Theatre in Victorian Britain,* 13–14. 72–74.

65. Norbert Lusk, "News and Gossip of Stage and Screen," *Los Angeles Times,* April 29, 1934, A3.

66. Review of *Rebecca of Sunnybrook Farm, Variety,* March 9, 1938, 14.

67. Gilbert Seldes, "Two Great Women," *Esquire,* July 1935, 86, 143.

68. George Custen insinuates that Seldes is arguing that men responded to Temple in a pedophilic way. See Custen, *Twentieth Century's Fox: Darryl F. Zanuck and the Culture of Hollywood* (New York: Basic Books, 1997), 206. Hatch depends on a similar reading to argue for a major change in the 1930s in the understanding of Temple in relation to pedophilia. Both seriously misread Seldes, who does not characterize male reaction to Temple as "defined by sexual desires that can only be expressed in an inarticulate growl," as Hatch claims. See Hatch, "Playing Innocent," 189. Ara Osterweil also mentions the "growl" to support her claim of Temple's construction of a male "fantasy of the child-woman's sex appeal, sweetness, and availability" (Osterweil, "Reconstructing Shirley," 3–4).

69. Seldes, "Two Great Women," 86, 143.

70. See Philip Jenkins, *Moral Panic: Changing Concepts of the Child Molester in Modern America* (New Haven, CT: Yale University Press, 1998), 49–50.

71. Ibid., 52–53.

72. "Medicine: Pedophilia," *Time,* August 23, 1937, 42–44.

73. Jenkins, *Moral Panic,* 52.

74. Solomon, "On Kitsch and Sentimentality," 5.

75. "The Screen: Shirley Temple and the Pearls," *New York Times,* June 30, 1934, 18.

76. Child-watching as entertainment has been usefully discussed by Carolyn Steedman within a nineteenth-century British stage context in *Strange Dislocations: Childhood and the Idea of Human Interiority, 1780–1930* (Cambridge, MA: Harvard University Press, 1995); and by Rose, *The Case of Peter Pan,* 90–102.

77. "The Screen: Shirley Temple and the Pearls," 18.

78. Abel, review of *Curly Top, Variety,* August 7, 1935, 21.

79. Smith, *Children, Cinema and Censorship,* 27. The claim that Temple was less popular with children than with men is in Haskell, *From Reverence to Rape,* 123.

80. Gaynor's version makes an interesting revision in which Judy Abbott could have been adopted out, but the orphanage selected another girl in her stead because, out of economic self-interest, they wanted to keep Judy for her working skills.

81. Review of *Poor Little Rich Girl, Variety,* July 1, 1936, 12.

82. Steedman argues that Goethe's *Wilhelm Meister's Apprenticeship* was crucial because the "story was used to develop new notions and conventions of childhood that were displayed in dramatic performance throughout the century" (Steedman, *Strange Dislocations,* 145).

83. Karen Sanchez-Eppler, *Dependent States: The Child's Part in Nineteenth-Century American Culture* (Chicago: University of Chicago Press, 2005), 71–72; see also Hatch, "Playing Innocent," 163–65.

84. Hatch, "Playing Innocent," 163–65.

85. Sanchez-Eppler, *Dependent States,* 71–72. For a temperance film in which the daughter saves the father from alcoholism see D.W. Griffith's one-reeler *A Drunkard's Reformation* (1909). In *M'Liss* Pickford's heroine lives with her drunkard father, who "takes his own zoo with him" via the D.T.s. In one comic scene she waters down his liquor but otherwise exerts no effort to get him off the booze. His alcoholism is played for comedy throughout.

86. As Gladys Smith, Mary Pickford appeared onstage as the "Baby" in *Bootles' Baby.* See Eileen Whitefield, *Pickford: The Woman Who Made Hollywood* (New York: Faber and Faber, 1997), 31.

87. On the similarities between this novel and play and Goethe's *Wilhelm Meister's Apprenticeship* see Steedman, *Strange Dislocations,* 145–48.

88. Winter, *Bootles' Baby,* 17–21.

89. Ibid., 31.

90. Ibid., 52, 54.

91. On cosseting see Hunter, *How Young Ladies Became Girls,* 122–23.

92. Winter, *Bootles' Baby,* 87.

93. For the claim that an assistant director "dubbed her 'Butch,'" see Dorothy Spensley, "The Life and Loves of Shirley Temple," *Motion Picture,* July 1936, 35.

94. Rudyard Kipling, "Wee Willie Winkie," from *Wee Willie Winkie and Other Children's Stories,* www.readbookonline.net/readOnLine/8178/.

95. Greene, "*Wee Willie Winkie, The Life of Emile Zola,*" in Greene, *The Graham Greene Film Reader,* 234.

96. In this respect Priscilla anticipates Captain Kirby York (John Wayne) in *Fort Apache* (dir. John Ford, 1948). York attempts to prevent war with the Apaches through negotiation, but his efforts are thwarted by Colonel Thursday (Henry Fonda). In that film Temple is cast as Thursday's sixteen-year-old daughter, Philadelphia.

97. "My all-time favorite photo: waif in *Little Miss Marker,* 1934" (caption to photo in Black, *Child Star,* n.p.).

98. See Carol Mavor on the relationship between imaginary and real girls, male vision and the female child before the photographic camera. Mavor, "Dream-Rushes: Lewis Carroll's Photographs of the Little Girl," in *The Girl's Own: Cultural Histories of the Anglo-American Girl, 1830–1915,* ed. Claudia Nelson and Lynne Vallone (Athens: University of Georgia Press, 1994), 156–93.

## CHAPTER 3

*Epigraph.* Frederick Lewis, "The Private Life of Deanna Durbin," *Liberty,* July 3, 1937, 55.

1. Durbin was born December 4, 1921, in Winnipeg, Canada. Some reports say that Edna Mae Durbin was renamed "Deanna" while she was at MGM, but her one film appearance for that studio in *Every Sunday* gives her screen credit under her birth name of "Edna Mae." The review of *Three Smart Girls* in *Time* says Universal changed her name. See "The New Pictures," *Time,* Dec. 21, 1936, 22. Jeanine Basinger says that when Rufus LeMaire was searching for a girl to play the contralto Ernestine Schumann-Heink as a child in an MGM biopic called "Gram," he happened to talk to a friend about "the Ralph Thomas school and the little girl he had heard sing there." Basinger's account overlooks the more intricate web of Hollywood talent peddling in Durbin's discovery revealed in testimony during a lawsuit brought in 1938, by Mrs. Olive White against two Hollywood agents. See "Young Star's Earnings Told," *Los Angeles Times,* June 16, 1938, A3; and "Court Decides for Writer in Deanna Durbin Suit," *Los Angeles Times,* June 17, 1938, A1, A2. Jeanine Basinger, *The Star Machine* (New York: Alfred A. Knopf, 2007) 258–59.

2. Douglas Churchill, not the most reliable of commentators on the star, claims that producer Joe Pasternak's request for a budget expansion of *Three Smart Girls* was aided by Joseph Breen, who praised the scenario submitted for approval to the Production Code Administration. See Douglas W. Churchill, "A Corner on Hollywood Talent," *New York Times,* Dec. 13, 1936, X7.

3. "Deanna Durbin in *Three Smart Girls,*" *Film Daily,* Jan. 20, 1937, *Three Smart Girls* file, unpaginated clipping, Academy of Motion Picture Arts and Sciences Special Collections (hereafter AMPAS).

4. For one account of Mayer's reaction to Durbin's "Il Bacio" audition for MGM see John Franchey, "One Smart Girl," *Los Angeles Times,* August 20, 1944, F17. "Bubbles" (Beverly) Sills, the future star and artistic director of the New York City Opera, sings "Il Bacio" as an eight-year-old in *Uncle Sol Solves It,* a short film released by 20th Century–Fox in 1938. Eight-year-old Sills has an impressive vocal instrument, musical technique, poise, and charm. The former Belle Silverman also has Shirley Temple–styled curls and a New York accent revealed in her speaking part. On Sills's development as a singer and her early career on the radio, including appearances on *Major Bowes' Amateur Hour* and other programs, see Winthrop Sargeant, *Divas: Impressions of Six Opera Superstars* (1959; New York: Coward, McCann and Geoghegan, 1973), 87–88.

5. On her career at Universal see William K. Everson, "Deanna Durbin," *Films in Review* 27, no. 9 (1976): 513–14.

6. Durbin's vocal teacher, Andreas de Segurola, a former member of the Metropolitan Opera and internationally acclaimed basso profundo, was featured in a comic and singing supporting role in Grace Moore's vehicle *One Night of Love.* The timing and reasons for Durbin's arrival at Universal have frequently been mischaracterized. Jeanine Basinger says, "After the successful release of *Every Sunday* in October 1936, Durbin again began to prepare for 'Gram'" (262). She claims that Durbin was let go when the studio cancelled the Schumann-Heink biopic in the wake of the opera singer's death. Basinger's account perpetuates erroneous elements found in the late 1930s in pieces like Jim Tully's "Fifteen and Famous," *Los Angeles Times,* Nov. 28, 1937, J4. The *New York Times* reported on July 1, 1936, that Durbin had signed with Universal to do *Three Smart Girls.* According to the *American Film Institute Catalog, Three Smart Girls* was in production between September 10 and October 22 and was released on December 20, 1936. This means that Durbin completed filming her first Universal release by the time Schumann-Heink died, on November 17, 1936. See also "Deanna's Diary," of Nov. 17, 1936 (AMPAS); Basinger, *The Star Machine,* 260–63; "*Three Smart Girls,*" in *American Film Institute Catalogue of Motion Pictures Produced in the United States, Feature Films, 1931–1940,* ed. Patricia King Hanson (Berkeley: University of California Press, 1993), 2202–203.

7. "As usual we become acquainted only too intimately with the hideous cavern of the human mouth," snips Greene of Durbin's *Three Smart Girls* performance. See Graham Greene, "Three Smart Girls," in *The Graham Greene Film Reader,* ed. David Parkinson (New York: Applause, 1994), 185.

8. See Jeremy Tambling, *Opera, Ideology, and Film* (New York: St. Martin's, 1987), 47.

9. Fred C. Othamm, untitled review of *First Love, Los Angeles Herald,* Oct. 9, 1939, n.p., Durbin clipping files, AMPAS.

10. William K. Everson says that Durbin's films were consistent top box-office moneymakers but that they also were important in keeping Universal from almost complete artistic collapse as it struggled under an administration that sought to eliminate A productions. See Everson, "Deanna Durbin," 513–14.

11. David Shipman, "Deanna Durbin," *The Great Movie Stars: The Golden Years* (New York: Bonanza, 1970), 175. See also Edwin Schallert, "Author Says Scarlett Has Charm of Irish," on Durbin's high polling in Britain, *Los Angeles Times,* Jan. 18, 1939, 10; and Edwin Schallert, "While the Films Reel By," *Los Angeles Times,* May 19, 1940, C3. Durbin's great popularity in Britain was also noted by Eddie Cantor in an episode of *Texaco Town.*

12. Durbin's image or endorsement was associated with dolls from Ideal Novelty and Toy Co., as well as with robes, coats, rainwear, perfume, cologne, soap, dresses, handbags, millinery, and sheet music. See press book for *Three Smart Girls Grow Up* (1939), 6–7, AMPAS.

13. Sheila Graham, "Hays Office Battles to Maintain Screen Purity: Kid Stars Making Hit in Hollywood," *Los Angeles Times,* Feb. 7, 1937, C1. Anticipating Graham, Churchill reports in 1936 that Durbin's success lifted "the ban from half-grown girls. . . . Girls in their early and mid 'teens have never inter-

ested producers" (Douglas Churchill, "A Corner on Hollywood Talent," *New York Times,* Dec. 13, 1936, X7).

14. In the postwar period the quality of her films began to slide. Most of them made money, but Everson suggests that *Lady on a Train* (dir. Charles-Henri David, 1945) "was her last really top film, and her career spiraled downhill from that point." (527). Everson, like Durbin herself, claims a change in postwar tastes contributed to the obsolescence of her type of films, but musicals flourished in the postwar period, and those with classical music were sustained, especially through Joe Pasternak's productions at MGM. Unhappy with the artistic limitations placed on her by Universal and Hollywood 's lack of privacy, Durbin relocated to France, where she remarried (her third try), raised a family, and refused all intrusions into her new life. She never made another film or sought the attention of the public again in any way. See Everson, "Deanna Durbin," 528–29; and "Deanna Durbin Happy at 35 in French Village," *Chicago Sunday Tribune,* April 20, 1953, pt. 1, 20H.

15. Edward Baron Turk, "Deriding the Voice of Jeanette MacDonald: Notes on Psychoanalysis and the American Film Musical," *Camera Obscura* 9, nos. 1–2.25–26 (1991): 224–49, 224. Turk calls Jeanette MacDonald "Hollywood's most successful soprano." There is, however, an argument to be made that Durbin was the American film industry's most successful soprano. Unlike MacDonald, who was paired with equally or more important male vocalists, Durbin achieved her popularity in films in which she was almost always the only vocal attraction. Also, unlike MacDonald's, Durbin's voice influenced the training and subsequent vocal style of a number of lyric sopranos, including Kiri Te Kanawa. Cellist Mstislav Rostropovich regarded her as a musical inspiration in her "purity." See Lynn Darling, "Song of Slava," *Washington Post,* 1983, www.washingtonpost.com/wp-dyn/articles/A51083-2004Jul15.html.

16. Turk, "Deriding the Voice of Jeanette MacDonald." Turk's central claim regarding male derision of classically trained sopranos is not well supported. On MacDonald's career see Edward Baron Turk, *Hollywood Diva: A Biography of Jeanette MacDonald* (Berkeley: University of California Press, 1998).

17. See Everson, "Deanna Durbin," 513–29; Basinger, *The Star Machine,* 256–96; and Georganne Scheiner, "The Deanna Durbin Devotees: Fan Clubs and Spectatorship," in *Generations of Youth: Youth Cultures and History in Twentieth-Century America,* ed. Joe Austin and Michael Nevin Willard (New York: New York University Press, 1998), 181–94.

18. See Frank Nugent, "The Screen," review of *Three Smart Girls Grow Up, New York Times,* March 18, 1939, 9; Basinger, *The Star Machine,* 267.

19. Sigmund Freud, "The Uncanny," in *The Standard Edition of the Complete Psychological Works of Sigmund Freud,* ed. James Strachey (London: Hogarth, 1953–74), 17:219–56.

20. Patrick Galway of the *New Statesman,* quoted in David Shipman, *The Great Movie Stars: The Golden Years* (New York: Bonanza, 1970), 176.

21. Ilana Nash, *American Sweethearts: Teenage Girls in Twentieth-Century Popular Culture* (Bloomington: Indiana University Press, 2006), 86.

22. Grace Palladino, *Teenagers: An American History* (New York: Basic Books, 1996), 52–55.

23. Leslie Hohman, "As the Twig Is Bent," *Ladies' Home Journal,* Oct. 1939, 67.

24. Nash, *American Sweethearts,* 85–90.

25. Ibid., 100.

26. Norbert Lusk, "Durbin Film Scores Hit in New York," *Los Angeles Times,* Sept. 26, 1937, D3.

27. See newsletters of the Deanna Durbin Devotees housed at AMPAS; and Scheiner, "The Deanna Durbin Devotees," 100; see also "Deanna Durbin Happy at 35 in French Village," 20H.

28. Patricia Robinson, quoted in Jackie Stacey, *Star Gazing: Hollywood Cinema and Female Spectatorship* (New York: Routledge, 1994), 139.

29. Roland Barthes, *S/Z,* translated by Richard Miller (New York: Hill and Wang, 1974), 110.

30. Taylor protested the kind of "musical baby kissing" as programming practice among classically trained singers in recital that consisted of mixing "high-class trash that any night-club singer or instrumentalist could perform better" with serious music in order to "lighten the program" (Deems Taylor, *The Well-Tempered Listener* [New York: Simon and Schuster, 1940], 180).

31. Roland Barthes, *L'obvie et l'obtus* (Paris: Seuil, 1982), 238, 243, cited in Mladen Dolar, "The Object Voice," in *Gaze and Voice as Love Objects,* ed. Renata Saleci and Slavoj Žižek (Durham, NC: Duke University Press, 1996), 7–31, 10.

32. Dolar, "The Object Voice," 10. See also "The Grain of the Voice," in Roland Barthes, *Image/Music/Text,* trans. Stephen Heath (New York: Hill and Wang, 1977), 86.

33. Joan Riviere, "Womanliness as a Masquerade," in *Psychoanalysis and Female Sexuality,* ed. Hendrik M. Ruitenbeek (New Haven, CT: College and University Press, 1966), 209–20. In feminist film theory perhaps the most cited articulation of the masquerade has come from Mary Ann Doane, "Film and the Masquerade: Theorising the Female Spectator," *Screen* 23, nos. 3 and 4 (1987): 74–87.

34. Joan Riviere, "Womanliness as a Masquerade," 215.

35. Peter Brooks, "Body and Voice in Melodrama and Opera," in *Siren Songs: Representations of Gender and Sexuality in Opera,* ed. Mary Ann Smart (Princeton, NJ: Princeton University Press, 2000), 122.

36. Ibid., 123.

37. Ibid., 122.

38. Deanna Durbin confirms that Disney rejected her because she sounded too mature for *Snow White* in a 1983 interview with David Shipman. See "Nostalgia: Deanna Durbin," *Films & Filming,* no. 382 (Dec. 1983): 25.

39. Dolar, "The Object Voice," 16.

40. Britta Sjogren, *Into the Vortex: Female Voice and Paradox in Film* (Urbana: University of Illinois Press, 2006), 25.

41. Photo clipping in Life Story of Deanna Durbin scrapbook, comp. Anne Cogley, Special Collections, AMPAS; and unidentified fan magazine article in Deanna Durbin scrapbook II, comp. Anne Cogley, Special Collections, AMPAS.

42. Rosemarie Garland Thomson, "Introduction," *Freakery: Cultural Spec-*

*tacles of the Extraordinary Body* (New York: New York University Press, 1996), 3.

43. Lewis, "The Private Life of Deanna Durbin," 55.

44. On Durbin's fashion influence on a female member of the British "Deanna Durbin Society" see Stacey, *Star Gazing,* 200–201. On her playing young see Norbert Lusk, "'Her Butler's Sister' Wins Critics to Durbin Anew," *Los Angeles Times,* Jan. 6, 1944, A9; and Bosley Crowther, "The Screen," *New York Times,* Dec. 30, 1943, 13.

45. See the many articles and newspaper photos in Deanna Durbin scrapbook II, AMPAS. The quotation is from "Movie Life of Deanna Durbin," unidentified clipping in Deanna Durbin scrapbook II, AMPAS.

46. "The Truth about Deanna's Divorce," unidentified article in ibid.

47. "Sidelights of the Week," *New York Times,* Nov. 7, 1937, 66.

48. Michele Hilmes, *Radio Voices: American Broadcasting, 1922–1952* (Minneapolis: University of Minnesota Press, 1997), 113.

49. Ibid., 118.

50. See Michele Hilmes, *Hollywood and Broadcasting: From Radio to Cable* (Urbana: University of Illinois Press, 1990), esp. chap. 3, "Radio Goes Hollywood, 1928–38" (49–77).

51. Moore made two films at MGM—*A Lady's Morals* (dir. Sidney Franklin, 1930) and *New Moon* (dir. Jack Conway, 1930)—before she was fired by Irving Thalberg. She then signed with Columbia, where she made a spectacular comeback with *One Night of Love,* which earned her an Academy Award nomination in the Best Actress category (among six nominations for the film). On Moore's tenure at MGM see Turk, *Hollywood Diva,* 142–43, 150.

52. Michel Chion, *Audio-Vision: Sound on Screen,* edited and translated by Claudia Gorbman (New York: Columbia University Press, 1994), 97.

53. Hilmes, *Radio Voices,* 20.

54. To hear Durbin's "One Night of Love," reportedly sung as a thirteen-year-old, go to www.youtube.com/watch?v=AgNmvVG2pB4.

55. Paul Young, *The Cinema Dreams Its Rivals: Media Fantasy Films* (Minneapolis: University of Minnesota Press, 2006), 81.

56. The citation of the huge response to the program is given on the website for the Deanna Durbin Devotees, deannadurbindevotees.com/radio-fo/the-eddie-cantor-show.

57. This claim is made on the website for the Deanna Durbin Devotees: deannadurbindevotees.com. Issues of the devotees' newsletter from the 1940s document the participation of males as well as females in her fan base; many of these letters are housed at AMPAS.

58. Joseph Horowitz, *Classical Music in America: A History of Its Rise and Fall* (New York: Norton, 2005), 398.

59. Hilmes, *Radio Voices,* 189; see also Horowitz, *Classical Music,* 198–99.

60. See "We Applaud," *Radio Guide,* May 1, 1937, 25.

61. On one much-publicized remote broadcast see "Texas Honors Deanna Durbin," *Los Angeles Times,* March 10, 1937, A21.

62. See comment by Devotee #1 on Jan. 22, 2008, www.deannadurbindevo-

tees.com/radio-f9/the-eddie-cantor-show. Cantor also stated this in an episode on the air.

63. "Photo," *New York Times,* Oct. 11, 1936, X12.

64. Photograph, "Two potential opera stars . . . ," *Motion Picture,* August 1937, 65. Demonstrating the problem of authenticity and radio, another member of the *Texaco Town* family, violinist Dave Rubinoff, had to have his thickly accented speaking voice replaced on the program, first with Cantor speaking Rubinoff's lines in a Russian accent and later with an actor (Lionel Stander) speaking them. Bobby Breen had a successful career as a child star at RKO, where he made nine films, starting with *Let's Sing Again* (dir. Kurt Neumann, 1936) and ending with *Johnny Doughboy* (dir. John Auer, 1942).

65. "Sidelights of the Week," *New York Times,* Nov. 7, 1937, 66; "Deanna Durbin Scales Screen Heights to Stardom in 'Three Smart Girls,'" *Los Angeles Times,* Dec. 2, 1936, 11; Douglas Churchill, "One Smart Girl," *New York Times,* Sept. 17, 1939, 17.

66. Matthew Murray, "'The Tendency to Deprave and Corrupt Morals': Regulation and Irregular Sexuality in Golden Age Radio Comedy," in *Radio Reader: Essays in the Cultural History of Radio,* ed. Michele Hilmes and Jason Loviglio (New York: Routledge, 2002), 135.

67. Ibid., 141.

68. Basinger, *The Star Machine,* 271.

69. Wayne Koestenbaum, *The Queen's Throat: Opera, Homosexuality, and the Mystery of Desire* (New York: Da Capo, 1993), 155.

70. For a discussion of cultural theorists like Benjamin, Adorno, and Brecht on this issue see Tambling, *Opera, Ideology, and Film,* 91–100.

71. In its review *Time* magazine seemed not to take the film seriously, calling it "the daintiest, quaintest, most hygienic little musicomedy of the season" but then concedes that the film was "first-rate entertainment" ("The New Pictures," *Time,* review of *Three Smart Girls,* Dec. 21, 1936, 22).

72. Edwin Schallert, "Durbin Plays Match-Maker in Latest," *Los Angeles Times,* March 17, 1939, 21.

73. Donald O'Connor's supporting role in *Something in the Wind* allows him an eccentric specialty dance number. He is not the romantic lead.

74. In the 1920s the studios had recognized the potential of radio to help the film industry, evidenced in the purchase of radio stations by Warner Bros. and Paramount. Tensions did arise, however. In 1932, operating under pressure from exhibitors, Hollywood temporarily banned its stars from making radio appearances, but this was an attempt at appeasement defied almost immediately by some studios and universally abandoned in less than one year. See Hilmes, *Hollywood and Broadcasting,* 55–60.

75. Leopold Stokowski, *Music for All of Us* (New York: Simon and Schuster, 1943), 221, 234–35.

76. Theodor Adorno, "On the Fetish Character of Music and the Regression of Listening," in *The Essential Frankfurt School Reader,* ed. Andrew Arato and Eike Gebhardt (New York: Continuum, 1982), 270–99, 271.

77. On the foundational importance of heterosexual coupling to the film

musical see Rick Altman, *The American Film Musical* (Bloomington: Indiana University Press, 1987), 28–58.

78. Susan J. Douglas, *Listening In: Radio and the American Imagination* (New York: Random House, 1999), 150.

79. In this vein Nash has referred to Durbin's screen character as "a spotless force for moral good" and unrealistically "angelic," but she appears to confuse the impression left by the actress's "angelic" voice with Durbin's assertive if not outright bratty characters. See Nash, *American Sweethearts,* 85–91.

80. Ibid., 150.

81. On women's suffering in opera see Catherine Clément, *Opera: The Undoing of Women,* translated by Betsy Wing (Minneapolis: University of Minnesota Press, 1999), 11.

82. The quotation is from Frank Nugent, "The Screen" [review of *Three Smart Girls Grow Up*"], *New York Times,* March 18, 1939, 9. In his review the next week, Nugent says Durbin has brought "freshness," "gay vitality," "artful artlessness," and "youthful radiance" to the screen and doesn't need a cheapening Hollywood epithet like "glamorous." See Frank Nugent, "A Universal Error about Glamour," *New York Times,* March 26, 1939, 137. On the many commentaries detailing Universal's clumsy attempts to have Durbin grow up glamorously, see Edwin Schallert, "Drama and Film: New Deanna Durbin Brought to Screen," *Los Angeles Times,* August 1, 1943, C2.

83. Richard Griffith, "Deanna Durbin's Maturing Worries New York Critics," *Los Angeles Times,* April 7, 1941, 16. See also John Scott, "Puppy Love Big Problem for Studios," *Los Angeles Times,* May 1, 1938, C3.

84. On this issue see Tambling, *Opera, Ideology, and Film,* 51.

85. Altman, *American Film Musical,* 107.

86. Brooks, "Body and Voice in Melodrama and Opera," 125.

87. Barthes, *S/Z,* 25.

88. Koestenbaum, *The Queen's Throat,* 43.

## CHAPTER 4

1. John Scott, "Juveniles Bidding," *Los Angeles Times,* March 13, 1938, C1; Edwin Schallert, "Jane Withers Picture Given Budget Boost," *Los Angeles Times,* June 3, 1940, 9.

2. Richard Schickel, *The Stars: The Personalities Who Made the Movies* (New York: Bonanza, 1962), 280. Alexander Walker recounts this story and also details the role of Hedda Hopper in Taylor's discovery, as well as the dropping of her option by Universal in February of 1942. See Alexander Walker, *Elizabeth: The Life of Elizabeth Taylor* (New York: Grove, 1990), 32–33.

3. *National Velvet* press book, microfiche, Margaret Herrick Library, Academy of Motion Picture Arts and Sciences (hereafter AMPAS); Schickel, *The Stars,* 278; and Walker, *Elizabeth,* 33.

4. Quoted in Larissa Branin, *Liz* (New York: Courage Books, 2000), 23. Taylor's association with Lassie in two films would appear to be worth considering in light of the role played by animals, especially domesticated pets, in eighteenth- and nineteenth-century high-art representations of girls. However,

Taylor's character in *Lassie Come Home* has only one scene in which she very briefly interacts with the dog. It is not her love for Lassie that is important. The film is about the love of Joe (McDowall) and Lassie, a love that compels Lassie to walk all the way from Scotland back to Yorkshire and Joe. Priscilla helps to facilitate their reunion by opening the gate to allow Lassie to escape and through encouraging her grandfather to hire Joe's unemployed father at his kennels. The final shot of the film shows Lassie's puppies following Priscilla and Joe as they ride bicycles. Unlike the films I discuss in this chapter, *Courage of Lassie* (dir. Fred M. Wilcox, 1946) does not play on Englishness: Taylor plays an American who rescues a dog named Bill (played by Lassie) near a lake somewhere in the U.S. West.

5. Raymond Williams, *The Long Revolution* (London: Chatto and Windus, 1961), 53.

6. Letter to Betty Marsh, Jan. 14, 1915, vertical file, folder 32, AMPAS.

7. "A 'Broncho Billy' Turns Murderer," *Decatur Daily Review*, Sept. 22, 1914, 11. My thanks to Courtney Andree for this information and for delineating the issue of "movieitis" and aberrant or even criminal male responses to early film in her paper "Broncho Billy and the Problem of the Male Fan" [unpublished seminar paper, Dec. 2010].

8. Lionel Lambourne, *Victorian Painting* (London: Phaidon, 1999), 170.

9. Quoted in Malcolm Warner, "John Everett Millais's *Autumn Leaves*: 'A Picture Full of Beauty and without Subject,'" in *Pre-Raphaelite Papers*, ed. Leslie Parris (London: Tate Gallery, 1984), 137.

10. Leslie Williams, "The Look of Little Girls: John Everett Millais and the Victorian Art Market," in *The Girl's Own: Cultural Histories of the Anglo-American Girl, 1830–1915*, ed. Claudia Nelson and Lynne Vallone (Darby, PA: Diane, 1994), 149.

11. For a definition of *fancy pictures* see Ellis Waterhouse, "Gainsborough's 'Fancy Pictures,'" *Burlington Magazine for Connoisseurs*, June 1946, 135.

12. Waterhouse, "Gainsborough's 'Fancy Pictures,'" 131.

13. Patmore, quoted in Tate Gallery, *Pre-Raphaelites* (London: Allen Lane, 1984), 86.

14. Williams, "The Look of Little Girls," 131.

15. Ibid., 124.

16. Viviana A. Zelizer, *Pricing the Priceless Child: The Changing Social Value of Children* (Princeton, NJ: Princeton University Press, 1985), 11.

17. Laura Bradley, "From Eden to Empire: John Everett Millais's 'Cherry Ripe,'" *Victorian Studies* 34, no. 2 (1991): 192.

18. Pamela Tamarkin Reis, "Exchange: Victorian Centerfold; Another Look at Millais's *Cherry Ripe*," *Victorian Studies* 35, no. 2 (1992): 201.

19. Bradley, "From Eden to Empire," 179.

20. Ibid., 182, 190.

21. Reis, "Exchange," 201.

22. Nina Auerbach, *Romantic Imprisonment: Women and Other Glorified Outcasts* (New York: Columbia University Press, 1986), 24.

23. Charlotte Brontë, *Jane Eyre* (1847; New York: Modern Library, 2000), 96.

24. Ibid., 96, 106.

25. Ibid., 117.

26. Theodora A. Jankowski, "Pure Resistance: Queer(y)ing Virginity in William Shakespeare's 'Measure for Measure' and Margaret Cavendish's 'The Convent of Pleasure,'" *Shakespeare Studies* 26 (1998): 218.

27. Ibid., 219.

28. Brontë, *Jane Eyre*, 95–96.

29. Millais, quoted in Warner, "John Everett Millais's *Autumn Leaves*," 137–38.

30. Elisabeth G. Gitter, "The Power of Women's Hair in the Victorian Imagination," *PMLA* 99, no. 5 (1985): 938. See also Galia Ofek, *Representations of Hair in Victorian Literature and Culture* (Burlington, VT: Ashgate, 2009).

31. "The New Pictures: *National Velvet*," *Time*, Dec. 25,1944, 44.

32. Manny Farber, "Crazy over Horses," *Nation*, Feb. 3, 1945, 175.

33. James Agee, "*National Velvet*," *Nation*, Dec. 23, 1944; repr. in *Cinema Nation: The Best Writing on Film from "The Nation," 1913–2000*, ed. Carl Bromley (New York: Thunder's Mouth, 2000), 373.

34. Farber, "Crazy over Horses," 175.

35. *National Velve*t press book, AMPAS.

36. Mary Beth Haralovich, "Advertising Heterosexuality," *Screen* 23, no. 2 (1982): 50–60.

## CHAPTER 5

*Epigraph*. George Du Maurier, *Trilby* (1894; New York: Harper and Brothers, 1895), 458. On the importance of the Svengali-Trilby story to Victorian mythmaking focused on the woman as victim see Nina Auerbach, *Woman and the Demon: The Life of a Victorian Myth* (Cambridge, MA: Harvard University Press, 1982), 15–22.

1. Jones's first contract was dated July 23, 1941. Selznick renamed her in January of 1942. See Jennifer Jones Correspondence file for Selznick memos related to the contract particulars, July 28, 1941, memo to Dan O'Shea and Katharine Brown. David O. Selznick Collection, Harry Ransom Center for the Humanities, University of Texas, Austin (hereafter DOS).

2. "Jennifer Jones," *Current Biography: Who's News and Why, 1944*, ed. Anna Rothe (New York: H.W. Wilson, 1945), 328–30.

3. Quotation from review by T.S., "*Claudia* at the Music Hall," *New York Times*, Nov. 5, 1943, 23. *Claudia* is a frothy comic take on the misunderstandings surrounding an extremely naive young bride who doesn't understand her impact on others, especially men. She grows up in reaction to learning that her mother is dying. Dorothy McGuire (another Selznick contractee) won the title role in the film. She played the role on Broadway. Jones auditioned for the Chicago run of the play but lost out to Phyllis Thaxter. See Selznick to Katharine Brown, memo, August 27, 1941, Jennifer Jones Correspondence file, DOS.

4. Selznick to Brown, memo, Sept. 19, 1941, DOS.

5. Selznick to Dan O'Shea, memo, Feb. 2, 1942. DOS.

6. "The New Pictures," *Time,* Feb. 7, 1944, 56. Jones failed to mention a Republic contract to Selznick until the month after she had signed with him. Under her birth name of Phylis Isley she made three pictures at Republic in 1939: *New Frontier* (with John Wayne), a Dick Tracy serial, and a Roy Rogers picture in which Jones claimed she appeared in the background (as an Indian). Republic did not exercise its option on her six-month contract. Selznick had his people investigate to make sure she had no remaining obligation with the studio, and then they "let the matter die." Daniel O'Shea to Selznick, memo, Oct. 27, 1941, DOS. The fact that Jones had been at Republic leaked out when *The Song of Bernadette* was going into release and being advertised as her debut film. By 1949 the official biography for Jones constructed by Howard Strickland for MGM (where she was filming *Madame Bovary*) was forthright about the actress having first spent a short time in B pictures. Jennifer Jones Special Collection file, 15.13 Biography, Margaret Herrick Library, Academy of Motion Picture Arts and Sciences (hereafter AMPAS).

7. Jones was born March 2, 1919. In 1952 Selznick remarked, "Jennifer can when necessary play a very young girl" (Selznick to Charles Feldman, memo, March 19, 1952, DOS). Joan Fontaine, who was contracted with Selznick at the time, played the fourteen-year-old in *The Constant Nymph* (dir. Edmund Goulding, 1943) who falls in love with a concert pianist; a few years later, she played the role of yet another young girl who falls in love with a concert pianist in *Letter from an Unknown Woman* (dir. Max Ophuls, 1948).

8. It is unclear what age the heroine of *Love Letters* is, but one review called her a "youngster." See Howard Barnes review, *New York Herald Tribune,* n.d., n.p., *Love Letters* file, AMPAS; Georganne Scheiner, *Signifying Female Adolescence: Film Representations and Fans, 1920–1950* (Westport, CT: Praeger, 2000), 138–44; Ilana Nash, *American Sweethearts: Teenage Girls in Twentieth-Century Popular Culture* (Bloomington: Indiana University Press, 2006), 117–67.

9. Other vision-related symptoms included eyelid twitching, temporary blindness, and changes in color or spatial perception. See Georges Didi-Huberman, *Invention of Hysteria: Charcot and the Photographic Iconography of the Salpêtrière,* trans. Alisa Hartz (Cambridge, MA: MIT Press, 1982), 135, 137.

10. "*Portrait of Jennie,*" in *American Film Institute Catalog of Motion Pictures Produced in the United States, Feature Films, 1941–1950,* ed. Patricia King Hanson (Berkeley: University of California Press, 1999), 1872.

11. Peter Brooks, *The Melodramatic Imagination: Balzac, Henry James, Melodrama, and the Mode of Excess* (New Haven, CT: Yale University Press, 1976); Geoffrey Nowell-Smith, "Minnelli and Melodrama," in *Imitations of Life: A Reader on Film and Television Melodrama,* ed. Marcia Landry (Detroit: Wayne State University Press, 1991), 272; Thomas Elsaesser, "Tales of Sound and Fury: Observations on the Family Melodrama," in *Home Is Where the Heart Is: Studies in Melodrama and the Woman's Film,* ed. Christine Gledhill (London: British Film Institute, 1987), 43–69, repr. from *Monogram* 4 (1972): 2–16.

12. Nowell-Smith, "Minnelli and Melodrama," 272.

13. Sigmund Freud, *Fragments of an Analysis of a Case of Hysteria (1905)* (New York: Touchstone, 1997).

14. Didi-Huberman, *Invention of Hysteria,* 159.

15. Robin Wood, "*Duel in the Sun:* The Destruction of an Ideological System," in *The Book of Westerns,* ed. Ian Cameron and Douglas Pye (New York: Continuum, 1996), 189. See also Robin Wood, "Minnelli's *Madame Bovary,*" repr. in *Vincente Minnelli: The Art of Entertainment,* ed. Joe McElhaney (Detroit: Wayne State University Press, 2009), 157.

16. Catherine Clément and Hélène Cixous, *La jeune née* (Paris: 10/18, 1975), 283, quoted in Charles Bernheimer, "Introduction: Part One," in *In Dora's Case: Freud-Hysteria-Feminism,* ed. Charles Bernheimer and Claire Kahane (New York: Columbia University Press, 1985), 1.

17. Nitza Yarom, *Matrix of Hysteria: Psychoanalysis of the Struggle between the Sexes as Enacted in the Body* (London: Routledge, 2005), 1–9.

18. Laura Mulvey, "'It Will Be a Magnificent Obsession': The Melodrama's Role in the Development of Contemporary Film Theory," in *Melodrama: Stage, Picture, Screen,* ed. Jacky Bratton, Jim Cook, and Christine Gledhill (London: British Film Institute, 1994), 132.

19. Yarom, *Matrix of Hysteria,* 20–37.

20. Aljean Harmetz says that Jones "never set her own course. . . . The screen image was always as molded by Selznick" (Aljean Harmetz, "Jennifer Jones, Postwar Actress, Dies at 90," *New York Times,* Dec. 17, 2009, www.nytimes.com/2009/12/18/movies/18jones.html). On Selznick's "Svengalian grasp" on Jones, see David Thomson, *Showman: The Life of David O. Selznick* (New York: Alfred A. Knopf, 1992), 48. Elsa Maxwell mentions the "mesmeric attraction" between Jones and Selznick in "New Horizons," *Photoplay,* Nov. 1949, 100.

21. Shirley Temple Black recounts the office setup and fending off Selznick's sexual advances while she was under contract to him; see Shirley Temple Black, *Child Star: An Autobiography* (New York: Warner Books, 1988), 357, 436.

22. Quoted in "Oscar Winning Actress Jennifer Jones Dies at 90," stupidcelebrities.net/2009/12/oscar-winning-actress-jennifer-jones-dies-at-90/.

23. Quoted in Florabel Muir, "6 to 5 on Jones," *Modern Screen,* April 1947, 38–39.

24. Thomson, *Showman;* Edward Z. Epstein, *Portrait of Jennifer: A Biography of Jennifer Jones* (New York: Simon and Schuster, 1995); Beverly Linet, *Star-Crossed: The Story of Robert Walker and Jennifer Jones* (New York: G.P. Putnam's Sons, 1986), 125; Irene Mayer Selznick, *A Private View* (New York: Alfred A. Knopf, 1983); John Huston on Jones and Selznick, in Linet, *Star-Crossed,* 217.

25. Louella O. Parsons, "I Predict a Honeymoon," *Photoplay,* Feb. 1949, 32–33.

26. On the similarities between *Duel in the Sun* and *Ruby Gentry* see Raymond Durgnat and Scott Simmon, *King Vidor, American* (Berkeley: University of California Press, 1988), 286.

27. Selznick remarked more than once that Jones had very good judgment about film properties. She was scheduled to play the female lead in *The Country*

*Girl* (1954), but to protect her pregnancy, she dropped out. The role was filled by Grace Kelly, who won the Academy Award for best actress. Jones was considered for the lead role of the woman with multiple personalities in *The Three Faces of Eve*. See Thomas M. Pryor, "Actress Famine Hits Hollywood," *New York Times,* Sept. 14, 1956, 27. She declined. Joanne Woodward went on to win an Academy Award for portraying Eve. Jones bought the rights to *Terms of Endearment* but was supposedly muscled out of the deal on the argument that she was too old to play Miranda; Shirley MacLaine filled the role.

28. One of Selznick's colleagues told him that the problem in getting any productions for Jones in England was that British filmmakers could not afford her (at US$150,000 a film) and were afraid of dealing with him. See Jenia Reissar to Selznick, memo, March 20, 1945, DOS.

29. Selznick feared Jones's "excessive modesty" made people think "that she is not up to playing this kind of role [in *St. Joan*], but it's one of the problems I always have to face in Jennifer . . . even though inevitably it is going to cost her many opportunities. . . . I want to be very sure that Jennifer is treated as what she is—a tremendous drawing card and an established star of the first rank" (Selznick to Nancy Stern, memo, Jan. 4, 1952, DOS).

30. William Dieterle: "Jennifer was a creative actress. She came to work prepared. . . . Her instincts were good" (quoted in Epstein, *Portrait of Jennifer,* 156). Dieterle claims there was no interference from Selznick on *Love Letters* since Hal Wallis produced. On Jones's opinions being expressed in private see Epstein, *Portrait of Jennifer,* 182. For Joan Fontaine on Selznick as a smothering man—including sexually—see Epstein, *Portrait of Jennifer,* 158.

31. Selznick to Dan O'Shea, memo, Oct. 19, 1949, DOS.

32. Selznick claims that Jones was very enthusiastic after reading the book and seeing the Gary Cooper/Helen Hayes version of *A Farewell to Arms* (dir. Frank Borzage, 1933). She was interested in working with Elia Kazan on *A Streetcar Named Desire* but did not like the role of Blanche, and Tennessee Williams thought her too young for it. See Selznick to Dan O'Shea, memo, March 23, 1950, DOS.

33. Selznick to Anita Colby, McNamara, etc., memo, Sept. 16, 1946, DOS. On Jones's fear of making stills see Selznick to Ben Washer, memo, March 21, 1945, DOS.

34. John Cromwell, quoted in Linet, *Star-Crossed,* 124–25 (my emphasis).

35. Black, *Child Star,* 360.

36. Cotten, quoted in Linet, *Star-Crossed,* 125.

37. Harmetz, "Jennifer Jones, Postwar Actress, Dies at 90." By the time Selznick begged John Huston to direct Jones in *A Farewell to Arms,* he was complaining that no good director wanted to work with him. That did not keep him from firing Huston.

38. Earl Wilson, *New York Post,* Dec. 15, 1945 (cited in Epstein, *Portrait of Jennifer,* 184).

39. "Movies," *Newsweek,* July 10, 1944, 86.

40. Maxine Arnold, "Jennifer—The Fabulous Life of a Girl Named Jones," *Photoplay,* Sept. 1947, 120–21. The article notes that "she and David O. Selznick may be man and wife after his marital problems have been cleared up."

Other than mentioning Jones's romantic relationship with a married man, this article is a clichéd blueprint for "how to construct a new female star" as modest, hardworking, devoted to her family and old friends, grateful to be working, and average in her tastes. It relies on the testimony of Anita Colby, identified as a close friend of Jones (as she was), but a woman who also was in charge of Jones's education into stardom within the Selznick organization.

41. Elsa Maxwell, "Hollywood Show-Offs," *Photoplay*, Dec. 1949, 35, 104.

42. Henry Willson, former Selznick talent scout: "I always thought Selznick made Jennifer nervous in public. . . . He was such a perfectionist. . . . He was always criticizing how she looked, how she spoke" (quoted in Epstein, *Portrait of Jennifer*, 185).

43. Ibid., 223–24.

44. On Jones's reported first suicide attempt in response to Earl Wilson's column that implied she and Selznick were living together, see Thomson, *Showman*, 462–63; and Epstein, *Portrait of Jennifer*, 184. According to Epstein, Anita Colby denied that Jones attempted to throw herself out of a moving taxi in 1947, as reported by Irene Selznick (*A Private View*, 292) and discussed, with Colby, by Epstein (*Portrait of Jennifer*, 205); see also Otto Friedrich, *City of Nets: A Portrait of Hollywood in the 1940s* (New York: Harper and Row, 1987), 228; and Linet, *Star-Crossed*, 191. Jones's suicide attempt of 1967 was reported widely in newspapers; see also, Thomson, *Showman*, 696.

45. Edgar Morin, *The Stars*, trans. Richard Howard (New York: Grove, 1960), 37.

46. For her role as Jane Hilton, Jones was nominated for Best Supporting Actress by the Academy of Motion Picture Arts and Sciences. "Cinema," *Time*, July 17, 1944, 96.

47. Epstein, *Portrait of Jennifer*, 286.

48. Referring to "bewildering nervous moves and grimaces" is Bosley Crowther, "The Screen: David Selznick's 'A Farewell to Arms,'" *New York Times*, Jan. 25, 1958, 14. On *Tender Is the Night* see "Cinema: A Fatal Desire to Please," *Time*, Jan. 26, 1962, 55. On Jones's "imbuing the nurse with a sense of neurosis and foreboding," see review of *A Farewell to Arms*, *Variety*, Dec. 25, 1957, 6.

49. "Cinema: A Fatal Desire to Please," 55.

50. Irene Selznick, *A Private View*, 235–36. Friedrich, *City of Nets*, 221–24.

51. Thomson, *Showman*, 422–29.

52. Yarom, *Matrix of Hysteria*, 35.

53. In addition to *Since You Went Away*, Raoul Walsh's *The Man I Love* (1946) offers an interesting take on curing a war veteran with psychological problems. See Maria Santos, *The Dark Mirror: Psychiatry and Film Noir* (New York: Lexington, 2011).

54. Franz Werfel, *The Song of Bernadette*, trans. Ludwig Lewisohn (1942; San Francisco: Ignatius Press, 1970), 372–81.

55. For a concise overview of the origins of psychoanalysis, with emphasis on Freud's study of men in relation to his theorization of hysteria, see Mark S. Micale, *Hysterical Men: The Hidden History of Male Nervous Illness* (Cambridge, MA: Harvard University Press, 2008), 228–75.

56. See Sigmund Freud, "Hysterical Phantasies and Their Relation to Bisexuality" (1908), *The Standard Edition of the Complete Psychological Works of Sigmund Freud*, ed. James Strachey (London: Hogarth, 1959), 9:161.

57. See Nancy Rubino, "Impotence and Excess: Male Hysteria and Androgyny in Flaubert's Salammbô," *Nineteenth-Century French Studies* 29, no. 1/2 (2000–2001): 1–3.

58. Ulrich Baer, "Photography and Hysteria: Toward a Poetics of the Flash," *Yale Journal of Criticism* 7, no. 1 (1994): 44.

59. Elaine Showalter, *The Female Malady: Women, Madness, and English Culture, 1830–1980* (New York: Penguin, 1985), 154; on "arresting the symptom" through photography for diagnostic purposes see Baer, "Photography and Hysteria," 44–45.

60. Charcot reported that Augustine's hysterical attacks started after she was raped at age thirteen by a man who was her mother's lover and in whose home she lived; this "stepfather" first attempted to seduce her with gifts, but meeting resistance, he forced alcohol on her and then violently raped her. See Charcot, quoted in Désiré Magloire Bourneville and Paul Regnard, *Iconographie photographique de la Salpêtrière* (Paris: Bureaux du Progrès médical/Delahaye and Lecrosnier, 1878), 126–27 (quoted in Didi-Huberman, *Invention of Hysteria,* 157). On cultural performances of madness see Showalter, *The Female Malady,* 154.

61. Didi-Huberman, *Invention of Hysteria,* 115. The four stages of the hysterical attack were (1) "epileptoid," which looked like a familiar epileptic fit; (2) "clownism," involving violent, distorting bodily contortions evidencing no logic with "tetanism," contractures that rendered parts of the body rigidly immobile (hysterical contracture); (3) plastic poses or "*attitudes passionnelles,*" in which an imaginary scenario (expressing memory of trauma?) is acted out; and (4) "delirium," marked by the flow of talk (and sometimes explosive anger or rebuttal) from the hysteric. Augustine experienced deliria of being raped (160–61). On memory and *attitudes passionnelles* see 115, 152, 154.

62. On Charcot's attempts to use photography to defend himself against skeptical reactions, see Andrew Scull, *Hysteria: The Biography* (Oxford: Oxford University Press, 2009), 124. On British reactions to Charcot, and the proliferation of hysteria in nineteenth-century France, see Showalter, *The Female Malady,* 150–51.

63. On Augustine's escape from confinement see Showalter, *The Female Malady,* 154; and Didi-Huberman, *Invention of Hysteria,* 275.

64. On Charcoat, Cristina Mazzoni, *Saint Hysteria: Neurosis, Mysticism, and Gender in European Culture* (Ithaca, NY: Cornell University Press, 1996), 39. On Augustine as Charcot's most photographed patient see Baer, "Photography and Hysteria," 47.

65. Charcot, quoted in Didi-Huberman, *Invention of Hysteria,* 144.

66. Hanne Blanke, *Virgin: The Untouched History* (New York: Bloomsbury, 2007), 153.

67. Mazzoni, *Saint Hysteria,* 41.

68. Showalter, *The Female Malady,* 56.

69. Julia Kristeva, "Adolescence: A Syndrome of Ideality," *Psychoanalytic Review* 94, no. 5 (2007): 724, 717.

70. On Francisca Badia and other female visionaries see Stephen Haliczer, *Between Exaltation and Infamy: Female Mystics in the Golden Age of Spain* (New York: Oxford University Press, 2002), 85.

71. Didi-Huberman, *Invention of Hysteria,* 142. On the extravagant ecstasies of English mystic Margery Kempe see Blanke, *Virgin,* 153.

72. Blanke, *Virgin,* 130–36.

73. See Blanke, *Virgin,* 154–56.

74. In 1945 a nine-year-old boy named Joseph Vitolo Jr. started seeing the Virgin Mary at a vacant lot in the Bronx and said she told him that a spring would appear. Thousands of people arrived to keep vigil for the sixteen nights that the boy said he was told to return. No spring appeared. Some thought *The Song of Bernadette* influenced the child's vision, but he denied having seen the film. The Catholic Church refused to endorse his claims. See John T. McGreevy, "Bronx Miracle," *American Quarterly* 52, no. 3 (2000): 405–43; for a rather class-biased contemporary account see "Shrine in the Bronx," *Time,* Nov. 26, 1945, 27.

75. Selznick to Darryl Zanuck, Jan. 26, 1944, DOS.

76. Thomas Elsaesser refers to the convergence of the woman's film and melodrama; he mentions actresses like Bette Davis and Joan Crawford as icons of the woman's picture, but his exemplar of the classic woman's film during the war years is *Since You Went Away* rather than better-known film melodramas such as *Now, Voyager* (dir. Irving Rapper, 1942) or *Mildred Pierce* (dir. Michael Curtiz, 1945). See Elsaesser, "Tales of Sound and Fury," 58.

77. Temple would play Corliss Archer, twice, in *Kiss and Tell* and in its sequel, *A Kiss for Corliss* (dir. Richard Wallace, 1948).

78. The quotation is from the introduction to the Corliss Archer radio series. See Nash, *American Sweethearts,* 151.

79. Letters to the editor, *Seventeen*, Nov. 1944, 4 (quoted in Grace Palladino, *Teenagers: An American History* [New York: Basic Books, 1996], 105).

80. Palladino, *Teenagers,* 23.

81. For an extended discussion of Herbert's characters, comedies, and career see Nash, *American Sweethearts,* 150–54.

82. Palladino, *Teenagers,* 74–75.

83. Eleanor Lake, "Trouble on the Street Corners," *Reader's Digest,* May 1943, 43.

84. Rachel Devlin, "Female Juvenile Delinquency and the Problem of Sexual Authority in America, 1945–1965," in *Delinquents and Debutantes: Twentieth-Century American Girls' Cultures,* ed. Sherrie A. Innes (New York: New York University Press, 1998), 99. See also Scheiner, *Signifying Adolescence,* 9, 11–12.

85. In a passing remark, Wood seems to misremember *Since You Went Away.* He refers to Jones's "disruptive" presence in an otherwise conservative film, and "the big hysterical scene that follows the revelation that Robert Walker has been killed in action" ("Minnelli's *Madame Bovary,*" 157).

86. Robert Lang, *American Film Melodrama* (Princeton, NJ: Princeton University Press, 1989), 191.

87. Selznick to Don King, memo, June 14, 1944, *Since You Went Away* publicity files, DOS.

88. Frank Tuttle, *"Daddy's Gone to War": The Second World War in the Lives of America's Children* (New York: Oxford University Press, 1995), 189.

89. Ibid.

90. On this point see William Paul, *Ernst Lubitsch's American Comedy* (New York: Columbia University Press, 1987), 100.

91. Lang makes a similar observation about the interrelatedness of sexuality and sociality in *Ruby Gentry:* "The way in which the film handles the issue of social class reveals that sexual difference as a problem is, wherever possible, pressed into class terms" (*American Film Melodrama,* 154).

92. Robin Wood also points in the direction of an embodied struggle when he calls attention to the dichotomy in Jones's persona of "innocence" and "sensuality," but what I am arguing is that this is not, as he implies, a struggle in which the halves or "twin poles" are necessarily separated, with one acted out in one film and then another.

93. Kristeva, "Adolescence," 717.

94. Ibid., 720–21.

95. Joan Copjec, "More! From Melodrama to Magnitude," in *Endless Night: Cinema and Psychoanalysis, Parallel Histories,* ed. Janet Bergstrom (Berkeley: University of California Press, 1999), 260.

96. Lang says Ruby is so disruptive because her tomboy, phallic sexuality is coupled with a "drowning sexuality" associated with uncontrolled nature. *American Film Melodrama,* 156–57.

97. Mulvey, "'It Will Be a Magnificent Obsession,'" 126, 132. Mulvey says psychic processes reveal the social through an "inscribed absence" in which the domestic replaces the political with psychic traces of the past (trauma); she suggests that by such means, melodrama offers a "cultural symptomatic" (126).

98. Ron Haver summarizes the difficulties of production, most of which he attributes to Selznick's obsessive perfectionism. King Vidor walked off the production but was credited onscreen, after arbitration, as the film's director. See Ron Haver, *David O. Selznick's Hollywood* (New York: Bonanza, 1980).

99. Sen. John Rankin quoting Lloyd T. Binford, chief censor of the city of Memphis, TN, in letter to Joseph Breen regarding a resolution to ban *Duel in the Sun* in Washington, DC. Congressional record on June 19, 1947, p. 7456. See PCA file for *Duel in the Sun,* AMPAS.

100. On the film's box-office ranking see www.filmsite.org/boxoffice.html, which ranks it no. 91 in domestic gross of any U.S. film (as of this writing). *Duel in the Sun* comes in as no. 150 (adjusted domestic gross) at Boxoffice.com.

101. Selznick to Don King, memo, Nov. 27, 1944, DOS.

102. Bazin defined the "super Western" as a postwar phenomenon in which westerns were not satisfied just to be westerns but sought justification by adding "supplements from outside the genre." See André Bazin, *What Is Cinema?* trans. Hugh Gray (Berkeley: University of California Press, 1971), 2:149–62. Mark Williams defines the "supra-western" as films of the 1950s "involving new subject matter and aesthetic pressures (especially . . . via the casting of major female stars) that stretch and make apparent generic boundaries that otherwise

might seem impermeable" (Mark Williams, "Get/Away: Structure and Desire in *Rancho Notorious,*" in *Dietrich Icon,* ed. Gerd Gemünden and Mary R. Desjardins [Durham, NC: Duke University Press, 2007], 261–62). Williams does not discuss *Duel in the Sun* as a supra-western, and, unlike the films he discusses, it achieved great box-office success.

103. Thomson, *Showman,* 445; Friedrich, *City of Nets,* 226–27.

104. Molly Haskell, *From Reverence to Rape: The Treatment of Women in the Movies,* 2nd ed. (1974; Chicago: University of Chicago Press, 1987), 200–201. See also Miriam Bale, "Basic Instinct," Film Society of Lincoln Center, www.filmlinc.com/film-comment/article/basic-instinct-jennifer-jones-retrospective

105. Laura Mulvey, "Afterthoughts on 'Visual Pleasure and Narrative Cinema' Inspired by *Duel in the Sun* (King Vidor, 1946)," *Framework* 15–17 (summer 1981): 12.

106. Julia Kristeva, *New Maladies of the Soul,* trans. Ross Mitchell Guberman (New York: Columbia University Press, 1995), 73.

107. Ibid., 71.

108. On the masculinization of Emma Bovary through psychological traits see Dorothy Kelly, *Fictional Genders: Role and Representation in the Nineteenth-Century French Narrative* (Lincoln: University of Nebraska Press, 1989).

109. Didi-Huberman, *Invention of Hysteria,* 170.

110. Ibid., 171.

111. Kristeva, *New Maladies of the Soul,* 70.

112. Didi-Huberman, *Invention of Hysteria,* 167.

113. Robin Wood, "*Duel in the Sun,*" 189.

114. Maria Ramas, "Freud's Dora, Dora's Hysteria," in Bernheimer and Kahane, *In Dora's Case,* 151.

115. In the original novel Pearl walks away from the mountain after she has shot Lewt dead and marries Jesse. They take part in a free-land run and start to build an empire. Selznick considered this ending but rejected it. See Niven Busch, *Duel in the Sun* (1944; New York: Popular Library, 1963), 197–99. On the role of Josef von Sternberg in visually eroticizing Pearl/Jones in *Duel in the Sun* see Durgnat and Simmon, *King Vidor, American,* 239.

116. On the contributions of the many different directors and three cinematographers who worked on the film, see Durgnat and Simmon, *King Vidor, American,* 239–55; and program in *Duel in the Sun* publicity file, DOS. On "The Degradation Scene" see Durgnat and Simmon, *King Vidor, American,* 242; and Haver, *Selznick's Hollywood,* 353.

117. Didi-Huberman, *Invention of Hysteria,* 200.

118. Ibid., 162. The scene also echoes the scene in which Laura Belle makes her way across her bedroom to her wheelchair-bound husband in an attempt at reconciliation before she dies, and it anticipates the final scene of the film at Squaw's Head rock.

119. Kristeva, *New Maladies of the Soul,* 73.

## CHAPTER 6

1. Radie Harris, "Audrey Hepburn—The Girl, the Gamin [*sic*] and the Star," *Photoplay,* March 1955, 61. See also Earl Wilson, "Is Hollywood Shifting Its

Accent on Sex?" *Silver Screen,* July 1954, 40. On big breasts as a 1950s "fashion imperative" that "shaped the experience of adolescence of both genders," see Joan Jacob Brumberg, *The Body Project: The Intimate History of American Girls* (New York: Vintage Books, 1998), 108–18. Molly Haskell addresses stars in relation to "breast fetishism" in 1950s Hollywood films in *From Reverence to Rape: The Treatment of Women in the Movies,* 2nd ed. (Chicago: University of Chicago Press, 1987), 235–52. For a discussion of 1950s comedy in relation to voluptuous female stars see Ed Sikov, *Laughing Hysterically: American Screen Comedy of the 1950s* (New York: Columbia University Press, 1995), 1–15.

2. Alfred C. Kinsey and the staff of the Institute for Sex Research, Indiana University, *Sexual Behavior in the Human Female* (Philadelphia: Saunders, 1953). On the impact of Kinsey's study see John D'Emilio and Estelle B. Freedman, *Intimate Matters: A History of Sexuality in America* (New York: Harper and Row, 1989), 295–97.

3. Grace Palladino, *Teenagers: An American History* (New York: Basic Books, 1996), 168–69.

4. "Cinema: The New Pictures," *Time,* Sept. 10, 1956, 116.

5. Angela Taylor, "Audrey Hepburn Tries on a Swinging Image," *New York Times,* Dec. 27, 1966, 39. In 1967 a review of *Two for the Road* suggested, "Miss Hepburn is amazing in her ability to portray a very young girl" ("*Two for the Road,*" *Variety,* May 3, 1967, 6). A *New York Times* review of *Breakfast at Tiffany's* called Hepburn's Holly "a genuinely charming, elfin waif" (A.H. Weiler, "The Screen: *Breakfast at Tiffany's,*" *New York Times,* Oct. 6, 1961, 28).

6. Stanley Donen, quoted in Ian Woodward, *Audrey Hepburn* (New York: St. Martin's, 1984), 183.

7. See Gaylyn Studlar, "'Out-Salomeing Salome': Dance, the New Woman, and Fan Magazine Orientalism," in *Visions of the East: Orientalism in Film,* ed. Matthew Bernstein and Gaylyn Studlar (New Brunswick, NJ: Rutgers University Press, 1997), 114–16.

8. Linda Mizejewski, *Ziegfeld Girl: Image and Icon in Culture and Cinema* (Durham, NC: Duke University Press, 1999), 21, 95.

9. Ibid., 99.

10. "Mary Pickford in New Summer Clothes Made Specially for Her by Lanvin of Paris," *Ladies' Home Journal,* June 1921, 40–43.

11. Mary B. Mullett, "Dressing the Movie Stars," *Woman's Home Companion,* August 1926, 13–14.

12. Jackie Stacey, *Star Gazing: Hollywood Cinema and Female Spectatorship* (London: Routledge, 1994), 196–97.

13. On Taylor imitating Jones, to the consternation of MGM executives, see C. David Heymann, *Liz: An Intimate Biography of Elizabeth Taylor* (1995; New York: Atria, 2001), 61.

14. Kelly Schrum, *Some Wore Bobby Sox: The Emergence of Teenage Girls' Culture, 1920–1945* (New York: Palgrave Macmillan, 2004), 139–42.

15. Richard Corliss, "Audrey Hepburn: Still the Fairest Lady," *Time,* Jan. 20, 2007, www.time.com/time/arts/article/0,8599,1580936,00.html.

16. Snow was said to have declared, "It's quite a revolution, dear Christian, your dresses have such a new look" (quoted in Katell le Bourhis, "The Elegant

Fifties: When Fashion Was Still a Dictate," in *New Look to Now: French Haute Couture, 1947–1987*, ed. Stephen de Pietri and Melissa Leventon [New York: Rizzoli, 1989], 14).

17. Christian Dior, *Christian Dior and I* (New York: E.P. Dutton, 1957), 35.

18. Christian Dior, *Talking about Fashion* (New York: G.P. Putnam's Sons, 1954), 23.

19. Cristóbal Balenciaga, quoted in Sandra Barwik, *A Century of Style* (London: George Allen and Unwin, 1984), 165. On the financial crisis in couture in the 1960s see Francoise Giraud, "After Courrèges, What Future for the Haute Couture?" *New York Times Sunday Magazine,* Sept. 12, 1965, 50–51, 109–12.

20. For a discussion of how postwar couture was sold in the United States through the custom salon see Melissa Leventon, "Shopping for Style: Couture in America," in *New Look to Now: French Haute Couture, 1947–1987,* ed. Stephen de Pietri and Melissa Leventon (New York: Rizzoli, 1989), 23–27. For a wonderfully engaging and thorough examination of the marketing of couture in North America, emphasizing the Canadian market, see Alexandra Palmer, *Couture and Commerce: The Transatlantic Fashion Trade in the 1950s* (Vancouver: University of British Columbia, 2001).

21. Givenchy's success with American women was predicted in "De Givenchy, a New Name in Paris," *Life,* March 3, 1952, 61–64.

22. Maureen Turim, "Designing Women: The Emergence of the New Sweetheart Line," in *Fabrications: Costume and the Female Body,* ed. Jane Gaines and Charlotte Herzog (New York: Routledge, 1990), 215–19.

23. Cobina Wright, "How Low Will They Go?" *Modern Screen,* August 1948, 42–43, 72.

24. Marlene Dietrich went straight to Dior for her New Look wardrobe featured in *No Highway in the Sky* (1951) and *Stage Fright* (1950), but these films were shot in Britain. Hepburn's recounting of how Givenchy's work came to be used for *Sabrina* appears in a 1962 *Cine-Revue* interview in which she states, "For *Sabrina,* Billy Wilder agreed to let me add a few Parisian costumes to the ones created by Edith Head. The dresses put forward by Hubert de Givenchy were divine. I felt as though I had been born to wear them. My dearest wish . . . was that Billy would allow me to keep them" (Hubert de Givenchy and Musée de la mode et du costume, *Givenchy: Forty Years of Creation* [Paris: Paris-Musée, 1991], 116).

25. Hubert de Givenchy, quoted in Warren G. Harris, *Audrey Hepburn: A Biography* (New York: Simon and Schuster, 1994), 129.

26. Barry Paris, *Audrey Hepburn* (New York: G.P. Putnam's Sons, 1996), 123.

27. Barry Paris reports that Hepburn finally strayed from wearing Givenchy because the cost of buying from his collection became too much for her when she was not working and that, living in Italy as the wife of Italian psychiatrist Andrea Dotti, she felt she had some obligation to use Italian designers. Ibid., 255–56.

28. Audrey Hepburn, "The Costumes Make the Actors: A Personal View," in *Fashion in Film,* ed. Regine Engelmeier and Peter W. Engelmeier, rev. ed. (Munich: Prestel, 1997), 10.

29. Cecil Beaton, quoted in Nicholas Drake, ed., *The Fifties in "Vogue"* (New York: Henry Holt, 1987), 76.

30. See, e.g., a model used for "Black, White: Brightest Young Colours in Town," *Vogue,* April 1, 1955, 155; and an advertisement for a Junior Sophisticate dress in *Vogue,* May 15, 1955, 13. On store window mannequins being patterned after the actress see Virginia Lee Warren, "Beauty of Mannequins in Store Window Often Draws Its Pattern from Real Life," *New York Times,* Sept. 16, 1964, 14.

31. Givenchy and Musée de la mode et du costume, *Givenchy,* 117.

32. Mizejewski, *Ziegfeld Girl,* 24.

33. Joshua Zeitz, *Flapper* (New York: Crown, 2006), 162–69.

34. Françoise Giraud, "Backstage at Paris' Fashion Drama," *New York Times Magazine,* Jan. 27, 1957, 24.

35. See Valerie Steele, *Paris Fashion: A Cultural History* (New York: Oxford University Press, 1988), 276; Richard Donovan, "That Friend of Your Wife's Named Dior," *Collier's,* June 10, 1955, 34–39.

36. "Gee, Is She Sophisticated!" *Seventeen,* Jan. 1946, 82.

37. Philip T. Hartung, "Companion Family-Approved Movies: *Sabrina,*" *Women's Home Companion,* Sept. 1954, 10.

38. Rosalind Coward, *Female Desires: How They Are Sought, Bought, and Packaged* (New York Grove, 1985), 31–32.

39. Jack Moffitt, "*Sabrina,*" *Hollywood Reporter,* Sept. 1954, n.p., *Sabrina* clipping file, Academy of Motion Picture Arts and Sciences (hereafter AMPAS).

40. Jennifer Craik, *The Face of Fashion: Cultural Studies in Fashion* (London: Routledge, 1994), 105.

41. Weiler, "The Screen: *Breakfast at Tiffany's,*" 28 (see note 5 above).

42. Jane Gaines, "Introduction: Fabricating the Female Body," in Gaines and Herzog, *Fabrications,* 19. Written after the initial appearance of this chapter in article form in 2000, Rachel Moseley's *Growing Up with Audrey Hepburn* (Manchester: Manchester University Press, 2002) acknowledges my work and parallels some of the arguments I make about the visualization of costuming in *Sabrina.*

43. Molly Haskell, "Our Fair Lady Audrey Hepburn," *Film Comment* 27, no. 2 (1991): 10.

44. Review of *Sabrina, Los Angeles Times,* Sept. 23, 1954, n.p., *Sabrina* clipping file, AMPAS.

45. Stacey, *Star Gazing,* 181, 192–95.

46. Richard Dyer, "Social Values of Entertainment and Show Business" (PhD diss., Birmingham University, Center for Contemporary Cultural Studies, 1972), 339.

47. Mark Shaw, "Audrey Hepburn, Many-Sided Charmer," *Life,* Dec. 7, 1953, 128.

48. Ibid., 32.

49. On the fashion rules that the chic American woman needed to follow in the 1950s see le Bourhis, "The Elegant Fifties," 16–19.

50. Vanessa Schwarz, *It's So French!* (Chicago: University of Chicago Press, 2005), 23–53.

51. Ibid., 27–38.

52. "Chi-Chi Cinderella," *Look,* May 14, 1957, 116.

53. "Young Idea," *Vogue,* Sept. 1, 1954, 111.

54. For example, one fashion article emphasized the "youthful freshness" of Italian fashion and even used a Hepburn look-alike as a model, but the suits featured hardly seem "casual" and "easy-moving" as the text suggests. See "Italian Collections, Their New Young Look," *Vogue,* March 15, 1955, 84–87. Fifty-eight-year-old Madeleine Carroll's return to Broadway was compared to the change in her private life by her move from Balenciaga to Givenchy because of the "young-looking fluid clothes he has designed for Miss Hepburn." See Gloria Emerson, "Couturier's Fluid Styles Suit Madeleine Carroll," *New York Times,* August 20, 1964, 32.

55. Angela Taylor, "Audrey Hepburn Tries on a Swinging Image," *New York Times,* Dec. 27, 1966, 39. "Look at Audrey Hepburn Now!" *Ladies' Home Journal,* Jan. 1967, 59–60, 110–11. The article reacts to her costumes in *Two for the Road* with "Audrey Hepburn swings? You're kidding" (59).

56. Publicity also helped in this. Some *Funny Face* film advertisements featured Hepburn in Givenchy's wedding gown. Paramount produced sketches of Sabrina's "little black dress" affixed with Edith Head's signature, and in the wake of great enthusiasm for the film and its dresses, publicity left the impression that Head, not Givenchy, had designed it. See "*Sabrina*" file, core collection, AMPAS.

57. Clayton Cole, "*Sabrina,*" *Films and Filming,* Nov. 1954, 20.

58. Haskell, *From Reverence to Rape,* 268. Similar explanations have been given to account for Twiggy's popularity as a model for young women of the 1960s. See Craik, *The Face of Fashion,* 84.

59. Haskell, "Our Fair Lady Audrey Hepburn," 10.

60. Nora Sayre, *Running Time: Films of the Cold War* (New York: Dial, 1982), 133–34.

61. Stacey, *Star Gazing,* 197.

62. Ibid., 198.

63. Ibid., 205, 200, 201. The interest in Hepburn has found numerous consumer modes of expression in recent years through everything from Hepburn calendars and a collectable doll outfitted in a tiny reproduction of the little black dress from *Breakfast at Tiffany's* to posters and coffee table picture books.

64. "How Does a Girl Become a Woman?" *Photoplay,* May 1955, 68–69.

65. *Funny Face* press book, 25, AMPAS. *Vogue* anticipated the film's "Think Pink" musical number with a similarly conceived though decidedly nonsatirical fashion feature in 1955. See "Vine Rose," *Vogue,* Nov. 15, 1955, 128–33. For a discussion of First Lady Mamie Eisenhower's predilection for pink and the "decisive moment" in 1955, "when the rest of America went pink, too," see Karal Ann Marling, "Mamie Eisenhower's New Look," in *As Seen on TV: The Visual Culture of Everyday Life in the 1950s* (Cambridge, MA: Harvard University Press, 1994), 8–49.

66. *Funny Face* press book, 25, 26, AMPAS.

67. Ibid., 40.

68. Shaw, "Audrey Hepburn, Many-Sided Charmer," 127–35. In all of the

photos in the layout she wears pants. Hepburn's casual wear in magazine layouts anticipates the big-sweater/tight-pants look assumed by Brigitte Bardot, the bad girl of 1950s French cinema. Bardot's voluptuous femininity was combined with childlike qualities that led Simone de Beauvoir to label her an "erotic hoyden." Beauvoir thought that Bardot and Hepburn were alike in showing the triumph of the "child-woman" and age difference as a means of spurring male desire. See Simone de Beauvoir, "Brigitte Bardot and the Lolita Syndrome," trans. Bernard Fretchman, *Esquire,* August 1959, 32–38.

69. *Life,* Dec. 7, 1953, cover; Shaw, " Audrey Hepburn, Many-Sided Charmer," 127–35. Elizabeth Wilson, "Audrey Hepburn: Fashion, Film and the 50s," in *Women and Film: A Sight and Sound Reader,* ed. Pam Cook and Philip Dodd (Philadelphia: Temple University Press, 1993), 40, 36–38.

70. See, esp., Thomas Doherty, *Teenagers and Teenpics: The Juvenilization of American Movies in the 1950s* (Boston: Unwin Hyman, 1988).

71. *How to Steal a Million* press book, AMPAS.

72. Givenchy and Musée de la mode et du costume, *Givenchy,* 111.

73. "Audrey Hepburn at 40," *McCall's,* July 1969 (quoted in Steele, *Paris Fashion,* 255).

74. Givenchy and Musée de la mode et du costume, *Givenchy,* 127. "Jackie" appeared in a Givenchy advertisement for a sweater ensemble in *Vogue,* March 1, 1955: "Expect More Than the Traditional . . . When Givenchy Creates the Sweatered Look in Orlon" (32). Hepburn was not necessarily Givenchy's most famous client (the Duchess of Windsor and Grace Kelly were also customers), but she was definitely among the most influential fashion leaders to wear his designs. Jackie Kennedy wore Givenchy designs on a visit to Versailles in 1961. See "Givenchy," *Look,* Nov. 21, 1961, 110–13.

75. Fashion layout, *Vogue,* Nov. 1, 1964, 142–51.

76. *Vogue,* Oct. 15, 1964, 29–49.

77. "*How to Steal a Million,*" *Los Angeles Magazine,* Oct. 1966, n.p., *How to Steal a Million* clipping file, AMPAS.

78. Philip K. Scheuer, "Audrey Charms in 'Steal a Million,'" *Los Angeles Times,* July 14, 1966, n.p., *How to Steal a Million* clipping file, AMPAS.

79. "Counterfeit Comedy," *Newsweek,* July 25, 1966, n.p., *How to Steal a Million* clipping file, AMPAS.

80. Sayre, *Running Time,* 134.

81. Gloria Emerson, "Co-Stars Again: Audrey Hepburn and Givenchy," *New York Times,* Sept. 8, 1965, 54.

82. Ibid. On mink lining as reflecting the ultimate measure of a refined woman see Giraud, "After Courrèges, What Future for the Haute Couture?" 112.

83. Ibid.

84. Taylor, "Audrey Hepburn Tries on a Swinging Image," 39.

85. Ibid.

86. See Susan Cheever, "Twiggy: A Stick Figure," in *Heroine Worship: Inventing an Identity in the Age of Female Icons,* special issue, *New York Times Magazine,* Nov. 24, 1996, 74, www.nytimes.com/specials/magazine4/articles/twiggy.html.

87. See Elizabeth Wilson, *Adorned in Dreams: Fashion and Modernity* (London: Virago, 1985), 222.

## CONCLUSION

1. Quoted in Benjamin DeCasseres, "In Mary's Eyes," *New York Times,* March 3, 1922, 90.

2. Thomas H. Ince, "The Star Is Here to Stay," *Munsey's Magazine,* Nov. 1918, 346.

3. Pickford acknowledged the "problem of the voice" for the stage actress who attempts a child role; see Mary Pickford, "The Portrayal of Child Roles," *Vanity Fair,* Dec. 1917, 75.

4. "Mary Pickford Secretly Has Her Curls Shorn; Forsakes Little-Girl Roles to Be 'Grown Up,'" *New York Times,* June 23, 1928, 1.

5. Mary Pickford, "Why I Have Not Bobbed Mine," *Pictorial Review,* April 1927, 9; reproduced online at http://historymatters.gmu.edu/d/5117/.

6. Adela Rogers St. Johns, "Why Mary Pickford Bobbed Her Hair," *Photoplay,* Sept. 1928, 33.

7. Quoted in Cynthia Felando, "Hollywood in the 1920s: Youth Must Be Served," in *Hollywood Goes Shopping,* ed. David Desser and Garth Jowett (Minneapolis: University of Minnesota Press, 2001), 82–107, 97.

8. Frederick Lewis Allen, quoted in Heather Addison, *Hollywood and the Rise of Physical Culture* (New York: Routledge, 2003), 36.

9. "Clara Bow Leads Film List," *Los Angeles Times,* Jan. 3, 1929, A3. Joan Crawford, who would become Pickford's stepdaughter-in-law in June of 1929 (as the bride of Douglas Fairbanks Jr.), was ranked tenth.

10. "Mary Pickford's Voice Comes to the Screen," advertisement for Gala World Premiere at the Rivoli, untitled newspaper clipping, April 5, 1929, 29, clipping file, Academy of Motion Picture Arts and Sciences (hereafter AMPAS).

11. Review of *Coquette, Evening World,* quoted in Donald Crafton, *The Talkies: American Cinema's Transition to Sound, 1926–1931* (New York: Charles Scribner's Sons, 1997), 298.

12. Mordaunt Hall, review of "*Kiki,*" *New York Times,* March 6, 1931, 16.

13. Clare Boothe Brokaw, "Mary Pickford: The End of an Era," *Vanity Fair,* August 1932, 53.

14. "Deanna's First Kiss," *Picturegoer,* Dec. 30, 1939, quoted in Annette Kuhn, *Dreaming of Fred and Ginger: Cinema and Cultural Memory* (New York: New York University Press, 2002), 120–21.

15. "The Amazing Mrs. Holliday," in *American Film Institute Catalog: Within Our Gates; Ethnicity in American Feature Films, 1911–1960,* ed. Alan Gevinson (Berkeley: University of California Press, 1997), 26.

16. Deanna Durbin, quoted in "The Role I Liked Best," unsourced clipping, n.d., n.p., in the Life Story of Deanna Durbin scrapbook, comp. Anne Cogley, Special Collections, AMPAS.

17. Shirley Temple, *Child Star: An Autobiography* (New York: Warner Books, 1988), 357.

18. Selznick's high loan-out price (more than $100,000 per film) for Temple

guaranteed that he would make a great deal of money from her appearances in films made for others, but increasingly, studios like Warner Bros. balked at her price in comparison with projected box-office revenue for her films, especially ones in which Temple was not surrounded by other stars. Temple complained about being loaned out instead of being cast in Selznick-supervised productions but to no avail. See Temple, *Child Star,* 356–62.

19. Simone de Beauvoir, "Brigitte Bardot and the Lolita Syndrome," trans. Bernard Fretchman, *Esquire,* August 1959, 32–38.

20. See Annette Kuhn, *Dreaming of Fred and Ginger;* and Jackie Stacey, *Star Gazing: Hollywood Cinema and Female Spectatorship* (New York: Routledge, 1994). On the advantages and drawbacks of ethnographic study that depends on viewers' memories see Kuhn, *Dreaming of Fred and Ginger,* 7–12, 218–20.

21. My thoughts on this issue have been influenced by Vivian Sobchack's *Carnal Thoughts: Embodiment and Moving Image Culture* (Berkeley: University of California Press, 2004); and by Nicola Bown, "Tender Beauty: Victorian Painting and the Problem of Sentimentality," *Journal of Victorian Culture* 16, no. 2 (2011): 214–25, esp. 217–22.

22. See Gaylyn Studlar, *This Mad Masquerade: Stardom and Masculinity in the Jazz Age* (New York: Columbia University Press, 1996), 10–89.

# Selected Bibliography

ARCHIVES

AMPAS Margaret Herrick Library, Fairbanks Study Center, Academy of Motion Picture Arts and Sciences, Beverly Hills, CA.

DOS David O. Selznick Collection, Harry Ransom Research Center, University of Texas, Austin.

ARTICLES AND BOOKS

*Fan magazine, newspaper, general interest, and trade magazine articles and reviews are listed in notes.*

Addison, Heather. *Hollywood and the Rise of Physical Culture.* New York: Routledge, 2003.

Adorno, Theodor. "On the Fetish Character of Music and the Regression of Listening." In *The Essential Frankfurt School Reader,* edited by Andrew Arato and Eike Gebhardt, 270–99. New York: Continuum, 1982.

Adorno, Theodor, and Max Horkheimer. *Dialectic of Enlightenment.* 1947. New York: Continuum, 1995.

Altman, Rick. *The American Film Musical.* Bloomington: Indiana University Press, 1987.

Auerbach, Nina. *Romantic Imprisonment: Women and Other Glorified Outcasts.* New York: Columbia University Press, 1985.

———. *Woman and the Demon: The Life of a Victorian Myth.* Cambridge, MA: Harvard University Press, 1982.

Baer, Ulrich. "Photography and Hysteria: Toward a Poetics of the Flash." *Yale Journal of Criticism* 7, no. 1 (1994): 41–77.

Balio, Tino. *Grand Design: Hollywood as a Modern Business Enterprise, 1930–1939.* Berkeley: University of California Press, 1993.

Barnes, Elizabeth. "Affecting Relations: Pedagogy, Patriarchy, and the Politics of Sentiment." *American Literary History* 8, no. 4 (1996): 597–614.

Barthes, Roland. *Image/Music/Text.* Translated by Stephen Heath. New York: Hill and Wang, 1977.

———. *S/Z.* Translated by Richard Miller. New York: Hill and Wang, 1974.

Barwik, Sandra. *A Century of Style.* London: George Allen and Unwin, 1984.

Basinger, Jeanine. *Shirley Temple.* New York: Pyramid, 1978.

———. *The Star Machine.* New York: Alfred A. Knopf, 2007.

Beauvoir, Simone de. "Brigitte Bardot and the Lolita Syndrome." Translated by Bernard Fretchman. *Esquire,* August 1959, 32–38.

Berebitsky, Julie. *Like Our Very Own: Adoption and the Changing Culture of Motherhood, 1851–1950.* Lawrence: University Press of Kansas, 2000.

Bergman, Andrew. *We're in the Money: Depression America and Its Films.* 1971. Chicago: Ivan R. Dee, 1992.

Black, Shirley Temple. *Child Star: An Autobiography.* New York: Warner Books, 1988.

Blanke, Hanne. *Virgin: The Untouched History.* New York: Bloomsbury, 2007.

Bodnar, John. *Blue-Collar Hollywood: Liberalism, Democracy, and Working People in American Film.* Baltimore: Johns Hopkins University Press, 2003.

Bordwell, David, Janet Staiger, and Kristin Thompson. *The Classical Hollywood Cinema: Film Style and Mode of Production to 1960.* New York: Columbia University Press, 1985.

Bown, Nicola. "Tender Beauty: Victorian Painting and the Problem of Sentimentality." *Journal of Victorian Culture* 16, no. 2 (2011): 214–25.

Bradley, Laurel. "From Eden to Empire: John Everett Millais's *Cherry Ripe.*" *Victorian Studies* 34, no. 2 (1991): 179–203.

Bratton, Jacky, Jim Cook, and Christine Gledhill, eds. *Melodrama: Stage, Picture, Screen.* London: British Film Institute, 1994.

Brontë, Charlotte. *Jane Eyre.* 1847. New York: Modern Library, 2000.

Brooks, Peter. *The Melodramatic Imagination: Balzac, Henry James, Melodrama, and the Mode of Excess.* New Haven, CT: Yale University Press, 1976.

Brownlow, Kevin. *Mary Pickford Rediscovered.* New York: Abrams, 1999.

Brumberg, Joan Jacobs. *The Body Project: An Intimate History of American Girls.* New York: Vintage, 1987.

Cary, Diana Serra. *Hollywood's Children: An Inside Account of the Child Star Era.* 1978. Dallas: Southern Methodist University Press, 1997.

Chion, Michel. *Audio-Vision: Sound on Screen.* Edited and translated by Claudia Gorbman. New York: Columbia University Press, 1994.

Cleghorn, Cassandra. "Chivalric Sentimentalism: The Case of Dr. Howe and Laura Bridgman." In *Sentimental Men: Masculinity and the Politics of Affect in American Culture,* edited by Mary Chapman and Glenn Hendler, 163–80. Berkeley: University of California Press, 1999.

Clément, Catherine. *Opera: The Undoing of Women.* Translated by Betsy Wing. Minneapolis: University of Minnesota Press, 1999.

Cohen, Robert, ed. *Dear Mrs. Roosevelt: Letters from Children of the Great Depression.* Chapel Hill: University of North Carolina Press, 2002.

Craik, Jennifer. *The Face of Fashion: Cultural Studies in Fashion*. London: Routledge, 1994.

Custen, George F. *Twentieth Century's Fox: Darryl F. Zanuck and the Culture of Hollywood*. New York: Basic Books, 1994.

deCordova, Richard. "Ethnography and Exhibition: The Child Audience, the Hays Office and Saturday Matinees." *Camera Obscura* 8, no. 2.23 (1990): 90–107.

———. *Picture Personalities: The Emergence of the Star System in America*. Urbana: University of Illinois Press, 1990.

D'Emilio, John, and Estelle B. Freedman. *Intimate Matters: A History of Sexuality in America*. New York: Harper and Row, 1989.

Didi-Huberman, Georges. *Invention of Hysteria: Charcot and the Photographic Iconography of the Salpêtrière*. Translated by Alisa Hartz. Cambridge, MA: MIT Press, 1982.

Dijkstra, Bram. *Idols of Perversity: Fantasies of Feminine Evil in Fin-de-siècle Culture*. New York: Oxford University Press, 1986.

Dior, Christian. *Christian Dior and I*. New York: E.P. Dutton, 1957.

———. *Talking about Fashion*. New York: G.P. Putnam's Sons, 1954.

Doane, Mary Ann. "Film and the Masquerade: Theorising the Female Spectator." *Screen* 23, nos. 3 and 4 (1987): 74–87.

Doherty, Thomas. *Teenagers and Teenpics: The Juvenilization of American Movies in the 1950s*. Boston: Unwin Hyman, 1988.

Dolar, Mladen. "The Object Voice." In *Gaze and Voice as Love Objects*, edited by Renata Saleci and Slavoj Žižek, 7–31. Durham, NC: Duke University Press, 1996.

Douglas, Susan J. *Listening In: Radio and the American Imagination*. New York: Random House, 1999.

———. *Where the Girls Are: Growing Up Female with the Mass Media*. New York: Random House, 1995.

Drake, Nicholas, ed. *The Fifties in "Vogue."* New York: Henry Holt, 1987.

Durgnat, Raymond, and Scott Simmon. *King Vidor, American*. Berkeley: University of California Press, 1992.

Dyer, Richard. "The Colour of Virtue: Lillian Gish, Whiteness and Femininity." In *Women and Film: A Sight and Sound Reader*, edited by Pam Cook and Philip Dodd, 1–9. Philadelphia: Temple University Press, 1993.

———. "Entertainment and Utopia." In *Movies and Methods II*, edited by Bill Nichols, 221–32. Berkeley: University of California Press, 1985.

———. *Stars*. London: British Film Institute, 1979.

Eckert, Charles. "Shirley Temple and the House of Rockefeller." *Jump Cut* 2 (July-August 1974): 17–20. Repr. and abr. in *Stardom: Industry of Desire*, edited by Christine Gledhill, 60–73. London: Routledge, 1991.

Edwards, Anne. *Shirley Temple: American Princess*. New York: William Morrow, 1988.

Elder, Glen H., Jr. *Children of the Great Depression: Social Change in Life Experience*. Chicago: University of Chicago Press, 1974.

Elsaesser, Thomas. "Tales of Sound and Fury: Observations on the Family Melodrama." In *Home Is Where the Heart Is: Studies in Melodrama and the*

*Woman's Film,* edited by Christine Gledhill, 43–69. London: British Film Institute, 1987.

Epstein, Edward Z. *Portrait of Jennifer: A Biography of Jennifer Jones.* New York: Simon and Schuster, 1995.

Everson, William K. "Deanna Durbin." *Films in Review* 27, no. 9 (1976): 513–29.

Fass, Paula. *The Damned and the Beautiful: American Youth in the 1920s.* New York: Oxford University Press, 1977.

Fleischhauer, Carl, and Beverly W. Brannan, eds. *Documenting America, 1935–1943.* Berkeley: University of California Press, 1988.

Freedman, Russell. *Children of the Great Depression.* New York: Clarion, 2005.

Freud, Sigmund. "Hysterical Phantasies and Their Relation to Bisexuality." 1908. In *The Standard Edition of the Complete Psychological Works of Sigmund Freud.* Edited by James Strachey. Vol. 9, 155–67. London: Hogarth, 1959.

———. "The Uncanny." 1919. In *The Standard Edition of the Complete Psychological Works of Sigmund Freud.* Edited by James Strachey. Vol. 17, 219–56. London: Hogarth, 1953–74.

Gaines, Jane. "Introduction: Fabricating the Female Body." In *Fabrications: Costume and the Female Body,* edited by Jane Gaines and Charlotte Herzog, 1–27. New York: Routledge, 1990.

Gitter, Elisabeth G. "The Power of Women's Hair in the Victorian Imagination." *PMLA* 99, no. 5 (1984): 936–54.

Givenchy, Hubert de, and Musée de la mode et du costume. *Givenchy: Forty Years of Creation.* Paris: Paris-Musée, 1991.

Greene, Graham. *The Graham Greene Film Reader: Reviews, Essays, Interviews, and Film Stories.* Edited by David Parkinson. New York: Applause, 1994.

Griswold, Robert L. *Fatherhood in America: A History.* New York: Basic Books, 1993.

Hammontree, Patsy Guy. *Shirley Temple Black: A Bio-bibliography.* Westport, CT: Greenwood Press, 1998.

Harris, Warren G. *Audrey Hepburn: A Biography.* New York: Simon and Schuster, 1994.

Hartley, John. "Juvenation: News, Girls and Power." In *News, Gender and Power,* edited by Cynthia Carter, Gill Branston, and Stuart Allen, 47–70. London: Routledge, 2000.

———. "'When Your Child Grows Up Too Fast': Juvenation and the Boundaries of the Social in the News Media." *Continuum: Journal of Media and Cultural Studies* 12, no. 1 (1998): 9–30.

Haskell, Molly. *From Reverence to Rape: The Treatment of Women in the Movies.* 2nd ed. Chicago: University of Chicago Press, 1987.

———. "Our Fair Lady Audrey Hepburn." *Film Comment* 27, no. 2 (1991): 9–17.

Hastie, Amelie. "History in Miniature: Colleen Moore's Dollhouse and Historical Recollection." *Camera Obscura* 16, no. 3.48 (2001): 112–57.

Hatch, Kristen Lee. "Playing Innocent: Shirley Temple and the Performance of Girlhood, 1850–1989." PhD diss., University of California, Los Angeles, 2006.

Haver, Ron. *David O. Selznick's Hollywood.* 1980. New York: Bonanza, 1985.

Hawes, Joseph M. *Children between the Wars: American Childhood, 1920–1940.* New York: Twayne, 1997.

Hepburn, Audrey. "The Costumes Make the Actors: A Personal View." In *Fashion in Film,* edited by Regine Engelmeier and Peter W. Engelmeier, 9–11. Rev. ed. Munich: Prestel, 1997.

Hesse-Biber, Sharlene Nagy. *The Cult of Thinness.* 2nd ed. New York: Oxford University Press, 2007.

Heymann, C. David. *Liz: An Intimate Biography of Elizabeth Taylor.* 1995. New York: Atria Press, 2001.

Hilmes, Michele. *Hollywood and Broadcasting: From Radio to Cable.* Urbana: University of Illinois Press, 1990.

———. *Radio Voices: American Broadcasting, 1922–1952.* Minneapolis: University of Minnesota Press, 1997.

Hilmes, Michele, and Jason Loviglio, eds. *Radio Reader: Essays in the Cultural History of Radio.* New York: Routledge, 2002.

Horowitz, Joseph. *Classical Music in America: A History of Its Rise and Fall.* New York: Norton, 2005.

Howard, June. "What Is Sentimentality?" *American Literary History* 11, no. 1 (1999): 63–81.

Hunter, Jane H. *How Young Ladies Became Girls: The Victorian Origins of American Girlhood.* New Haven, CT: Yale University Press, 2002.

Innes, Sherrie A., ed. *Delinquents and Debutantes: Twentieth-Century American Girls' Cultures.* New York: New York University Press, 1998.

Jankowski, Theodora A. "Pure Resistance: Queer(y)ing Virginity in William Shakespeare's 'Measure for Measure' and Margaret Cavendish's 'The Convent of Pleasure.'" *Shakespeare Studies* 26 (1998): 218–55.

Johansen, Shawn. *Family Men: Middle-Class Fatherhood in Early Industrializing America.* New York: Routledge, 2001.

Johnston, Annie Fellows. *The Little Colonel.* 1895. Boston: L.C. Page, 1922. www.digital.library.upenn.edu/women/johnston/colonel/colonel.html.

Kelly, Dorothy. *Fictional Genders: Role and Representation in the Nineteenth-Century French Narrative.* Lincoln: University of Nebraska Press, 1989.

Kett, Joseph P. *Rites of Passage: Adolescence in America, 1790 to the Present.* New York: Basic Books, 1977.

Kincaid, James. *Erotic Innocence: The Culture of Child Molesting.* Durham, NC: Duke University Press, 1998.

King, Barry. "The Star and the Commodity: Notes Towards a Performance Theory of Stardom." *Cultural Studies* 1, no. 2 (1987): 145–61.

King, Rob. "The Kid from *The Kid:* Jackie Coogan and the Consolidation of Child Consumerism." *Velvet Light Trap* 48 (fall 2001): 4–19.

Kinsey, Alfred C., and the staff of the Institute for Sex Research, Indiana University. *Sexual Behavior in the Human Female.* Philadelphia: Saunders, 1953.

Kitch, Carolyn. *The Girl on the Magazine Cover: The Origins of Visual Stereo-*

*types in American Mass Media*. Chapel Hill: University of North Carolina Press, 2001.
Kivy, Peter. *Sound Sentiment: An Essay on the Musical Emotions*. Philadelphia: Temple University Press, 1989.
Klinger, Barbara. "'Local' Genres: The Hollywood Adult Film in the 1950s." In Bratton, Cook, and Gledhill, *Melodrama: Stage, Picture, Screen*, 134–46.
Koestenbaum, Wayne. *The Queen's Throat: Opera, Homosexuality, and the Mystery of Desire*. New York: Da Capo, 1993.
Kristeva, Julia. "Adolescence: A Syndrome of Ideality." Translated by Michael Marder and Patricia I. Vieira. *Psychoanalytic Review* 94, no. 5 (2007): 715–25.
———. *New Maladies of the Soul*. Translated by Ross Guberman. New York: Columbia University Press, 1995.
Lambourne, Lionel. *Victorian Painting*. London: Phaidon, 1999.
Lang, Robert. *American Film Melodrama: Griffith, Vidor, Minnelli*. New York: Columbia University Press, 1989.
LaRossa, Ralph. *The Modernization of Fatherhood: A Social and Political History*. Chicago: University of Chicago Press, 1997.
le Bourhis, Katell. "The Elegant Fifties: When Fashion Was Still a Dictate." In *New Look to Now: French Haute Couture, 1947–1987*, edited by Stephen de Pietri and Melissa Leventon, 13–22. New York: Rizzoli, 1989.
Leppert, Richard. *The Sight of Sound: Music, Representation, and the History of the Body*. Berkeley: University of California Press, 1993.
Leventon, Melissa. "Shopping for Style: Couture in America." In *New Look to Now: French Haute Couture, 1947–1987*, edited by Stephen de Pietri and Melissa Leventon, 23–27. New York: Rizzoli, 1989.
Lindsay, Vachel. *The Art of the Moving Picture*. 1915. New York: Liveright, 1970.
———. *Complete Poems*. New York: Macmillan, 1925.
———. "Queen of My People." *New Republic*, July 17, 1917, 280–81.
Linnet, Beverly. *Star-Crossed: The Story of Robert Walker and Jennifer Jones*. New York: G.P. Putnam's Sons, 1986.
Lubbe, Trevor. "Diagnosing a Male Hysteric: Don Juan–Type." *International Journal of Psychoanalysis* 84, no. 4 (2003): 1043–59.
MacLeod, Anne Scott. "The *Caddie Woodlawn* Syndrome: American Girlhood in the Nineteenth Century." In *A Century of Childhood, 1820–1920*, edited by Mary Lynn Stevens Heininger et al., 97–119. Rochester, NY: Margaret Woodbury Strong Museum, 1984.
Macleod, David. *The Age of the Child: Children in America, 1890–1920*. New York: Twayne, 1998.
Marling, Karal Ann. *As Seen on TV: The Visual Culture of Everyday Life in the 1950s*. Cambridge, MA: Harvard University Press, 1994.
Mavor, Carol. *Becoming: The Photographs of Clementina, Viscountess Hawarden*. Durham, NC: Duke University Press, 1999.
———. "Dream-Rushes: Lewis Carroll's Photographs of the Little Girl." In Nelson and Vallone, *The Girl's Own*, 156–93.

McDonald, Tamar Jeffers, ed. *Virgin Territory: Representing Sexual Inexperience in Film*. Detroit: Wayne State University Press, 2010.

McElhaney, Joe, ed. *Vincente Minnelli: The Art of Entertainment*. Detroit: Wayne State University Press, 2009.

Melosh, Barbara. *Strangers and Kin: The American Way of Adoption*. Cambridge, MA: Harvard University Press, 2002.

Merish, Lori. "Cuteness and Commodity Aesthetics: Tom Thumb and Shirley Temple." In *Freakery: Cultural Spectacles of the Extraordinary Body*, edited by Rosemarie Garland Thomson, 185–203. New York: New York University Press, 1996.

Micale, Mark S. *Hysterical Men: The Hidden History of Male Nervous Illness*. Cambridge, MA: Harvard University Press, 2008.

Mintz, Stephen. *Domestic Revolutions: A Social History of American Family Life*. New York: Free Press, 1989.

———. *Huck's Raft: A History of American Childhood*. Cambridge, MA: Belknap Press of Harvard University Press, 2004.

Mitchell, Sally. *The New Girl*. New York: Columbia University Press, 1996.

Mizejewski, Linda. *Ziegfeld Girl: Image and Icon in Culture and Cinema*. Durham, NC: Duke University Press, 1999.

Moseley, Rachel. *Growing Up with Audrey Hepburn*. Manchester: Manchester University Press, 2002.

Mulvey, Laura. "Afterthoughts on 'Visual Pleasure and Narrative Cinema' Inspired by *Duel in the Sun*." *Framework* 15–17 (summer 1981): 12–15.

———. "'It Will Be a Magnificent Obsession': The Melodrama's Role in the Development of Contemporary Film Theory." In Bratton, Cook, and Gledhill, *Melodrama: Stage, Picture, Screen*, 121–33.

———. "Visual Pleasure and Narrative Cinema." *Screen* 16, no. 3 (1975): 6–18.

Murray, Matthew. "'The Tendency to Deprave and Corrupt Morals': Regulation and Irregular Sexuality in Golden Age Radio Comedy." In Hilmes and Loviglio, *Radio Reader*, 135–56.

Nash, Ilana. *American Sweethearts: Teenage Girls in Twentieth-Century Popular Culture*. Bloomington: Indiana University Press, 2006.

Nelson, Claudia, and Lynne Vallone, eds. *The Girl's Own: Cultural Histories of the Anglo-American Girl, 1830–1915*. Athens: University of Georgia Press, 1994.

Nowell-Smith, Geoffrey. "Minnelli and Melodrama." In McElhaney, *Vincente Minnelli*, 99–105.

———. "On Kiri Te Kanawa, Judy Garland, and the Culture Industry." In *Modernity and Mass Culture*, edited by James Naremore and Patrick Brantlinger, 70–79. Bloomington: Indiana University Press, 1991.

Osterweil, Ara. "Reconstructing Shirley: Pedophilia and Interracial Romance in Hollywood's Age of Innocence." *Camera Obscura* 24, no. 3.72 (2009): 1–39.

Palladino, Grace. *Teenagers: An American History*. New York: Basic Books, 1996.

Palmer, Alexandra. *Couture and Commerce: The Transatlantic Fashion Trade in the 1950s*. Vancouver: University of British Columbia Press, 2001.

Paris, Barry. *Audrey Hepburn*. New York: G.P. Putnam's Sons, 1996.

Parris, Leslie, ed. *Pre-Raphaelite Papers.* London: Tate Gallery, 1984.

Polhemus, Robert M. "John Millais's Children: Faith and Erotics; *The Woodman's Daughter* (1851)." In *Victorian Literature and the Victorian Visual Imagination,* edited by Carol T. Christ and John O. Jordan, 290–312. Berkeley: University of California Press, 1995.

Pritchard, Susan Perez. *Film Costume: An Annotated Bibliography.* Metuchen, NJ: Scarecrow Press, 1981.

Reis, Pamela Tamarkin. "Exchange: Victorian Centerfold; Another Look at Millais's *Cherry Ripe.*" *Victorian Studies* 35, no. 2 (1992): 201–5.

Riviere, Joan. "Womanliness as Masquerade." In *Psychoanalysis and Female Sexuality,* edited by Hendrik M. Ruitenbeek, 209–20. New Haven, CT: College and University Press, 1966.

Robson, Catherine. *Men in Wonderland: The Lost Girlhood of the Victorian Gentleman.* Princeton, NJ: Princeton University Press, 2001.

Rose, Jacqueline. *The Case of Peter Pan; or, The Impossibility of Children's Fiction.* Philadelphia: University of Pennsylvania Press, 1984.

Sammond, Nicholas. *Babes in Tomorrowland: Walt Disney and the Making of the American Child, 1930–1960.* Durham, NC: Duke University Press, 2002.

Sánchez-Eppler, Karen. *Dependent States: The Child's Part in Nineteenth-Century American Culture.* Chicago: University of Chicago Press, 2005.

Sayre, Nora. *Running Time: Films of the Cold War.* New York: Dial, 1982.

Scheiner, Georganne. "The Deanna Durbin Devotees: Fan Clubs and Spectatorship." In *Generations of Youth: Youth Cultures and History in Twentieth-Century America,* edited by Joe Austin and Michael Nevin Willard, 181–94. New York: New York University Press, 1998.

———. *Signifying Female Adolescence: Film Representations and Fans, 1920–1950.* Westport, CT: Praeger, 2000.

Schickel, Richard. *The Stars: The Personalities Who Made the Movies.* New York: Bonanza, 1962.

Schrum, Kelly. *Some Wore Bobby Sox: The Emergence of Teenage Girls' Culture, 1920–1945.* New York: Palgrave Macmillan, 2004.

Segurola, Andreas de. *Through My Monocle: Memoirs of the Great Basso Andreas de Segurola.* Edited by George R. Creegan. Steubenville, OH: Crest, 1991.

Selznick, Irene Mayer. *A Private View.* New York: Alfred A. Knopf, 1983.

Shary, Timothy, *Generation Multiplex: The Image of Youth in Contemporary American Cinema.* Austin: University of Texas Press, 2002.

Shipman, David. *The Great Movie Stars: The Golden Years.* New York: Bonanza, 1970.

Showalter, Elaine. *The Female Malady: Women, Madness, and English Culture, 1830–1980.* New York: Penguin, 1987.

Sikov, Ed. *Laughing Hysterically: American Screen Comedy of the 1950s.* New York: Columbia University Press, 1995.

Silverman, Kaja. *The Acoustic Mirror: The Female Voice in Psychoanalysis and Cinema.* Bloomington: Indiana University Press, 1988.

Sjogren, Britta. *Into the Vortex: Female Voice and Paradox in Film.* Urbana: University of Illinois Press, 2006.

Smart, Mary Ann, ed. *Siren Songs: Representations of Gender and Sexuality in Opera*. Princeton, NJ: Princeton University Press, 2000.

Smith, Sarah J. *Children, Cinema and Censorship: From Dracula to the Dead End Kids*. London: I.B. Tauris, 2005.

Solomon, Robert. "On Kitsch and Sentimentality." *Journal of Aesthetics and Art Criticism* 49, no. 1 (1991): 1–14.

Stacey, Jackie. *Star Gazing: Hollywood Cinema and Female Spectatorship*. London: Routledge, 1994.

Staiger, Janet. "Seeing Stars." *Velvet Light Trap* 20 (summer 1983). Repr. in *Stardom: Industry of Desire*, edited by Christine Gledhill, 1–16. New York: Routledge, 1991,

Stamp, Shelley. *Movie-Struck Girls: Women and Motion Picture Culture after the Nickelodeon*. Princeton, NJ: Princeton University Press, 2000.

Steedman, Carolyn. *Strange Dislocations: Childhood and the Idea of Human Interiority, 1780–1930*. Cambridge, MA: Harvard University Press, 1995.

Steele, Valerie. *Paris Fashion: A Cultural History*. New York: Oxford University Press, 1988.

Stokowski, Leopold. *Music for All of Us*. New York: Simon and Schuster, 1943.

Studlar, Gaylyn. "Max Op(h)uls Fashions Femininity." *Arizona Quarterly* 60, no. 5 (2004): 65–86.

———. *This Mad Masquerade: Stardom and Masculinity in the Jazz Age*. New York: Columbia University Press, 1996.

Tambling, Jeremy. *Opera, Ideology, and Film*. New York: St. Martin's, 1987.

Tate Gallery. *Pre-Raphaelites*. London: Allen Lane, 1984.

Temple, Mrs. Gertrude, as told to Mary Sharon. *How I Raised Shirley Temple*. Akron, OH: Saalfield, 1935.

Thomson, David. *Showman: The Life of David O. Selznick*. New York: Alfred A. Knopf, 1992.

Thomson, Rosemarie Garland, ed. *Freakery: Cultural Spectacles of the Extraordinary Body*. New York: New York University Press, 1996.

Turim, Maureen. "Designing Women: The Emergence of the New Sweetheart Line." In *Fabrications: Costume and the Female Body*, edited by Jane Gaines and Charlotte Herzog, 212–28. New York: Routledge, 1990.

Turk, Edward Baron. "Deriding the Voice of Jeanette MacDonald: Notes on Psychoanalysis and the American Film Musical." *Camera Obscura* 9, nos. 1–2.25–26 (1991): 224–49.

———. *Hollywood Diva: A Biography of Jeanette MacDonald*. Berkeley: University of California Press, 1998.

Varty, Anne. *Children and Theatre in Victorian Britain: "All Work, No Play."* Houndmills, UK: Palgrave Macmillan, 2008.

Vered, Karen Orr. "White and Black in Black and White: Management of Race and Sexuality in the Coupling of Child-Star Shirley Temple and Bill Robinson." *Velvet Light Trap* 39 (spring 1997): 52–65.

Vicinus, Martha. " The Adolescent Boy: Fin-de-siècle Femme Fatale?" In *Victorian Sexual Dissidence*, edited by Richard Dellamora, 83–106. Chicago: University of Chicago Press, 1999.

Wagenknecht, Edward. *The Movies in the Age of Innocence.* Norman: University of Oklahoma Press, 1962.

Warner, Malcolm. "John Everett Millais's *Autumn Leaves:* 'A Picture Full of Beauty and without Subject.'" In Parris, *Pre-Raphaelite Papers,* 126–42.

Watkins, T.H. *The Hungry Years.* New York: Henry Holt, 1999.

Webb, Jessica. "Why Women Fell: Representing the Sexual Lapse in Mid-Victorian Art (1850–65)." *eSharp,* no. 9 (spring 2007): 1–13. www.gla.ac.uk/media/media_41222_en.pdf.

Werfel, Franz. *The Song of Bernadette.* Translated by Ludwig Lewisohn. 1942. San Francisco: Ignatius, 2006.

Whitfield, Eileen. *Pickford: The Woman Who Made Hollywood.* New York: Faber and Faber, 1997.

Williams, Leslie. "The Look of Little Girls: John Everett Millais and the Victorian Art Market." In Nelson and Vallone, *The Girl's Own,* 124–55.

Wills, Nadine. "'110 Per Cent Woman': The Crotch Shot in the Hollywood Musical." *Screen* 42, no. 2 (2001): 121–41.

Wilson, Elizabeth. *Adorned in Dreams: Fashion and Modernity.* London: Virago, 1985.

———. "Audrey Hepburn: Fashion, Film and the 50s." In *Women and Film: A Sight and Sound Reader,* edited by Pam Cook and Philip Dodd, 36–40. Philadelphia: Temple University Press, 1993.

Winter, John Strange. *Bootles' Baby: A Story of the Scarlet Lancers.* 1885. London: Frederick Warne, 1891. Facsimile. La Vergne, TN: Nabu Public Domain Reprints, 2010.

Wood, Robin. "*Duel in the Sun:* The Destruction of an Ideological System." In *The Book of Westerns,* edited by Ian Cameron and Douglas Pye, 189–95. New York: Continuum, 1996.

———. "Minnelli's *Madame Bovary.*" In McElhaney, *Vincente Minnelli,* 154–66.

Woodward, Ian. *Audrey Hepburn.* New York: St. Martin's, 1984.

Wurlitzer, Steve J. *Electric Sounds: Technological Change and the Rise of Corporate Mass Media.* New York: Columbia University Press, 2007.

Yarom, Nita. *Matrix of Hysteria: Psychoanalysis of the Struggle between the Sexes as Enacted in the Body.* London: Routledge, 2005.

Young, Paul. *The Cinema Dreams Its Rivals: Media Fantasy Films.* Minneapolis: University of Minnesota Press, 2006.

Zeitz, Joshua. *Flapper.* New York: Crown, 2006.

Zelizer, Viviana A. *Pricing the Priceless Child: The Changing Social Value of Children.* 1985. Princeton, NJ: Princeton University Press, 1994.

Zukor, Adolph, with Dale Kramer. *The Public Is Never Wrong: The Autobiography of Adolph Zukor.* New York: G.P. Putnam's Sons, 1953.

# Index

*Italic numbers indicate illustrations*